Suspended Prison Sentences

This book uncovers the controversies around the suspended prison sentence, its main aims and features, and the role that it occupies within the wider criminal justice context. Suspended prison sentences were introduced in Central and Eastern European (CEE) states as alternatives to short prison sentences: although they were initially generally conceived of as exceptional penal tools, over time, they became the most imposed and dominant penal sanctions and, in that sense, a defining feature of criminal justice systems in the region.

The book provides a rich source of information about the development and features of suspended sentences in eight CEE countries, a topic that, although of great importance due to their frequency, has received only scant academic attention. Employing a legal, socio-legal, and criminological approach, it achieves this goal through individual chapters on eight countries (Czechia, Estonia, Hungary, Poland, Romania, the Russian Federation, Serbia, and Slovenia), and also through three general chapters, which outline the main specificity of the region as a whole but also present nuances between different countries.

The book will be of interest to a wide variety of academic researchers who study crime, punishment, and the penal system, and especially to those interested in sentencing. Given the huge discrepancy in the frequency of use of this sanction in CEE countries and the frequency of use of parole in contemporary practice, the work provides unique insights into the potential and desirability of its wider use, particularly due to the minimal supervision that it requires in examined countries. The book therefore seeks to critically inform current thinking on the value and appropriateness of particular forms of sanctions in responding to crime.

Jakub Drápal is Associate Professor at Charles University specialising in sentencing in continental Europe, particularly in Central and Eastern Europe. He primarily uses quantitative and doctrinal methods to examine judicial discretion and promote principled sentencing – the central focus of his ERC-funded project *Re-Constructing Sentencing.*

Krzysztof Krajewski is Professor Emeritus at the Jagiellonian University in Krakow, former Head of the Criminology Department at that university. He published on penal policy and sentencing issues, a.o. in *Crime & Justice: A Review of Research*, *European Journal of Criminology*, and *European Journal on Criminal Policy and Research.*

Milena Tripković is Senior Lecturer in Criminology at the University of Edinburgh. Milena's current research concerns the relationship between punishment and belonging. Her notable publications include the book *Punishment and Citizenship*, as well as articles in journals such as the *British Journal of Criminology*, *Punishment and Society,* and *Journal of Applied Philosophy*.

Innovations in Corrections

An emphasis on innovation is evident in the field of corrections. While changes in policies and public opinion regarding sentencing philosophies such as mass incarceration bump up against the reality that budgets continue to be tightened and the division of these revenues is more competitive, innovative strategies become all the more valuable. The premise behind innovation is effecting improvements without sacrificing the overall safety and security of the institution. Through research and evaluation, we seek to identify what works and what does not work.

1. Hallett et al, *The Angola Prison Seminary: Effects of Faith-Based Ministry on Identity Transformation, Desistance, and Rehabilitation*
2. Shah, *The Meaning of Rehabilitation and its Impact on Parole: There and Back Again in California*
3. Pealer, *Correctional Rehabilitation and Therapeutic Communities: Reducing Recidivism Through Behavior Change*
4. Ward, *Rural Jail Reentry: Offender Needs and Challenges*
5. Pedlar et al, *Community Re-Entry: Uncertain Futures for Women Leaving Prison*
6. Cross, *Juvenile Justice and Expressive Arts: Creative Disruptions through Art Programs for and with Teens in a Correctional Institution*
7. Roush, *Recalibrating Juvenile Detention: Lessons Learned from the Court-Ordered Reform of the Cook County Juvenile Temporary Detention Center*
8. Middlemass & Smiley, *Prisoner Reentry in the 21st Century: Critical Perspectives of Returning Home*
9. Birch and Sicard, *Prisons & Community Corrections: Critical issues and emerging controversies*
10. Urrutia-Moldes, *Health and Well-Being in Prison Design: A Theory of Prison Systems and a Framework for Evolution*
11. Evans, *Transformation During Incarceration: Breaking the System*
12. Drápal et al, *Suspended Prison Sentences: Elusive Punishment in Central and Eastern Europe*

Suspended Prison Sentences

Elusive Punishment in Central and Eastern Europe

Edited by Jakub Drápal, Krzysztof Krajewski and Milena Tripković

Routledge
Taylor & Francis Group
NEW YORK AND LONDON

First published 2026
by Routledge
605 Third Avenue, New York, NY 10158

and by Routledge
4 Park Square, Milton Park, Abingdon, Oxon, OX14 4RN

Routledge is an imprint of the Taylor & Francis Group, an informa business

ISBN: 978-1-032-94050-2 (hbk)
ISBN: 978-1-032-94051-9 (pbk)
ISBN: 978-1-003-56866-7 (ebk)

DOI: 10.4324/9781003568667

Typeset in Times New Roman
by Deanta Global Publishing Services, Chennai, India

Contents

Figures

Tables

Contributors

Gennady Esakov, Faculty of Law, Lomonosov Moscow State University, Russian Federation, is a Visiting Professor who previously led the criminal law department at HSE University. His research focuses on economic and comparative criminal law, and he has published extensively in English, German, and Russian, including books and legal commentaries.

Jaan Ginter is a Professor Emeritus at the School of Law of the University of Tartu (Estonia). He is serving as the European Criminal Law Academic Network Contact Point for Estonia. His research and writing encompass criminology, judicial system, ethics, criminal law, and procedure. For his research and publications see https://www.etis.ee/CV/Jaan_Ginter/eng/.

Aleksej Jankovič was an Assistant Researcher at the Institute of Criminology at the Faculty of Law, University of Ljubljana (Slovenia) and has since moved on to work as a legal practitioner and entrepreneur.

Ekaterina Khodzhaeva holds a PhD-equivalent in sociology from Kazan State University. She has studied policing, courts, and legal professions in Russia, with fellowships in Germany, the US, and France. From 2013 to 2024, she worked at the Institute for the Rule of Law, European University at Saint Petersburg (Russian Federation); in 2024–2025, she was a fellow at Nantes IEA.

Krisztina Lukács is a Senior Counsel at the Constitutional Court of Hungary and Assistant Professor at the University of Miskolc (Hungary). She is a Lecturer at Eötvös Loránd University (Hungary) and the secretary of the Prison Law Subcommittee of the Hungarian Academy of Sciences. She holds PhD and MA degrees.

Barbara Mohácsi is an Assistant Professor in criminal procedure law and prison law at Eötvös Loránd University (Hungary) and Senior Counsel at the Constitutional Court of Hungary. She holds PhD and MA degrees from Eötvös Loránd University.

Gabriel Oancea, Bucharest Probation Service, Romania, has over 20 years of experience in probation, developing rehab programmes, legislation, and reintegration networks. He trains magistrates and officers, and has served internationally as an expert (CoE, EU), contributing to probation reform in Moldova, N. Macedonia, Kazakhstan. A PhD and Law holder, he lectures at Bucharest University and publishes on criminology and probation.

Mojca M. Plesničar, Institute of Criminology, Faculty of Law, University of Ljubljana, Slovenia, is a Senior Research Associate at the Institute of Criminology and an Associate Professor at the University of Ljubljana. Her research focuses on sentencing, criminal justice decision-making, and penal policy. She currently leads the ERC-funded project Sentrix, exploring sentencing architectures and decision-making in European criminal justice systems.

Foreword

Sentences promote the objectives of sentencing by imposing hard treatment of one kind or another. This hard treatment may involve confinement in a penal institution, deprivation of financial resources, a requirement of unpaid work, to name a few penal impositions. Suspended sentences, in contrast, seek to achieve the same objectives – desistance for example – through the mere threat of punishment. The potential advantages of a suspended punishment are clearest with regard to suspended imprisonment. A 12-month prison sentence imposes great hardship on the prisoner as well as their family and dependants. The cost to the State is also a consideration. In England and Wales, imprisoning an adult for a year costs almost 75,000 euros.

If a suspended prison sentence can achieve the same outcomes through the threat rather than the execution of punishment, the benefits are obvious. In addition to the human and fiscal savings, suspending rather than executing prison sentences is consistent with the long-standing principle of parsimony or penal restraint. The sentence imposed should be that which achieves the objectives of sentencing in the way that imposes least suffering on the defendant. All this explains the powerful and cross-jurisdictional appeal of suspended sentences, particularly in Europe and the Nordic countries. Who would deprive an individual of his or her liberty if the threat of such a deprivation is sufficient?

So far so good. Devising and implementing a successful suspended sentence regime, however, has proved very challenging, to say the least. Almost all Western jurisdictions have created or currently operate some form of suspended sentence. These sentences vary greatly in the ambit of offences for which they are available, as well as the requirements imposed on offenders and the nature of judicial response to breach of those requirements. Curiously, there has been little comparative research, and less "learning from each other". As a result, we have no clear idea of what an ideal suspended sentence might look like.

The benefits of suspended sentences also create problems. A suspended sentence – particularly a suspended prison sentence – will normally carry less "penal weight" and have less censuring power than penal sequestration. This lack of equivalence undermines parity at sentencing – a requirement of proportional sentencing. In addition, when a defendant receives a suspended prison sentence, community reaction is often negative. The public see a suspended prison sentence as a mitigated sentence – "Imprisonment lite" if you will. Public criticism grows when the suspended sentence is imposed for a relatively serious crime.

Jurisdictions have responded to the lack of parity in a number of ways, including introducing strict requirements on the offender serving a suspended prison sentence in the community. Protracting the length of the period of suspension is another strategy to attempt to create some rough equivalence between prisoners and offenders receiving suspended prison sentences. A six-month immediate prison sentence may be matched by a 12-month suspended sentence. Both strategies create their own difficulties. For example, piling on conditions and requirements during the period of suspension may lead to breach, and subsequently committal to custody – this defeats the whole purpose of the suspended sanction. How to increase the penal "bite" of a suspended sentence is one of the key questions addressed in this volume.

The concept of suspending sentence raises many important questions at the level of penal theory, sentencing law, and judicial practice. Most of the literature has been jurisdiction specific. Until now. The present volume is therefore a landmark addition to the field. In addition, most of the literature has focused on a small number of countries, Finland, the United Kingdom, and Australia in particular. This collection of essays presents the experience in continental jurisdictions that have been insufficiently discussed in the English language. This oversight is particularly striking since the origins of suspended sentences are found in the continental systems of justice.

The book draws upon research across a range of jurisdictions, and the contributions will be of great interest to readers not just across Europe, but around the world. In this respect, the editors have produced a truly international volume that represents a great step forward in our understanding of this creative, yet often controversial sanction.

Julian V. Roberts, K.C. (Hon.)
University of Oxford

Acknowledgements

This book grew out of the efforts and generosity of many people. We are especially thankful to the authors from across Central and Eastern Europe, who took on the challenge of exploring topics that had remained largely untouched – never an easy task. Anna Barton kindly proofread all the chapters and offered thoughtful first-round feedback to the contributors; her help made the book far more readable, and we are truly grateful for her dedication. We also owe thanks to our colleagues who shared their insights along the way, in particular the participants of the 2022 workshop on suspended prison sentences in post-communist Europe, hosted by Charles University, Eurocrim conferences, presentations in Ljubljana, Krakow, Greifswald, Edinburgh, and Leiden, as well as the reviewers of our book proposal. Filip Švestka was a great help in preparing the manuscript according to the submission guidelines, and we much appreciated his patience and precision. Last but not least, we are very grateful to the Routledge team for their support and guidance throughout the publication process. Finally, the writing of this book was supported by the Grant Agency of the Czech Republic (Grantová agentura České republiky) through grant no. 21-19485S, "Suspended Prison Sentences in Post-Communist Europe: The Unexplored Behemoth", carried out at the Faculty of Law, Charles University.

Part I

1 Introduction

Jakub Drápal, Krzysztof Krajewski, and Milena Tripković

Introduction

The suspended prison sentence is one of the most controversial criminal sanctions in modern history. It has been enacted and abolished in multiple countries, in some cases more than once. It has been described both as a complete exoneration and as excessively punitive and a contributing factor to large prison populations. Suspended sentences are, paradoxically, imposed both for the least serious offences and for very serious offences – both for stealing a chocolate bar and for serious cases of rape. Controversial though it is, the suspended prison sentence is currently one of the most frequently used sanctions in Europe: in 2015 it was imposed in around one million cases across Europe (about 1.4 times more frequently than non-suspended prison sentences) and its use is particularly high in several Central and Eastern European countries, where over half of all convicted offenders receive this sanction (Aebi et al., 2021, p. 217; Krajewski, 2014).

Given the extent of its use, it is surprising how little knowledge we have about suspended prison sentences. Consider a few anecdotal examples. In the *Encyclopedia of Criminology*, the entry for "suspended sentences" simply refers the reader to the entry on probation, despite the fact that these are two vastly different penal institutions (indeed, if the reader were to look up the entry for "probation", they would find nothing about the continental form of suspended prison sentences (Décarpes & Durnescu, 2014)). At the Annual conferences of the European Society of Criminology between 2012 and 2024, only 11 presentations were given on suspended prison sentences: fewer than one per year and less than one per about a thousand abstracts of presentations.[1] Most criminological scholarship written in English on the topic of suspended prison sentences focuses on suspended prison sentences in common law countries,[2] despite the fact that suspended sentences were originally a "continental" invention and tend to be used more frequently in continental criminal justice systems.

This means that new, thorough study is needed to provide a better understanding of suspended prison sentences and their place in continental criminal justice systems, in particular focusing on the Central and Eastern European countries, where suspended prison sentences are used the most. The frequency of their use in this region is so high that some scholars have argued that suspended sentences

DOI: 10.4324/9781003568667-2

constitute a defining feature differentiating "western" from "eastern" European criminal justice systems (Krajewski, 2007, 2014). Even so, there is almost no existing literature in English on suspended prison sentences in continental Europe: the last book written on the subject was published in 1971 (Ancel, 1971). What scarce continental scholarship there is has, furthermore, focused predominantly on Western Europe, and there is almost no literature in English explaining the use, history and development of suspended prison sentences in Central and Eastern Europe.

This book aims to remedy this situation. First, it presents and critically assesses the (dis)advantages of suspended prison sentences as they are typically applied in Central and Eastern Europe (we delineate this region by the inclusion of the former USSR, the former Warsaw Pact countries and the former Yugoslav countries).[3] Following this general introduction, authors from the individual Central and Eastern European countries present the use of suspended prison sentences in their jurisdictions, as well as the historical development of suspended prison sentences from both legal and practical perspectives. This approach, combining the theory and practice of suspended prison sentences in each individual country, not only enables an overview of the use of these sanctions and the problems associated with them, but – given the fact that suspended prison sentences dominate the penal sphere in Central and Eastern Europe – also provides a new perspective on penal policy and its development in this region. The book concludes by presenting and analysing the key features of suspended sentences as they operate in the examined region, articulating some of the convergent and divergent elements in their history, and by outlining a solution to the problems identified during the previous chapters, proposing a way of remodelling suspended prison sentences in order to make them better aligned with the need for a just and principled sentencing system.

The remainder of this introductory chapter is structured as follows. First, we provide a definition of the suspended prison sentence, contrasting it with the more familiar institute of probation and with other similar sanctions. Then, to introduce the reader to the context within which this book is set, we briefly discuss criminal justice systems in Central and Eastern Europe more broadly. We conclude our introduction by outlining the structure of the individual national chapters, which form the backbone of this book. Our aim is to highlight the key issues that are discussed in this book and to enable the reader to navigate with ease to the topics that interest them the most.

Defining features of suspended prison sentences and the glossary of terms

Before embarking on a thorough discussion of suspended prison sentences, we must first clarify what we mean when we use this term and other related terminology. A *suspended prison sentence* is a prison sentence that is imposed with a set length of imprisonment but is not enforced (executed); imprisonment is deferred on condition that the offender does not re-offend during a set period (the *operational period*). Its counterpart, the *non-suspended prison sentence* (in other words, *imprisonment*), is a prison sentence that is intended to be enforced from the very beginning (and not suspended). A *partly suspended prison sentence* is a sanction in between these two, which involves the imposition of a prison sentence the first part of which is to be served immediately (in prison): after release from this first period, an operational period begins subject to which the remainder of the sentence is suspended.

Upon suspending a prison sentence of a specific length, the court sets an *operational period.* This is a set period of time during which, if the convicted person re-offends, the suspension of the prison sentence may (or in some cases must) be revoked and the sentence must then be executed (i.e. the offender imprisoned). In Slavic languages, this operational period is commonly called a "test period". In this book, we refrain from using the term "probationary period", which is often used in related literature in English, since this term presupposes probationary supervision, which is not an integral part of suspended prison sentences. However, (*probationary*) *supervision* may be imposed alongside a suspended prison sentence. We refer to this as "probationary supervision", a term closely related to that used in some Slavic languages for this concept.[4]

For a suspended prison sentence to be completed without imprisonment, the convicted person must not commit a new offence during the operational period of the suspended sentence and must not breach other set conditions. If the offender complies with these obligations during the operational period, the suspended prison sentence is considered completed as soon as the operational period ends. Any non-compliance with the conditions of the suspension is considered a *breach*. This constitutes grounds for the suspension to be *revoked* and the previously suspended prison sentence enforced. Alternatively, if the court decides not to revoke the suspension of the sentence in such a case, it may *prolong/extend* the operational period or impose additional conditions.

There are two main differences between a suspended prison sentence and probation. First, in the case of a suspended prison sentence, the court begins by setting the length of the prison sentence that will be executed if a breach occurs during the operational period and the court revokes the suspension. Probationary supervision is an element that is only added to a suspended prison sentence if it is deemed necessary. Probation entails the supervision of the offender by a probation officer and, when imposed without a suspended sentence, allows the judge to impose any sentence upon revocation that was initially available at the time the probation was imposed (Petersilia, 1997).[5] These two legal approaches originate from two different doctrinal views of criminal law among scholars at the end of the 19th century. Continental lawyers considered that a decision on guilt should always be followed immediately by a decision on a (specific) sentence. The suspended prison sentence was conceived as a sanction for first-time offenders, for whom its deterrent effect was deemed sufficient and supervision was not deemed necessary. There were also practical reasons for avoiding sentences with supervision, as there was a lack of social workers and at the time, probationary supervision could only be carried out by the police (Ancel, 1971, p. 23).

Though the distinction between probation and suspension was therefore clear at first, it has become more blurred over time. Some features of probation – such as supervision – have since been incorporated into suspended prison sentences, while certain features of suspended prison sentences – such as setting the length of the prison sentence at the outset – have found their way into specific variations of probation (Frase, 2019). Additionally, various new penal instruments that bear some resemblances to suspended prison sentences or probation have been enacted over time. For example, in continental systems, prosecutors and judges sometimes have the authority to either conditionally defer sentencing or impose conditional discharge upon sentencing. The term *conditional deferral* used in this book thus refers to a situation in which the accused makes a declaration of guilt and the proceedings are deferred for a set period (operational period) after which, if the accused does not re-offend, the case is considered closed. In the case of conditional deferral, the court does not pass a verdict of guilt or impose a sentence unless the conditions of the deferral are breached. Alternatively, in the case of *conditional discharge*, a guilty verdict is made, but no sentence is imposed: instead, an operational period begins, after which the case is dismissed and no sentence is imposed provided that the offender has not committed a further offence. Conditional discharge is thus very similar to probation, especially if it is combined with probationary supervision.

The enactment of new institutes similar to probation and the introduction of some features of probation into suspended prison sentences did not, however, change the basic structure of this sanction. A suspended prison sentence still entails the imposition of a prison sentence of a specific length and the suspension of its execution, having confidence in the deterrent effect of an individualised threat, which suspension is revoked in full in case of a breach, unless the court considers it suitable to prolong the operational period. The original conception remains very much alive in many respects and continues to dominate the criminal justice systems of the region we focus on in this book. It is for this reason that we are interested in assessing how it has developed, how it functions today, and how its use impacts the criminal justice systems of the region.

The broader sentencing context in continental and Central and Eastern Europe

To properly understand a particular type of penal sanction, one must examine it within the broader context of criminal justice. To help readers understand how and why suspended prison sentences came to be used as they are today, we present this context on three levels. We begin by outlining the basic features of continental sentencing systems and the specificities of the Central and Eastern European countries. We then divide this group of countries into three broad regions, within each of which are countries sharing certain cultural and legal commonalities: the countries of the former USSR, the countries of the former Warsaw Pact and the countries of the former Yugoslavia. We provide a brief introduction to the societal and legal history of each of these regions. Last but not least, the detailed context of each country's criminal justice system is presented in the relevant national chapter.

Typically, any continental sentencing system is grounded in a penal (or criminal) code that establishes basic sentencing rules in a general part and defines individual criminal offences and applicable sentencing ranges (sentence minimums and maximums) in a special part. The sentencing rules in the general part of the penal code typically outline basic sentencing principles, such as aggravating and mitigating circumstances, rules governing multiple offending, and the conditions for the imposition of individual types of sanctions. With just a few exceptions (such as Scandinavia), the hierarchy of sentencing rationales is not mentioned or elaborated in the penal code. As far as the content of the special part is concerned, sentencing range minimums are often more important than the maximums, since sentences are typically imposed much closer to the minimum than to the maximum for the given offence (Drápal, 2018; Hinkkanen & Lappi-Seppälä, 2011). No thorough theory of sentencing ranges has, however, been elaborated to date, and it is often unclear, for instance, whether the imposition of a sentence below the sentencing range minimum should be an exception or the norm (Drápal & Plesničar, 2023); theory and practice can further differ in this respect. In most continental systems, no additional guidance is provided to judges beyond these basic rules, although some countries (e.g. Finland and the Netherlands) offer sentence orientations (starting points).

What sentences are eventually imposed is further shaped by the procedure, which is typically regulated by a code of criminal procedure. The vast majority of cases are decided by judges, while prosecutors are typically able to divert a smaller number of (mostly simple and not serious) cases. In some jurisdictions (such as Switzerland or the Netherlands) prosecutors have wider powers and can themselves impose sentences. Guilty pleas and plea bargaining, once unfamiliar in continental Europe, are now being introduced gradually across the region, although with substantial variation in their implementation and use so far (Langer, 2021). The typical continental instrument for shortening the length of judicial proceedings is the penal order (although it is not used in all systems). This involves the judge making a decision on guilt and on the sentence, without seeing the accused; the decision is then delivered to the defendant by mail. If the defendant does not object, the decision is final. If an objection is filed, the full court procedure and oral hearings take place.

Decisions on guilt and on the sentence to be imposed are typically made at the same time, within a single oral hearing. In most cases, judges have to provide (written or oral) reasons for their decision. The quality of these decisions varies, and it is often impossible to decipher why a judge made a certain decision (Drápal et al., 2025; Killias, 1994; Schuyt, 2010). There are substantive opportunities for appeal, yet appellate courts typically do not discuss principles in sufficient detail to guide first-level courts (Drápal & Vanča, 2025).

It could be said, then, that sentencing in continental Europe prioritises the individualisation of sentences over consistency, although there is significant variation across Europe. In France, for example, individualisation is the key principle and the system is not particularly concerned by disparities, while in Finland the uniformity of sentencing practices is prescribed by law (Hinkkanen & Lappi-Seppälä, 2011; Hodgson & Soubise, 2016). The level of discretion provided to judges across Europe by penal codes has, however, not yet been empirically analysed.

Over time, the Central and Eastern European countries have experienced various other problems that have complicated their route to principled sentencing. Most of these countries have experienced multiple regime changes in their (relatively) recent history, which have often had a detrimental effect on legal and criminological research: in some countries criminology almost ceased to exist as a discipline, since it was believed that crime would disappear in a classless society (Drápal, 2019). Ideological influences during the mid-20th century and the (very) limited financing of social sciences after 1989 resulted in rather limited and underdeveloped sentencing scholarship focused on Central and Eastern Europe. For instance, there are no sentencing textbooks and sentencing training for judges and prosecutors is limited (Drápal & Plesničar, 2023). Legal practitioners often have more influence on how sentencing policies are shaped than academics, which results in the enactment of incoherent measures and insufficiently considered judicial tools (Drápal, 2023; Krajewski, 2016).

Societal mistrust towards the executive branch and its tendency to influence the judiciary, which originated during the communist period and was deepened both by abuses of power during the 1990s and by the more recent phenomenon of democratic backsliding in many countries of the region, significantly undermines these countries' abilities to produce further sentencing guidance to instruct their judges. Sentencing commissions of the kind that exist in England and Wales, for instance, would likely be regarded with mistrust and as interfering with judicial independence by both the general public and judges themselves, who would consider these an undue limitation of their powers. As a result, judges often enjoy broad discretion in sentencing, which is cloaked in the discourse of individualisation but is so extensive that it would likely be viewed critically in Northern and Western Europe (Drápal & Plesničar, 2023).

Given these problems, it is not surprising that unprincipled sentencing outcomes are present in particular criminal justice systems in Central and Eastern

Europe (Drápal et al., 2025; Drápal & Šoltés, 2024; Skugarevskiy, 2017). In addition, systems of sanctions and sentencing principles might appear incoherent, and thorough empirical analysis of how criminal justice systems function has been absent. Changes that are introduced might seem erratic (or even chaotic) and complex theory-informed complex reforms are rare or non-existent; within some countries, the situation is further aggravated by penal populism, which is often incited by a single event that leads to public uproar (Drápal & Plesničar, 2023). The lack of both theoretical and empirical scholarship further complicates discussions of current and historical sentencing trends.

The structure of the national chapters

The majority of this book consists of a set of chapters pertaining to the theory and practice of suspended prison sentences in individual countries of the examined region. To help readers grasp the substance of these chapters and to direct their attention to the issues that may interest them the most, we outline below the common structure of these national chapters. In developing them, our main motivation was to select the most important features of each jurisdiction's approach to suspended prison sentences, which can help us understand our own systems without comparing them to or criticising other systems. Since suspended prison sentences dominate most criminal justice systems in Central and Eastern Europe, we wanted to provide evidence that shows how they are used, why and how their use has developed as it has, and whether problems related to their use are present across the entire region or whether they are more limited in scope. By keeping to a common structure in these chapters, we enable a comparative analysis that allows the identification of pertinent commonalities and differences and reflection upon whether there may be a common solution to the identified challenges that is suitable for all Central and Eastern European countries, or whether different criminal justice systems require distinct solutions.

Each national chapter begins with a brief presentation of the criminal justice system it focuses on, in particular the sentencing system. Two main sections follow, in which the authors specifically discuss suspended prison sentences. The first of these sections describes the use of suspended prison sentences today, outlining the applicable provisions and the frequency with which such sentences are used. The second section then discusses the historical development of suspended prison sentences, from legislative, scholarly and practical perspectives. In addition, each chapter seeks to answer a set of questions, which we present below in the order in which they are typically responded to in the chapters. As we mentioned above, the availability of relevant data is poor and many of the authors faced a substantial lack of data and of empirical research pertaining to these questions. Where no reliable empirical research is available, the authors offer their own perspectives, which they clearly state as their own opinions.

The first main section of each chapter (pertaining to the use of suspended prison sentences today) begins by specifying the main characteristics of suspended prison sentences in the jurisdiction described: is there a custodial threshold that determines the possibility of its use and do judges officially decide on suspension only after determining to impose a prison sentence of a particular length? Individual features of suspended prison sentences are then discussed. These include:

- *Positive definition*: Which sanctions and of what length can be suspended or imposed as a suspended sentence?
- *Negative definition*: Are certain offences or offenders (for example, recidivists) ineligible for a suspended prison sentence?
- *The decisive factor*: Which considerations influence the decision whether to suspend a prison sentence? Is it a favourable prognosis of not reoffending or something more demanding?
- *Exceptionality:* Is the suspension of prison sentences considered exceptional (to be applied only rarely or in very specific situations)?
- *Two-stage imposition*: Does the law instruct judges to determine first that a prison sentence is warranted and what its length should be, and *only then* to decide on the mode of execution (suspended or non-suspended)? In systems where a suspended prison sentence is not considered a prison sentence, how is the length of a suspended prison sentence determined?
- *Partly suspended sentences*: Does the system permit the partial suspension of a sentence?
- *Procedure during decision*: Can a special hearing be held at which a decision is made *only* on the suspension of a prison sentence? Can a suspended prison sentence be imposed via penal order, and if so, are there any limitations to this? Are judges procedurally incentivised to suspend prison sentences?
- *Sanctions imposed alongside suspended prison sentences*: Which other sanctions can be imposed alongside a suspended prison sentence, and can these be suspended as well?
- *Suspension (operational) period*: How long can the operational period be? Are there any principles guiding judges in determining it?
- *Conditions and measures*: What types of conditions and measures can be imposed alongside suspended prison sentences? Do any particular requirements need to be fulfilled for such additional conditions to be imposed?
- *Breach*: What constitutes a breach of a suspended prison sentence? Is re-offending the only means of breach, or can other behaviour result in a breach as well?
- *Decisions subsequent to breach*: What options do judges have when deciding how to respond to a breach? Are they obliged to revoke the suspension of the prison sentence or can they, alternatively: (i) prolong the supervision period

and/or impose new obligations, (ii) order only part of the prison sentence to be executed, or (iii) make some other arrangements?

- *Sentencing multiple conviction offenders*: Can a judge, when imposing a sentence for a new offence committed during the operational period of a previously imposed suspended sentence, consider the fact that the offender will likely have to serve the previously imposed prison sentence?
- *Criminal record*: When is the criminal record of a suspended prison sentence erased?

In the second main section of the chapter authors subsequently discuss the historical development of suspended prison sentences in the focus jurisdiction. They describe when and how suspended prison sentences were introduced and the vision behind their initial introduction, focusing on any differences between that original conception and the current system. They then discuss subsequent legislative amendments and the rationales behind any major changes as presented in the explanatory memoranda to enacted laws, scholarship and other sources. This is followed by a discussion of the use of suspended prison sentences in practice and of the possible reasons for the frequency of their use. Finally, attempts made in the country to reduce the use of suspended prison sentences (if any) are presented.

Notes

1 Authors' own calculations.
2 See for example articles in *Law and Contemporary Problems* Vol. 82, No. 1.
3 There is no term that accurately represents the region in question. While we have opted for "Central and Eastern Europe", we are aware that this term geographically includes Germany and Austria, which are countries we do not study here. An alternative term, "post-communist countries" would also include Germany, but would moreover exclude the countries of former Yugoslavia (which experienced state socialism rather than communism per se). "Former socialist countries" (a term used by Drápal & Plesničar (2023)) could be problematic for the purposes of this current research, since it could also be associated with Scandinavian countries or even with national socialism in Nazi Germany. For these reasons, we opted to use "Central and Eastern Europe", albeit with the caveat that we do not discuss Austria or Germany.
4 In French, where the suspended prison sentence was first conceived, the equivalent is *sursis probatoire* or the more antiquated *sursis avec mise à l'épreuve*; a suspended prison without such supervision would be labelled as *sursis simple*.
5 This type of probation is, however, not the only one currently used even in common law countries. For example, in some U.S. states courts also impose a specified prison term and then suspend it entirely or in part (Frase, 2019).

References

Aebi, M. F., Caneppele, S., Harrendorf, S., Hashimoto, Y. Z., Jehle, J.-M., Khan, T. S., Kühn, O., Lewis, C., Molnar, L., Smit, P., & Þórisdóttir, R. (2021). *European sourcebook of crime and criminal justice statistics, 2021*. Göttingen University Press. https://www.univerlag.uni-goettingen.de/handle/3/isbn-978-3-86395-519-9

Ancel, M. (1971). *Suspended sentence*. Heinemann.

Décarpes, P., & Durnescu, I. (2014). Probation and community sanctions. In G. Bruinsma & D. Weisburd (Eds.), *Encyclopedia of criminology and criminal justice* (pp. 3957–3963). Springer. https://doi.org/10.1007/978-1-4614-5690-2_568

Drápal, J. (2018). Individualizace v České republice: Jak určujeme tresty a co o tom víme? *Státní zastupitelství, 15*(1), 9–23.

Drápal, J. (2019). Vývoj kriminologie na právnických fakultách v Praze v letech 1918-2018. *Česká Kriminologie, 4*(1), 1–23.

Drápal, J. (2023). Punitive by negligence? The myths and reality of penal nationalism in the Czech Republic. *European Journal of Criminology, 20*(4), 1549–1567. https://doi.org/10.1177/14773708211063753

Drápal, J., Bolocan-Holban, A., Ginter, J., Plesničar, M. M., Tomšů, K., & Vidaicu, M. (2025). Sentence justification in first-level courts in post-communist Europe. In J. Drápal (Ed.), *Justification of Punishment: Perspectives from Post-Communist Europe* (pp. 39–62). Routledge.

Drápal, J., & Plesničar, M. M. (2023). Sentencing elsewhere: Structuring sentencing discretion in post-communist Europe. *European Journal on Criminal Policy and Research, 31*, 251–270. https://doi.org/10.1007/s10610-023-09568-4

Drápal, J., & Šoltés, M. (2021). Rozdíly v ukládání a navrhování trestů: Výsledky dvou experimentů. In T. Gřivna (Ed.), *V upomínku na Marii Vanduchovou* (pp. 51–69). Wolters Kluwer.

Drápal, J., & Šoltés, M. (2024). Sentencing decisions around quantity thresholds: Theory and experiment. *Journal of Experimental Criminology, 20*(4), 1323–1367. https://doi.org/10.1007/s11292-023-09568-8

Drápal, J., & Vanča, T. (2025). Justifying sentence changes at appellate courts. In J. Drápal (Ed.), *Justifying punishment: Perspectives from post-communist Europe* (pp. 63–79). Routledge.

Frase, R. S. (2019). Suspended sentences and free-standing probation orders in U.S. guidelines systems: A survey and assessment. *Law and Contemporary Problems, 82*(1), 51–79.

Hinkkanen, V., & Lappi-Seppälä, T. (2011). Sentencing theory, policy and research in the Nordic countries. *Crime and Justice, 40*(1), 349–404.

Hodgson, J., & Soubise, L. (2016). Understanding the sentencing process in France. *Crime and Justice, 45*(1), 221–265.

Killias, M. (1994). Sentencing reform—From rhetorics to reducing sentencing disparity. *European Journal on Criminal Policy and Research, 2*(1), 19–28.

Krajewski, K. (2007). Too many suspended sentences? Polish or Central and Eastern European problem? *Sociologija. Mintis ir veiksmas, 2*, 109–121.

Krajewski, K. (2014). Different penal climates in Europe. *Kriminologijos Studijos, 1*, 86–111.

Krajewski, K. (2016). Sentencing in Poland: Failed attempts to reduce punitiveness. *Crime and Justice, 45*(1), 175–218. https://doi.org/10.1086/685539

Langer, M. (2021). Plea bargaining, conviction without trial, and the global administratization of criminal convictions. *Annual Review of Criminology*, *4*(1), 377–411. https://doi.org/10.1146/annurev-criminol-032317-092255

Petersilia, J. (1997). Probation in the United States. *Crime and Justice, 22*, 149–200. https://doi.org/10.1086/449262

Schuyt, P. M. (2010). *Verantwoorde straftoemeting*. Kluwer.

Skugarevskiy, D. (2017). *Essays in law and economics of enforcement*. Graduate Institute of International and Development Studies in Geneva.

2 Key features of suspended prison sentences and some associated problems[1]

Jakub Drápal

Introduction

For a sanction to lead to just outcomes, its features must be fair and principled, and their interaction should produce the desired response. This is no easy task. It requires a thorough theoretical foundation, attentiveness to sentencing rationales, consideration of front-door and back-door sentencing (decisions on imposition and execution) and an awareness of practical issues and possible misuses of the sanction. This may be more easily accomplished when a sanction is first introduced – when detailed thought is given to the detail of the relevant legislation – than when later legislative amendments are made and context changes. Such amendments may be especially problematic when institutional memory has lapsed and limited resources are available for consideration of how changing one feature of a particular sanction might influence other aspects of the same sanction. In this chapter, I argue that although the original conception of suspended prison sentences was coherent and led to just outcomes, subsequent changes to the individual features of the sanction were not considered with sufficient care and negatively impacted the overall functioning of the sanction. This has resulted in unprincipled sentencing and undesired responses to criminal offences.

I begin by describing the original conception of the suspended prison sentence and the legal and societal context within which this sanction originated. This allows the reader to understand how the various features of suspended prison sentences interacted with one another and how they were designed to fulfil one specific objective: to offer offenders another chance while at the same time seeking to deter them. In most countries, this original approach has not been maintained: the original conception has gradually given way to broader sentencing rationales, including rehabilitation, incapacitation, and hard treatment that communicate censure. This has resulted in various changes to the functioning of the sanction. Additionally, suspended prison sentences have become a key instrument for reducing the prison population, which has widened its scope even further. At the same time, however, the principles governing the imposition of suspended prison sentences have not changed. The side effects of this situation have typically not been considered.

DOI: 10.4324/9781003568667-3

To demonstrate the problems caused by the changes that have been made to the provisions governing suspended prison sentences, I proceed to discuss four key aspects of suspended prison sentences from a judicial perspective and to outline, in relation to each one, the issues arising from changes made without a holistic reimagining of the suspended prison sentence as a concept. I discuss the factors influencing the imposition of suspended prison sentences, the determination of their length, the imposition of additional measures alongside suspended prison sentences, and the revocation of suspension. I explore how changes made in each of these areas have – in particular in their interactions – led to disproportionate sentences and unprincipled sentencing. I conclude by suggesting why suspended prison sentences might be seen as more problematic in post-communist European countries than in the rest of Europe.

The origins of suspended prison sentences

It seems almost futile to repeat that in order to understand where we are, we need to look at where we came from. Surprisingly, we often fail to do so, and the resulting lack of comprehension of how things were established and how they developed into what we now know prevents us from understanding why we are now facing particular problems and whether the reforms required to remedy those problems are minor or more substantive. I thus begin this chapter with an extensive discussion of the context in which suspended prison sentences were originally conceived and introduced, and of the dominant sentencing rationales that they were supposed to achieve. In doing so, I consider the European context generally and Central and Eastern European countries in particular.

The societal and legal context

The concept of the suspended prison sentence first emerged in the context of legal theories that became dominant at the turn of the 20th century. While criminologists have sometimes considered its origin to be earlier (Ancel, 1971, p. 4; Milota, 1919, p. 8), suspended prison sentences as we now know them were first formulated in France during the 1880s. Their initial adoption there was driven by perceptions of the sanction's effectiveness, the limited availability of other types of sanctions (at the time, only imprisonment or fines), the short lengths of prison sentences imposed by judges, and specific legal dogmas. After their adoption in France (1891) and Belgium (1888), suspended prison sentences spread quickly across the European continent and enthusiasm for their introduction was substantial; for instance, a Czechoslovak MP responsible for its enactment in 1919 described the suspended prison sentence as "the most beautiful advancement of modern criminology".[2] This enthusiasm seems to have vanished long ago; nowadays, multiple sentencing scholars consider the suspended prison sentence to be the most controversial and problematic alternative to imprisonment (Bagaric, 1999; Freiberg, 2019; Irwin-Rogers & Roberts, 2019).

Historical context is necessary to understand the substantial growth in the use of suspended prison sentences during the 20th and 21st centuries. At the end of the 19th century, when the concept of the suspended sentence was first introduced, *there were practically only two sanctions available to sentencers in continental Europe: imprisonment and fines.* Fines had not yet been enacted in the form of day-fines (Drápal, 2021a), so they were not imposed in proportion to the offender's economic situation, which meant that it was often impossible to impose them on poor offenders. Imprisonment was thus the only option for many, especially poor, offenders. Imprisonment itself, however, also looked very different then than it does today. Prison sentences were much more common, but were also much shorter. As an illustration, consider the Czechoslovak data from 1923 (representative of the entire period[3]), during which 172,385 sentences were imposed in Czechia (i.e. the regions of Bohemia, Moravia, and Silesia). 25% of those sentences were fines, while 74% were prison sentences. Prison sentences of one week or less constituted 66% of prison sentences and only 13% of all prison sentences were longer than 1 month.[4] The dominant sanction was therefore a very short prison sentence.

At the time, prison sentences, especially if very brief, were criticised for their criminogenic effects. The idea that prison was capable of reforming offenders effectively had already been consigned to history, partly thanks to Franz von Liszt's 1882 lecture (Dünkel, 2019, p. 38). The detrimental effect of short prison sentences was virtually a paradigm[5] of the end of the 19th century (Ancel, 1971, p. 11; O'Brian, 1995; Zucker, 1891, p. 8). Alongside it another paradigm of highly effective deterrence was often mentioned: Criminologists simply assumed the deterrent effects of suspended prison sentences without critically considering their mechanisms or effectiveness (Ancel, 1971, p. 18; Kallab, 1904, p. 21; Zucker, 1891). Imprisonment was thus considered harmful, but the *threat* of imprisonment was seen as effective. Consequentialist rationales were popular at the time and principles of proportionality were as yet underdeveloped – that only changed in the second half of the 20th century. Indeed, it was not until the 21st century that criminological scholars came to a consensus over the fact that hard treatment has a stronger effect than sentence pronouncement (von Hirsch, 2019). Hence, at the end of the 19th century, the theoretical shift away from counterproductive short prison sentences and towards the deterrent effect of threat provided the perfect context within which to introduce the suspended prison sentence, which consists of a sentence being pronounced but not carried out. A suspended prison sentence threatens the offender and expresses the amount of appropriate censure, responding to the seriousness of the offence, yet avoids the negative effects of incarceration.

The introduction of the suspended prison sentence in France and subsequently across Europe was not the first attempt to tackle the problems of short prison sentences. In the USA, a system of probation was introduced a decade earlier. Although the concept of the suspended prison sentence took some of its inspiration from probation, it was conceived as a separate institute for primarily doctrinal reasons. Continental doctrinal criminal lawyers opposed the introduction of probation on the grounds that probation consisted in deciding only on the offender's guilt, but not on any punishment. Doctrinal lawyers at the time were persuaded that it was necessary to pronounce a sentence: the execution of the sentence could be suspended, but its imposition should not be (Ancel, 1971, p. 23; Kallab, 1904, p. 7), because an offence required a tangible reaction, not merely an undefined threat. The rigidity of legal academia in Europe was likely strengthened by the absence of social work. In the United States, probation had originated from interested citizens, i.e. from the bottom-up (Vanstone, 2008), whereas any such approach from the top would require supervision of offenders by the police (Ancel, 1971, p. 23), and the result would have been quite different in character from the American concept of probationary supervision designed to help the offender, which was not considered appropriate by scholars (Solnař & Vanduchová, 2009, p. 102).

In other words, it is crucial to understand the original introduction of suspended prison sentences in continental Europe within the context of the period and the scholarly and societal attitudes of the time, themselves intrinsically linked to the continental legal system (Radzinowicz, 1971). Prior to the introduction of suspended prison sentences, short prison sentences dominated the criminal justice system, but they were criticised for being criminogenic. Suspension of the execution of such prison sentences seemed like it could solve that problem: it was a sufficiently specific response, whose negative effects ultimately depended on the offender's self-restraint, and no state-financed response was required. It represented a theoretically sound sanction that could occupy the place of the least worst sanction. The technique of its imposition – imposing a prison sentence and suspending its execution at the same time – was a compromise between the original inspiration found in probation and what was achievable given the existing resources and organisational structure, as well as academic opposition to probation. Suspended prison sentences made a lot of sense in the context of the late 19th century.

The original conception of suspended prison sentences

Originally, suspension of a prison sentence was to be applied exceptionally. It was a measure deemed exceptional not only by scholars (Ancel, 1971, p. 22; Horváth, 1969; Kallab, 1904, p. 22; Milota, 1919, p. 12), but also in the legislative provisions that limited its use. Suspension was available to offenders with (i) no or limited criminal history, (ii) who were handed very short prison sentences and (iii) who were sentenced for a select group of offences (alternatively, suspension could not be applied for select offences). All these conditions indicated that that suspension was only intended for those for whom imprisonment would have a detrimental effect, whose crime was not serious and for whom the risk of re-offending was low.

Originally, suspended prison sentences were designed "for the *first offender*" (Ancel, 1971, p. 27). Different legal systems expressed this differently. In Belgium, any previous conviction barred suspension, while in France, the requirement was that an offender had not previously been imprisoned.[6] Countries that adopted suspended prison sentences later on did not always enact legislative provisions to restrict their use to particular groups of offenders based on their criminal history; one such example is Israel (Enker, 1979, p. 376). Other countries sometimes adopted an in-between strategy. In 1919, Czechoslovakia adopted a provision barring suspension if an offender had previously been sentenced for a felony to imprisonment of at least three months. Although "first-time offender" meant slightly different things in the early years of suspended prison sentences, there was a shared idea of suspending a sentence for offenders who were worthy of another chance.

While the French original conception did not contain any strict limitations on the length of sentence that could be suspended, the Belgian law was stricter: suspension was only for sentences shorter than 6 months (Ancel, 1971, p. 26).[7] Similarly, proposals (unsuccessfully) made to the Parliament of the Austro-Hungarian empire in 1889 and 1891 considered suspension of prison sentences of up to 1, 3 or 6 months (Kallab, 1904, p. 10). Later on, in Hungary, suspension was initially introduced for prison sentences not exceeding one month (raised to three months in 1930; Horváth, 1969). When Germany enacted suspended prison sentences in 1953, it allowed for the suspension of prison sentences of up to 9 months (Dünkel, 2019). Even in countries that enabled the suspension of longer sentences, judges suspended only very short prison sentences in practice. For instance, in Czechoslovakia, which enabled suspension of up to 1 year, most sentences that were suspended were very short (weeks, or at most a few months; see the chapter 4 on Czechia). Some countries further limited the suspension of prison sentences imposed for certain types of offences (Ancel, 1971, p. 25), for instance, if an offence was committed with a dishonest motive.[8] All this means that the prison sentences that were suspended were those that did not result from serious offences.

The rules governing the suspension of prison sentences mirrored lawmakers' intention of avoiding the criminogenic effects of imprisonment, while also not having to rehabilitate the offender: this would be achieved by threatening the offender, while offering them another chance, which should be sufficient to fulfil sentencing rationales. The decision as to whether or not to suspend a prison sentence (assuming the above criteria were met) was to be made solely on the grounds of the offender's prospects of re-offending. The seriousness of the offence was *not* to affect this decision (Ancel, 1971, p. 27; Milota, 1919, p. 14). In some countries, this feature was a matter of contention from the outset. In

Czechoslovakia, for example, both academics and the Ministry of Justice battled with the judiciary over whether the "public interest" – entailing offence seriousness – could be considered when deciding on suspension (Takáč & Svitok, 1946, p. 17). The Czechoslovak Supreme Court repeatedly ruled that offence seriousness was not to be considered.[9]

To assist offenders in leading law-abiding lives, any other sanctions accompanying the suspended prison sentence were also suspended (apart from forfeiture of property or restitution of damages); in addition, the criminal record was not disclosed opposite to other sanctions, so as to preclude detrimental effects on offenders' lives (Takáč & Svitok, 1946, pp. 104–112). Upon being granted suspension, offenders were expected to abstain from further offending. Revocation of the suspended prison sentence was "not a question of bad behaviour" (Ancel, 1971, p. 36), but only occurred if the offender committed another offence within the operational period; revocation operated automatically in many countries. Elsewhere it was less automatic: in Czechoslovakia, if the new offence resulted in another suspended sentence or was categorised as a misdemeanour, the judge was not obliged to revoke the original suspension; this was obligatory only if the offender was handed a non-suspended prison sentence for the new offence.

The presupposition behind this original conception was that suspended sentences would be handed to rarely-erring offenders, whose personality was central to the decision on suspension. Suspension was suited to offenders "not yet corrupted by imprisonment" (Ancel, 1971, p. 36), who "succumbed only as a result of sudden weakness and not as a result of a permanent moral defect" (Kallab, 1904, p. 20). The threat of imprisonment was considered a sufficient deterrent for such offenders, along with the benefits of avoiding the criminogenic effects of imprisonment. The exceptional nature of suspended prison sentences, however, allows for wider use if the word "exception" is not taken literally, but rather as describing the conditions which do not have to be exceptions (offending is the exception). I do not believe such an interpretation reflects what its creators meant, but such an extensive interpretation can be used to justify frequent suspension of prison sentences, while arguing it is for exceptionally erring offenders.

Key features

In this part of the chapter, I argue against the common view that the original conception of suspended prison sentences was doomed from the outset, as the two-stage process of fixing a prison sentence of a certain length and then suspending its execution is unprincipled and impossible to carry out (Bartels, 2009; Gemmell, 1997; Webster & Doob, 2019). I believe that the original conception of the suspended prison sentence as an exceptional instrument capable of giving another chance to those sentenced to short prison sentences was in itself a sound solution that did not hamper principled sentencing. Instead, I argue that the multiple problems associated with these sentences were caused by the broadening of the suspended prison sentence's parameters, much wider use of suspension, open abandonment of certain principles, addition of new ones, and failure to adjust key principles to the broadened parameters. To explain this, I discuss separately four key decisions that judges (and penal systems) need to make when imposing a suspended prison sentence: (a) what factors should govern the suspension of a prison sentence, (b) how the length of the sentence is to be set, (c) whether to impose measures alongside a suspended prison sentence and (d) whether and how to revoke suspension. Within each topic, I briefly outline the main changes that have taken place and discuss their consequences.

The nature of the suspended prison sentence and factors governing its imposition

A crucial question about what should influence the imposition of a suspended prison sentence concerns the understanding of its nature: is it an independent sanction or merely a mode of execution for a prison sentence? The difference between these two perspectives can also be reflected in the language we use: should scholars discuss factors influencing the imposition of a suspended prison sentence or factors influencing the suspension of a prison sentence? The answer to the question of the nature of the suspended prison sentence will, among other things, determine for which offences the suspended prison sentence can be imposed, what factors should influence its imposition, and how the court should set its length. There are advantages and disadvantages to both approaches.

Suspended prison sentences were initially conceived as a mode of execution of imprisonment. The suspension was to be imposed as a second step in the sentencing process: the court would first decide on a prison sentence of a specific length and would subsequently decide whether it was to be served immediately or suspended. This can be compared, for example, with contemporary decisions on whether prison sentences are to be served at home (home detention) or in prison, which is a decision made in some countries after the prison sentence in question has been imposed. A two-step process of this kind reflects two different types of individualisations – individualisation at sentencing and individualisation of sentence execution – which in turn reflect different sentencing rationales.

If the decisions on the imposition and suspension of a prison sentence are separate, various factors will have different impacts on each of the two steps. During the first step, the court considers all factors pertinent to sentencing, whereas in the second step, only a selection of factors play a role. As described above, the expectation that the offender would be able to lead a law-abiding life was initially the only relevant factor determining the suspension of a prison sentence. Offence seriousness was not considered in the decision whether to suspend or not (although greater seriousness might have resulted in a prison sentence length beyond the upper limit for suspension).

The main possible criticism of such a two-step process is the fact that the decisions on the imposed sentence and on its execution (i.e. suspension) are, in many countries, made simultaneously, by the same person, and announced at the same time. In such a situation, the court has to invest significant effort into distinguishing between the two steps, since they become part of the same thought process, which might lead the court to merge the two steps into one. This could be intentional, especially if the judges disagree with the notion of two separate steps: they may find it problematic to consider the same factors twice (e.g. once to mitigate a prison sentence's length, and then to suspend its execution) or they might dislike the two-stage system for other reasons. If judges are not required to provide thorough reasoning for their sentencing decision(s), it becomes simpler for judges to decide in one step, rather than two (or indeed, they might begin by deciding whether they want to incarcerate the offender or not). The two-step process can also fade away unintentionally, since it is not an intuitive way of sentencing, but a structured approach that requires specific training and instruction. Unless the two-step process is both taught and enforced, therefore, it will likely be disparately or rarely applied, resulting in practice in judges considering suspended prison sentences as a separate type of sentence, rather than a mode of executing a prison sentence.

A disadvantage of the two-step process is that suspension could be seen as a let-off: the offender is not incarcerated, despite being handed a prison sentence. Symbolically, the most punitive sanction is imposed, yet in practice the offender's life is minimally impacted. This might not have been such an important issue when the suspended prison sentence was first conceived, since it was intended for only exceptional use and only for very short prison sentences (typically of up to one month). However, if suspension becomes the norm and long prison sentences are suspended, the fact that offence seriousness is not considered when deciding on suspension becomes more problematic, as it can easily distort the proportionality of the resulting sentence. This highlights the necessity of considering interactions between the individual parameters set when imposing suspended prison sentences (e.g. the length of prison sentences that can be suspended) and the principles governing their imposition. A two-step process in which the decision on suspension is made based only on the predicted risk of re-offending can be considered appropriate when only short prison sentences are suspended, and infrequently, yet the same principles can be considered problematic if long prison sentences are regularly suspended.

To summarise the previous discussion, the two-step process requires mental subscription to a particular process and set of parameters, if unjust sentences are to be avoided. Where such subscription is absent, the two-step process is easily misused. Abandoning the two-step process and rendering suspended prison sentences a distinct type of sanction, however, brings additional difficulties. First, it potentially renders the sanction dishonest: in some systems, it is called a suspended prison sentence, yet is imposed in situations in which a non-suspended prison sentence would never be considered (various alternative sanctions would be imposed if suspension was not an option). Second – and more practically – it becomes less clear when suspended sentences should be imposed, for which offences and which offenders. This is especially problematic in systems that subscribe symbolically to the two-step process, but in which judges in fact make their decision in one step. Where the penal code prescribes a two-step process, developing principled jurisprudence for a one-step process is virtually impossible.

Where the two-step process is fully abandoned, even conceptually, it becomes challenging to determine what length of suspended prison sentence to impose. In the two-step process, the length of the prison sentence is the same regardless of the mode (the decision to suspend does not alter its length). In a one-step process, there is no necessity to base the length on a custodial sentence. Suppose that a judge wishes to impose a suspended prison sentence in a case in which, were the offender to be incarcerated immediately, he/she would impose a seven-month prison sentence. The suspended prison sentence does not need to be seven months long; the judge must consider what constitutes a just and proportionate response, and that might entail a suspended sentence of a different length; since the suspended prison sentence is not perceived as a prison sentence, the lengths of the two should not be the same. In this scenario, further specific guidance is needed for judges to know what length of suspended prison sentence to apply; if such guidance is missing, they may end up imposing inconsistent sentences, or sentences that are overly harsh when suspension is revoked.

Sentence length: least punitive upon imposition, unduly punitive upon revocation

The difficulty in *setting* the length of suspended prison sentences in the one-step approach is best illustrated by research into public opinion on sanction equivalency. When professionals and the general public were asked about the equivalency of various sanctions, they considered a suspended prison sentence of 12 months to be equivalent to approximately 1–2 months of imprisonment and a suspended prison sentence of 36 months to equate to 3–6 months of imprisonment (Pina-Sánchez & Gosling, 2020; Sebba, 1978; Sebba & Nathan, 1984). The reasoning behind these ratios is straightforward: sentence suspension is often perceived as allowing the offender to "walk free" (Freiberg, 2019), and is represented as such in popular culture, including in the opening scene of *The Godfather* where these exact words are used. Neither the public nor the professional respondents approved of the two-step approach when applied widely, as they view suspended prison sentences as the least punitive sanction upon imposition. This issue becomes even more important if the parameters of suspended prison sentence are broadened (enabling longer sentences to be suspended): the difference between a week in prison and a week of a suspended prison sentence is not as substantial as the difference between two years in prison and a suspended prison sentence of two years.

This dissonance between the theoretical sanction equivalency provided by the two-step approach and the survey respondents' perspectives leads to sentence inflation. Judges impose longer sentences when suspending than they would if they were not deciding to suspend, because the threat of punishment communicated by the suspended sentence does not correspond to the punishment of imprisonment (Freiberg, 2019). So far, there exists very limited empirical evidence of this sentence inflation (Bottoms, 1979; Tait, 1995). To investigate it, I carried out two experiments in 2021 and 2022, both in Czechia, which formally operates a two-step process, but in which judicial practice resembles the one-step process. The results reveal that when presented with the same case, judges and prosecutors would impose a 7-month sentence when directed to impose a non-suspended prison sentence, and a 14-month sentence when directed to impose a suspended prison sentence. Similar differences were found across three different scenarios – theft, fraud and driving without a licence after a ban – as displayed in Figure 2.1.

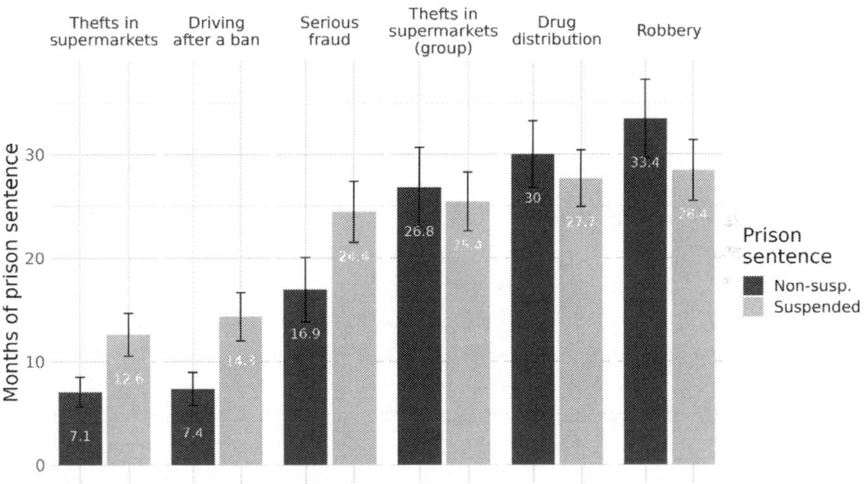

Figure 2.1 Sentence inflation and sentence deflation.

Note: Criminal justice practitioners were asked to set either a suspended or a non-suspended prison sentence for the same vignette. Vignettes were designed to be on the borderline for immediate incarceration, featuring offenders with an intermediate criminal history. Two separate sets of three vignettes (the first three and the second three) were presented to different groups of practitioners in September 2021 (N = 34) and March 2022 (N = 40). Average values and confidence intervals are reported.

This sentence inflation appears, however, to affect only cases in which short non-suspended prison sentences would be imposed (these are the most commonly imposed sentences). In other cases, the exact opposite occurs: sentence deflation, due to the cap on the length of prison sentences that can be suspended. In Czechia, under current rules, only prison sentences of up to 3 years may be suspended. Imagine an offence for which the sentencing range minimum is 3 years. A judge willing to imprison the offender immediately might impose a sentence of 4 years (for instance). Meanwhile, the only possible sentence that is within the sentencing range and can be suspended is a sentence of 3 years; hence a judge wishing to avoid incarcerating the offender immediately may be willing to impose a shorter sentence so as to enable its suspension (Harrendorf, 2017). This is the mechanism behind sentence deflation.

A third problem can be observed, which is that suspended prison sentences of similar lengths are imposed for offences of different seriousness, for which non-suspended prison sentences of different duration would be imposed. As I demonstrate in Figure 2.1, suspended prison sentences of 25 months would be considered equivalent to non-suspended prison sentences of both 17 and 27 months. This is a logical consequence of sentence inflation and of the cap on the length of prison sentence that can be suspended. I mention this primarily in order to show that various injustices arise in relation to fixing the length of suspended prison sentences: sentence inflation is only one of these.

Sentence inflation (and sentence deflation) leads to unjust sentences being imposed and potentially served when suspension is revoked. If the suspended sentence is inflated, then supposing that the convicted person reoffends and the suspension is revoked, the resulting prison sentence is unduly punitive. The length of the sentence cannot be changed at the point of revocation; hence neither inflation nor deflation can be corrected should the offender end up serving the sentence in prison. These difficulties are necessary consequences of the penological paradox of suspended prison sentences both being and not being prison sentences (Gemmell, 1997).

Sentence inflation is problematic especially for its effect on proportionality: it leads to overly punitive sentences upon revocation, which disproportionately impact low-level offenders such as repeat thieves.[10] Meanwhile, those who commit serious offences might benefit from a sentence deflation: for instance, instead of a non-suspended prison sentence of 36–40 months, they might receive a suspended prison sentence of 32–36 months. The disproportionate effect of suspended prison sentences on small-scale thieves and serious offenders is substantive. Both receive the benefit of a prison sentence suspension, yet that benefit is greater for serious offenders, because their sentence is longer. Moreover, prison sentences for small-scale offenders are inflated, while serious offenders' sentences may be partly deflated. Third, if low-level offenders re-offend more commonly than serious offenders, they would have their suspended prison sentences revoked more frequently. Thus, while the difference between the "punitive bite" of the suspended prison sentence and the penal value (i.e. the punitive bite that should be communicated to the offender as a matter of proportionality) will be greater for serious offenders than for low-level offenders, this disproportionality is more problematic in the case of low-level offenders because it is likely to result in overly harsh sentences (e.g. due to sentence inflation) and because there are many more low-level offences than serious offences.

Conditions imposed during the operational period

Originally, suspended prison sentences were designed to provide offenders with a "second chance", another opportunity to lead a law-abiding life. The idea was that by figuratively hanging Damocles' sword over the offender's head, such a sentence would deter the offender from further criminal activity without the need for any other measures or conditions. Before long, however, states began to work with offenders to guide them towards making certain life changes or prevent them from re-offending via means additional to the threat of imprisonment. Probationary supervision, which may be imposed alongside suspended prison sentences in several jurisdictions, is one such means, as are prohibitions from various activities and similar restrictive measures. Meanwhile, various other measures aimed at increasing the punitive bite of suspended prison sentences (Drápal, 2021b). These include the possibility of home detention or community work as part of a suspended prison sentence, which can be seen as a response to the low punitive bite of (especially longer) suspended prison sentences. Over time, rehabilitative, incapacitative and punitive measures thus began to be imposed alongside suspended prison sentences to fulfil multiple sentencing rationales.

The main problem with these measures is that upon a breach of the suspension conditions, no alterations can be made to the length of the originally imposed prison sentence, and no compensation can thus be made for punitive intrusions into offenders' lives during the operational period (including not only punitive or incapacitative measures, but also the punitive effects of rehabilitative measures). When suspended prison sentences were initially conceived, their punitive bite during the operational period was as low as possible. Offenders would undergo criminal proceedings,[11] would be found guilty of particular offences – and thus labelled as offenders – and would be warned that if they continued to offend, they would be required to serve a prison sentence of a given length. The threat of imprisonment was unpleasant and their criminal record might result in "invisible punishments" (Fitrakis, 2018), such as obstacles in getting employed, but in other respects their standard of life (von Hirsch & Jareborg, 1991) was not altered.[12]

After the introduction of additional measures applicable during the operational period, the punitive bite during the operational period increased, in some cases significantly (e.g. long home detention). For the suspended prison sentence to remain a proportionate sentence, I propose that courts should have the opportunity to shorten the prison sentence upon revocation to account for the "punitive bite" caused by various restrictions endured during the operational period. Such provisions are rare to date, because they arguably undermine the very basic conception of suspended prison sentences of deterrence (Bottoms, 1979). One way around this is the German solution of enabling a reduction in the sentence to be executed provided that an offender has fulfilled certain conditions (Harrendorf, 2017).

However, as I outline in the final chapter (Chapter 15), I believe that such provisions are necessary because no court can predict at the time of imposing a sentence (and deciding on its suspension) whether or how the offender will comply with the imposed measures. Imagine two offenders – Jose and Mojca – both of whom receive suspended prison sentences whose conditions include spending one year under house arrest. Jose completes the one-year house arrest, but later during the operational period of his suspended sentence re-offends, while Mojca re-offends right away and does not spend a single day under house arrest. The punitive bite of Jose's sanction will be higher than the punitive bite experienced by Mojca. If at the time of imposing the sentence, the judge had reduced the sentence length to reflect the simultaneous imposition of house arrest, Mojca will end up experiencing a disproportionately low punitive bite. If the judge did not impose a lower sentence initially, then Jose's punitive bite will be disproportionately high. Unless the court has the option to change the length of the prison sentence to be served at the moment of revoking the suspension, it is impossible to reconcile the punitive bite of measures attached to suspended prison sentences and proportionality requirements.

This is one example of a problem that has arisen from the changing parameters of suspended prison sentences over time, without any change to the principles of such sentences. As the maximum length of prison sentence that can be suspended gradually increased, suspension began to look increasingly like a let-off. This logically drove an increase in provisions enabling the imposition of additional punitive sanctions alongside suspended prison sentences, as well as rehabilitative and incapacitative measures. While the principles of the suspended prison sentence remained the same, and did not permit any consideration of the punitive bite of the suspended prison sentence and its associated measures upon revocation, that punitive bite became potentially more significant.

So why did judicial systems not respond by making changes that would enable the length of the sentence to be reassessed when suspension is revoked? My perception is that few people were aware of this issue, or considered that such changes might be effective. Suspended prison sentences had always been of a fixed length, with only the mode of serving the sentence changing dependent on the offender's fulfilment of suspension conditions. Changing the length of the sentence if served in prison would make suspended sentences less understandable, lower their deterrent effect and result in the necessity of formulating principles governing how such sentence reductions should be decided, and by how much they might be reduced. Nevertheless, the failure of most judicial systems to implement any such changes is primarily to offenders' detriment and deserves thorough attention.

Suspension revocation and other responses to breaches

The original rationale of specific deterrence required the (semi)automatic revocation of suspension upon re-offending. The deterrent effect would be lower if there were a high chance of the offender not being incarcerated even if they re-offended (Wasik, 1994). Semi-automatic revocation is not especially problematic for as long as the suspended prison sentences are of a few weeks. If a revoked (previously suspended) prison sentence of this length is served together with a second sentence of a similar length, this results in the offender being incarcerated for at most a few months, which may easily be considered a just sanction – not disproportionate or unjustly harmful. However, if this practice is applied to sentences of several months or even years, the same cannot be said to be true.

Imagine a longer suspended prison sentence – two years – is imposed with an operational period of four years. If the offender commits a new non-serious offence towards the end of the operational period, the judge might be hesitant to revoke the sentence, because the long imprisonment that would be prompted as a result by a non-serious offence would be perceived as disproportionate, especially given that the offender had led a law-abiding life for a substantial period of time. However, if the judge decided to give the offender a second chance (or perhaps even a third one), this might give both the offender and the public a feeling of impunity.[13] Neither of these options constitutes a good solution, and in a system that imposes longer suspended prison sentences, it is hard to resolve this. It can be partly remedied by the revocation of suspension being sometimes mandatory and sometimes optional, yet this might introduce different problems of its own: if, for example, it was mandatory to revoke suspension and enact the original prison sentence only when a non-suspended prison sentence was imposed for the new offence, judges might avoid imposing non-suspended prison sentences for re-offenders. A similar mechanism has been observed for serious offences in Israel (Gazal-Ayal & Emmanuel, 2023).

Judges' unwillingness to revoke suspension and execute the original prison sentence may also be bolstered by sentence inflation and net-widening. For instance, as we saw above, a suspended prison sentence of 14 months is often imposed when the length of a proportionate non-suspended prison sentence would be 7 months. When there is no possibility to shorten the sentence upon revocation of suspension, judges might avoid ordering the execution of the sentence because it is disproportionately long. Another non-custodial sanction (i.e. another suspended prison sentence or alternative sanction) offers a possible route out of this conundrum. Similarly, if a suspended prison sentence is imposed in a cases in which a non-suspended prison sentence would never normally be imposed, although the law allows one (which is a common scenario for non-serious offences committed by first-time offenders), judges might not be persuaded that incarceration is necessary even if the offender commits a second low-level offence. For example, judges are usually reluctant to incarcerate offenders who have (even repeatedly) driven without a licence, especially if the sentence would be semi-long. Instead, they tend to impose another non-custodial sanction for the re-offence.

The result of all this is that judges pile on multiple non-custodial sanctions, which is problematic especially if the pile includes more than one suspended sentence. An offender can easily end up with multiple suspended prison sentences, each of which is inflated. Upon any further re-offending, such an offender runs the risk that the judge(s) might revoke the suspension of one or perhaps all of those sentences such that the offender goes from having multiple suspended prison sentences – experiencing a low punitive bite – to serving multiple prison sentences in a row and thus experiencing a strong (and often disproportionate) punitive bite.[14] This accumulation of prison sentences often results in offenders serving very long prison sentences for (multiple) offences of low-seriousness (Drápal, 2020). Ironically, this is the result of repeated efforts not to incarcerate these offenders, but without sufficient consideration of the consequences of using a tool that was not designed for longer or multiple sentences.

Re-offending during the operational period of a (longer) suspended prison sentence represents a particular challenge for principled approaches to sentencing. How should a previously imposed, currently suspended prison sentence influence the imposition of a new sanction for a re-offence, and who should decide on the new sanction? Traditionally – even before the introduction of suspended prison sentences – criminal law distinguished between recidivism (multiple offences with separate convictions for each) and multiple offending (multiple offences committed prior to conviction). Suspended prison sentences distorted this distinction, since when sentencing an offender for a new offence committed during the operational period of a previously imposed suspended sentence, the new offence was committed after the previous conviction, but before the offender has experienced any hard treatment (Drápal, 2023).

The original conception of suspended prison sentences provided for the imposition of longer sentences to offenders who re-offended after receiving a suspended prison sentence; indeed, this was reflected in the name of the original French bill on suspended prison sentences ("on mitigation and aggravation of punishments"). Yet this seems to be out of touch with today's proportionality scholarship: censure theorists argue that the amount of disapproval communicated solely by the pronouncement of a sentence, without inflicting hard treatment, is limited, and this view has led to greater emphasis on the resulting hard treatment of revoking suspension more than on the pronouncement of the suspended sentence (von Hirsch, 2019). The likely result of this shift is a move towards the opposite of the original approach, i.e. towards imposing shorter sentences for offenders who have previously been handed suspended sentences and will thus (likely) have to serve multiple custodial sentences as a result of their re-offence. This is a substantial move away from the original theory of the suspended prison sentence, which was built on the idea that the pronouncement of the sentence was effective, even without the hard treatment itself. If a different perspective on the defining elements of punishment is adopted, this should be reflected in a re-evaluation of the choices made in the sentencing system.[15]

Subsequent sentencing of offenders with previous convictions is also problematic from a procedural perspective. In many countries (though not all, see e.g. chapter 12 on Serbia), two different judges make separate decisions about the revocation of suspension in relation to the existing prison sentence(s) and on the new sentence. Imagine, for instance, a case in which one judge (Ales) decides on a suspended prison sentence for a first offence, and a second judge (Marta) decides on a new sanction for an offence committed during the operational period of the suspended prison sentence imposed by Ales. Ales and Marta decide separately and independently. Marta must decide first, since Ales cannot (and has no reason to) revoke suspension unless the offender has been found guilty of a new offence.[16] Marta must thus impose a sentence for the new offence without knowing whether Ales will order the execution of the originally suspended prison sentence. Marta might be willing to give the offender another chance by imposing a second suspended prison sentence, but if Ales decides to imprison the offender, then Marta's attempt was not only futile, but she also cannot order the execution of the suspended prison sentence that she imposed unless the offender re-offends again, because the offender is leading a law-abiding life after being imposed a second suspended prison sentence. This would moreover result in the offender serving time in prison during the operational period of the second suspended prison sentence, which is counterintuitive.[17]

If Marta decides, on the other hand, to impose a non-suspended prison sentence, she must decide its length. If she expects Ales to revoke the original suspension and serve the previously imposed sentence (which is rather long), she may impose only a short non-suspended prison sentence. Yet Ales, considering that the new sentence is rather short, may in fact decide not to order the execution of the suspended prison sentence, and instead to prolong the operational period of the original suspension; as a result, the conception that Marta had in mind upon sentencing will not be realised. The only scenario in which Marta can be reasonably sure what Ales will do is that in which Marta imposes a longer non-suspended prison sentence for the new offence. Ales could then be expected to order the execution of the previous (suspended) prison sentence, and the offender will serve the two prison sentences concurrently, resulting in a substantial length of time in prison. It is hard to find any balance of certainty that would lead to the imposition of a just sentence in such a system. This problem might be solved by an unofficial agreement between the two judges, but this is not how the law is supposed to work.

Why do these two judges need to make independent decisions? Typically, post-communist continental criminal justice and sentencing systems are designed to ensure that the same judge hears the case, decides on guilt, imposes the sentence and decides on its execution; the only exception to this is parole decisions, which can be made by a different judge. Adding a second exception for suspension revocation – which is in many ways different from parole – would require resolving significant practical and theoretical issues and relying much more on written evidence. However, it may be necessary to ensure principled decision-making on suspended prison sentences.

Parameters and principles: cumulative problems of suspended prison sentences'

To recap, the original conception of the suspended prison sentence was not problematic, but the way in which its parameters have broadened over time, and the changes that have been made to it in many jurisdictions, have led to multiple flaws. In particular, the option to suspend longer prison sentences than the original conception envisioned and the (very) frequent imposition of suspended prison sentences have resulted in situations that were beyond the scope of the original conception. Further changes that have complicated the concept of suspended prison sentences to a lesser extent include the imposition of rehabilitative, incapacitative and punitive measures alongside suspended prison sentences and tendencies away from revoking suspension when the offender re-offends. Many of these changes have – to a varying degree – taken place across the post-communist countries. In the following chapters, I and my fellow authors take a closer look at how suspended prison sentences are designed and implemented in individual jurisdictions, how they were originally conceived and how they have changed over time.

In doing so, we discuss to what extent the issues I have described in this chapter arise, whether they are considered problematic, and which solutions (if any) have been proposed or implemented.

Given the extent of the difficulties these texts point out, readers would be excused for wondering why it is that these problems have not been addressed in sentencing scholarship relating to continental Western Europe (both Southern Europe and Scandinavia). To date, there has been very little published scholarship on the topic of suspended prison sentences (in English), hence I can only hypothesise. I believe that this has not been considered a crucial focus for scholarship primarily because suspended prison sentences are used less frequently in Western European jurisdictions and because there are more checks in place. Furthermore, the use of fines and other alternative sanctions as the primary go-to sanction for first-time offenders in many Western European countries avoids many of the difficulties associated with the cumulation of suspended prison sentences, which – if revoked – can result in very long prison sentences being served.

No doubt, some of the issues identified in this book also affect Western European legal systems, but have not yet been studied there since suspended prison sentences are less frequently used. Anecdotal evidence supports this: when I gave a presentation about sentence inflation in Czechia at a German university, participants were intrigued and mentioned that the same could be happening in Germany – but it has never yet been studied. This book could well serve as the inspiration for studies looking into similar issues in Western European countries.

It is also possible that Western European countries have taken a more experimental approach to suspended prison sentences than the post-communist countries have. For example, Sweden introduced a true suspended sentence, which is not a prison sentence (no length of imprisonment is set[18]). The Netherlands, Austria, and France all enable partly-suspended prison sentences, which can offset some of the issues mentioned above, if employed correctly. In Switzerland, a single judge sentences an offender for a new offence and also decides on the revocation of the previous suspended prison sentence. In Germany, the probation service works with serious and recidivist offenders and the number of suspension revocations is low (Dünkel, 2019). In Finland, suspended prison sentences are frequently combined with various other sanctions or treatments (Lappi-Seppälä, 2019). Given how little has been written in English about suspended prison sentences in these countries (and the little empirical attention paid to them), it is, however, difficult to ascertain which of these options have resulted in just sentences and which of them lead to additional problems of their own. New contributions to the literature on suspended prison sentences in Western Europe are needed, both to identify issues and solutions, and to serve as inspiration for other scholars.

One possible reason why suspended prison sentences have not been seen as controversial or deserving of attention in Western European jurisdictions may be that the sentencing rules in Western European jurisdictions keep lower limits on sentence length. While there has been no thorough examination of sentencing ranges across Europe, there is suggestive evidence of those ranges being higher in post-communist Europe compared with Western Europe (Kert et al., 2015). Lower ranges – especially lower sentencing range minimums – lead to shorter sentences. When shorter prison sentences are imposed, fewer problems arise from their suspension.

Again, this brings us back to the importance of considering suspended prison sentences in context: whether we should praise or condemn the use of suspended prison sentences depends entirely on how they are defined and how they are used.

Conclusion

In this chapter I have outlined the theoretical consequences of broadening the parameters of the suspended prison sentence, presupposing conditions that are present to a varying degree in many Central and Eastern European countries. Context matters. The proportion of suspended prison sentences in a particular jurisdiction strongly influences the risk of their accumulation; similarly, other difficulties do not arise if only a few suspended prison sentences are imposed. The outlined consequences will likely appear in individual countries at different levels depending upon the specific form of their legal provisions and other contextual features. Meanwhile, minuscule changes may make a substantial difference. For example, the accumulation of suspended prison sentences is approached differently in the former Yugoslavian countries, because they consider re-offending as the committal of multiple crimes rather than as recividism (Drápal, 2023). This approach likely results in significantly shorter prison sentences when suspension is revoked.

My hope, in outlining the original conception of the suspended prison sentence, the changes that we have seen to its principles and parameters over time in many Central and Eastern European countries, and the issues that arise from those changes, is that it will help readers to approach the next section of the book, in which the authors explore the design and use of suspended sentences in their countries of specialism, focusing in particular on the issues outlined in this chapter. In some countries, the original 1880s conception of suspended prison sentence was never implemented, and the suspended prison sentence introduced in the 1920s was already significantly different. Others followed the original conception closely and adopted more gradual changes. Nevertheless, similar issues have arisen across the post-communist countries. The national chapters are also important for what they do not say: the absence of a certain debate can reveal plenty about a particular country's attitudes or concerns.

Notes

1 Several parts of this chapter overlap slightly with a previously published paper (Drápal, 2025).
2 Parliamentary proceedings on 17 October 1919, available from https://www.psp.cz/eknih/1918ns/ps/stenprot/084schuz/s084011.htm.
3 With similar developments in Europe at the end of the 19th century (Faraldo Cabana, 2015).
4 These figures are based on official data (Státní úřad statistický, 1923, 1925, 1931, 1937), for further details see (Drápal, 2021b).
5 In the Kuhnian sense.
6 La loi Bérenger (loi du 26 mars 1891 sur l'atténuation et l'aggravation des peines), s. 1.
7 Such limitations persisted for a long time: David Thomas suggested a similar maximum in 1974 for England and Wales.

8 Czech law no. 562/1919 Coll. on conditional sentence and release, s. 2/1.
9 Decision made 20 June 1929, n. Zm I 386/29, decision made 9 October 1929, n. Zm I 60/29 or decision made 13 August 1927, n. Zm II 94/27.
10 Sentence inflation often goes unchallenged because offenders – rejoicing in not being incarcerated – are unlikely to appeal against the length of suspended prison sentences (Sentencing Advisory Council, 2006, p. 33).
11 This has sometimes been considered punitive in itself (Feeley, 1979).
12 At the time of its conception, the suspended prison sentence was even less punitive than this, since the criminal record did not have to be disclosed and any measures and sanctions imposed alongside a suspended prison sentence were also suspended.
13 Even if the penal code requires judges to revoke the suspension of a previously imposed prison sentence upon re-offending, judges might find a workaround. In Czechia, where revocation was mandatory for a long time, judges were willing to overlook certain breaches so that they would not have to send offenders to prison, even risking disciplinary proceedings for doing so (Lata, 2008).
14 In many European countries, prison sentences cannot be served concurrently.
15 This relates primarily to continental legal systems; common law systems can technically solve this problem easily via concurrent or partly concurrent sentences (Sentencing Advisory Council, 2006, p. 108), albeit this solution is not without its own issues (Bottoms, 1981).
16 Decision n. I. ÚS 1202/17 made 15. 8. 2017 (N 151/86 SbNU 527), s. 16-18.
17 A partial solution to this could be a ban on the imposition of further suspended prison sentences if an offender already has one (as in Poland, see chapter in this volume). Yet a very similar problem could result from the imposition of community sentences or fines.
18 See Chapter 27 of the Swedish Penal Code.

References

Ancel, M. (1971). *Suspended sentence*. Heinemann.

Bagaric, M. (1999). Suspended sentences and preventive sentences: Illusory Evils and Disproportionate Punishments. *UNSW Law Journal*, *22*(2), 535–563.

Bartels, L. (2009). To suspend or not to suspend: A qualitative analysis of sentencing decisions in the Supreme Court of Tasmania. *The University of Tasmania Law Review*, *28*(1), 23–62.

Bartels, L. (2010). An examination of the arguments for and against the use of suspended sentences. *Flinders Law Journal*, *12*, 119–172.

Bottoms, A. E. (1979). The Advisory council and the suspended sentence. *Criminal Law Review*, 437–446.

Bottoms, A. E. (1981). The suspended sentence in England, 1967-1978. *The British Journal of Criminology*, *21*(1), 1–26. https://doi.org/10.1093/oxfordjournals.bjc.a047193

Drápal, J. (2020). Ukládání trestů v případě jejich kumulace: Jak trestat pachatele, kteří spáchali další trestný čin předtím, než vykonali dříve uložené tresty. *Jurisprudence*, *29*(2), 1–17.

Drápal, J. (2021a). Day fines. In B. Huebner (Ed.), *Oxford bibliographies. Criminology*. Oxford University Press. https://doi.org/10.1093/obo/9780195396607-0303

Drápal, J. (2021b). Podmíněné odsouzení: Jeho účel a vývoj na území Česka. *Státní Zastupitelství*, *19*(6), 18–35.

Drápal, J. (2023). Sentencing multiple conviction offenders. *European Journal of Criminology*, *20*(1), 142–160. https://doi.org/10.1177/1477370821996903

Drápal, J. (2025). Suspended prison sentences in Czechia: How they came to dominate the penal landscape and their consequences. *Criminal Law Forum*. https://doi.org/10.1007/s10609-025-09515-4

Dünkel, F. (2019). Reforms of the criminal sanctions system in Germany – Achievements and unresolved problems. *Juridica International*, *28*, 37–48.

Enker, A. (1979). The suspended sentence: Israel's experience. *Israel Law Review*, *14*, 369–381.

Fairbanks, R. A. (1975). Suspension of execution of sentence: An examination of judicial power. *Tulsa Law Review*, *11*(1), 26–44.

Faraldo Cabana, P. (2015). A certain sense of fairness? Why fines were made affordable. *European Journal of Criminology*, *12*(5), 616–631. https://doi.org/10.1177/1477370815587765

Feeley, M. M. (1979). *The process is the punishment: Handling cases in a lower criminal court*. Russell Sage Foundation.

Fitrakis, E. (Ed.). (2018). *Invisible punishments. European dimension – Greek perspective*. National Printing House.

Frase, R. S. (2019). Suspended sentences and free-standing probation orders in U.S. guidelines systems: A survey and assessment. *Law and Contemporary Problems*, *82*(1), 51–79.

Freiberg, A. (2019). Suspended sentences in Australia: Uncertain, unstable, unpopular and unnecessary? *Law and Contemporary Problems*, *82*(1), 80–109.

Gazal-Ayal, O., & Emmanuel, N. (2023). How minimum sentences benefit offenders—The case of suspended sentences. *Law & Social Inquiry*, *48*(3), 847–880.

Gemmell, J. (1997). The new conditional sentencing regime. *Criminal Law Quarterly*, *39*(3), 334–361.

Harrendorf, S. (2017). Sentencing thresholds in German criminal law and practice: Legal and empirical aspects. *Criminal Law Forum*, *28*(3), 501–539. https://doi.org/10.1007/s10609-017-9331-x

Hodgson, J., & Soubis, L. (2016). Understanding the sentencing process in France. *Crime and Justice*, *45*(1), 221–265.

Horváth, T. (1969). Suspended sentence under Hungarian criminal law. *Acta Juridica Academiae Scientiarum Hungariae Tomus*, *11*(1–2), 61–80.

Irwin-Rogers, K., & Roberts, J. V. (2019). Swimming against the tide: The suspended sentence order in England and Wales. *Law and Contemporary Problems*, *82*, 137–162.

Kallab, J. (1904). Doporučuje se v Rakousku uvedení instituce podmínečného odsouzení? In *Spisy II. sjezdu právnického* (pp. 1–38).

Kert, R., Slot, B., Vernimmen, G., Lehner, A., & Schellekens, J. (2015). *Study on minimum sanctions in the EU Member States*. European Commission. https://doi.org/10.2838/596957

Lappi-Seppälä, T. (2019). Community sanctions as substitutes to imprisonment in the Nordic countries. *Law and contemporary problems*, *82*(1), 17–50.

Lata, J. (2008). Několik poznámek k problematice ukládání trestů začínajícím delikventům. In *Pocta Otovi Novotnému k 80. Narozeninám* (pp. 158–165). ASPI.

Milota, A. (1919). *Podmíněné odsouzení a propuštění (Výklad zákona)*. Nákladem Karla Beníška.

O'Brian, P. (1995). The prison on the continent: Europe, 1865–1965. In N. Morris & D. J. Rothman (Eds.), *The Oxford history of the prison* (pp. 199–225). Oxford University Press.

Osborough, N. (1969). The emergence of the suspended sentence in England. *The Irish Jurist*, *4*(1), 23–35.

Osborough, N. (1982). A Damocles' sword guaranteed Irish: The suspended sentence in the Republic of Ireland. *Irish Jurist*, *17*(2), 221–256.

Pifferi, M. (2016). *Reinventing punishment: A comparative history of criminology and penology in the nineteenth and twentieth centuries*. Oxford University Press.

Pina-Sánchez, J., & Gosling, J. P. (2020). Tackling selection bias in sentencing data analysis: A new approach based on a scale of severity. *Quality & Quantity*, *54*(3), 1047–1073. https://doi.org/10.1007/s11135-020-00973-z

Radzinowicz, L. (1971). Foreword. In M. Ancel (Ed.), *Suspended setnence* (pp. vi–viii). Heinemann.

Roach, K. (2000). Conditional sentences, restorative justice, net-widening and aboriginal offenders. *The changing face of conditional sentencing*, 25–38.

Sebba, L. (1978). Some explorations in the scaling of penalties. *Journal of Research in Crime and Delinquency*, *15*(2), 247–265. https://doi.org/10.1177/002242787801500209

Sebba, L. (2013). Is sentencing reform a lost cause? A historical perspective on conceptual problems in sentencing research. *Law and Contemporary Problems*, *76*(1), 237–264.

Sebba, L., & Nathan, G. (1984). Further explorations in the scaling of penalties. *The British Journal of Criminology*, *24*(3), 221–249. https://doi.org/10.1093/oxfordjournals.bjc.a047451

Sentencing Advisory Council. (2006). *Suspended sentences: Final report part 1*. https://www.sentencingcouncil.vic.gov.au/sites/default/files/2019-08/Suspe1nded_Sentences_Final_Report_Part_1.pdf

Solnař, V., & Vanduchová, M. (2009). *Systém českého trestního práva: Tresty a ochranná opatření*. Novatrix.

Státní úřad statistický. (1923). *Trestní statistika z Čech, Moravy a Slezska v letech 1913–1918*. Bursík a Kohout.

Státní úřad statistický. (1925). *Trestní statistika z Čech, Moravy a Slezska v letech 1919–1922*. Bursík a Kohout.

Státní úřad statistický. (1931). *Trestní statistika z republiky Československé v letech 1923–1927*. Bursík a Kohout.

Státní úřad statistický. (1937). *Trestní statistika republiky Československé za léta 1928–1931*. Bursík a Kohout.

Tait, D. (1995). The invisible sanction: suspended sentences in Victoria 1985–1991. *Australian & New Zealand Journal of Criminology*, *28*(2), 143–162. https://doi.org/10.1177/000486589502800202

Takáč, M., & Svitok, J. (1946). *Podmienečné odsúdenie a prepustenie*. Právnická jednota v Bratislavě.

Vanstone, M. (2008). The international origins and initial development of probation: An early example of policy transfer. *British Journal of Criminology*, *48*(6), 735–755. https://doi.org/10.1093/bjc/azn070

von Hirsch, A. (2019). Censure and hard treatment in the general justification for punishment: A reconceptualisation of desert-oriented penal theory. In A. du Bois-Pedain & A. E. Bottoms (Eds.), *Penal censure: Engagements within and beyond desert theory* (pp. 87–92). Hart Publishing.

von Hirsch, A., & Jareborg, N. (1991). Gauging criminal harm: A living-standard analysis. *Oxford Journal of Legal Studies*, *11*(1), 1–38.

Wasik, M. (1994). Sentencing guidelines: The problem of conditional sentences. *Criminal Justice Ethics*, *13*(1), 50–57. https://doi.org/10.1080/0731129X.1994.9991960

Webster, C. M., & Doob, A. N. (2019). Missed opportunities: A postmortem on Canada's experience with the conditional sentence. *Law and Contemporary Problems*, *82*(1).

Zucker, A. (1891). *Podmíněné odsouzení*. Bursík a Kohout.

Part II

Part IIa

Suspended sentences in the former Warsaw-pact countries

3 Countries of the former Warsaw Pact

Krzysztof Krajewski

Historical background

This brief introduction outlines the histories of six countries in Central Europe and the Eastern Balkans: Bulgaria, Czechia, Hungary, Poland, Romania, and Slovakia.[1] All six are former members of the Warsaw Pact, also known as the Soviet Bloc. Before 1990 they were commonly referred to in communist newspeak as "people's democracies" (to differentiate them from the "bourgeois democracies" of the West). Since the late 1940s they had been governed by communist parties dependent on Moscow and were effectively Moscow's satellites. Their sovereignty was substantially limited, in some cases by the continual presence of the Red Army, as well as by Soviet military interventions to discipline unruly allies (Hungary in 1956; Czechoslovakia in 1968). However, unlike Belarus, Estonia, Latvia, Lithuania, Moldova, and Ukraine, these six countries were not governed directly from Moscow as Soviet Republics. This had various important consequences for those countries and for their criminal law and criminal justice policies. Despite being members of the Soviet Bloc they enjoyed, for the most part – and especially after 1956 – a somewhat larger margin of freedom than the Soviet Republics.

The 45 years these countries spent as members of the Soviet Bloc is not their only common historical experience. Various earlier historical ties existed between them, not least dynastic connections: Czechs and Hungarians became Polish kings, and members of Polish royal dynasties became kings of Czechia and Hungary. Moreover, throughout the 19th century (and sometimes earlier), all six of these countries were either directly ruled or heavily influenced by the European powers of that time: Russia, Germany (earlier Prussia), Austria, or Turkey. None of these countries were fully independent in this period.

Bulgaria and Romania succeeded in regaining their independence – at least partially – from Turkish rule in the second half of the 19th century. Under the constitution adopted in 1879, Bulgaria became a constitutional monarchy, although between the two world wars it evolved into an authoritarian royal dictatorship. Bulgaria was a member of the Axis during the Second World War but declined to participate in the German invasion of the Soviet Union.

DOI: 10.4324/9781003568667-6

The foundations of contemporary Romania were established in 1856 with the union of the two Danubian principalities: Moldavia and Wallachia. The new state was given the name Romania in 1866 and gained its full independence from the Ottoman Empire in 1877. Until the end of the Second World War, Romania operated as a constitutional monarchy, albeit one that became increasingly authoritarian in the interwar period. During the Second World War, Romania was allied with Nazi Germany and took part in the invasion of the Soviet Union.

Czechia, Hungary and Slovakia share a substantial common history as lands of the Habsburg monarchy from the 16th century until 1918. Following the Austrian-Hungarian compromise in 1867, a dual Austro-Hungarian monarchy was established; this was a constitutional monarchy of rather liberal character that had – in addition to the shared monarch – a common foreign policy, common currency, and common army. In all other respects the Austrian part (including Czechia, south-eastern Poland, and south-western Ukraine), and the Hungarian part (including Slovakia), were separate and enjoyed broad autonomy, each with their own constitution, parliament and separate legal, and judicial system.

The collapse of the Habsburg monarchy after the First World War resulted in its member nations regaining their independence and establishing their own states. Independent Hungary, whose territory had been substantially diminished, was established as a kingdom without a king (governed by a regent). In 1941 it joined the German invasion of the Soviet Union. Independent Czechoslovakia was proclaimed in October 1918 and was probably the only country in Central Europe that was governed truly democratically between the two world wars. As a consequence of the Munich Agreement in 1938, it lost a substantial part of its territory that was inhabited by the German minority, and in March 1939 the remnants were dismembered: following German occupation of the newly created Protectorate of Bohemia and Moravia, Hungary annexed Carpathian Ruthenia, and Poland annexed *Záolží* (Polish: *Zaolzie*), a region around the city of *Těšín* (Polish: *Cieszyn*). Slovakia was proclaimed to be an independent state but it was in fact totally dependent on Nazi Germany. Like the other countries of Central Europe, the Czechoslovak territories were "liberated" by the Red Army in 1944–1945.

The Polish-Lithuanian Commonwealth lost its independence during the 18th century as a consequence of three consecutive partitions (1772, 1791, and 1795). The southern part, known as *Galicja* (German: *Galizien*, English: *Galicia*), became part of the Habsburg empire. The western part around the city of *Poznań* (German: *Posen*) became part of Prussia and was later incorporated into unified Germany. The central and eastern parts were incorporated into Russia. It was the collapse of the three partitioning powers as a result of the First World War that led, as in other countries of the region, to Polish independence. Nevertheless, parliamentary democracy in Poland survived for only a couple of years, until a coup d'état in 1926 (in which the right-wing government was toppled by the military, led by formerly socialist marshal Josef Piłsudski, who is considered the father of Polish independence in 1918). During the years that followed, Poland's government became increasingly authoritarian. The German attack on Poland on 1 September 1939 – joined on 17 September by the Soviet Union – crushed Poland's independence. Poland was "liberated" by the Red Army in 1944–1945 and its territory shifted several hundred kilometres west in the Potsdam agreements between the Allies: it lost its pre-war territories east of the River Bug and acquired new – formerly German – territories to the east of the *Odra* (German: *Oder*) and *Nysa Łużycka* (German: *Lausitzer Neiße*, English: *Lusatian Neisse*) rivers.

One shared feature in the recent history of Czechia, Bulgaria, Hungary, Poland, Romania, and Slovakia is their "liberation" from Nazi occupations by the Red Army. Between 1945 and 1948, the Soviets took advantage of this "liberation" to impose their rule over these countries, either in overt, communist arranged coups, or via phony elections. During the late 1940s and until 1956–1957, communist rule in these countries amounted to a reign of terror in which thousands of people were killed and hundreds of thousands repressed in other ways. After Stalin's death these countries gradually liberalised slightly. Their governments were still authoritarian in character, but repression became less widespread. The system of government closely resembled the Soviet model, albeit with some specific local features. For example, Hungary was allowed a somewhat unorthodox economic policy, commonly referred to as "goulash communism", providing better supply of consumer goods. In Poland the strong and unbroken position of the Roman Catholic Church, paired with the government's inability to implement collectivised land ownership, meant that the communist grip over the country was never quite complete. Romania, meanwhile, enjoyed a certain leeway when it came to foreign policy, although this came at a price: the country was entirely in the grip of one of the most bizarre of communist dictators, Nicolae Ceaușescu. The "people's democracies", therefore, were by no means a uniform group of countries functioning on the same set of principles (as they were often perceived to be in the West). What they were, however, is a set of communist dictatorships that only survived politically thanks to "brotherly" Soviet support.

The origins of modern criminal law

These countries' specific historical experience during the 19th century had a strong impact on their legal culture and legal systems. All six countries belonged and continue to belong to the continental, civil law tradition. However, in most cases, the development of their own legal systems and traditions has been interrupted in the 19th century as they had legal systems imposed by foreign powers or were strongly influenced by foreign examples. This is true even of the countries that regained full or partial independence in the second half of the 19th century. For instance, Bulgaria's legal system was originally imposed by the

Ottoman Empire, but at a time when Turkish penal law was strongly influenced by the French *Code Napoleon*. As Russia's support was of crucial importance for Bulgaria in regaining its independence from Turkey, Russian influences on the Bulgarian legal system were also strong. This was especially visible in the code of criminal procedure adopted in 1897, although at that time Russian procedure was itself strongly influenced by the French model (Gruev, 2008, p. 153). The first Bulgarian criminal code was adopted in 1896 and was influenced by both Russian and German legislation. It took a rather classical approach to criminal responsibility, based on the offender's culpability and a retributive understanding of punishment, although the influence of the Italian positive school was also visible (Dolaptchieff, 1932, p. 1014). This code remained in force in Bulgaria until the second half of the 1940s.

Romania provides a clear-cut example of a system heavily and directly influenced by French substantive and procedural regulations. This was a result of the cultural links and influences and linguistic connections between the Roman nations. The first Romanian penal code of 1864, known also as the *Cuza Code*, was "substantially a faithful translation of the *Code Napoleon* of 1810" (Rinceanu, 2009, pp. 792–793). There can be no doubt that this code was primarily inspired by the classical school of penal law. It remained in force until 1936, when it was substituted by a new code prepared under the leadership of prominent legal scholar Vintilă Dongoroz. This new code was once again heavily influenced by foreign legislation, but this time that was the Italian Rocco Code (*Codice Rocco*) of 1930. As Rinceanu notes, the Rocco Code was an "authoritarian, although not totalitarian code" (Rinceanu, 2009, p. 793). The Italian influence likely arose not only as a result of the two countries' linguistic and cultural relationship, but also from the strong reputation enjoyed at that time by the positive school of penal law in general and the Italian *scuola positiva*, as represented by Enrico Ferri et al., in particular. It was also true that Mussolini's Italy exerted a strong political impact on Romania. Romania's 1936 penal code remained in force in its original form until 1947, when it was substantially modified; the updated version then remained in force until 1968.

Another country in the region that was able to develop its own penal legislation in the second half of the 19th century was Hungary. Despite not being a fully independent nation, from 1867 onwards Hungary became one of the two equal parts of the Austro-Hungarian monarchy; as such, it enjoyed broad autonomy, which extended to its penal legislation and criminal justice system. The new Hungarian penal code was adopted in 1878. It was commonly referred to as the *Csemegi Kodex* (Csúri, 2014, p. 510), after Károlyi Csemegi, a prominent judge, later president of the Hungarian Supreme Court, who led the committee drafting the code. According to Schafer, the code "was strongly influenced by foreign legislation; indeed parts of foreign statutes (mostly German and Belgian) were incorporated almost verbatim" (Schafer, 1959, p. 164). The code was modified several times but remained in force in Hungary until the middle of the 20th century. Its special part containing definitions of offences ceased to have effect in 1950, but the more general provisions, including rules of criminal responsibility and sentencing guidance, remained in force until 1962 (Csúri, 2014, p. 510). Despite its somewhat eclectic character, *Csemegi Kodex* "was progressive compared with contemporaneous codes" (Schafer, 1959, p. 164). It is important to note that the 1878 Hungarian penal code was in force beyond the borders of modern-day Hungary, as it applied to all Hungarian-ruled parts of the Austro-Hungarian Empire; these included what is now Slovakia, as well as parts of modern-day Croatia, Serbia, and Romania.

In the 19th century, the remaining countries of the region had no penal legislation of their own. In Czechia and Galicia (now south-eastern Poland and south-western Ukraine), which were governed directly from Vienna, the Austrian penal code of 1852 applied. This code was not new: it was a compilation of earlier Austrian penal codes, including the famous 1787 Josephina legislation and the subsequent penal code of 1803. It was by no means a modern penal code (Olechowski, 2010, p. 339). It was adopted at a time when Austria was still ruled in a rather authoritarian manner following the events of the Spring of Nations in 1848–1849, and there was no room for liberal reforms. This Austrian penal code of 1852 remained in force even after the end of the Austro-Hungarian Empire in 1918: it continued to apply in southern Poland until 1932, in Czechia until 1950, and in Austria itself until it was completely rewritten during the reform of 1972. In consequence, its impact on the legal culture and jurisprudence of the region was very significant.

Penal legislation in 19th century Poland constitutes a somewhat special case. Because Poland was partitioned between three powers, its territory came under the jurisdiction of three different legal systems. As mentioned earlier, Galicia was subject to Austrian legislation, i.e. the 1852 Austrian penal code. Western Poland, which was under German rule, was subject to Prussian law and later on the German penal code of 1871. The central and eastern parts of Poland were governed by Russia and were in principle subject to Russian law. However, the situation was more complicated in reality: the Vienna Congress of 1815 established in the central part of the country Kingdom of Poland which was ruled as a monarchy by the Russian tsar. The Kingdom had, in principle, a liberal constitution and should have enjoyed broad autonomy, but this was not respected by the tsar and his government. It also had its own penal law, codified in the Punishing Code of the Kingdom of Poland, which was adopted in 1818 and considered at the time to be a rather modern piece of legislation. That code remained in force until 1847, i.e. beyond 1831, when the Kingdom lost most of its autonomy. It was then replaced by the new Russian penal code of 1845, known as the Code of Capital and Correctional Punishments. The latter was generally considered to be a very inflated and casuistic code constituting a clear step back in comparison with its predecessor (Timasheff, 1953, p. 442). In 1903, a new penal code entered partly into force in the Russian Empire, known as the *Tagancev Code*, which was considered to be a relatively modern example of penal legislation (Potseluev, 2016). However, it only entered into force on the Polish territories in 1917. Ironically, this was the result of a decision taken by the German administration: central Poland was occupied by Germany after the Russian army was pushed eastwards in the first months of the First World War (Timasheff, 1953, pp. 443–444).

After 1918, the Bulgarian code of 1898 and the Hungarian *Csemegi Kodex* remained in force, although they were amended several times. In Romania, a new penal code was adopted in 1936. Czechoslovakia retained its Austro-Hungarian penal legislation during the interwar period, which meant that on the territory of the new Czechoslovakia two penal codes remained in force: the Hungarian code in the Slovak part, and the Austrian code in the Czech one. Penal law was thus never unified in democratic Czechoslovakia (Karabec, 2011, p. 6).

The most complicated situation was in newly independent Poland, whose territory remained under jurisdiction of three legal systems: Russian, German, and Austrian.[2] There was discussion about an eventual extension of one of these penal codes to the entire Polish territory, and the prime candidate for this was the Russian code of 1903, as the most recent and most modern code. Serious consideration was also given to the Austrian code of 1852, mainly due to the liberal tradition of the Austrian government in Galicia and the fact that most prominent Polish legal scholars in the area of penal law at that time had been educated in Austria, and often had judicial or other practical experience from that jurisdiction. What spoke against this latter solution was the fact that the Austrian code was the oldest of the three and was considered eclectic and outdated. The least considered candidate for the proposed extension was the German code of 1871. Eventually, the new Polish authorities decided instead to draw up completely new penal legislation. This was drafted by a committee led by Juliusz Makarewicz, a professor of penal law at the university in *Lwów* (Ukrainian: *Lviv*, German: *Lemberg*) and a representative of the sociological school strongly influenced by the ideas of Franz Liszt. The new penal code was entered into force in 1932. Commonly referred to as the *Makarewicz Code*, it was considered to be a very modern piece of penal legislation providing clear options for individual prevention in its penal policies and giving judges rather broad discretionary powers when it came to sentencing offenders, while introducing protective measures for repeat and dangerous offenders (Busch, 1936; Makarewicz, 1933).

Soviet influence

The Soviet-inspired and -led communist takeovers in the region's countries between 1945 and 1948 had significant consequences for these countries' penal law and criminal justice systems. On the one hand, those takeovers and the resulting changes in the political, economic, and social landscapes of Central Europe were referred to as "proletarian revolutions" involving a complete break with the "bourgeois" past and justifying the use of force to defeat "class enemies". This was supported by Stalin's thesis about the intensification of the class struggle with the progress of the proletarian revolution, and resulted in intensive political repression. Within this framework, penal law became an instrument of crude, mass terror in most instances. On the other hand, the new communist authorities very often sought some sort of formal legitimacy and pretended that their takeovers had taken place through democratic procedures under the countries' pre-war legal systems (Plachta, 1990).

This gave rise to two alternative approaches. The first was to "revolutionise" everything as quickly as possible, i.e. to get rid of all "bourgeois" legislation, including the existing penal codes, and substitute them with new, "revolutionary" and "truly proletarian" codes inspired by Soviet penal legislation. The second was to retain the existing penal codes but either to make intensive amendments to them or to introduce a substantial number of new by-laws regulating certain areas of criminal responsibility, including new offences definitions based on Soviet principles. The majority of the region's countries took the first of these two approaches, quickly introducing new penal codes at the beginning of the 1950s and often replacing these with even newer ones during the 1960s. The latter move was thanks to a process of partial liberalisation that took place after Stalin's death in 1953, during which penal law gradually lost its explicitly terrorist character. Hence, socialist Bulgaria adopted two new penal codes (1951 and 1968) and two codes of criminal procedure (1952 and 1968); Czechoslovakia adopted two penal codes (1950 and 1961) and three codes of criminal procedure (1950, 1956, 1961); Hungary adopted three penal codes (1950 – special part only, 1961 and 1968) and three codes of criminal procedure (1951, 1962, 1974). Such frequent recodifications of penal law had been practically unknown earlier. The region's remaining two countries were more frugal in introducing changes: "socialist" Romania adopted only one new penal code, in 1968, which interestingly enough was heavily influenced by the same Vintilă Dongoroz (Rinceanu, 2009, p. 794) who had been responsible for the previous 1936 code. Similarly, Poland's 1932 code remained in force until 1969, albeit supplemented by many additional laws. The new Polish code entered into force in 1970 (Kubiak, 1987).

Penal legislation in the socialist countries was often categorised as belonging to a separate type of legal system, the "socialist law system" (Frankowski, 1987). Whether "socialist" law really deserved to be categorised as such remains an open question. There is no doubt, though, that this legislation was strongly influenced by Soviet legal ideas, in particular ideas about crime and punishment. It is therefore both possible and relevant to speak about the sovietisation of the legal systems, including penal law, in these countries. However, the intensity of this sovietisation and the countries' eagerness to introduce ideas and provisions of Soviet provenience varied, and those countries that preserved their existing pre-war penal legislation for a relatively longer time were probably able to prevent their criminal justice systems from experiencing the deep sovietisation observed in others (Frankowski & Wąsek, 1993). For instance, the rules of penal responsibility in the Polish code of 1969 did not differ substantially from the regulations in its former 1932 code, and many of the changes were technical rather than ideological in character. Nevertheless, none of those countries remained free of the Soviet influence.

There were many features characteristic of socialist penal law, although – interestingly enough – these usually overlapped with the typical features of authoritarian penal law. They included vague and imprecise definitions of offences – allowing for "flexible" application – and the introduction of specific types of offences, such as "social parasitism" and "hooliganism", which enabled vicarious criminal repression of political opponents. Socialist penal law also provided special protections for state or collective property and for the governing communist parties' political interests, including new types of economic crimes specific to the context of centrally planned economies that were, both in theory and practice, subject to extremely harsh penalties (Pomorski, 1981). The main socialist penal law "innovation", although it was by no means original, was the introduction of material or substantive definition of offence: in accordance with the materialist principles of Marxist philosophy, it specified that for an act to constitute an offence, it must be socially dangerous; it was not sufficient for it to be formally prohibited under the law.[3] In other words, formally prohibited acts that were not socially dangerous did not constitute offences. This idea was already implemented in the earliest Soviet penal codes in 1922 and 1926.

Apart from Marxist ideology, the socialist countries' penal legislation was also strongly influenced by the ideas of the sociological school in penal law and criminology (Pomorski, 1981). But ideas underlying that school were often adopted out of political necessity and for political expediency, rather than for their penological value. Nevertheless, in practice this meant that the "socialist" states often paid more attention to the *social dangerousness of the offender* than to the *social dangerousness of the offence* (Pomorski, 1981). Whether this was a deliberate adoption of the sociological school's teachings or a distortion of those ideas is another matter. In practice, it was one of the main reasons why socialist penal law became extremely punitive, even though the sanction systems in these countries did not differ enormously from Western ones (Szwarc, 1987). All this went on amid constantly repeated claims of upholding "socialist humanitarianism" and insistence that the rehabilitation of offenders was a pillar of "socialist criminal justice" (Marek, 1986). Despite those, and despite claims that in abolishing capitalism the countries had disposed of the main causes of crime and would become crime free, all the countries of the region – not to mention the Soviet Union itself – "enjoyed" extremely high incarceration rates pre-1989[4] that were well above the average in the "crime-ridden" capitalist countries of Western Europe, and were higher even than the rate in the US at that time[5] (Jasiński, 1976; Pomorski, 1981, pp. 22–25; Grajewski & Lammich, 1981; Krajewski, 2023).

After the fall of the Iron Curtain

1989 brought fundamental change to the region. The progressive collapse of the Soviet Union also resulted in the collapse of the communist regimes in its satellites. The countries of Central Europe regained their independence and started a very complicated, sometimes very painful process of political, economic, and social transformation. All that had been destroyed in the communist takeovers of the late 1940s and early 1950s could now be reinstated: all of our focus countries wished to reestablish themselves as liberal democracies governed by the rule of law and based on the market economy. This required sweeping legal reforms, not least to their penal law and criminal justice systems (Doss et al., 2001; Frankowski & Wąsek, 1995; Kerezsi & Lévay, 2008; Krajewski, 2004) Those reforms were substantially reinforced and accelerated by the fact that all of these countries joined the Council of Europe in the early 1990s and aspired to European Union membership. As their transformation was supposed to be evolutionary rather than revolutionary, the "socialist" legal systems were retained in principle, although they were very quickly modified. The priority was to remove all provisions constituting the most blatant violations of the principles of the rule of law. In penal law, this was usually done very gradually, although work on preparing new codes began very soon in some countries. One such example is Poland, where the new penal code was adopted as early as 1997 and entered into force in 1998 (Weigend, 1998). In other countries, the new penal legislation took longer to prepare: new penal codes entered into force in Slovakia in 2005 (Strémy & Ozoráková, 2020); in Czechia in 2010 (Herczeg, 2008); in Hungary in 2012 (Csúri, 2014); in Romania in 2014 (Avriceanu, 2017). Of the six countries of focus in this chapter, only Bulgaria is still using its 1968 "socialist" penal code to this day, although it has been heavily amended in the meantime.[6]

The adoption of new penal codes (and other criminal justice legislation) more or less compatible with modern international standards meant at least a formal overhaul of the communist inheritance in the region's criminal law. However, this does not mean that all the problems of these countries' criminal justice systems have been solved. One of the main tasks of penal law reform in the Central European countries was to reduce its enormous punitiveness. Although much has changed in the region, incarceration rates in these countries still remain excessively high, and higher than in most countries of Western Europe (Krajewski, 2014). To date, their attempts to reduce punitiveness have clearly largely failed. There have been various attempts to explain this phenomenon. One theory suggests that it is due to the persistence of communist patterns of thinking about crime and its control in the post-communist societies (Krajewski, 2013). Another refers to specific local nationalist traditions resulting in attempts to stand out from the West (Haney, 2016). A third hypothesis posits that – at least in Czechia – the persisting punitiveness is a result of legislative neglect rather than any intentional action (Drápal, 2023). A more detailed discussion of these issues is well beyond the scope of this chapter (see: Krajewski, 2023). It is, however, worth noting that populist and illiberal tendencies have grown in the region, especially in the past ten years. Hungary since 2012 (Boda et al., 2022; Gönczöl, 2022) and Poland in the years 2015–2023 (Sulikowski, 2020), are no doubt the most conspicuous examples, but none of the focus countries are free of these tendencies, and they have had a strong impact on these countries' penal law and criminal justice systems (Škvain, 2014; Strémy & Ozoráková, 2020; Doss et al., 2001; Oancea & Neculcea, 2022). It seems that the original "liberal optimism" in relation to criminal justice reform and the possibility of becoming truly European countries in that respect that was so widespread and seemingly prevalent in the region during the 1990s and early 2000s, has – unfortunately – largely evaporated.

Notes

1 From 1918 until 1 January 1993, Czechia and Slovakia constituted a single country: Czechoslovakia.
2 As a matter of fact, on the small territory of *Spisz i Orawa* (*Spiš a Orava* in Slovak and Czech) bordering on Czechoslovakia, the fourth penal code was in force, namely Hungarian.
3 In the first half of the 1950s, some countries abandoned the principle *nullum crimen sine lege* altogether, and analogy was permitted and broadly used. But this changed, at least in principle, in the second half of the 1950s.
4 A detailed comparative analysis of sentencing outcomes in the region before 1989 is no easy task, as most basic statistical data on criminal justice systems in the "socialist" states were either secret or very difficult to obtain. Hungary and Poland represented an exception to this rule, and data for Czechoslovakia were available for the time before the Soviet invasion in 1968.
5 Not to mention the fact that none of those countries, with the exception of East Germany, managed to abolish the death penalty. On the contrary, capital punishment was used rather frequently.
6 Most of the focus countries, including Bulgaria (Gruev, 2008), also have new codes of criminal procedure.

References

Avriceanu, T. (2017). Hat man in Rumänien einen Straftatbegriff gefunden? Wege und Irrwege einer missglückten Rezeption. *Zeitschrift für die gesamte Strafrechtswissenschaft*, *129*, 825–850.

Boda, Z., Tóth, M., Hollán, M., & Bartha, A. (2022). Two decades of penal populism – The case of Hungary. *Review of Central and East European Law*, *47*, 115–138.

Busch, R. (1936). Kritische Bemerkungen zum polnischen Strafgesetzbuch. *Zeitschrift für die gesamte Strafrechtswissenschaft, 55*, 621–640.

Csúri, A. (2014). Der lange Weg zum neuen ungarischen Strafgesetzbuch von 2012. *Zeitschrift für die gesamte Strafrechtswissenschaft, 126*, 509–538.

Dolaptchieff, N. (1932). Criminal law in Bulgaria. *The Journal of Criminal Law and Criminology, 23*(Spring), 1012–1019.

Doss, M. T., Bowers, S. R., & Hanganu, C. (2001). The transformation of the Romanian criminal justice system. *International Journal of Police Science & Management, 3*, 226–245.

Drápal, J. (2023). Punitive by negligence? The myths and reality of penal nationalism in the Czech Republic. *European Journal of Criminology, 20*(4), 1549–1567.

Frankowski, S. J. (1987). Poland. In G. F. Cole, S. J. Frankowski, & M. G. Gertz (Eds.), *Major criminal justice systems: A comparative survey* (2nd ed.). Sage.

Frankowski, S., & Wąsek, A. (1993). Evolution of the Polish criminal justice system after World War Two – An overview. *European Journal of Crime, Criminal Law and Criminal Justice, 1*, 143–166.

Frankowski, S., & Wąsek, A. (1995). Polish criminal law and procedure. In S. Frankowski & P. B. Stephan (Eds.), *Legal reform in post-communist Europe: The view from within*. Martinus Nijhoff.

Gönczöl, K. (2022). "Let there be order!": Rising criminal populism in Hungary. *Archiwum Kryminologii, 44*(1), 107–122.

Grajewski, J., & Lammich S. (1981). Criminal policy in Poland in light of the criminal code of 1969. *Review of Socialist Law, 7*, 407–423.

Gruev, L. (2008). Grundzüge der Bulgarischen Strafprozessordnung von 2005. *Zeitschrift für die gesamte Strafrechtswissenschaft, 120*, 153–179.

Haney, L. (2016). Prisons of the past: Penal nationalism and the politics of punishment in Central Europe. *Punishment and Society, 18*, 346–368.

Herczeg, J. (2008). Der allgemeine Teil des tschechischen StGB-Entwurfs. *Zeitschrift für die gesamte Strafrechtswissenschaft, 120*, 90–107.

Jasiński, J. (1976). The punitiveness of the criminal justice systems (A cross-national perspective). *The Polish Sociological Bulletin, 4*, 43–51.

Karabec, Z., & Vlach, J. (2011). *Criminal justice system in the Czech Republic* (Research report). Institute of Criminology and Social Prevention. https://www.ok.cz/iksp/docs/386.pdf

Kerezsi, K., & Lévay, M. (2008). Criminology, crime, and criminal justice in Hungary. *European Journal of Criminology, 5*, 239–260.

Krajewski, K. (2004). Crime and criminal justice in Poland. *European Journal of Criminology, 1*, 377–407.

Krajewski, K. (2013). Penal developments in Poland: New or old punitiveness? In T. Daems, D. van Zyl Smit, & S. Snacken (Eds.), *European penology?*. Hart Publishing.

Krajewski, K. (2014). Different penal climates in Europe. *Kriminologijos Studijos, 2*, 86–111.

Krajewski, K. (2023). Penal exceptionalism in countries of Central Europe: Why is the region different? *Archiwum Kryminologii, 45*(2), 171–211.

Kubiak, J. R. (1987). Internal and external factors influencing the operation of criminal justice systems of socialist European countries. *Review of Socialist Law, 13*, 5–59.

Makarewicz, J. (1933). Das Strafgesetzbuch für die Republik Polen. *Zeitschrift für Ostrecht, 7*, 316–331.

Marek, A. (1986). Resozialisierung und wechselnde Strategien der Bestrafung. Einige Anmerkungen in Bezug auf Polen. *Monatsschrift für Kriminologie und Strafrechtsreform, 69*, 138–146.

Olechowski, T. (2010). Zur Entstehung des österreichischen Strafgesetzes 1852. In A. Lengauer, Ch. Neschwara, & T. Olechowski (Eds.), *Grundlagen der österreichischen Rechtskultur: Festschrift für Werner Ogris zum 75. Geburtstag*. Verlag Österreich.

Oancea, G., & Neculcea, S. A. (2022). The compensatory appeal in the face of political populism. *Archiwum Kryminologii, 44*(1), 147–171.

Plachta, M. (1990). The formation of the Polish legal system during the changes in the structure of the government: 1944–1949 (with special emphasis on the criminal justice system). *Review of Socialist Law, 16*, 57–79.

Pomorski, S. (1981). Communists and their criminal law: Reflections on Igor Andrejew's "Outlines of the criminal law of socialist states". *Review of Socialist Law, 7*, 7–34.

Potseluev, E. (2016). Das russische Strafgesetzbuch (Ugolovnoje Uloženje) vom 22. März 1903: Ursachen der Verabschiedung und Geschichte der Ausfertigung. *Jahrbuch der Juristischen Zeitgeschichte, 17*, 211–236.

Rinceanu, J. (2009). Auf der Suche nach einem Straftatbegriff in Rumänien. *Zeitschrift für die gesamte Strafrechtswissenschaft, 121*, 115–134.

Schafer, S. (1959). Some basic principles of Hungarian criminal law. *The Modern Law Review, 22*, 164–174.

Škvain, P. (2014). Physical (Surgical) Castration as treatment of male sex offenders? Recent developments in legislation in the Czech Republic. *Monatsschrift für Kriminologie und Strafrechtsreform, 97*, 40–47.

Strémy, T., & Ozoráková, L. (2020). The new act amending the criminal legislation in Slovakia and the possible impact of the new crime of abuse of law on the independence of judiciary. *Pécs Journal of International and European Law, 6(*2), 66–77.

Sulikowski, A. (2020). The return of forgotten critique: Some remarks on the intellectual sources of the Polish populist revolution. *Review of Central and East European Law, 45*, 376–401.

Szwarc, A. J. (1987). The system of penalties in the 1969 Polish criminal code. *Review of Socialist Law, 13*, 217–239.

Timasheff, N. S. (1953). The impact of the penal legislation of Imperial Russia on the Soviet penal law. *The American Slavic and East European Review, 12*, 441–462.

Weigend, E. (1998). Das neue polnische Strafgesetzbuch von 1997. *Zeitschrift für die gesamte Strafrechtswissenschaft, 110,* 114–142.

4 Suspended prison sentences in Czechia[1]

Jakub Drápal

Introduction

If we are to understand the development of suspended prison sentences in Czechia and the discussion surrounding it, we must first gain at least a basic understanding of the relevant historical context. Until 1938, Czechoslovakia held a prominent position among the European nations: it was one of the most developed and prosperous nations in Europe, and in the interwar years, it was the only democratic rule-of-law country in Central Europe (Rotschild, 1988, pp. 86–87, 100). The Czechoslovak criminal justice system was widely discussed and studied from the perspectives of both criminal law and criminology (Drápal, 2019), usually in connection with similar studies of the German and Austrian systems. This era is characterised by a large number of high-quality scholarly and jurisprudential sources.

The subsequent German occupation, communist putsch, totalitarian regime and Soviet occupation between 1938 and 1989 thoroughly changed the country's criminal justice landscape. Universities closed or were altogether dissolved, the remaining academic community was heavily purged, and criminology was banned as a discipline throughout the 1950s (Drápal, 2019; Scheinost, 2010). Arguably the hardest blows to society were experienced following the Soviet occupation, in the period familiarly referred to as "normalization": 1969–1989. At the beginning of this period, ideological purges were conducted at all levels of society: 20% of university lecturers were fired (Urbášek, 2012), usually for failing to declare their agreement with the Soviet invasion. The era was symbolised by the verbalisation and proclamation of mottos everyone knew to be false – even those expressing them. This is best expressed in Václav Havel's essay "The Power of the Powerless", where he gives the example of a greengrocer displaying a sign with the words "Workers of the World, Unite!", albeit personally resenting the phrase. Unable to attend conferences abroad (especially in Western Europe) and not having access to foreign scholarship, researchers in the social sciences, including criminology, were crippled (Drápal, 2019).

In the aftermath of the 1989 Velvet Revolution, scholars' and reformers' focus turned initially to issues other than sentencing. Within the criminal justice system, effort was concentrated on the preparation of new criminal codes, criminal

DOI: 10.4324/9781003568667-7

law and criminology textbooks and criminal law commentaries. Empirical research was – especially at the faculties of law – non-existent or marginalised, as was thorough comparative or theoretical research. Furthermore, in the early 1990s "suddenly almost every essential scientific element of [academic] life had to be obtained and implemented" (Kutsar & Kovács, 2010, p. 2); this was hampered by the severe underfunding of the social sciences. Low wages resulted in criminal law scholars working as attorneys, judges, prosecutors or public officials alongside their academic positions. The number of criminal law scholars who are practitioners is high (see Richter, 2013 for statistics about academics working as attorneys), which disincentivises them from conducting thorough empirical, comparative or theoretical research.

The conception, development and study of suspended prison sentences has taken place against this background, which may – to some extent – explain why there has been a lack of sufficient consideration of the consequences of proposed changes, insufficient empirical research documenting even the basic use of suspended prison sentences, ideological disruptions relating to suspended prison sentences, and changes to the provisions governing suspended prison sentences made by uninformed practitioners or scholars. Unfortunately, some of these deficiencies persist today. The low level of knowledge about suspended prison sentences and the problematic provisions governing them are symptoms of a wider societal issue, which is also responsible for the large prison population: Czechia is "punitive by negligence" (Drápal, 2021c) owing to its insufficiently elaborated approach to criminal law.

Sentencing overview and current sentencing practice

The Czech penal code provides basic sentencing guidance by setting very general limits; judges thus have broad discretion when it comes to choosing the type and amount of a sanction. A special part of the penal code defines individual offences, usually divided into several subsections based on the seriousness of the offence, with specific sentencing ranges for each subsection. Judges are normally bound by the sentencing range minimum, although they may impose sentences below the stipulated minimum if they deem the case to be extraordinary and a prison sentence at the sentencing range minimum to be disproportionately harsh. To guide sentencing decisions, the penal code enumerates mitigating and aggravating factors. In a move that was criticised by scholars, the creators of the 2009 Penal Code deliberately refrained from including any sentencing rationale, arguing that the code's individual provisions capture it sufficiently (Drápal, 2018).[2]

There are two types of offences: délits (přečiny) and crimes (zločiny). Délits include all negligent offences and offences with a sentencing range maximum of no more than five years; this encompasses 90.7% of all tried cases.[3] Crimes are all other offences. For délits, judges can impose:

- a prison sentence in non-suspended (custodial) or suspended form (prison sentences of up to three years can be suspended, with or without probationary supervision);
- home detention (for up to two years with a default prison sentence of up to one year);
- community service (in the range 50–300 hours with a default prison sentence calculated using the ratio of 1 hour to 1 day of imprisonment); or
- a day fine (20–730 day fine units, with a default prison sentence calculated using the ratio of 1 day fine unit to 2 days of imprisonment).

The non-suspended prison sentence is the most punitive sanction, and the penal code states that this should be imposed for délits only if it is clear that if handed any other sanction, the offender is likely to re-offend. There is no other official hierarchy of sanctions. All sanctions other than prison sentences can be imposed as the sole sanction if – for the given offence and offender – the court considers there is no need to impose another type of sanction as well. The same general guidance is provided for all the non-custodial sanctions. No additional guidance is provided (Drápal, 2022c).

For crimes, virtually the only sanction that can be imposed is a prison sentence, which can be imposed either in its suspended form or in non-suspended (custodial) form. This provides a strange conundrum for judges: they are not allowed to impose sanctions with a larger penal bite upon imposition than a suspended prison sentence – such as home detention – when sentencing for more serious offences. This goes against the intention of the legislature, since home detention was introduced in order to be imposed in more serious cases than a suspended prison sentence, yet the provisions do not allow it. This serves as an example of the state's negligence in designing the criminal justice system (Drápal, 2022c). The longest prison sentence that can be imposed for crimes is either up to 30 years or for life. Finally, for both délits and crimes, various auxiliary punishments, such as bans on particular activities or locations, seizures, and extradition can be imposed.

Suspended prison sentences dominate the sentencing practice, as is evident from Figure 4.1: suspended sentences were imposed for 53.2% of offenders, 86.7% of them without probationary supervision. While shorter suspended sentences (of up to six months) were frequent, longer ones (between six months and two years in duration) were equally common, and sentences longer than two years were also frequently suspended. Non-suspended prison sentences were imposed on 20.2% of offenders, meaning that 116.2 non-suspended prison sentences were imposed per 100,000 inhabitants. These non-suspended prison sentences were primarily of medium duration (longer than six months); only 20.7% of non-suspended prison sentences were short sentences of up to six months. Fines were imposed as the main sanction for 13% of offenders and community service for 9.9% of offenders. Other sanctions were rare (3.8% of offenders).

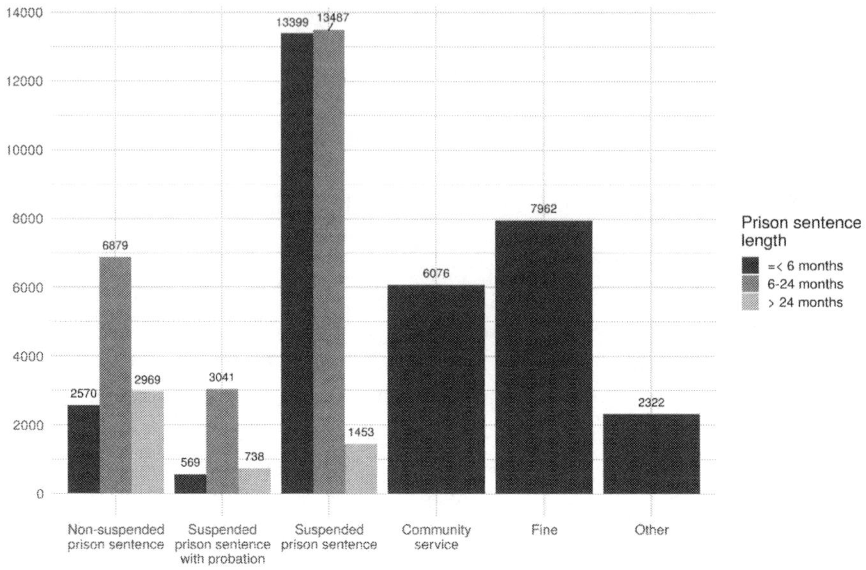

Figure 4.1 Main sanctions imposed in 2019 by type and length.

Note: Official court-level 2019 data.

The sentencing procedure is typical of continental systems, although gradually influenced by elements of common law systems. Judges decide on guilt and on the sentence at the same time, and there are no separate sentencing hearings. The preferred way to shorten the criminal procedure is to impose a penal order: a verdict of guilt that specifies the offence and the sanction imposed, but does not contain reasoning. The penal order is usually delivered by mail (there is no hearing), and the offender can file a protest against it, following which the case will be heard in a full criminal procedure. In 2019, 55.4% of guilty verdicts were concluded by penal order. Another measure enabling judges to shorten criminal proceedings is plea-bargaining (introduced in 2012). In 2020, plea bargain possibilities widened with the introduction of guilty pleas and pleas declaring certain facts as uncontested. These changes will likely impact sentencing practice, although unfortunately the reformers did not provide any guidance as to how such pleas should influence sentencing. Guilty pleas in particular will likely partly replace penal orders, but it is unclear whether they will also lead to an increase in the use of shorter sentences or a decrease in the use of non-suspended prison sentences. Finally, both prosecutors and judges can employ several types of diversion; in 2021, the prosecution applied a diversion in 6.4% of cases (NSZ,

2022), the most common being conditional deferral: if the offender does not re-offend during a specified operational period, the criminal charges are dropped.

The primary sentencing players are the first-level courts. The Supreme Court has ruled that it does not decide on sentencing principles, and there are no sentencing councils or commissions (Drápal, 2018). Appellate courts can easily overturn sentences, and indeed do so rather frequently (appeals are filed in 13.5% of cases and in 19.3% of these the appeal court changes only the sentence), partly due to the fact that it is not possible to impose a harsher punishment if only the defendant appeals. The role of the appellate courts is, however, complicated by the fact that first-level courts often fail to provide specific reasons for their sentencing decisions, despite being obliged to do so by the law (see Tomšů & Drápal, 2019). Not surprisingly, appellate courts may not sufficiently promote principled sentencing (Vanča & Drápal, 2023). First-level courts are thus entrusted with very broad discretion, yet their decision-making is almost unsupervised. Finally, prosecutors are also important actors in the sentencing process, since they recommend sanctions; their recommendations have been found to influence sentence choice substantially (Drápal & Dušek, 2025), yet they are given less training in sentencing than judges.

The broad discretion, very general sentencing principles set out in the criminal code, and lack of unifying jurisprudence or sentencing scholarship (e.g. there is no sentencing textbook) inevitably result in substantial sentencing disparities, which are documented at both judge and court levels (Drápal, 2020a; Drápal & Šoltés, 2021). While certain measures have been proposed as suitable for reducing sentencing disparities in the Czech criminal justice system (Drápal, 2020a, 2021b), these have not been implemented to date.

The Czech criminal code prescribes generous parole conditions: based on whether the offender committed a délit, a crime or an especially serious crime, he/she may be granted parole after 1/3, 1/2 or 2/3 of the imposed prison sentence, and in some cases even earlier. The prediction of leading an orderly life is the main criterion on which the parole decision should be based. However, despite this consequentialist regulation, parole decisions are in reality very formalistic: judges decide primarily based on the offender's previous criminal history and on the number of commendations or transgressions he/she has accrued while serving the prison sentence (Drápalová & Drápal, 2022).

Principles governing suspended prison sentences at presentIn Czech law, a suspended prison sentence is a prison sentence by name ("trest odnětí svobody") whose execution is conditionally postponed; the penal code recognises it as a type of prison sentence. Sentence suspension is not discussed alongside other sanctions in the penal code, but in a specific chapter of its own, which is followed by a chapter on parole. In other words, the structure of the penal code tacitly indicates that suspension is a decision about the execution of the prison sentence and not a separate sanction in its own right.

That being said, many people do not consider suspended prison sentences to be prison sentences. The Supreme Court has ruled repeatedly that even the shortest possible non-suspended prison sentence is more punitive than the longest possible suspended prison sentence,[4] essentially considering a suspended prison sentence to be a specific, different sanction. Similarly, criminal law scholars have suggested that suspended prison sentences constitute a specific type of sanction (Solnař & Vanduchová, 2009, p. 104), and some have argued that this is the least serious type of sanction, even less punitive than a fine (Kalvodová, 2002, p. 249), while others have noted difficulties in comparisons between these sanctions (Ščerba, 2014, pp. 36–37). It is not surprising, then, that the term "suspended sentence" ("podmíněné odsouzení") is widely used in place of the more technically correct "suspended prison sentence", or that suspended prison sentences are imposed for even the very least serious offences, when no custodial threshold can conceivably have been crossed: suspended prison sentences are the most typical sanction imposed on first-time offenders (65.1% of whom were handed suspended prison sentences in 2019, when first-time offenders constituted 16.6% of all offenders sentenced). However, there is no official *custodial threshold* relevant to suspended prison sentences: the only custodial threshold mentioned in the penal code refers to the imposition of non-suspended prison sentences (for offences with a sentencing range maximum of five years such sentences should be imposed only if it is clear that any other punishment would not result in the offender leading a law-abiding life).

The penal code stipulates that prison sentences of up to three years' duration can be suspended (this is the *positive definition*) and no offenders are excluded (i.e. there is no *negative definition*). The decisive factor in determining whether a prison sentence may be suspended is whether imprisonment is necessary in order for the offender to lead an orderly life. The current provision, which enables a specific consequentialist rationale to be taken into account, differs from the general set of punishment goals referred to in previous pre-2009 provisions. It is therefore disturbing that pre-2009 Supreme Court decisions that took offence seriousness into account when deciding on suspension are still being cited by the Supreme Court, jurisprudence, and commentaries (Drápal, 2022a). It is unclear in practice what factors currently influence decisions about sentence suspension.

Suspending a prison sentence is optional: the court "may" suspend a prison sentence, according to the 2009 Penal Code. This language was already used when suspended prison sentences were first introduced in 1919, when it was considered appropriate to provide judges with unfettered discretion in this respect (Drápal, 2021a). It is unclear how this provision is to be interpreted within the contemporary rule-of-law, principled-sentencing climate (Drápal, 2022a) and whether "may" might not here indicate "must", as the Czech Constitutional Court has ruled in the case of a similarly worded provision regarding parole.[5] The code does not consider the suspension of a prison sentence *exceptional*.

The *two-stage* imposition process – in which the prison sentence is decided first, and whether it is to be suspended or not follows in a second step – is not mentioned in the scholarship, despite the fact that the above-mentioned jurisprudence on the punitiveness of suspended prison sentences directly contradicts it. No wonder sentence inflation – imposition of longer prison sentences instead of shorter non-suspended prison sentences – has been empirically documented (Drápal, 2025). *Partly-suspended* prison sentences cannot be imposed and have never been seriously considered, although this option has recently been mentioned by several politicians.

Regarding procedural requirements, no specific evidence needs to be presented in order to suspend a prison sentence and no specific hearing can be held to decide on the suspension. Prison sentences of up to one year can be imposed via a *penal order*. In 2019, 55.4% of cases were concluded by penal orders. These may also be suspended; in 2019, 27.8% of offenders sentenced via penal order received a suspended prison sentence without any additional sanctions or measures, while a further 15.7% were handed suspended prison sentences combined with a prohibition from driving via penal order (see Table 4.1 for further statistics). Penal orders have a substantial impact on sentencing: judges sometimes prefer not to incarcerate offenders if this enables a speedier procedure via penal order (Drápal, 2017).

A wide variety of *sanctions* can be *imposed alongside* a suspended prison sentence; these include day-fines, seizures of property or possessions, prohibitions of particular activities, stays, or entries, and deportation. Community service and home detention cannot be imposed alongside a suspended prison sentence (which, in this respect, is still considered a prison sentence), but various limitations and obligations can be imposed on the offender or home arrest

Table 4.1 Conditions imposed alongside suspended prison sentences, by procedure type

Sanction/conditions	*Via penal order*	*Otherwise*
Suspended prison sentence alone	9,460 (15.4 %)	4,172 (6.8 %)
Suspended prison sentence with:		
· fine	355 (0.6 %)	383 (0.6 %)
· driving prohibition	5,339 (8.7 %)	1,134 (1.8 %)
· additional limitations	2,735 (4.5 %)	968 (1.6 %)
· other measures	2,354 (3.8 %)	1,439 (2.3 %)
· probationary supervision only	1,176 (1.9 %)	738 (1.2 %)
· with probation supervision and other measures	1,277 (2.1 %)	1,157 (1.9 %)
Non-suspended sanctions (primarily non-suspended prison sentences, fines and community service)	11,357 (18.5 %)	17,421 (28.3 %)

Note: Offenders sentenced in 2019 (including aggregate and conjoint punishments, excluding young offenders), N: 61,465. 34,053 cases (55.4 %) were concluded by penal order.

of up to one year. Various other *conditions,* such as the obligation to undergo a course of therapy, to compensate the victim, or to refrain from drinking alcohol or using drugs, can also be imposed.

The frequency with which such conditions are imposed is presented in Table 4.1. Suspended prison sentences are often imposed without any additional measures or sanctions (to 41.7% of all offenders handed suspended prison sentences in 2019). 19.8% of suspended sentences were issued together with a prohibition to drive, 2.3% with an additional fine and 11.3% with other limitations or obligations defined by the judge. Combinations of multiple sanctions or measures were imposed alongside the suspended sentence in 11.6% of cases. This means that a substantial share of all suspended prison sentences carry only the limited penal bite communicated by the suspended prison sentence itself, and the majority of suspended prison sentences result in very limited hard treatment for offenders.

Probationary supervision can also be imposed alongside a suspended prison sentence. Officially, this then constitutes a separate type of prison sentence, yet since the provisions are identical with the exception of the inclusion (or not) of probationary supervision and law makes no real distinction between the two sanctions, I refer to probationary supervision as a specific condition applicable alongside a suspended prison sentence. Probationary supervision was imposed on 13.3% of offenders who were handed suspended prison sentences in 2019; in 44.2% of these cases, this was the only condition imposed alongside the suspended prison sentence.

The *operational period* can be set for a period between one and five years. There is very little guidance as to how to set it; the only condition (introduced in 2022) is that this period cannot be shorter than the prison sentence itself. During the operational period, the offender must *lead an orderly life* and abide by other requirements. What is an orderly life? In 2017, the Constitutional Court stated that we are living in a pluralistic society in which there is no dominant ideology, and therefore unless clearly stated otherwise, offenders can only be required to obey the law, i.e. they must not re-offend or commit any administrative offence. If the court wishes the offender to lead a good life in other respects, it can do so, but in such a case it must clearly state what such a good life should look like.[6]

When the conditions of a suspended prison sentence are *breached* – especially if offenders re-offend – judges have two options: first, they may revoke the suspension, meaning that the offender must then serve the originally imposed prison sentence in full, notwithstanding any hard treatment he/she has undergone during the operational period (e.g. probationary supervision measures akin to a home arrest or community service). Second, the judges may decide not to revoke the suspension but instead to prolong the operational period by up to two years (not exceeding five years in total) and/or to impose additional obligations, including probationary supervision, alongside the suspended sentence. In 2019, suspended prison sentences were revoked following a breach in 7.4% of cases, while in 8.5% they were not revoked despite a breach of the original conditions (Drápal & Vanča, 2024).

When sentencing an offender who has re-offended during the operational period of a suspended prison sentence, the length of the original suspended prison sentence can be considered when fixing the sanction for the new offence. This new option, introduced in 2020, directs judges not to impose sanctions that would result in a disproportionately severe sentence when combined with previously imposed but not yet served suspended prison sentence(s). However, it remains challenging to ensure that offenders are handed punishments that fit the committed offences in their totality, as the decisions are made by independent judges who may take rather different perspectives and approaches to sentencing (Drápal, 2020b, 2021d).

If offenders are *not found in breach* during the operational period, then at the end of the operational period, a judge may declare that they have fulfilled all the conditions of the suspended sentence (they have proved successful). Alternatively, if such a decision is not made within a year after the operational period ended, a legal fiction deems such a decision to have been made. For 18.2% of those who were not found in breach, the decision was made via this legal fiction (Drápal & Vanča, 2024). The period of one year does not, however, apply if criminal proceedings are underway (a breach resulting from re-offending occurs only following a guilty verdict that has acquired legal force – the presumption of innocence is invoked[7] = and so the operational period may end apparently without breach before such a verdict is made). Once the judge – or the fiction – has confirmed that all conditions were met, the *criminal record* is hidden and can be accessed only by specific entities.

How and why has the system developed?

The approach to suspended prison sentences in what is now Czechia has changed substantially over the last 135 years. I present the development of the provisions relating to them for three distinct periods: from the first ideas and propositions in 1889 until the German occupation of Czechoslovakia (1938), during the communist authoritarian regime (1948–1989), and from the Velvet Revolution until the present day.

Early beginnings: 1889–1938

The introduction of suspended prison sentences in the Austrian-Hungarian Empire was first suggested as early as 1889 and 1891 by the then Minister of Justice, Bedřich Schönborn, who was an aristocrat of Czech origin. The possibility of introducing suspended prison sentences was debated within Czech legal circles in the following decades, and legal scholars generally supported this measure (Kallab, 1904; Vaněk, 1890; Zucker, 1891). Although the suspension of prison sentences was not enacted in Cisleithania (the "Austrian" part of the Austrian-Hungarian Empire, of which Bohemia, Moravia, and Silesia were part), these discussions paved the way for its introduction after the formation of independent Czechoslovakia in 1918.

Less than a year after the independent Czechoslovak Republic was established, the Czechoslovak Parliament passed a law that enabled both the suspension of prison sentences and parole. In Czech, the link between these two institutes is clearer as both include the term "conditional" in their names: "podmíněné odsouzení" (conditional conviction) and "podmíněné propuštění" (conditional release). The 1919 law subscribed to the original French-Belgian conception of suspended prison sentences, although it differed from the French-Belgian provisions in several ways, primarily as a result of interventions by members of Parliament amending the original draft of the law. Specifically, whereas the draft stated – in line with the previous suggestions in 1889 and 1891 – that suspension should be used only exceptionally and that its use should be more strictly limited for recidivists, these provisions were not included in the enacted law. These changes caused some confusion, and, e.g. during the 1920s the Czechoslovak Supreme Court consistently ruled that suspension should be exceptional (Drápal, 2021a), depsite the fact that the law did not state so.

The lower courts did not share the Supreme Court's position, and prison sentences were suspended extremely frequently. In 1920, just a year after their introduction, suspended prison sentences became the most frequently imposed sanction, as is evident from Figure 4.2: 51.1 % of prison sentences were suspended and 49.1% of offenders were handed a suspended prison sentence or suspended fine.[8] Suspension applied primarily to the shortest prison sentences: almost four-fifths of all prison sentences lasting one month or less were suspended, while only slightly less than one-fifth of prison sentences longer than 3 months were suspended. Given that very short prison sentences were dominant at this time, the result was a very high frequency of suspended prison sentences. Additionally, as Figure 4.3 suggests, prison sentences were not the only measures that were frequently suspended at this time: suspended fines gradually came to be imposed twice as frequently as non-suspended fines.

While suspension was not as exceptional as scholars had initially advised, the Czechoslovak law was otherwise written to comply with the original French-Belgian conception. The person of the offender was to influence the decision whether to suspend the sentence, and the seriousness of the offence was not to be taken into consideration when deciding on suspension. Suspension was forbidden for a few offences and for certain groups of recidivists. Procedurally, suspension could not be imposed via the shortened procedure of penal order, since it was considered necessary for the judge to personally meet the offender in order to decide on suspension. Imposition of a suspended prison sentence was a two-step process consisting of a first decision on the prison sentence and its length and a second decision on its suspension, which could have been taken

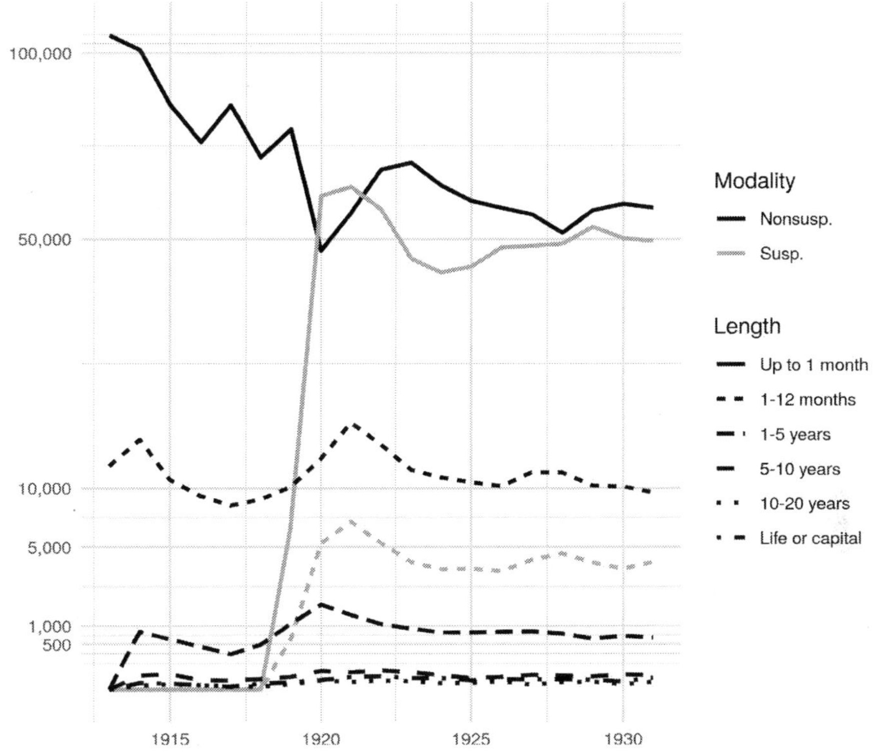

Figure 4.2 Prison sentences imposed 1913–1922.

Note: All types of offences – contraventions, délits and crimes (přestupky, přečiny, zločiny) – are included. The y-axis has been log-transformed.

in a special follow-up hearing; similarly, if an appellate court decided on the length of the prison sentence, the first-level court then decided whether or not to suspend it (see Milota, 1919; Takáč & Svitok, 1946 for detailed commentaries of the provisions).

Suspension in Czechoslovakia was designed to offer the offender a true second chance: all auxiliary sanctions were suspended along with the prison sentence, with the sole exception of seizure of a possession, which, however, could also be suspended under specified conditions. Offenders handed suspended sentences did not have these noted in their criminal record: suspended prison sentences were recorded separately and were only disclosed if revoked or if the offender applied for a public-sector job during the operational period. Apart from this exception, the law stated very clearly that "during the operational period, an

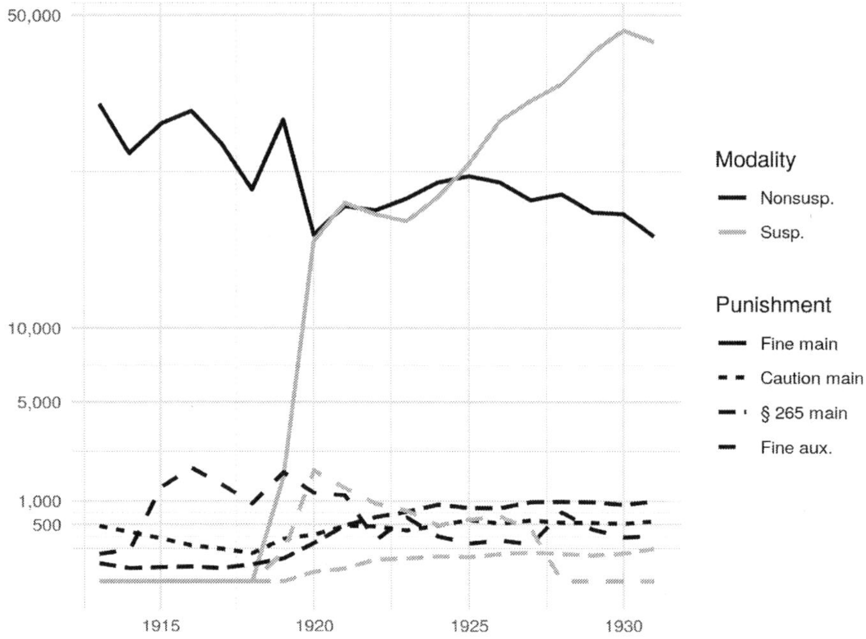

Figure 4.3 Sanctions other than prison sentences imposed 1913–1931.

Note: All types of offences – contraventions, délits and crimes (přestupky, přečiny, zločiny) – are included. § 265 refers to section 265 of the Code of Criminal Procedure, law n. 119/1873 Coll. and relates to aggregate punishments. The y-axis has been log-transformed.

offender is obliged to reveal the fact of being sentenced to a suspended prison sentence only upon a question posed by a court".[9]

Draft texts for the penal code dating from 1921, 1926 and 1937 all contain a very similar conception of suspended prison sentences, although they reveal efforts to limit the scope of their use: suspension was to become once again exceptional and should not be used in cases when it would be "against important public interest" (Drápal, 2021a). None of these drafts were, however, enacted and the original law on suspended prison sentences thus continued to apply until 1950.

Abandonment of the original conception: 1948–1989

In the two years that followed the 1948 communist putsch, a complete re-drafting of the main codes was undertaken. The 1950 Penal Code was "imperfect, quickly drafted following Soviet example, without deep knowledge of Soviet legislation, without unified philosophy" (Gřivna, 2009, p. 580). It was heavily ideological and prescribed disproportionately high penalties. In regard to suspended prison sentences, it – surprisingly – followed the ideas expressed in several unenacted drafts made during the interwar years.[10] Suspension was forbidden in cases when it would be "against important general interests" and any offender handed a suspended prison sentence must be assumed to have committed only an "exceptional deviation from otherwise orderly life" (Drápal, 2021a).[11] The 1950 criminal code did not otherwise aim to uphold the original conception of suspension. Notably, it removed the limitation on imposing suspended prison sentences to recidivists and made the suspension of auxiliary sanctions optional rather than mandatory.

A 1956 amendment designed to correct the biggest flaws of the 1950 code (Gřivna, 2009), brought about even larger changes in the use of suspended prison sentences. The possibility of suspending a prison sentence greatly expanded, first with the removal of the two limitations on suspension – the general interest and exceptional deviation clauses – and second with the removal of limitations on suspension for certain types of offences and lengths of sentence. Newly, suspension was permitted for sentences lasting up to two years. The rationale behind this increase was that the 1950 code had not allowed "cultivation of the educative function of penal law"; unfortunately, the legislature did not elaborate on this very vague term.[12] A new penal code in 1961 adopted the same principles, and in addition barred the court from suspending any auxiliary sanctions imposed alongside the suspended prison sentence.

The 1956 amendment brought about another change which the 1961 code then copied: rather stealthily, it deviated from the idea that the main factor to determine whether or not to suspend a prison sentence was supposed to be the prediction of the offender leading an orderly life. Instead, it stated that the court should suspend a prison sentence if punishment goals (sentencing rationales) would be fulfilled even without the execution of the prison sentence. The punishment goals expressed by the penal code were, however, multiple: protection of society, crime prevention, re-education and education of the public.[13] Which of these goals was to be considered when deciding on suspension? No-one knew. There was no longer clarity about which factors should determine whether a sentence was to be suspended.

Altogether, the changes brought in by the 1956 amendment and 1961 code destroyed the original theoretical conception of the suspended prison sentence and did not replace it with a coherent new conception. The emphasis on specific deterrence was gone, replaced by a vague reference to multiple punishment goals. Two-stage imposition was no longer an option. The decisive factor of whether to suspend a prison sentence became obscure. At the same time, the scope of suspended prison sentences substantially broadened, while any accompanying sanctions were no longer suspendable. The result was a sanction that was a jack of all trades and master of none.

The consequences of these changes are displayed in Figures 4.4 and 4.5. Following the 1956 amendment, very short prison sentences (up to 1 month) ceased to be imposed. While in 1955 the proportions of prison sentences imposed with durations up to 1 month and above one month were rather similar, from 1956 onwards longer prison sentences began to dominate. Longer suspended prison sentences – both between 1 and 12 months and between 12 and 24 months – were imposed widely from the early 1960s.

As there were no substantial changes made to suspended prison sentences between 1960 and the 1980s, changes in sentencing practices during this period likely relate primarily to overall societal developments. The Prague Spring is identifiable via a lower number of non-suspended prison sentences being imposed up to 1968. The Soviet occupation from 1968 to 1989 is then visible in the increased imposition of non-suspended prison sentences. Legislative provisions were not, however, fully followed in this period. For example, during the 1960s and 1980s, courts did not heed the official instruction to impose various additional measures alongside suspended prison sentences and virtually never imposed such measures (Fábry, 1983; Jestřáb, 1960).

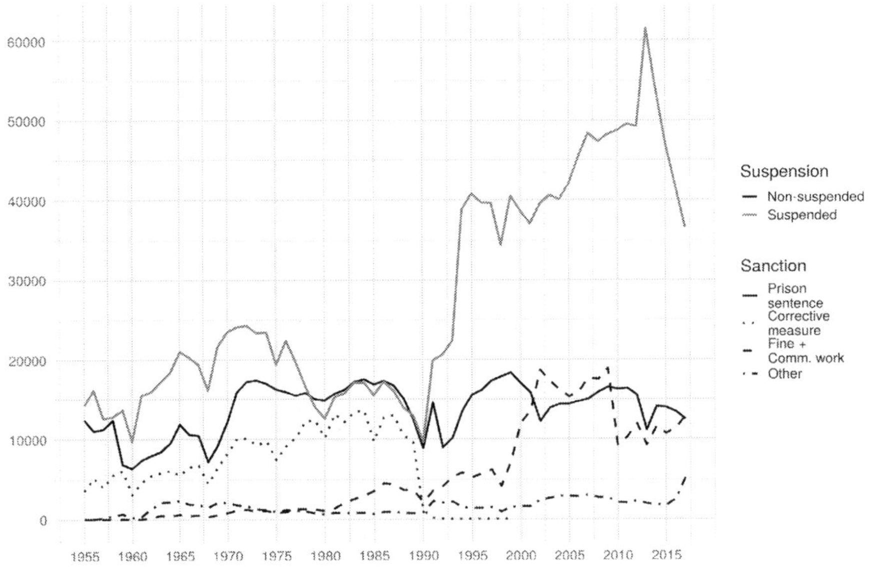

Figure 4.4 Main sanctions imposed 1955–2017.

Source: Criminal Records data, author's own calculations.

Note: Sanctions imposed for misdemeanors according to the 1969 lawn. 150/1969 Coll. are excluded.

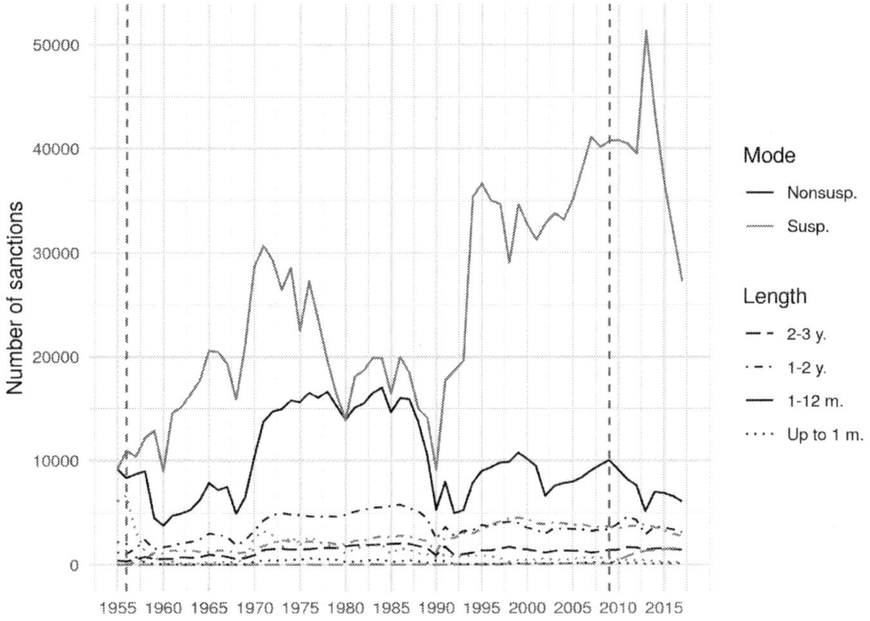

Figure 4.5 Prison sentences by length 1955–2017.

Source: Criminal Records data, author's own calculations.

Note: Sanctions imposed for misdemeanors according to the 1969 law n. 150/1969 Coll. were excluded. The vertical dashed lines signalize substantial increases in the scope of suspended prison sentences (to include prison sentences of up to 2 years from 1956 and prison sentences of up to 3 years from 2009).

Dominance of suspended prison sentences: 1989–2022

Suspended prison sentences came to dominate the Czech penal landscape following the 1989 Velvet revolution, as Figure 4.4 shows. The destruction of the original conception of suspension and the wide use of suspended prison sentences in the preceding decades provided the perfect groundwork for their wide, unprincipled use when the circumstances required it. There were likely two main reasons for suspended prison sentences acquiring dominance after 1989.

Firstly, no intermediate sanctions were available. In 1990, judges were obliged to choose between a prison sentence and a fine. Community service was not introduced until 1995, probationary supervision from 1997 and home detention as late as 2009. Restriction of liberty (known in Czech as a "corrective measure", "nápravné opatření"), which had been a typical communist sanction consisting of an obligation to work while having part of the salary deducted, was abolished in 1990. Additionally, fines were not imposed as day-fines, which limited the possibility of imposing them on poor offenders.

Secondly, courts needed to properly manage an increasing case load. After the revolution, crime rates increased (Marešová & Scheinost, 1994), while the capacities of the criminal justice system decreased: the process of transforming the existing, communist-party-directed police, prosecution and judiciary into a well-functioning rule-of-law criminal justice system necessitated at least partial replacement of the staff. Furthermore, the rapidly growing private sector lured many capable lawyers previously active as judges and prosecutors away from the judiciary into relatively better-paid private-sector jobs, which in turn led to lawyers of questionable quality being appointed to judicial positions in the early 1990s (Bobek, 2015). The criminal justice system needed to be able to act very efficiently with limited resources.

A natural solution to staffing shortages would be to employ a shortened procedure. However, at the beginning of the 1990s there was virtually none available: guilty pleas and plea bargains were not an option and penal orders were banned between July 1990 and December 1993. These were then reintroduced in 1994, but since 2002 judges have been prohibited from imposing non-suspended prison sentences via penal order[14]. They may, however, impose a suspended prison sentence of up to one year via penal order, which provides a further incentive to impose suspended prison sentences. There was no other restriction except that a penal order can be employed when an offender is found guilty of offences with sentencing range maximum up to five years (until 2012 up to three years). Empirical research has documented that judges were likely willing to impose suspended prison sentences via penal orders instead of non-suspended sentences, in order to shorten the criminal proceedings (Drápal, 2017). Penal orders, when available, thus contributed to the wide use of suspended prison sentences.

Another option – at times the only one – for judges wishing to lighten their loads was to appease all parties, especially the defendants (prosecutors were well aware of the issues the criminal justice system was facing and also needed to close their cases as quickly as possible). If both defendants and prosecutors waived their rights to appeal, judges did not need to provide reasoning for the guilty verdict. Suspended prison sentences, meanwhile, offered the best option for appeasing all parties. On one hand, a suspended prison sentence had very little penal bite and hence was considered favourable by defendants; on the other hand, it still officially constituted a prison sentence, which enabled prosecutors to claim a harsh response had been achieved – whether the hard treatment would be inflicted or not then depended entirely on the offender's behaviour. Until 1994, judges were further incentivised not to incarcerate offenders: when imposing a non-suspended prison sentence, they were obliged to provide reasoning, which they did not have to provide for suspended prison sentences provided that both parties waived their rights to an appeal. Overall, judges were substantially procedurally incentivised to impose suspended prison sentences, which seemingly became the least problematic sanction available.

Non-suspended prison sentences were, by contrast, complicated to impose and placed substantial strain on the country's resources. Fines, too, were arguably harder to impose than suspended prison sentences; they were also unsuitable for mid-serious offences (for which they may not constitute a proportionate response) and for poor offenders. Suspended prison sentences thus came to dominate the penal landscape, possibly not out of particular merit but because they were the best of a bad lot.

The scope of suspended prison sentences also broadened after the Velvet Revolution. In 1998, the option of imposing a suspended prison sentence with probationary supervision was introduced and applied to prison sentences of up to three years. The reasoning was that such enlargement does not lessen the level of penal repression since the probationary supervision will affect the offender.[15] In 2009, the new penal code enabled the suspension of prison sentences lasting up to three years even without probationary supervision, reasoning that judges had been imposing probationary supervision simply in order to be able to suspend prison sentences of between two and three years.[16] The reasoning provided did not cite any empirical (or even anecdotal) evidence, and its claims thus cannot be confirmed. The effect was a further broadening of the scope of suspended prison sentences, without sufficient heed for its consequences.

Another change introduced in 2002 was the possibility of prolonging the operational period of a suspended prison sentence if the offender did not lead an orderly life (re-offended). The introduction of this provision marked a return to the original 1919 legislature, which similarly allowed such extensions, albeit neither these historical provisions nor any theoretical considerations as to which cases such extensions should apply to are mentioned in the explanatory materials to the 2002 penal code amendment. The declared reasoning is that some re-offending is not very serious, and "so with a certain increase in punitiveness, the suspended sentence could be left unactivated".[17] This may have been a reaction to practitioners' unwillingness to revoke suspended prison sentences in cases they considered unjust, even when threatened with disciplinary proceedings (Lata, 2008).

The new penal code issued in 2009 re-introduced the "expectation of leading an orderly life" as the main – or more precisely the sole – decisive factor for whether or not to suspend a prison sentence. (This replaced the previous reference to the fulfilment of "punishment goals" introduced in 1956.) Surprisingly, no reasoning was provided for this change and it is not discussed at all in the explanatory memorandum to the penal code, leaving at least one key question unanswered: should offence seriousness be a factor determining the suspendability of an imposed prison sentence, even though the offence seriousness does not predict offenders' probability of leading an orderly life? Judges were thus presented with a conundrum: Should they ignore the letter of law and follow the – insufficiently elaborated – doctrine enabling consideration of various punishment goals when deciding on suspension, or should they follow the letter of law, albeit none knows whether it was the intention of the legislature and it might easily produce disproportionate outcomes (prison sentences of three years can be easily imposed for grievous bodily harm, rape or a serious white-collar crime and if it was suspended only based on the expectation to lead an orderly life it arguably would not be a sufficiently punitive reaction)? Twelve years later, the judiciary is still waiting for an answer to this question (Drápal, 2022a).

The dominance of suspended prison sentences post-1989 is visible in Figure 4.4. Figure 4.5 complements this story by explaining the length of the prison sentences that have been suspended. Prison sentences between 1 and 12 months are the most commonly suspended, and they have thus become *the* defining feature of the Czech criminal justice system. However, prison sentences between 1 and 2 years have also been suspended as frequently as not, which marks a substantial departure from the practices of the previous two decades, during which sentences of between 1 and 2 years were suspended only infrequently. Moreover, following the 2009 broadening of the suspension legislation, prison sentences between 2 and 3 years also very quickly came to be suspended as often as they are not.

Gradually, the dominance of suspended prison sentences came to be viewed as problematic. Efforts to impose sanctions other than suspended prison sentences for minor offences emerged. The low proportion of fines was a concern for the legislature, judiciary and prosecutors, who pushed for their wider imposition and eventually succeeded. Informal prosecutorial meetings and educational seminars for judges and prosecutors in 2016 and 2017 were key to achieving an increase in the fine imposition rate (Drápal & Dušek, 2025). Meanwhile, in 2020, the legislature enabled an increase in the punitive bite for suspended prison sentences with the introduction of a measure similar to home detention which, for up to one year, could be imposed alongside a suspended prison sentence (in 2025 the legislature enabled a quasi community service to be also imposed alongside a suspended prison sentence). However, the hard treatment of this measure is not taken into account in any way when such an offender re-offends (whereas e.g. an equivalent measure in Germany can result in a shorter prison sentence being ordered to be served if suspension is revoked). This apparent oversight is likely due to negligence on the part of the Czech legislators (Drápal, 2022c). Further re-imagination of the provisions governing suspended prison sentences in Czechia is necessary to achieve a principled sentencing system.

Conclusion

The development of the legislative provisions and practical use of suspended prison sentences in Czechia has been chaotic. The dramatic societal changes of the 20th century in particular, with their knock-on effects on the quality of academic research, legislature, executive decision-making and the judiciary, contributed substantially to the chaos. The present use of suspended prison sentences is dramatically different from how they were originally conceived. Suspended prison sentences are now imposed for a very broad array of offences and are no longer considered by many practitioners to be prison sentences. This change has taken place without any official re-imagination of the conception, and while the legal provisions governing sentence suspension have remained largely the same, its scope has gradually increased.

This unprincipled approach has resulted in various problems, including sentence inflation: ever longer suspended prison sentences are imposed. The legislature, with knowledge of the dominance of suspended prison sentences, has increased sentencing range minimums, likely more than it would have without such widespread suspension (Drápal, 2021a). The difficulty is that if – as is officially the case – the only deciding factor as to whether to suspend a prison sentence or not is the likelihood of re-offending, and suspension is possible even for longer sentences, then suspended prison sentences are regularly imposed for rather serious offences. The inattentiveness to the re-imagination of the institute while at the same time enlarging its scope produces the vicious cycle of suspended prison sentences.

Not surprisingly, there has been public criticism of suspended prison sentences in Czechia. The common imposition of suspended prison sentences for rape has been especially criticised by institutions focused on gender (Ježková, 2017, pp. 24–25; Šafařík, 2020) and indeed the NGO *Bez trestu* (English: *Without Punishment*) has been founded to focus specifically on this issue. Unfortunately, these critics largely focus on specific aspects of suspended sentence use, for example demanding further increases in the sentencing ranges for particular offences, and so far have not pushed for a more complex reform of sentencing practices, as I believe to be necessary. There has however been some sign in recent years that politicians, academics and practitioners are aware of the need for a thorough reform of suspended prison sentences (see e.g. Drápal, 2021a; Úřad vlády, 2022) and we may thus hope that such a reform will take place within the coming decade.

Notes

1 Several parts of this chapter overlap slightly with a previously published paper (Drápal, 2025).
2 Explanatory memorandum (*důvodová zpráva*) to Penal Code, law n. 40/2009 Coll., p. 214–215.
3 All guilty verdicts that acquired legal force in 2019 (N = 61,465) excluding youth offenders. Aggregate and conjoint punishments are included. For a further description of the dataset see Vanča and Drápal (2021). All data relating to current sentencing practice, unless otherwise specified, relate to this 2019 court dataset.
4 Decision of the Supreme Court on 17 October 2007, n. 5 Tdo 974/2007 and previous decisions cited in this decision.

5 Decision n. II. ÚS 482/18 made on 28. 11. 2018 (N 195/91 SbNU 411), point 12. The author of this chapter contributed to this decision as an assistant to the judge-rapporteur.
6 Decision of the Constitutional Court n. I. ÚS 1202/17 made on 15. 8. 2017 (N 151/86 SbNU 527), point 21. The author of this chapter contributed to this decision as an assistant to the judge-rapporteur.
7 Decision of the Constitutional Court n. I. ÚS 1202/17 made on 15. 8. 2017 (N 151/86 SbNU 527), points 12-18.
8 The data on the interwar period is based on official aggregated statistics (Státní úřad statistický, 1923, 1925, 1931, 1937), compiled by the author.
9 Law n. 562/1919 Coll., section 9/4.
10 Penal code drafts made in 1921, 1926 and 1937 (Drápal, 2021a).
11 These provisions were, however, very likely interpreted ideologically: the primary rationale of the 1950 Penal Code was to "destroy the enemies of the working class" (s. 17/1/a).
12 Explanatory memorandum to law no. 63/1956 Coll., Introduction.
13 S. 23/1 of 1961 Penal Code.
14 See development of sections 314d and 314e of the Czech Code of Criminal Procedure, law no. 141/1961 Coll.
15 Explanatory memorandum to law no. 253/1997 Coll., art. 1, points 4 and 5.
16 Explanatory memorandum to Penal Code, law n. 40/2009 Coll., p. 229.
17 Explanatory memorandum to law no. 265/2001 Coll., Second part, art. IV, point 16.

References

Bobek, M. (2015). Judicial selection, lay participation, and judicial culture in the Czech Republic: A study in a Central European (non)transformation. In S. Turenne (Ed.), *Fair reflection of society in judicial systems – A comparative study* (pp. 121–146). Springer. https://doi.org/10.1007/978-3-319-18485-2_6

Drápal, J. (2017). Vede větší užití trestních příkazů k ukládání méně nepodmíněných trestů odnětí svobody? *Jurisprudence*, (5), 5–17.

Drápal, J. (2018). Individualizace v České republice: Jak určujeme tresty a co o tom víme? *Státní Zastupitelství*, *XV*(1), 9–23.

Drápal, J. (2019). Vývoj kriminologie na právnických fakultách v Praze v letech 1918-2018. *Česká Kriminologie*, *4*(1).

Drápal, J. (2020a). Sentencing disparities in the Czech Republic: Empirical evidence from post-communist Europe. *European Journal of Criminology*, *17*(2), 151–174. https://doi.org/10.1177/1477370818773612

Drápal, J. (2020b). Ukládání trestů v případě jejich kumulace: Jak trestat pachatele, kteří spáchali další trestný čin předtím, než vykonali dříve uložené tresty. *Jurisprudence*, (2), 1–17.

Drápal, J. (2021a). Podmíněné odsouzení: Jeho účel a vývoj na území Česka. *Státní Zastupitelství*, *19*(6), 18–35.

Drápal, J. (2021b). Principiální a konzistentní ukládání trestů: Jak jej docílit v České republice? *Státní Zastupitelství*, *19*(1), 9–18.

Drápal, J. (2021c). Punitive by negligence? The myths and reality of penal nationalism in the Czech Republic. *European Journal of Criminology, 20*(4), 1549–1567. https://doi.org/10.1177/14773708211063753

Drápal, J. (2021d). Sentencing multiple conviction offenders. *European Journal of Criminology, 20*(1), 142–160. https://doi.org/10.1177/1477370821996903

Drápal, J. (2022a). Lze zohlednit závažnost při rozhodování o podmíněném odsouzení? *Státní Zastupitelství, 6*.

Drápal, J. (2022c). Za reformu systému trestů: Citelnost trestů, jejich ekvivalence a nekoncepčnost současného systému. *Státní Zastupitelství*, (2, 3), 8–17, 20–36.

Drápal, J. (2025). Suspended prison sentences in Czechia: How they came to Dominate the penal landscape and their consequences. *Criminal Law Forum*. https://doi.org/10.1007/s10609-025-09515-4

Drápal, J., & Dušek, L. (2025). Law or authority? How Czech penal elites shaped sentencing policy by non-binding interventions. *Journal of Quantitative Criminology*. https://doi.org/10.1007/s10940-025-09614-w

Drápal, J., & Šoltés, M. (2021). Rozdíly v ukládání a navrhování trestů: Výsledky dvou experimentů. In T. Gřivna (Ed.), *V upomínku na Marii Vanduchovou*. Wolters Kluwer.

Drápal, J., & Vanča, T. (2024). Osvědčit, nařídit či ponechat v platnosti: Rozhodnutí o výkonu podmíněného trestu (aneb z výjimky se stává pravidlo). In *Podmíněný trest odnětí svobody: Převládající, nepopsaný, nepřiměřený*. Wolters Kluwer.

Drápalová, J., & Drápal, J. (2022). Precedenční závaznost judikatury Ústavního soudu v praxi. *Bulletin Advokacie*, (7–8), 33–45.

Fábry, A. (1983). Poznatky o účinnosti podmienečného odsúdenia v okrese Bratislava – Vidiek. *Prokuratura*, (4), 62–71.

Gřivna, T. (2009). Trestní právo hmotné. In M. Bobek, P. Molek, & V. Šimíček (Eds.), *Komunistické právo v Československu* (pp. 553–581). Retrieved from www.komunistickepravo.cz

Jestřáb, M. (1960). Omezení, uložené podmíněně odsouzenému podle § 25 odst. 2 tr. z. *Právník*, (2), 113–116.

Ježková, V. (2017). *Jen ano je ano*. http://www.profem.cz/shared/clanky/550/A5-JenAnoJeAno_WEB.pdf

Kallab, J. (1904). Doporučuje se v Rakousku uvedení instituce podmínečného odsouzení? In E. Novák (Ed.), *Spisy II. právnického* (pp. 1–38).

Kalvodová, V. (2002). *Postavení trestu odnětí svobody v systému trestněprávních sankcí*. Masarykova univerzita.

Kutsar, D., & Kovács, I. P. (2010). Introduction. In D. Kutsar & I. P. Kovács (Eds.), *Internationalisation of social sciences in Central and Eastern Europe* (pp. 1–6). Routledge.

Lata, J. (2008). Několik poznámek k problematice ukládání trestů začínajícím delikventům. In *Pocta Otovi Novotnému k 80. narozeninám* (pp. 158–165). ASPI.

Marešová, A., & Scheinost, M. (1994). Současný stav kriminality v České republice. *Sociologický Časopis, 30*(2), 167–178.

Milota, A. (1919). *Podmíněné odsouzení a propuštění (Výklad zákona)*. Nákladem Karla Beníška.

NSZ. (2022). *Zpráva o činnosti státního zastupitelství za rok 2021*. https://verejnazaloba.cz/wp-content/uploads/2022/07/ZoČ_2021-textová_část.pdf

Richter, T. (2013). Koho chléb jíš, toho píseň zpívej: Konflikty vznikající při propojení právní praxe s právní teorií. *Právník*, (2), 124–137.

Rotschild, J. (1988). *East Central Europe between the two World Wars*. University of Washington Press.

Šafařík, R. (2020). Znásilnění: donucení k pohlavnímu styku násilím, či absence souhlasu? In K. Šimáčková, B. Havelková, & P. Špondrová (Eds.), *Mužské právo. Jsou právní pravidla neutrální?* (pp. 267–296). Wolters Kluwer.

Ščerba, F. (2014). *Alternativní tresty a opatření v nové právní úpravě* (2. vydání). Leges.

Scheinost, M. (2010). Kriminalita a kriminologie v České republice. In M. Scheinost (Ed.), *Kriminalita očima kriminologů* (pp. 7–18). IKSP.

Solnař, V., & Vanduchová, M. (2009). *Systém českého trestního práva: Tresty a ochranná opatření*. Novatrix.

Státní úřad statistický. (1923). *Trestní statistika z Čech, Moravy a Slezska v letech 1913-1918*. Bursík a Kohout.

Státní úřad statistický. (1925). *Trestní statistika z Čech, Moravy a Slezska v letech 1919-1922*. Bursík a Kohout.

Státní úřad statistický. (1931). *Trestní statistika z republiky Československé v letech 1923-1927*. Bursík a Kohout.

Státní úřad statistický. (1937). *Trestní statistika republiky Československé za léta 1928-1931*. Bursík a Kohout.

Takáč, M., & Svitok, J. (1946). *Podmienečné odsúdenie a prepustenie*. Právnická jednota v Bratislavě.

Tomšů, K., & Drápal, J. (2019). Odůvodňování trestů: Empirická studie rozhodnutí okresních soudů. *Státní Zastupitelství*, *6*, 9–21.

Úřad vlády. (2022). *Teze trestní politiky*. https://icv.vlada.cz/assets/ppov/rlp/vybory/Pro_trestni_politiku/Teze-trestni-politiky_1.pdf

Urbášek, P. (2012). Čistky na českých vysokých školách v letech 1945–1990. In M. Černá & J. Cuhra (Eds.), *Prověrky a jejich místo v komunistickém vládnutí: Československo 1948–1989* (pp. 121–138). Ústav pro soudobé dějiny AV ČR.

Vanča, T., & Drápal, J. (2021). Statistické listy trestní soudů: Ověření jejich spolehlivosti. *Česká Kriminologie*, *6*(1–2), 1–24. https://ceskakriminologie.cz/cs/archiv/2021-120132/statisticke-listy-trestni-soudu-overeni-jejich-spolehlivostispolehlivosti/Attachment

Vanča, T., & Drápal, J. (2023). Odůvodňování trestů odvolacími soudy. *Unpublished Manuscript*.

Vaněk, L. (1890). Zprávy o týdenních schůzích Právnické Jednoty v Praze. *Právník*, 63–68.

Zucker, A. (1891). *Podmíněné odsouzení*. Bursík a Kohout.

5 The development of suspended prison sentences in Hungary

Barbara Mohácsi and Krisztina Lukács

Introduction

Until the 18th century, there was no criminal code in Hungary, not even any attempt at codification. At the beginning of the 19th century, penal law was characterised by tradition, and criminal jurisprudence was regulated by customary law. The first Hungarian criminal code was the so-called Csemegi Code, which entered into force on 1st September 1880 and remained in force for more than seventy years. Suspended prison sentences were introduced through Act XXXVI of 1908, which was the first amendment to the Csemegi Code. At that time, short-term imprisonment was already recognised as inappropriate and harmful, and replacing it with non-custodial punishment, for example, through suspension, was seen as justifiable. This proved a successful legal instrument and has been in use ever since.

This chapter describes the characteristics of suspended prison sentences in Hungary. To this end, it presents in detail the current rules and regulations and highlights the importance of this sanction within the Hungarian penal system. In addition, we present practitioners' experience with this type of sanction and describe the history of suspended prison sentences and the evolution of the rules governing them, from 1908 until the present day.

Based on its historic development, we conclude that the suspended prison sentence sanction is not an independent type of punishment in the current Hungarian system of criminal sanctions. According to the provisions set out in the current Criminal Code (hereinafter CC), if the court delivers a sentence of imprisonment, the length of imprisonment must be determined without considering potential probation or parole (CC, § 80(4)). Furthermore, the Hungarian legislation currently in force does not regulate any mandatory case of suspended prison sentence. However, it cannot be considered an exceptional option, since the law requires only one condition for its application: the purpose of the punishment must be attainable even in the absence of imprisonment.

DOI: 10.4324/9781003568667-8

Current regime

Pursuant to the **Hungarian legal rules currently in force** (CC, §§ 85–88) suspension may only be applied to prison sentences, and not for fines or other types of sanctions.

(i) The execution of a term of imprisonment not exceeding two years' duration may be suspended for an operational period of between one and five years (CC, § 85). The court may decide to suspend the imprisonment if there is good reason to believe – particularly in view of the offender's personal circumstances – that the aim of punishment may be achieved without its execution. According to the Criminal Code of Hungary (CC, § 79), the aim of punishment is to deter the offender or any other person from committing a crime. The reasons given by Parliament to further specify this legal rule stipulate that the aim of the punishment is the protection of society, both in special and general terms. Through the use of the **pardoning power,** granted by the Fundamental Law (Fundamental Law, Art. 9(4)(g)), the president of the Republic may also suspend the execution of a penalty.[1]

Suspension of the execution of imprisonment is, then, an option rather than an obligation. As an option, it cannot be deemed exceptional, since its application is contingent upon the fulfilment of one single condition, which is its potential to achieve the aim of the punishment.

Detailed guidance for the courts on the criteria and principles for the application of suspended imprisonment is provided in the opinion of the Penal Collegium[2] no. 55/2007 on parole and the suspension of the execution of penalty. This opinion emphasises that a suspended sentence is not an independent type of punishment. The court should decide upon a term of imprisonment regardless of whether its execution will or will not be suspended. Compensating for the suspension of a sentence by imposing a longer term of imprisonment cannot be considered legal and would contradict the sentencing rules. The proper course of imposing a penalty is to first fix the term of imprisonment and afterwards – independently – decide on its eventual suspension (CC, § 80).

If the offender's personal circumstances are favourable, the court should in general impose imprisonment only for offences constituting significant danger to the society, in accordance with further guidelines stipulated in the opinion of the Penal Collegium no. 55/2007. For sentences not exceeding two years, the aim of punishment can usually be achieved by suspending the execution of imprisonment. However, according to the Penal Collegium, suspension of a prison sentence is not justified if the offender has committed a criminal offence of aggravated nature (such as a crime of a violent or vandalistic nature or a threat to public order), if the offender was grossly negligent and the offence had severe consequences, or if the crime was committed by a member of a criminal organisation. In such cases, suspending the imprisonment would go against societal values, as such conduct is too reprehensible. In other words, imprisonment may be suspended only if either the danger to society or the degree of culpability is low. Additionally, suspension is not generally permitted when the offender has an alcoholic lifestyle,[3] or immoral attitude, or has committed an offence that poses significant danger to the society, or if their personality is otherwise egregious to society.

Other sanctions can be imposed alongside suspended prison sentences, with the exceptions of custodial arrest[4] and community service. Fines, prohibitions from exercising professional activities, driving bans, prohibitions from residing in particular areas, bans from attending sporting events, and expulsion can be imposed in addition to suspended imprisonment. Deprivation of civil rights is not applicable to a suspended sentence.[5]

The number of custodial sentences imposed decreased steadily and significantly between 2013 and 2020, as shown in Table 5.1, with a slight increase in the two subsequent years. In comparison, the use of suspended prison sentences was balanced over the last ten years. Suspended prison sentences constituted between 61% and 67% of the total number of prison sentences imposed in this period, and there was no significant difference in any given year. The same was not true of the trends in community service and fines, however. The number of community service sentences imposed was stable in 2013 and 2014 but subsequently decreased and continued to drop until 2022. The number of fines increased gradually from 2013 to 2019 before falling somewhat in the following three years.

Pursuant to the opinion of the Penal Collegium no. 55/2007, any penalties applied in addition to a suspended prison sentence must be determined in such a way that their effect, together with the effect of the suspended prison sentence, supports the achievement of the purpose of the penalty. As a result, suspended prison sentences are typically imposed without any additional sanctions. However, the numbers of fines, prohibitions from exercising professional activities, and driving bans imposed alongside suspended prison sentences have been rising, while the number of expulsions has remained relatively stable.

In 2015, amendments were adopted which made it possible to suspend prison sentences longer than two years (but not exceeding five years) for certain criminal offences, namely: unlawful crossing of the border barrier (Section 352/A of CC), destruction of the border barrier (Section 352/B of CC) or obstruction of the construction or maintenance of the border barrier (Section 352/C of CC). This change was part of a broader set of amendments to legal rules that were aimed at managing mass immigration.

(ii) The **operational period** ranges from one to five years in general, but the Criminal Code may provide differently in individual cases. For instance, the operational period may exceed five years if the offender is sentenced to a further custodial sentence and therefore the suspended sentence cannot be executed (CC, § 86(2)–(4)). In such cases, the operational period is extended by the length

Table 5.1 Sanctions imposed between 2013 and 2022.

	2013	*2014*	*2015*	*2016*	*2017*	*2018*	*2019*	*2020*	*2021*	*2022*
Imprisonment	26256	26113	24144	22403	21858	20432	19186	15793	17399	18520
- of which suspended	17541 66,8%	17138 65,6%	15402 63,8%	14251 63,6%	14003 64,1%	12906 63,2%	12025 62,7%	10509 66,5%	11032 63,4%	11337 61,2%
Community service	13509	13607	12070	11599	10684	9780	9368	8106	7875	7390
Fine	15708	19723	20143	21591	22861	24409	24766	22765	22348	23573
Sanctions imposed alongside suspended prison sentences (in numbers and as a percentage of suspended prison sentences)										
Fine	244 1.4%	398 2.3%	445 2.9%	599 4.2%	565 4%	656 5.1%	725 6%	775 7.4%	888 8%	1212 10.7%
Prohibition to exercise professional activity	91 0.5%	139 0.8%	207 1.3%	223 1.6%	278 2%	320 2.5%	358 3%	294 2.8%	579 5.2%	705 6.2%
Driving ban	856 4.9%	1044 6.1%	1083 7%	1264 8.9%	1506 10.8%	1445 11.2%	1429 11.9%	1329 12.6%	1545 14%	1795 15.8%
Expulsion	151 0.9%	221 1.3%	212 1.4%	196 1.4%	153 1.1%	118 0.9%	88 0.7%	118 1.1%	178 1.6%	152 1.3%
Other	2	32	20	21	15	16	7	19	19	15

Source: National Office for the Judiciary (NOJ).
Note: Figures for 2022 are not final.

of the additional term of imprisonment. Furthermore, the operational period cannot be shorter than the length of the suspended prison sentence.

The length of the operational period is determined in deliberation by the court, in a process akin to that when deciding on suspension. However, the deliberation is different in character, with the following guidelines as per the opinion of the Penal Collegium no. 55/2007: if the offender's personal circumstances are favourable, the circumstances of the criminal offence come into prominence. All these circumstances are to be evaluated primarily from the standpoint of preventing recidivism, and the operational period should therefore be determined in line with individual circumstances.

The guidelines (CC, § 86(5)) include instructions for cases when an offender has been sentenced more than once to imprisonment that was suspended, and the operational period has not yet expired. In such cases, all of the operational periods pass concurrently.

As part of the migration-related amendments of 2015, the rules governing the terms of suspension for the three specific offences mentioned above were also amended. For these offences, the operational period may range from two to ten years but may not be shorter than the period of expulsion. Expulsion is obligatory for these offences when a custodial sentence is imposed (CC, § 60) and must be double the length of the prison sentence (and not shorter than two years). The enforcement of the expulsion takes place after the decision to suspend the prison sentence.

Probationary supervision may be ordered for the duration of a suspended prison sentence if supervision is deemed necessary to ensure the effectiveness of the suspension (CC, §§ 69, 86(6)). Probationary supervision is obligatory if the offender is a recidivist or has been sentenced to imprisonment for a violent crime against a family member, or for a criminal offence against sexual freedom, or for sexual offences committed against a minor. Supervision is also mandatory when suspended prison sentences are imposed on juvenile offenders (CC, § 119). When the courts decide on suspension with probationary supervision, they must primarily consider the nature of the criminal offence committed and the offender's personal circumstances.

(iii) In certain cases, the execution of a prison sentence **may not be suspended** (CC, § 86). These are cases in which the personality of the offender or the nature of the offence committed are such that suspension cannot be reasonably expected to result in the desired outcomes and aims, and they are cases involving:

- a repeat offender;[6]
- a member of a criminal organisation;[7] or
- a crime committed intentionally before a previous prison sentence had been fully served, or during the operational period of a suspended sentence (this provision does not apply to negligent offences).

(iv) The Criminal Code provides a list (CC, § 87) of cases in which the suspension of a prison sentence **must be revoked**.

The first such case is when, during the operational period, it is established that the execution of imprisonment was suspended despite the existence of one or more grounds for refusal as mentioned above.[8]

Second, suspension is revoked if the offender is sentenced to an executable imprisonment for a crime committed during the operational period. In this case, it is irrelevant whether the new offence was committed intentionally or through negligence, since the reason for revoking suspension is that it was incorrect to presume that the aim of punishment could be achieved without the execution of imprisonment. Note that suspension **cannot** be revoked if the offender receives any sentence other than executable imprisonment for the new offence.

Third, revocation occurs if the offender seriously breaches the conditions of probationary supervision. This case differs from those above, as it requires court discretion to decide whether the offender's conduct qualifies as an infraction whose severity justifies revocation.

Finally, suspension may be revoked if an offender who was deported for committing specific offences unlawfully returns to the territory of Hungary during the operational period.[9]

The history of the suspended sentence and the development of the current system

Until the 19th century, there were no attempts to codify criminal law in Hungary (Lőrincz & Mezey, 2019, pp. 59–60). The first Hungarian penal code was the 1878 Act "On crimes and délits", commonly referred to as the Csemegi Code, after its main creator. The Code entered into force on 1st September 1880, and remained in force for more than seventy years. Its greatest achievement was codification itself (Király, 1977, pp. 36–41). The Csemegi Code did not allow for the suspension of a prison sentence: while Károly Csemegi did suggest in 1890 that short-term imprisonment should be reconsidered and reconceived, he was against simple exoneration, i.e. "its replacement with no penalty" (Pálvölgyi, 2017, p. 76). Hence, no options for suspending sentences were included in the Code (Horváth, 1968, p. 13).

The introduction of suspended imprisonment

Act XXXVI of 1908 "On supplementing and amending the code of criminal procedure" (known as the 1st Amending Act) was the first to introduce the possibility of suspending a prison sentence. At that time, there was harsh opposition to the concept of a suspended sentence. Critics' main argument was that, since the aim of punishment is retribution, suspending punishment "*would compromise the belief in the necessary causal relationship between crime and penalty*"

(Földvári, 1970, p. 437). Supporters, on the contrary, argued that the threat of punishment would exert a deterrent impact (e.g., von Liszt & Irk, n.d.; see also Pálvölgyi, 2018b, pp. 75–76). Another argument in support of suspension was that first-time offenders who did not otherwise lead "criminal" lives should not be incarcerated: it was already recognised that short-term imprisonment was inappropriate and ineffective, and that replacing it with punishment not involving imprisonment could be justified (Földvári, 1970, p. 438; Edvi Illés, 1909, p. 606).

The legislator highlighted that an extraordinary emphasis should be put on the offender's personality; in other words, it was appropriate to treat first-time and occasional offenders, and those whose motivations were excusable or who acted without malice, differently from other offenders.[10] The legislator furthermore emphasised the economic and political benefits of suspension, since offenders whose prison sentences are suspended do not lose their jobs and are therefore not forced to reoffend by a loss of subsistence.

The 1st Amending Act provided for the possibility of suspending jail sentences[11] that did not exceed one month, in cases "deserving special consideration".[12] Suspension was conditional on due consideration of the conduct of the offender – his/her personality, life conditions, and all other circumstances of the case – and the expectation of a favourable outcome.[13] The court could also order suspension of a sentence in response to a request from the convicted offender or *ex officio*. Its decision had to detail the reasons and circumstances in view of which it had decided that suspension was justified. [14] The act did not specify exactly what must be taken into consideration when assessing the option of suspending a sentence, but the Reasons accompanying the Code highlighted some of these, such as the offender's personality, age, living circumstances, family circumstances, former conduct, reason for committing the offence, honest confession, and reparation of the damages or intent to do so (Edvi Illés, 1909, p. 612).

Suspension was seen as an individualised sentence corresponding to the personality of the offender, which could only benefit those who committed a criminal offence "imputably to the accidental coincidence of circumstances" (Edvi Illés, 1909, p. 606).

The Reasons attached to the Amending Act emphasise that suspension should not be used to mitigate a sentence. The court could not justify suspension on the basis of mitigating circumstances that it took into account when deciding on the length of imprisonment (Földvári, 1970, p. 440). For those who were considered suitable and worthy of it, however, suspension could be used irrespective of age, for both juveniles and adults.

The Amending Act restricted the possibility of suspension to jail sentences not exceeding one month, which in comparison with other solutions applied in Europe (usually limited to three or six months) seems to be more restrictive. However, suspension could also be applied for offences qualified as délits or contraventions, i.e. offences to be punished with jail or fines. Statistics suggest that the number of such offences was high, which confirms that the legislator did not intend suspension to be used minimally, but rather assigned it to a particular category of offences.[15] In the majority of such cases, the court-imposed jail sentences of less than one month (Edvi Illés, 1909, pp. 609–610).

The Amending Act also allowed for the option of suspending a fine, irrespective of its amount. This was applicable even to fines imposed as an additional penalty alongside another sentence, since their nature and aim were identical to that of fines imposed as the main penalty. Pecuniary sanctions were imposed only in the case of less severe offences where incarceration was not justified, and therefore it would have been unjust to prohibit suspension.[16]

The operational period determined by the Amending Act was three years for both imprisonment and fines, calculated from the first day on which the sentence could no longer be appealed. The Amending Act stipulated that the sentence imposed by the court must not be executed if the period of three years passed without any proceedings against the offender (1st Amending Act, § 3). Courts decided whether or not to suspend sentences, but they did not decide the length of the operational period, which was fixed. The Reasons explain that it was necessary to determine a uniform term of suspension because the introduction of a new legal institution might have led to legal uncertainty if judges were given discretion to determine the term of suspension (Edvi Illés, 1909, p. 669).

The Amending Act also determined the scope of the application of the suspended sentences by citing cases of offences and offenders for which it was not applicable. Suspension could not be applied for sentences imposed for acts or attempts punishable by penitentiary or correctional institution, nor for offenders who had committed the offences out of despicable motives. In principle, the Amending Act did not preclude the suspension of sentences for recidivists: it precluded suspension if the offender had already been sentenced for committing a crime, but allowed it if they had committed a délit. However, it also precluded suspension if the offender had previously been handed a sentence of jail longer than one month within the previous ten years. Recidivism was not a barrier to suspension if ten years had already passed since the previous jail sentence or custodial arrest, nor if the convict had been pardoned. A period of ten years without committing another offence was considered to indicate that the previous sanctions had achieved their aim. The legislator held that it was not reasonable to presume that any relation existed between the former and successive criminal offences if ten years had passed between them (1st Amending Act, § 2).

Revocation was obligatory if a new offence was committed during the operational period for which criminal proceedings were initiated prior to the end of the operational period, and in the course of the new proceedings, the offender was sentenced for a crime or sentenced to jail for deliberate délit. When suspension was revoked in such cases, the sentences were not merged: all periods of imprisonment had to be served consecutively (1st Amending Act, § 4, first sentence). As the Reasons explain, this was designed as a punishment for convicted offenders who turned out to be unworthy of the benefit of suspension.[17] In the case of other délits (e.g. a délit committed through negligence, which could be punished only by a fine or incarceration in a state-operated jail), the court could assess the possibility of the revocation (1st Amending Act, § 4, second sentence). In such cases, while assessing the circumstances of the case, the court could consider whether further offences committed during the operational period were merely incidental or whether they indicated more serious immoral conduct. If, during the operational period, criminal proceedings commenced against the offender for an offence that was committed before the suspended sentence became non-appealable, or the court became aware that a non-appealable prison sentence imposed earlier than the suspended sentence should be executed, these sentences had to be merged. If the necessary conditions were met, such merged sentences could also be suspended (1st Amending Act, § 5).

Because the institution of suspended sentences that was introduced in 1908 operated well in practice, the possible expansion of its application was soon considered. Firstly, the maximum eligible sentence length of one month began to be thought of as too short, and reasons to prolong it were considered. This was corroborated by the fact that the courts applied suspension in quite a moderate manner. Suspension had other benefits in terms of the criminal procedure, because it led to an increase in the number of cases completed in the first instance, which consequently diminished the courts' workload. [18]

Act XXXIV of 1930 on the simplification of jurisdiction emphasised the favourable impact of suspended prison sentences on the courts' workload and amended suspension conditions. Jail sentences not exceeding three months – instead of the previous one month – could now be suspended (Act XXXIV of 1930, § 124). This change also meant that suspension could be imposed not only for délits but also, under specific conditions, for some crimes.[19] At that time, although a more general review of the Criminal Code was on the agenda, the legislative body thought it appropriate to broaden the institution of suspension.

Suspended sentences in socialist criminal law

After the Second World War, Soviet criminal law, unlike the previous offender-focused system, placed greater emphasis on the criminal offence and on punishment. In this spirit, Act II of 1950, which contained the general part of the new Criminal Code (hereinafter 1950 Act), was passed. The new code sought to protect working people, educate offenders and prevent members of society from committing criminal offences. The 1950 Act abolished the distinction between crimes and délits and introduced a single form of incarceration, known as a correctional institution.[20]

In view of the harmful impacts of short-term imprisonment, the 1950 Act maintained and arguably expanded the possibility of suspending imprisonment by giving the court more discretion in deciding whether such suspension was appropriate.[21] The legal formulation of the assessment no longer referred to cases "deserving special consideration" but focused on the offender's "worthiness"[22] and the favourable impact that suspension might have on the offender's conduct (1950 Act, § 55(1)).

Both imprisonment and fines could still be suspended. Moving beyond the amended Csemegi Code, the 1950 Act further expanded the possibility of suspension to sentences of up to one year of imprisonment (1950 Act, § 55(3)). Sentences could not be suspended if they were accompanied by the deprivation of civil rights or prohibition from exercising professional activities, nor if the offender had been sentenced to imprisonment during the five-year period preceding the commission of the offence in question, the execution of which was suspended (1950 Act, § 55(3)(b)–(d). In such cases, the offender could not be considered "worthy" of a suspended sentence (Pálvölgyi, 2017., p. 124). The Reasons accompanying the code make clear that suspension was designed as a replacement for short-term imprisonment, and, in practice, it was readily applied as such. In the years following the enactment of the 1950 Act, a large proportion of sentences were suspended. For instance, 50% of all prison sentences of up to one year were suspended in 1951, 45.9% in 1952 and 38.7% in 1953 (Földvári, 1970, p. 442).

However, the downward trend in the use of suspension already observed in the early 1950s was soon confirmed by a conceptual decision[23] from the Supreme Court, no. X, in 1954, which stated that the suspension of a sentence for an operational period was to be considered an exceptional measure.[24] The use of suspended sentences dropped: in 1954, only 37.4% of all imprisonments with a term not exceeding one year were suspended, and in 1955 this rate was 29.6% (Földvári, 1970, p. 442).

This change in the courts' practice moved against the aims stipulated in the Criminal Code and against criminal policy, and consequently the Supreme Court subsequently issued a new conceptual decision, no. XX, in 1959, concerning the applicability of suspension. This decision emphasised that two conditions should be taken into account when considering whether suspension was justified: whether future favourable changes to the offender's conduct could be expected; and the offender's "worthiness".

Statistics demonstrating the efficiency of suspended sentences are unfortunately not available for this period. However, the number of criminal offences committed during the operational period of a suspended sentence was examined in 1951, when it was found that 14% of suspended sentences had to be executed (i.e. suspension revoked) due to recividism (Pálvölgyi, 2018a, p. 129).

In 1961, a new Criminal Code[25] was enacted, which designated the aim of criminal law as the protection of the State and of social and economic order. This Criminal Code maintained and further developed the institution of suspended sentences. It remained possible to suspend the execution of imprisonment not exceeding one year or of a fine (Act V of 1961, § 70(1)), but newly, in exceptional cases "deserving special consideration", the Code also allowed the suspension of imprisonment of up to two years (Act V of 1961, § 70(2)). There were two preconditions for suspending a prison sentence: first, consideration of the personal circumstances of the offender and the nature of the criminal offence, and second, an expectation that the aim of the punishment could be achieved without its execution. The CC of 1961 – in harmony with the provisions stipulated in 1950 Act – enabled the courts to take mitigating factors into consideration when considering whether or not to suspend a prison sentence. Suspension did not pertain to fines imposed as an additional penalty, alongside another sanction, because the execution of a fine imposed alongside a suspended prison sentence could benefit the achievement of the sentence's purpose (Act V of 1961, § 70(4)).

The 1961 Code allowed for more differentiation in operational periods than there had been previously. Fines were to be suspended for one year. Prison sentences not exceeding one year were to have an operational period of three years, while prison sentences of between one and two years were to be suspended for an operational period of between one and five years (Act V of 1961, § 70(3)). As previously, the 1961 Act stipulated specific grounds for refusing suspension, which were the same as those stipulated in the 1950 Act[26] A suspended sentence had to be revoked if it had been suspended despite the existence of grounds for refusal, or if the offender was sentenced to imprisonment for a criminal offence committed during the operational period, or if an imposed community service sentence was changed to a custodial sentence.[27] A new sentence of a fine or community service alone was not sufficient cause for revocation of suspension (Földvári, 1970, p. 456).

In 1962, the Supreme Court reconfirmed its conceptual decision no. XX of 1959. It emphasised that suspension of imprisonment should not be deemed exceptional, except in cases pertaining to prison sentences of between one and two years. Accordingly, suspension was increasingly applied in practice, mostly in cases involving criminal offences against bodily integrity and property. During the years following the enactment of the CC of 1961, 25–40% of imposed sentences were suspended, while in 1965 this rate increased to 51.6% (Pálvölgyi, 2018a, p. 128). The early 1960s can thus be seen as the starting point for the institution of suspended imprisonment as we currently know it.

The next act that amended the institution of suspended sentences was Law-decree no. 28 of 1971. This enabled further differentiation to reflect various degrees of criminal liability. The operational period of suspension was now to be tied more closely to the nature of the offence committed. In the case of prison sentences for délits, the operational period could range from one to three years, whereas in the case of prison sentences for crimes, it could range from one to five years. No longer was there any fixed operational period; instead, the act provided ranges within which the court could decide, with due consideration of the offender's personal circumstances, the nature of the criminal offence and the method of perpetration. In addition, the 1971 Law-decree amended the cases in which suspension was forbidden, which now only pertained to cases in which the new offence had been committed during an existing operational period, or in which the offender had committed another offence within a certain period preceding the new conviction (five years for a deliberate crime, three years for a deliberate délit) (Pálvölgyi, 2018a, p. 132). The amending act calculated this specific period of time not from the date of a non-appealable sentence being imposed, but from the last day of the served sentence or the date on which its executability was terminated, and stipulated different periods for criminal offences of various natures.

Suspended sentences according to Act IV of 1978

In 1978, a new Criminal Code (hereafter: 1978 Act) was adopted, largely based on the penal system created by the 1961 Act. Under the new rules, suspended sentences occupied an important place as a sanction not involving the deprivation of liberty. The 1978 Act regulated two forms of conditional (i.e. suspended) sentences: probation[28] and suspension. It stipulated that suspension was not a specific type of sanction, and it was therefore regulated among the provisions regarding the manner in which sentences were to be imposed. The case law remained clear on the principle that, when imposing a sentence, the degree of punishment should be determined prior to any consideration of whether suspension was applicable. This notion was codified in the 1978 Act.[29] Since suspended imprisonment was not an independent type of punishment, suspension could not be "counterbalanced" against a longer term of imprisonment.[30] In addition, the court issued another conceptual decision stating that in the specific case of an offender who committed an exceptionally brutal offence, short term incarceration (6 months) and suspension (for two years) violated the law.[31]

Suspension of fines and of prison sentences of less than one year remained an option if it could be expected that the aim of the punishment – specifically in view of the offender's personal circumstances – could be achieved even so.[32] Pursuant to the case law, suspension was not considered justified, despite the offender's favourable personal circumstances, in cases involving more severe offences, higher degrees of negligence, or severe consequences, or when the crime had been committed by a member of a criminal organisation (Opinion of the Penal Collegium No. 55/2007, § 153(2)(a)). Suspension was, however, permitted in cases involving offenders whose conduct was reprehensible, but where the degree of culpability was lower, or if the offence presented less of a danger to society. Offenders with reprehensible conduct were placed under probationary supervision. In general, sentences were not suspended for offenders whose alcoholic lifestyle or immoral attitude had caused them to commit an offence that was substantially dangerous to society (Opinion of the Penal Collegium No. 55/2007, § 153(2)(b)).

In "cases deserving special consideration", prison sentences of more than one year but not exceeding two years could also be suspended (Act 1978, § 89(2)). This special consideration related to the offender's characteristics (such as old age or severe illness), as well as e.g. a lesser degree of culpability, an excusable motive, or provocation by the victim.[33] For example, the court deemed that a case was worthy of special consideration in which an offender with no previous conviction had committed or attempted life-threatening battery while driven by emotions in a humanly understandable situation, with contributory behaviour from the victim, and where further mitigating circumstances were also present.[34]

Other types of sanction could not be suspended. When deciding on suspension, the offender's personal circumstances had to be taken into consideration. Therefore, suspension was primarily intended for offenders "who committed the criminal offence incidentally, but whose conduct is otherwise honourable".[35] Within this context, evidence of prior convictions was extremely important, although prior conviction itself did not constitute an obstacle to suspension.

Suspension was not possible if the offender had committed an intentional offence prior to the expiry of a previous sentence or during the operational period of a previous suspension, nor when the offender was a recidivist. Suspension had to be revoked (and the imprisonment executed) if it had been granted despite the existence of one or more grounds for refusal (Act 1978, §§ 90, 91(1)(a)). Suspension also had to be revoked if the offender was sentenced to a new custodial sentence for a criminal offence committed during the operational period, or if a community service sanction was substituted by imprisonment (Act 1978, § 91(1)(b); BH1982.364). However, if the offence committed during the operational period was negligent, the suspension did not necessarily have to be revoked.[36] Suspension was to be revoked in any case if the offender severely breached the rules of probationary supervision (Act 1978, § 91(1)(c)).

The operational period varied depending on both the type of sanction being suspended and the category of the offence. The possible length of the operational period remained the same as earlier. The court's discretion in determining the length of the operational period was restricted by the Act inasmuch as it stipulated that this must be determined in whole years (Act 1978, § 89(3)). Case law indicated that in cases involving intentional criminal offences and reprehensible conduct, longer operational periods were appropriate.[37] If the offender was subject to several operational periods, these could not be merged or served in parallel, but would be served consecutively.

In addition to suspended imprisonment, the offender could be placed under probationary supervision if the personality of the offender and the severity and nature of the criminal offence justified this. For instance, probationary supervision was routinely ordered in cases involving negligent criminal offences.[38]

Law-decree 19 of 1984, which amended Act IV of the 1978 Criminal Code, introduced strict community service under close confinement.[39] If the offender was sentenced to this sanction for an offence committed during the operational period of a suspended sentence, that suspension could consequently be revoked. Revocation of suspension was compulsory if the strict community service was later substituted by imprisonment.

The next amendment to the 1978 Act was passed in 1998 and this amendment changed the rules of suspension in two respects. First, it clarified that in the case of suspension of a sentence due to presidential pardon, the ordering of the execution of the punishment shall be subjected to the general rules.[40] Second, it increased the lower limit of the operational period for suspended sentences imposed for crimes, from one to two years, better expressing the difference between crimes and délits in relation to the operational period (of Act LXXXVII of 1998, § 23, "on the amendment of the criminal legal rules"). In addition, the amendment extended the scope of reasons in view of which a sentence could not be suspended: suspension was now forbidden for repeat offenders, offenders who committed the offence as members of a criminal organisations, and in cases involving a criminal offence that carried imprisonment of at least three years that was committed in criminal association (Act LXXXVII of 1998, § 24, "on the amendment of the criminal law rules").

In 2003, a further change in criminal policy occurred, which was no longer based on the idea that effective crime reduction depended on tougher penalties. The 2003 amendment repealed all provisions in the 1978 Act that unnecessarily restricted sentence suspension. Habitual criminality or offences subject to three or more years' imprisonment committed in criminal association were no longer outside the scope of suspension (Act II of 2003, § 88(e), "on the amendment of penal provisions and certain related acts").

Partial suspension of prison sentences

The next amendment to the 1978 Act, passed in 2010, introduced the possibility of partial suspension of the execution of imprisonment.[41] This amendment sought to further promote the criminal policy approach that custodial sanctions should only be executed if the aim of the punishment could not be achieved otherwise. The possibility of partially suspending imprisonment enabled better sentence differentiation and greater sanction individualisation. The 2010 amendment also abolished the possibility of suspending fines.

The 2010 amendment permitted the suspension of prison sentences longer than one year but not exceeding two years, without requiring any evidence that special consideration was due.[42] For prison sentences longer than two years, but not exceeding five years, the amendment introduced the possibility of part-suspension of the imprisonment: part of the term of imprisonment was executable, while the remainder of the term was suspended. The operational period would begin only after the executable part of the sentence had been served. During the executable term, conditional release was not permitted. The non-executed part of the sentence could be suspended for a period of between two and five years, although the operational period could not be shorter than the suspended part of the prison sentence. Probationary supervision could also be imposed for the duration of the operational period.[43] The grounds for refusing such suspension remained as in the previous regulations, both for suspended and partly suspended sentences, as did the rules on revocation.

Critics of the new possibility of part-suspension emphasised that while suspended imprisonment was a much more lenient sanction than imprisonment, this was not necessarily the case for partly suspended prison sentences. Partly suspended prison sentences bore substantial similarities to custodial (non-suspended) prison sentences, and in certain cases could even be considered to have more severe legal consequences because of the existence of the operational period. These criticisms hindered the practical use of partly suspended sentences. Another problem was that a legal institution designed to shorten imprisonment – conditional release – already existed and appeared to make partial suspension redundant, even though these two legal institutions differed in nature.[44] Furthermore, the executable part of a partly suspended sentence would sometimes be too short to fulfil the educative goal of punishment (Nagy, 2003, p. 30). In view of these various difficulties and criticisms, the subsequent amendment to the Criminal Code, known as Act C of 2012, did not prolong the use of partly suspended imprisonment. Partial suspension was thus in force in Hungary for only a very short period, from 1st May 2010 until 30th June 2013.

Conclusion

Since 1908, the development of suspended prison sentences in Hungary has been characterised by their gradual expansion. Because the sanction worked well in practice after its initial introduction, there was a strong inclination to expand its scope, and all subsequent amendments to the criminal code broadened the possibilities for its imposition. While a conceptual decision issued by the Supreme Court hindered its use temporarily, the Supreme Court subsequently confirmed that suspended sentences should not be considered an exception. Suspended sentences thus gradually grew in importance among the non-custodial criminal sanctions within the Hungarian system, and they remain important today.

Notes

1 CC, section 88 prescribes that if a prison sentence is suspended by presidential pardon, the general rules on revocation shall be applied accordingly. Thus, sentences suspended by presidential pardon shall be executed (the suspension revoked) if the offender is sentenced to further imprisonment during the operational period, or if the offender seriously breaches the rules of probationary supervision.

2 The Penal Collegium is a chamber of the Supreme Court that monitors the courts' practice and gives its opinion on disputed judicial issues in order to ensure uniform case law. The opinion of the Collegium is advisory and not binding for the courts.

3 I.e. has a problematic addiction to alcohol.

4 Custodial arrest was introduced into the system of sanctions on 1 July 2013. It is a custodial sanction mainly imposed on offenders for whom other sanctions are inappropriate in view of their social, economic, family situation or age, or for whom it can serve effectively as a specific preventive measure. The duration of detention ranges from five to ninety days.

5 CC, section 61: "Any person who is sentenced to executable imprisonment for an intentional criminal offence, and is deemed unworthy of the right to participate in public affairs, shall be deprived of these rights".

6 The CC defines a repeat offender as a perpetrator of an intentional crime who was previously sentenced to an executable term of imprisonment, if three years have not yet passed between the day the offender was released from prison or the day when imprisonment ceased to be enforceable and the commission of another criminal offence. CC, section 459, subsection 1, point 31.

7 The CC defines a criminal organisation as a hierarchical group of at least three persons conspiring to collaborate in the long term to deliberately engage in intentional criminal acts that are punishable by at least five years of imprisonment. CC, section 459, subsection 1, point 1.

8 BJD 9733.

9 Pursuant to the Criminal Code, these specific offences are: unlawful crossing of the border barrier (Section 352/A), destruction of the border barrier (Section 352/B), obstruction to the construction or maintenance of the border barrier (Section 352/C) or smuggling illegal immigrants (Section 353).

10 The Reasons accompanying the Code explained that in some cases the problems caused for the convicted offender, as well as for the state and society by even a few days of imprisonment exceed the expected beneficial outcomes (Irk, 1915, pp. 97–101).

11 The Csemegi Code defined four types of imprisonment. These were – from the most to the least severe – penitentiary, state-operated jail, correctional institution, and jail.

12 "Deserving special consideration" is a positive criterion, but its interpretation was left to the court.

13 Act XXXVI of 1908 "On supplementing and amending the code of criminal procedure", Section 1.

14 Section 9 of the 1st Amending Act supplemented the provisions stipulated in Act XXXIII of 1896 with procedural rules concerning suspension.

15 "The number of imposed jail sentences of less than one month, for offences qualified as délits, exceeded 40,000 per year; the number of imprisonment sanctions was approximately 7000, and the number of fines was almost 60,000. This meant that the courts might consider suspension in about 100,000 cases annually". Az Országgyűlés Képviselőházának Irományai XIV. kötet (Documents of the House of the Representatives of the Parliament), Budapest, Pesti Nyomda Részvénytársaság 1907. nos. 531–578, no. 566 p. 434. in: pálvölgyi: Doktori Értekezés (Doctoral thesis), p. 105.

16 Loss of savings could, in certain cases, cause further disadvantage or even lead to reoffending, which would contradict the aim of punishment. In: Az Országgyűlés Képviselőházának Irományai XIV. kötet (Documents of the House of the Representatives of the Parliament), Budapest, Pesti Nyomda Részvénytársaság 1907. nos. 531–578, no. 566. pp. 435–436. in: pálvölgyi: Doktori Értekezés (Doctoral thesis), p. 106.

17 In cases in which criminal proceedings began after the operational period, in respect of an offence committed during the operational period, the execution of the suspended

sentence could not be ordered; however, the fact that the offence was committed during the period of suspension was evaluated as an aggravating circumstance for the subsequent sentence. Pálvölgyi, 2018/2, p. 82.

18 Az Országgyűlés Képviselőházának Irományai (Documents of the House of the Representatives of the Parliament) vol. XX, Budapest, Atheneum Irodalmi és Nyomdai Részvénytársaság 1930. nos. 882–937. no., 388. in: pálvölgyi: Doktori értekezés (Doctoral thesis) p. 111.

19 According to Section 92 of the Csemegi Code, in case of momentous or several mitigating circumstances, the type of punishment in question could be mitigated to the minimum; thus, jail could be applied instead of a correctional institution.

20 The term of imprisonment was between 30 days and 15 years. 1950 Act, section 32, subsection 2.

21 Földvári, 1970, pp. 447.

22 "Worthiness" refers to exceptional circumstances under which the offender – according to the socialist society's moral perception and sense of justice – is considered worthy of conditionally avoiding the execution of the imposed sentence.

23 The Supreme Court may adopt a conceptual decision in a case that is relevant to the wider society or is of outstanding importance from the standpoint of public interest. In principle, such conceptual decisions are binding for the lower courts.

24 The court stated that "the decision whether the suspension of the sentence would exercise favourable impact on the conduct of the offender, and also, whether the offender is in the meantime worthy of the benefit, could be based on exceptional circumstances revealed with due foresight and procedural method". In: pálvölgyi: Doktori értekezés (Doctoral thesis) op. cit. p. 125.

25 Act V of 1961 "on the Criminal Code".

26 Act V of 1961, section 70, subsection 5, points (a)–(c). A sentence may not be suspended if imposed with deprivation of civil rights, prohibition of residing in a particular area, or expulsion, even if the criminal offence was committed before the termination of imprisonment or during the operational period of suspension. Suspension is not permitted if the perpetrator was previously sentenced fewer than five years prior to the commission of the criminal offence in question.

27 Act V of 1961, section 71: if an offender failed to comply with the conditions of a community service sentence, it was substituted by imprisonment.

28 Probation had previously been applicable only to juveniles; the 1978 Act expanded its use to adults.

29 Section 24 of Act LXXXVII of 1998 "on the amendment of the criminal legal rules" inserted subsection 4 into section 83 of CC, pursuant to which the court determines the degree of punishment regardless of the possibility of suspending its execution.

30 Opinion of the Penal Collegium no. 55/2007, section 153, point II.

31 BH1979. 352.

32 This was drafted in the Supreme Court's Conceptual Criminal Decision no. VII, in harmony with the permanent case law.

33 Opinion of the Penal Collegium no. 55/2007, section 153, subsection 3.

34 BH1988. 433; BH2000. 93.

35 Reasons attached to Act IV of the 1978 Criminal Code (hereinafter Reasons), detailed arguments attached to section 89.

36 Arguments attached to section 91.

37 Opinion of the Penal Collegium no. 55/2007, section 153, subsection 5.

38 Arguments attached to section 89.

39 It was a new type of punishment. This punishment involved the obligation to work, with restrictions on the personal liberty of the offender. It was possible to convert it into a custodial sentence.

40 Section 91/A of Act 1978 was included by virtue of Section 1 of Act XXII of 1998 "on the amendment of the criminal law".

41 Act LXXX of 2009 "on the revision of Act IV of 1978 on the Criminal Code".

42 Section 28 of Act LXXX of 2009 "on the revision of Act IV of 1978 on the Criminal Code".

43 Section 29 of Act LXXX of 2009 "on the revision of Act IV of 1978 on the Criminal Code" inserted the partial suspension of the execution of imprisonment into Section 90 of Act 1978.

44 When a prison sentence is partly suspended, circumstances existing prior to the non-appealable sentence are taken into consideration, while in the case of conditional release, the offender's conduct during his/her imprisonment is decisive.

References

Az Országgyűlés Irományai [Documents of the Parliament]. (1951). *Vol. I, Nos. 1–51* (No. 39, p. 189). Budapest.

Criminal Code, Act C of 2012. (2012). *Magyar Közlöny*, 2012/92. https://njt.hu/jogszabaly/2012-100-00-00

Edvi Illés, K. (1909). *A Magyar Büntetőtörvénykönyv magyarázata* [Explanations to the criminal code of Hungary]. Budapest.

Földvári, J. (1970). *A büntetés tana* [The science of penalty]. Közgazdasági és Jogi Könyvkiadó.

Fundamental Law. (2011). *Magyar Közlöny*, 2011/43. https://www.parlament.hu/documents/125505/138409/Fundamental+law/

Horváth, T. (1968). A feltételes elítélés a magyar büntetőjogban [Conditional sentencing in the penal code of Hungary]. *Jogtudományi Közlöny, 1968*(1).

Irk, A. (1915). *A büntetőjog átalakulása* [The development of criminal law]. Kolozsvár.

Király, T. (1977). *Fejezetek a magyar büntető eljárásjog tudományának történetéből* [Chapters from the science of penal procedures in Hungary]. Közgazdasági és Jogi Könyvkiadó.

Kónya, I. (Ed.). (2022). *Magyar büntetőjog I–IV. – új Btk. – Kommentár a gyakorlat számára* [Hungarian criminal law I–IV. – New CC – Commentary for practitioners]. ORAC.

Lőrincz, J., & Mezey, B. (2019). *A magyar börtönügy története* [History of imprisonment in Hungary] Dialóg Campus Kiadó.

Nagy, F. (2003). A büntetés végrehajtásának – részbeni – felfüggesztéséről [On the – partial – suspension of imprisonment]. *Büntetőjogi Kodifikáció, 2003*(3), 30–32.

Pálvölgyi, Á. (2017). *A büntetés felfüggesztése intézménye történetének és egyes büntetőjogi alapelvek értékelése a magyar büntetőjogban a Csemegi Kódextől napjainkig* [Evaluation of the history of the institution of suspended sentence and certain fundamental penal principles in the law of Hungary, from the Csemegi Code to date] [Doctoral dissertation, University of Pécs]. palvolgyi-akos-muhelyvita-ertekezes

Pálvölgyi, Á. (2018a). *A büntetés felfüggesztése: egy jogintézmény fejlődéstörténete (1878–1971)* [Suspension of sentences: A history of the development of a legal institution (1878–1971)]. Pécs.

Pálvölgyi, Á. (2018b). A feltételes elítélés, avagy a felfüggesztett büntetés intézménye a 1908. évi XXXVI. tc. az I. büntető novella és a törvénykezés egyszerűsítéséről szóló 1930. évi XXXIV. törvénycikk alkalmazásában [Conditional sentencing or the institution of suspended sentence as applicable under Act XXXVI of 1908 as amended by the 1st amending act, and under Act XXXIV of 1930 on the simplification of jurisdiction]. *Büntetőjogi Szemle*, *2018*(2).

Supreme Court of Hungary, Penal Collegium. (2007). *Opinion No. 55/2007.*

6 Suspended sentences as an alternative to imprisonment in Poland

Krzysztof Krajewski

Introduction

In the second half of the 17th century, the territories of the Polish-Lithuanian Commonwealth were partitioned between Austria, Germany and Russia. The Polish independent state reestablished in November 1918 was a highly diverse country troubled by various ethnic and class tensions, with a huge west-east gap in terms of its level of development. It also had a complicated political history. Real parliamentary democracy survived only until the 1926 military coup d'etat by Marshal Josef Pilsudski, which resulted in growing authoritarian tendencies and sometimes brutal repression of the opposition, especially during the 1930s.

In September 1939, after German and Soviet aggression and as a consequence of the "Ribbentrop-Molotov pact", the country was partitioned between two totalitarian powers yet again and subjected to a particularly brutal occupation. "Liberation" by the Red Army in 1944–1945 simply substituted the German occupation with a Soviet one. Moreover, as a consequence of the Potsdam accord of 1945, the entire country was shifted several hundred kilometres to the west, losing its pre-war territories to the east of the river Bug and acquiring new, formerly German lands to the east of rivers *Odra* (German *Oder*) and *Nysa Łużycka* (German *Lausitzer Neisse*). After the Soviet-assisted creeping communist coup d'etat in the years 1945–1948, the country was overwhelmed by Stalinist terror. After 1956, the communist party abandoned its most brutal methods of government and the system underwent a slight "liberalization". This was mainly due to the Catholic Church's strong, unbroken position and the regime's inability to collectivise land ownership. The communist authorities lacked legitimacy and popular support, in part due to notorious economic mismanagement. Therefore, the People's Republic of Poland experienced frequent protests by workers (in 1956, 1970 and 1976) and by intellectuals and students (in 1968). Some of these were bloodily suppressed. Another workers' protest at the Lenin Shipyard in Gdansk in August 1980 resulted in the creation of the independent trade union *Solidarność* (Solidarity). Although this was crushed by martial law in December 1981, it initiated the final demise of the communist regime, which was aggravated by the total collapse of the economy. In 1989, the communist party began to negotiate with the opposition and agreed to partially free elections in June of

DOI: 10.4324/9781003568667-9

that year, in which it lost power. A non-communist government was installed and the era known as the Third Republic began. The new state underwent a deep and at times a very painful process of political, economic and social transformation. Milestones that marked Poland's return to the Western World included the adoption of its new constitution in 1997, NATO membership in 1999, and accession to the EU in 2004. Unfortunately, in the years 2015–2023, the populist, nationalistic, and Eurosceptic government of political party *Prawo i Sprawiedliwość* (Law and Justice) seems to have put question marks over many of those achievements, and despite the change of government, a return to the principles of liberal democracy seems to be not a simple task.

Sentencing overview and current sentencing practice

At the end of the 18th century, the three partitioning powers imposed their own legal systems on the territories of the former Polish-Lithuanian Commonwealth. When independence was regained in November 1918, there were three penal codes in force: the Austrian penal code of 1852, the German penal code of 1871, and the Russian penal code of 1903. Penal law was the only branch of law to be relatively quickly and completely unified during the 20 years of independence between the two world wars. A new code of criminal procedure – modelled primarily on the French *Code d'Instruction Criminelle* – was adopted in 1928. In 1932, the new penal code and contraventions code entered into force. The penal code was significantly influenced by Juliusz Makarewicz, a professor of penal law at the University of *Lwów* (Ukrainian *Lviv*, German *Lemberg*) and by the sociological school and the ideas of Makarewicz's teacher, Franz von Liszt. It emphasised individual prevention as the main purpose of punishment and gave judges broad discretionary powers in sentencing offenders. It was recognised at the time as a very modern example of penal legislation (Busch, 1936; Glaser, 1933; Makarewicz, 1933).

Unlike many other countries in Central Europe, Poland retained its "bourgeois" penal code after the communist takeover: it remained in force until 1969. It remained practically without amendment during this time, but was supplemented by various additional special laws that rendered the penal law unequivocally authoritarian in character. Nevertheless, the fact that the old code remained in force provided a certain continuity in legal tradition. The new "socialist" penal code entered into force only in 1970 (Kennedy & Sadowski, 1973). Although it retained many provisions from the former code, especially the rules on criminal responsibility contained in the general part, it largely followed Soviet ideas about criminal responsibility and penal policy. With regard to sentencing, it limited judicial discretion by providing for various forms of mandatory penalty aggravation. Theoretically, it stressed rehabilitation as the main purpose of punishment, but in reality it contained many provisions mandating just harsh punishment. The most conspicuous example of this were its rigid provisions on sentencing recidivists, mandating harsher penalties for each consecutive conviction. Generally, the 1969 code is considered responsible for the growing punitiveness of Polish penal law during the 1970s and 1980s (Frankowski & Wąsek, 1993, 1995).

Criminal justice system reform was one of the most important tasks that the governments of post-communist countries faced after 1989. Relatively quickly, in 1997, a new penal code was adopted in Poland, along with a new code of criminal procedure and penal-executive code; these entered into force on 1 September 1998 (Weigend, 1998; Faulkner, 2012). The new penal code aimed to reduce the punitiveness of the criminal justice system, first of all by reducing the extremely high incarceration rates and prison overcrowding. For that purpose, the new code established the principle of proportionality between the penalty and the degree of the offender's guilt. It also returned broad judicial discretionary powers, expressed preference for non-custodial sanctions, and – in many instances – lowered statutory minima and maxima. Unfortunately, the new code entered into force at a time when the crime rate was increasing substantially, which created an ideal setting for penal populism (Krajewski, 2004). It immediately became the subject of widespread criticism, including accusations of unwarranted liberalism in times that required being "tough on crime" (Krajewski, 2016). The 1997 penal code has been amended several times since entering into force. Indeed, it is one of the most frequently amended laws, which has resulted in a patchwork of sometimes inconsistent provisions[1].

The code contains four types of criminal law response measures to offences: penalties, penal measures, compensatory measures, and forfeiture. The catalogue of penalties (Art. 32) lists: fine (*grzywna*); restriction of liberty (*ograniczenie wolności*); deprivation of liberty *(pozbawienie wolności*), i.e. a prison sentence; and deprivation of liberty for life. The increasingly harsh ordering of this list is intentional, indicating a general preference for non-custodial sanctions.

Fines are to be imposed in daily units, within the range 10 to 540 units, with one unit amounting to between 10 and 2000 PLN (2.5–450 €). This system, invented in Scandinavian countries, is designed to address the problem of inequality in fine application due to offenders' varied financial circumstances. It means that the sentencing process involves two steps. First, the judge decides on the number of daily units, which should be proportionate to the offence without any considerations regarding the offender, i.e. similar numbers of daily units should be allocated for similar offences. Second, the judge then sets the value of the daily unit to be applied in the given case, within the limits prescribed by the law, taking into account the offender's financial situation, so that the resulting sentence is proportionate to that financial situation. In other words, this system is designed to ensure that similar penalties are applied for similar offences, while considering each offender's financial situation (Drápal, 2018).

Restriction of liberty is equivalent to community service and is imposed for a number of whole months, where the minimum duration is 1 month and the maximum 2 years[2]. Under this penalty, the offender is obliged to perform unpaid, supervised work for community purposes for between 20 and 40 hours each month. If the offender in question is employed, the court may decide that instead of community work, 10–25% of their monthly earnings will be deducted and designated for community purposes. Prior to 1990, this second form prevailed, but nowadays it is rather uncommon.

Deprivation of liberty, the term used to refer to a prison sentence, may last up to 30 years[3], and is imposed in years and months. Life imprisonment is considered a separate type of sentence in the penal code.

For many of the less serious offences (*występki*[4]) provided for in the special part of the code, alternative sanctions are permitted: the court may choose between a fine, restriction of liberty, or deprivation of liberty – the latter (custodial) sanction being the last resort. For more serious *występki* and serious offences (*zbrodnie*[5]), deprivation of liberty is the sole available sanction. Nevertheless, the general part of the penal code provides various possibilities for substituting imprisonment with non-custodial sanctions.

All three Polish penal codes provided for the possibility of suspending a prison sentence.[6] Suspended prison sentence is not considered to be a separate type of penalty and is not mentioned in the catalogue of penalties. Instead, it is regulated by chapter VIII of the code, which contains provisions on probationary measures. In addition to sentence suspension (*warunkowe zawieszenie wykonania kary*), this chapter also regulates conditional discontinuance of proceedings (*warunkowe umorzenie postępowania*) and conditional release (*warunkowe przedterminowe zwolnienie*). These three measures all share the need for an operational period to be established and for potential further consequences dependent on the offender's behaviour during that period. Conditional discontinuance of proceedings[7] may be used in cases involving a maximum prison sentence of 3 years or less. If other conditions are met (including a positive criminological prognosis), proceedings may be suspended for an operational period of 1–2 years; this suspension may be accompanied by additional obligations. If the conditions are not breached during the operational period, the case is dismissed and the offender's criminal record is unaffected. Under the 1969 code, conditional discontinuance could be awarded not only by courts but also by public prosecutors (with the possibility of appeal to court) and, indeed, the overwhelming majority of such decisions were taken by public prosecutors. Since 1997, for constitutional reasons, this measure may only be awarded by the courts following a motion from the public prosecutor; this has substantially reduced the frequency of its use, as it is easier for public prosecutors to present their indictment and leave subsequent decisions to the court than to issue an additional motion for conditional discontinuance. Although it involves confirmation of the accused's guilt and is awarded by the court, conditional discontinuance is not considered equivalent to a conviction.

In addition to penalties and probationary measures, the penal code also provides for what it refers to as penal measures (*środki karne*), which were previously called supplementary penalties in the 1969 code. Art. 39 lists 11 such measures, including deprivation of public rights, disqualification from specific posts, professions or economic activities, bans on being present in certain communities or locations, injunctions against contacting specific individuals, bans on entering specific mass events, bans on entering gaming centres, orders to leave premises occupied by the victim, and disqualification from driving. In principle, these penal measures are to be imposed in addition to penalties; however, they may also accompany suspended prison sentences. The general part of the penal code also provides that under certain conditions such measures may constitute the sole sanction for an offence. The general part of the code also regulates compensatory measures (*środki kompensacyjne*), measures remedying damage, monetary performance (*nawiązka*), and forfeiture of objects or of material benefit from an offence.

Penalties and other penal measures in reaction to an offence must be imposed within the sentencing range specified in the special part of the code for the given offence, which stipulates the statutory minimum and maximum. When choosing penalties and other measures and determining their severity, judges are supposed to follow three sentencing principles (*zasady*): judicial discretion, individualisation of sentencing, and the determinate character of a sentence, as well as general or specific sentencing directives (*dyrektywy wymiaru kary*).

There are four general sentencing directives (Art. 53, § 1): the degree of guilt, the degree of social harm, preventive and rehabilitative tasks to be achieved in relation to the convicted person, and the need for shaping legal awareness in society. The last refers to what is known as positive general prevention, and means that the penal code in principle rejects negative general prevention or deterrence as the purpose of punishment.[8] A penalty may only be considered proportionate and just if it takes into account all four of these directives, and all aggravating and mitigating circumstances (although prior to 1 October 2023, the code did not contain any list of such circumstances). However, individual directives are not supposed to play the same role in every act of sentencing. Each directive may influence a concrete act of sentencing to a varying degree, allowing for individualisation in punishment. The above general directives are modified by special directives (Art. 54) in cases involving adolescent and juvenile offenders.[9] The main rationale of punishment for such offenders is their rehabilitation.

In addition to the above directives, there are also certain special directives or circumstances that the court must consider when sentencing. Art. 53, § 2 of the penal code lists the following: the offender's motivation and behaviour, any involvement of a juvenile, the type and degree of any breach of duties, the type and degree of any negative consequence of the offence, the offender's characteristics and personal circumstances, the offender's lifestyle before committing the offence, and his or her subsequent conduct, in particular any efforts to redress the damage or to satisfy the public sense of justice, and – last but not least – the conduct of the aggrieved party. These circumstances are considered relevant to ensure any punishment is proportionate to the degree of social harm, but the list is not exhaustive: the courts may also consider circumstances that are not specifically mentioned in this part of the penal code.

Sentencing practices changed substantially after 1990. Although there were no significant changes made between 1990 and 1997 to the provisions of the 1969 code on sentencing principles and directives,[10] the application of those provisions (and others) did change in practice. Under the new political and social circumstances, judges regained their judicial independence and began to apply the code's provisions rather differently, substantially altering sentencing patterns. Those changes are depicted in Figure 6.1.[11]

First of all, after 1990, we observe a substantial increase in the number of convictions, which accelerated enormously after the year 2000. That trend reversed in 2005, but a new increase came after 2013. These trends reflect changes in the rates of registered offences (Krajewski, 2004). While the scope of this chapter does not permit a detailed discussion of the reasons for those changes, the enormous increase in convictions between 2000 and 2005 was substantially influenced by a legislative change in the year 2000 that had profound consequences for the criminal justice system: driving under the influence of alcohol or narcotic drugs (or DUI) was reclassified as an offence punishable with up to 3 years' imprisonment. Previously, this act had been classified as a contravention and was punishable with a prison sentence of up to three months or a fine.[12] Data on contraventions are not included in registered offences statistics and conviction statistics, and hence this reclassification had a huge impact on the number of registered offences and convictions after the year 2000. Indeed, in the following years, convictions for DUI amounted – on average – for between one-fifth and one-third of all convictions.[13] Likewise, this had a substantial impact on sentencing patterns: most convictions for DUI resulted in suspended prison sentences rather than fines. Therefore, the increased use of suspended prison sentences after the year 2000 may be attributable primarily to this particular legislative change.

Besides these DUI-related changes, Figure 6.1 also reveals remarkable changes in the frequency with which various types of sanctions were imposed after 1990. First, the number of prison sentences gradually decreased, especially during the 1990s. Despite some increases later on, especially towards the end of the observed period, the frequency of their use remains lower than before 1990. Before 1989, suspended prison sentences were used on average somewhat more frequently than non-suspended prison sentences, but they did not dominate among sentencing outcomes. This changed radically after 1990, when suspended prison sentences began to be used more often. Their use further accelerated substantially after 2000, partly as a consequence of the aforementioned DUI reform. This trend reversed in 2010, and the reduction in the use of suspended sentences

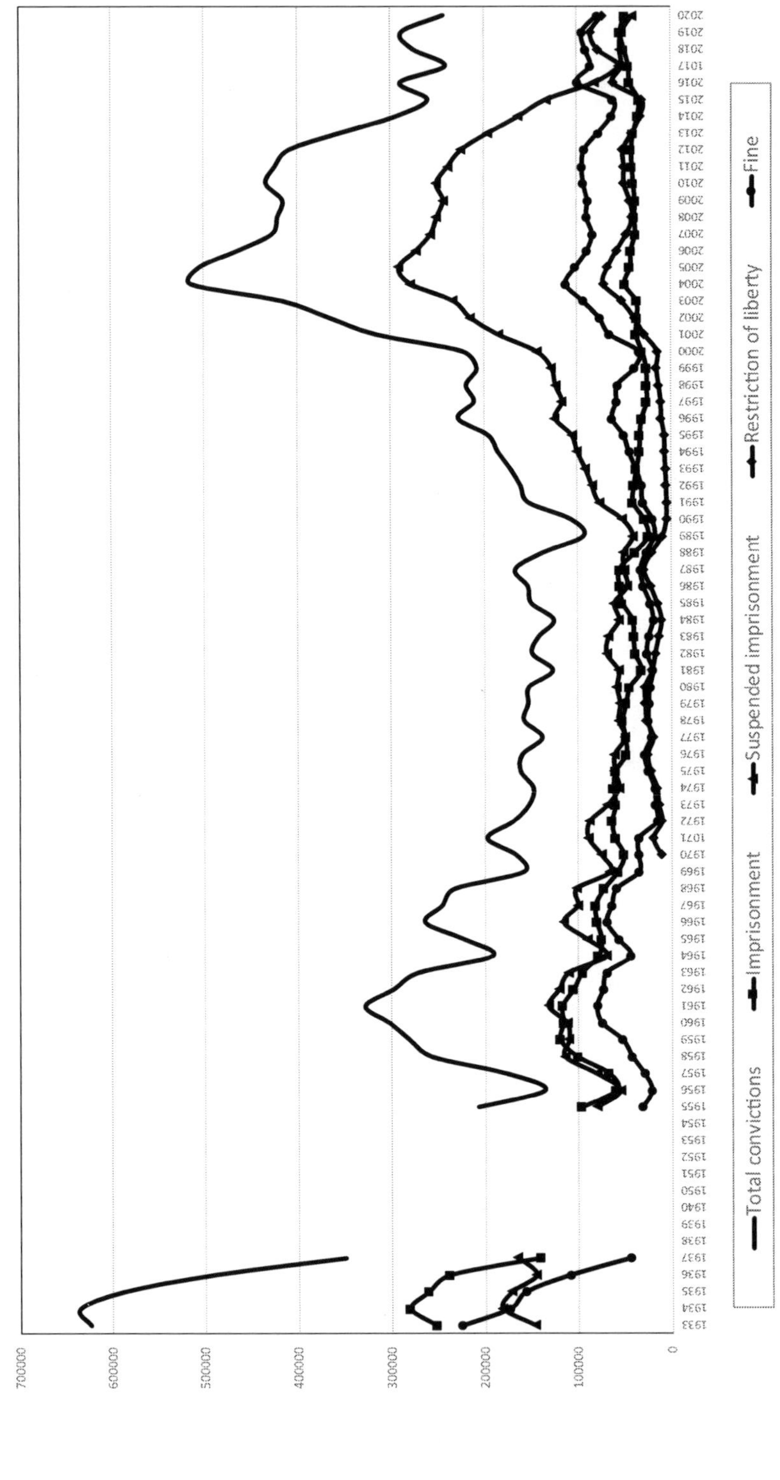

Figure 6.1 Convictions and the frequency of use of various sanctions in Poland.

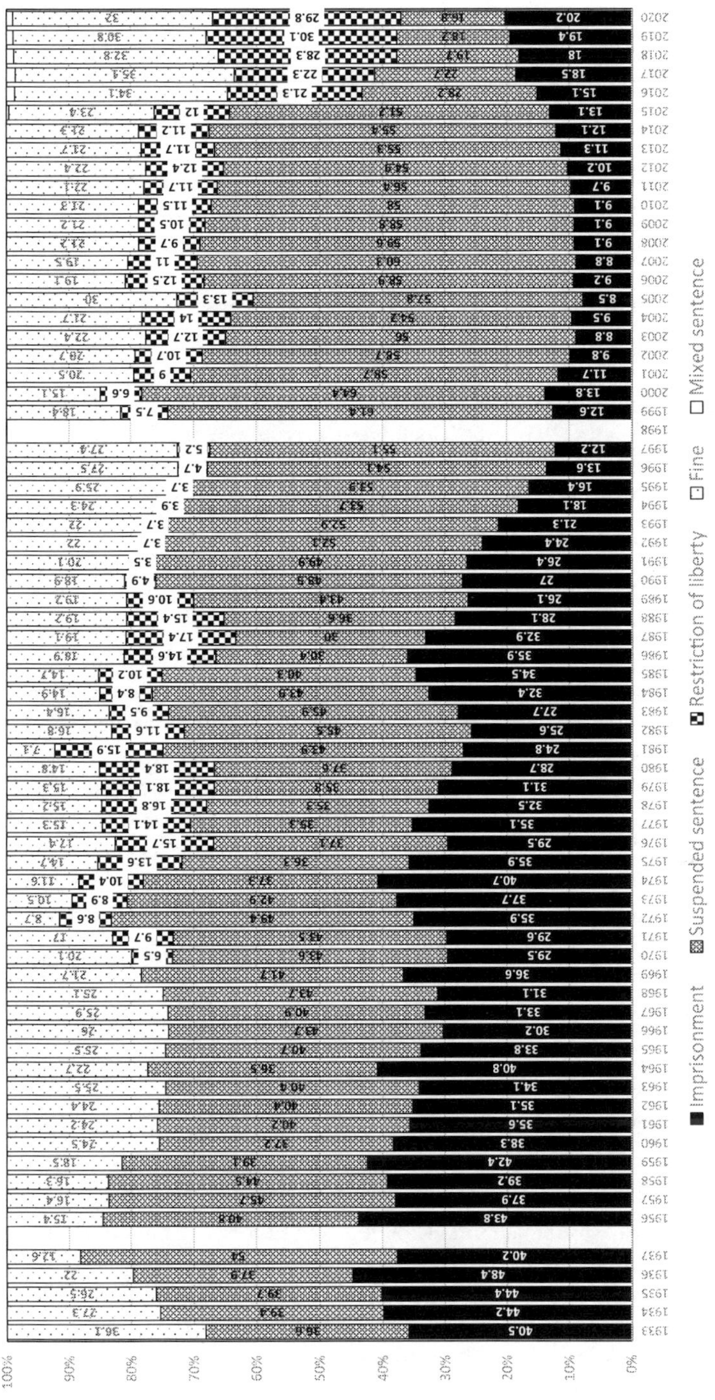

Figure 6.2 Structure of sanctions imposed by courts in Poland.

accelerated after 2015 as a result of a major reform aimed at curbing the use of suspended prison sentences, which we discuss further below.

The use of fines increased after 1989. From 1993 onwards, the number of fines issued has remained consistently higher than the number of convictions to imprisonment (with the exception of the year 2000). Since 2000, the number of convictions to restriction of liberty[14] has also frequently exceeded the number of convictions to imprisonment (with the exception of 2013–2016 and 2020). This indicates that since about 2000, the main burden of penal reaction to offences in Poland has been borne by various alternative sanctions, and not by prison sentences. Despite this, Poland still has one of the highest incarceration rates in the EU; we will return to this issue later.

A look at the structure of sanctions (Figure 6.2) further highlights these changes in the frequency of various penalties:

Between 1992 and 2016, the suspended prison sentence was undoubtedly *the* sanction used by Polish courts: it consistently accounted for more than 50% of all penalties imposed on convicted offenders; in some years (1999, 2000 and 2007) this proportion even exceeded 60%. Non-suspended prison sentences reached an all-time low in 2005, being applied in only 8.5% of all convictions. Since 2010, however, imprisonment has become more prominent again, and since 2013 it has regularly been used in more than 10% of convictions. After the 2015 reform this increased to about 20%, accompanied by a substantial decrease in the use of suspended prison sentences. Notwithstanding these recent changes, statistically imprisonment continues to play a relatively minor role in the Polish system of criminal justice.[15]

This may be further confirmed by data on the average length of prison sentences (Figure 6.3). Prior to the 2015 reform, prison sentences most frequently lasted between 1 and 2 years, and the use of shorter sentences of between 6 months and 1 year was increasing. Sentences longer than 3 years were not very frequent (accounting for less than 10% of all prison sentences), and sentences longer than 5 years even less so. After 2015, the number of very short prison sentences (less than 6 months) increased substantially. This was probably an unintended side effect of attempts to curb the use of suspended sentences (Krajewski, 2022).

Current principles governing suspended prison sentences

As we have already described, a legislative reform in 2015 led to substantial changes in the principles governing suspended prison sentences in Poland. As a result, any analysis of the use of suspended sentences in Poland during the past 20–30 years must be split into two parts, before and after the year 2015.

Before 2015, the provisions in the penal code regarding suspended prison sentences (Art. 69–76) followed the model established in the 1932 code and preserved in the 1969 code, under which it was possible to suspend any prison

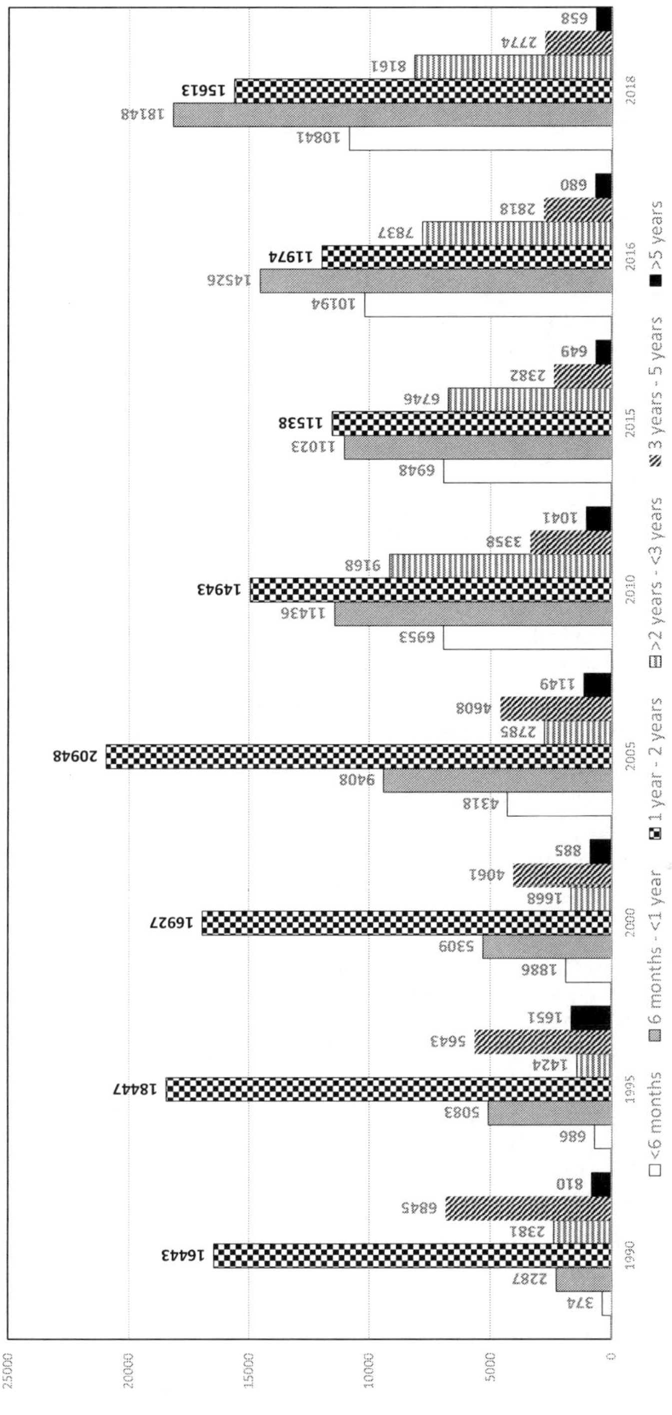

Figure 6.3 Length of prison sentences in Poland.

sentence of 2 years' duration or less, provided that all objectives of the penalty with respect to the offender, in particular preventing him/her from reoffending, would be achieved despite the suspension. This meant that suspended prison sentences were justifiable exclusively by taking into account individual preventive considerations and positive criminological prognosis. Before deciding to suspend a sentence, the judge had first to consider, for instance, the offender's attitudes, personal characteristics and circumstances, lifestyle, and conduct after committing the offence. If this examination supported the conclusion that the offender would not reoffend, even if not imprisoned, then suspension could be justified.[16] The only group of offenders explicitly excluded from suspended sentences was multiple recidivists, i.e. offenders convicted under special conditions defined in Art. 64, § 2 of the penal code. Even this exclusion was not absolute, however: under exceptional circumstances (described in a provision regarding the extraordinary mitigation of penalty), multiple recidivists could also be eligible for sentence suspension. Being convicted as a "simple" recidivist under Art. 64, § 1 of the penal code, meanwhile, did not preclude sentence suspension.

The operational period for a suspended sentence was set, in principle, within the range of 2 to 5 years. For adolescents and (in exceptional cases) multiple recidivists, the range was 3 to 5 years. Independently of all other provisions, it was always possible to impose a fine alongside a suspended sentence. The code further provided for the option of accompanying the suspended sentence with various additional measures during the operational period. The range of such measures, or obligations, has been substantially extended since the 1969 code.[17] Suspended sentences could also be accompanied by (probationary) supervision (*dozór*) for the duration of the operational period. In principle, probationary supervision should be exercised by a probation officer,[18] but it was also possible to appoint a person of public trust to exercise such supervision, or an association or organisation involved in crime prevention and support for offenders. Imposing probationary supervision was also always optional.

The 1997 code differentiated between mandatory and optional reasons for revoking suspension of a sentence, i.e. imposing imprisonment. It was mandatory to revoke suspension if the sentenced person committed a new offence during the operational period that was similar[19] to the original offence and received a sentence for the new offence involving deprivation of liberty, i.e. imprisonment. Like the previous penal code, the 1997 code did not specify whether a suspended prison sentence for the new crime also mandated the revocation of the original suspended sentence. This matter had already given rise to serious disputes since the 1960s (which will be presented in more detail below). Generally, it was assumed that a new suspended sentence required revocation of the previous suspension. If the offender committed an offence that was not similar to the first or, when convicted for a similar offence committed during the operational period, was sentenced to any other sanction (e.g. fine, restriction of liberty), or defaulted on a fine or evaded obligations accompanying their suspended sentence, revoking suspension was optional.

On 1 July 2015, sentencing provisions underwent a major reform, in particular those related to suspended sentences. This reform is often referred to as a complete overhaul of the 1997 provisions. It was aimed at limiting the use of suspended sentences and encouraging the use of other alternatives to imprisonment. As a result of this reform, since 2015 it has only been possible to suspend prison sentences whose duration does not exceed 1 year (Art. 61, § 1). This change alone should, at least theoretically, shrink the pool of eligible cases by half. Additionally, suspended prison sentences may now be imposed only for offenders who had not been handed any prison sentences for other offences at the time of their offence, whether suspended or otherwise. This constitutes a revolutionary limitation on eligibility for suspended prison sentences: in principle, any offender may only once be handed a suspended prison sentence. Reconviction precludes another suspended prison sentence, although it does not preclude the restriction of liberty or a fine. This limitation was brought in to end the earlier practice of suspending prison sentences for the same offender several times.[20]

Furthermore, the 2015 reform reduced the operational period for suspended sentences, which may now last between 1 and 3 years.[21] This change accompanied the move to limit eligibility for suspension, but was also intended to reduce the burden on the probation system and encourage the use of probationary supervision. Last but not least, the ongoing debates about mandatory revocation of suspended sentences were finally settled: under the amended provisions (Art. 75, § 1) it is clear that revocation is mandatory only if a new, similar offence committed during the operational period results in a non-suspended prison sentence. Otherwise, revocation is always optional, including the commission of an offence other than specified in Art. 75, § 1.

Other substantive conditions for suspending a prison sentence remained largely unchanged, including the requirement to establish a positive criminological prognosis and the possibility of imposing fines, penal measures, various obligations and probationary supervision alongside a suspended prison sentence. However, unless the court imposes a penal measure, it is now mandatory to impose at least one obligation to accompany a suspended prison sentence.

The 2015 reforms to the penal code also brought in changes in the use of fines and restriction of liberty, in an attempt to encourage the use of these alternatives to imprisonment, thereby changing sentencing patterns and reducing the incarceration rate. These changes were necessary in addition to limiting the use of suspended sentences, since otherwise the use of short-term custodial sentences could in fact have increased, worsening the incarceration rate.

The 2015 reforms were not born simply out of a conviction that using suspended sentences on such a broad scale is wrong. It was true that imposing a simple suspended sentence was in many cases the easiest and quickest option available to judges, and that this was not necessarily reasonable from a penological perspective. However, there were also long-term difficulties with the organisation and implementation of community service, and a huge proportion of fine defaults, both of which led to judges preferring to avoid these types of alternative sanctions: hence, if they did not want to incarcerate the offender, they had often no other option than to impose a suspended prison sentence. Indeed, without such broad use of suspended sentences, it is likely that the Polish incarceration rate would have been much higher (Krajewski, 2007).

The great paradox of Polish sentencing policies in the early 21st century seems to be the fact that the extremely high incarceration rate resulted from the frequent use, or even abuse, of suspended sentences as an alternative to imprisonment. Available statistical data for the years 2007–2013 show that almost half of the prison population (48.2% in 2007, 50.3% in 2009, and 49.5% in 2012) was made up of convicted offenders whose suspended sentences had been revoked (Krajewski, 2016; Mycka & Kozłowski, 2017, p. 19). When persons incarcerated following the revocation of conditional release decisions are added to this number, almost 60% of prisoners in Poland were "failed probationers", and this figure does not take into account fine defaulters or offenders incarcerated after evading obligations accompanying the restriction of liberty (community service). In other words, during this period, the generous use of alternatives to imprisonment, primarily suspended sentences, did not prevent incarceration but merely delayed it. This seems similar to the Czech situation that Drápal (2023) describes as "punitivity by negligence": the punitiveness of the Polish criminal justice system in recent decades seems to have been – at least partly – an unintended side effect of the generous use of suspended prison sentences.

That said, there were likely other factors that influenced the very high ratio of "failed probationers" in Poland. For example, the methods judges used to establish a positive criminological prognosis were (and still are) primarily based on intuition and as such probably inadequate. Moreover, in most instances, suspended imprisonment sentences were imposed without probationary supervision (Figure 6.4), which has been considered a problem for some time (Skupiński, 2009).

This policy emerged from the fact that the suspended prison sentence in the Polish penal code was based on the Franco-Belgian model. Although under the 1997 penal code suspended sentences were considered a type of probationary measure, they had little in common with the Anglo-American concept of probation. The overwhelming majority of convicted offenders serving suspended sentences were not supervised by a probation officer during the operational period, and were just left alone with their eventual problems. Moreover, the few offenders who were subject to probationary supervision could hardly count on any intensive assistance from their overworked probation officers: again, they were largely left alone and often ended up reoffending. This situation could raise penological questions, since it means that such offenders suffered practically no consequences for their original lawbreaking behaviour, and their sentences

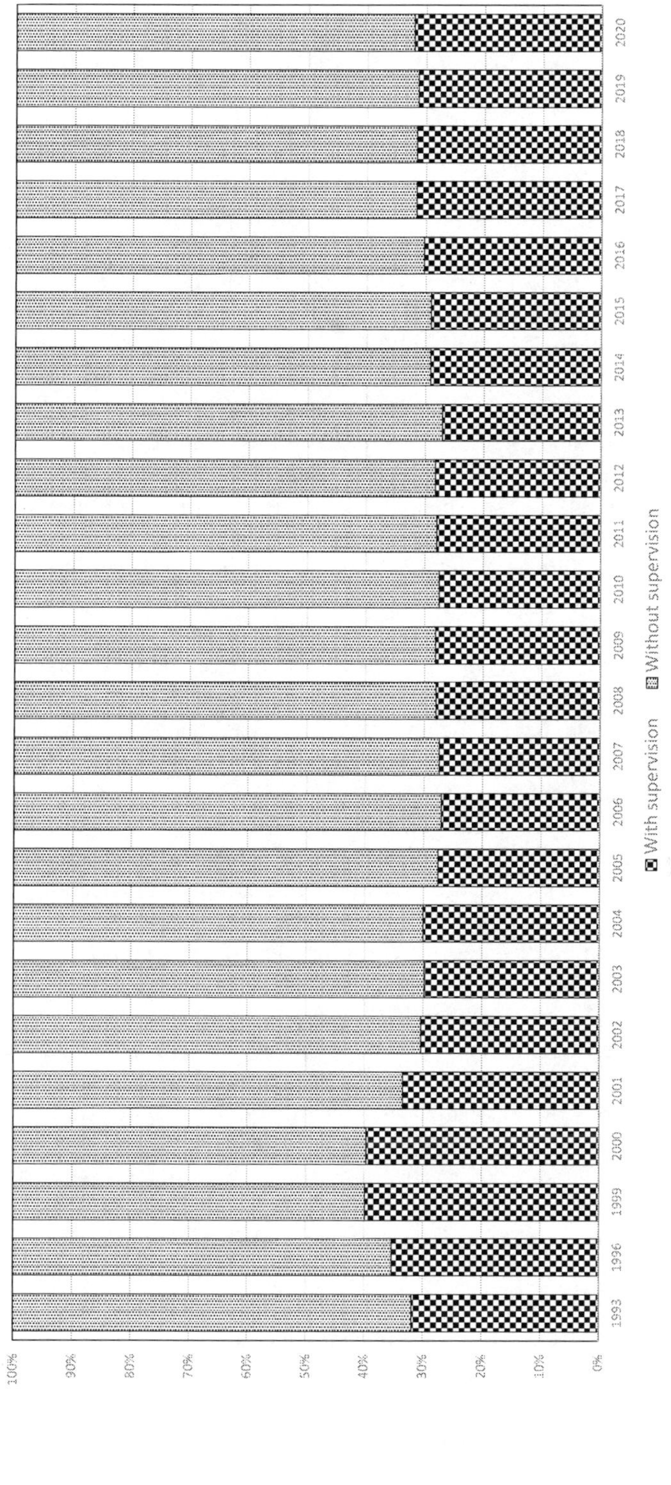

Figure 6.4 Suspended sentences with and without probationary supervision.

lacked any penal bite. Indeed, this also led to a public perception that offenders were "getting away" with their crimes on a massive scale, and that the criminal justice system was unduly lenient.

The 2015 reform had far-reaching consequences on sentencing patterns. The number of suspended prison sentences dropped substantially during the years that followed, while the use of restriction of liberty and fines increased (Figure 6.1), becoming dominant alternatives to imprisonment. Unfortunately, the number of custodial sentences also increased. This can be seen clearly from the data on the structure of sanctions (Figure 6.2). The proportion of suspended prison sentences dropped in 2016, further falling to below 20% after 2018, and has continued to decrease since. In 2020, restriction of liberty and fines constituted more than 60% of all sanctions imposed, while the share of custodial sentences reached 20% for the first time since the beginning of the 1990s. Data on the length of prison sentences (Figure 6.3), show that in 2016 and 2018 there were substantial increases in the number of short prison sentences: those lasting less than 6 months, and especially those lasting between 6 months and 1 year. The reform was successful in reducing the number of suspended sentences, but contrary to the intention behind it, these were not replaced only by fines and restriction of liberty, but were in some cases substituted with short-term imprisonment. From a practical perspective, this represents a huge problem: the 2015 reform sought to limit the use of suspended imprisonment sentences and in doing so reduce the incarceration rate, which was seen as excessively high. Unfortunately, although the structure of sanctions has changed, the incarceration rate remains one of the highest in Europe, partly as a result of an increased use of short-term imprisonment.[22]

The 2015 reform was also designed to solve the problem of an overburdened probation service. A reduction in the number of suspended sentences combined with an increase in the proportion of such sentences that are accompanied by probationary supervision ought to increase the effectiveness of such supervision and, as a result, reduce the number of revoked suspended prison sentences, which were one of the main causes of the high incarceration rate in previous years. Unfortunately, it seems that this was only partially successful: despite the enormous drop in the number of suspended prison sentences (from 133,076 in 2015 to 54,302 in 2018 and 41,973 in 2020), the proportion of such sentences accompanied by probationary supervision increased only slightly, and still oscillates around one-third (Figure 6.4). In absolute numbers, the drop in supervision orders has thus been substantial (from 38,661 in 2015 to 13,434 in 2020; for comparison, in 2005 there were 80,148 such orders), hence theoretically the burden on the probation system has been relieved, which ought to make it possible for a higher proportion of cases to be accompanied by supervision. Yet this has not happened, which may indicate that the probation system in Poland – and possibly more widely across Central Europe (van Kalmthout et al., 2003) – is struggling and unable to play an appropriate role. It seems that the system is primarily focused on (ineffectively) supervising offenders' behaviour, while elements of social work and assistance are rather neglected. It may also suggest that the probation system's capacity was not the main reason for the rather infrequent use of supervision in previous years. In this respect, proposals have been made to take the probation service out of the court system and remodel it as a separate type of social service similar to the social welfare system (Stępniak, 2005).

How and why has the system developed?

As I explained in the introduction, in the 19th century, three different penal codes were in force on the territory of what was to become Poland. This remained the case after Polish independence in November 1918 until the new penal code entered into force in 1932. The existing codes – the Austrian penal code of 1852, the German code of 1871, or the Russian codes of 1845 and 1903 – were all rooted in classical thinking about penal responsibility and punishment, and none of them provided for the possibility of suspending a prison sentence. This possibility was subsequently introduced via special legislation pertaining to the separate territories of each of the former partitions: during the First World War, the Russian part was the first to obtain such regulation. Before the war, the Polish territories belonging to Russia were under the jurisdiction of the old Russian code of 1845. In 1915, the German occupational administration decided to substitute this with the Russian penal code of 1903 (known as the *Tagancev* code). Subsequently, on 7 August 1917, the Provisional Council of State for the Kingdom of Poland, a body consisting of Polish representatives appointed by German and Austrian-Hungarian authorities, issued special regulations to implement the 1903 Russian code; those regulations also contained provisions on suspended sentences, which were modelled on the French system of conditional conviction, and were intended to be applied in limited and exceptional situations only, especially for offenders under the age of 21 years. It was possible to suspend a sentence of up to 6 months of imprisonment provided a positive criminological prognosis, referred to as an expectation of generally good behaviour in the future, was established. Offenders who had previously been convicted to imprisonment were excluded from suspension.

In the formerly Austrian parts of southern Poland and today's Western Ukraine called *Galicja* (Galicia in English or *Galizien* in German), sentence suspension was introduced by special legislation on 10 June 1926. The provisions were partly modelled on the regulations that had by then been in force for 10 years in the former Russian part (i.e. sentences up to 6 months were eligible). However, these new regulations permitted a broader use of suspension. For a positive criminological prognosis, the only requirement was an expectation that the accused would not reoffend, and not the former much broader expectation of generally good behaviour. Moreover, the use of suspended prison sentences was not limited to young offenders. One year later, on 17 September 1927, the

President of the Republic issued a decree introducing sentence suspension into the provisions in force in the formerly German territories of western Poland. The new provisions were modelled on the regulations previously adopted in the former Austrian part.

There is no comprehensive statistical data on the application of suspended prison sentences under the aforementioned three regulations, although we do have access to fragmentary data on particular court districts. These latter suggest that in the formerly Russian part of Poland, suspended sentences were used sparingly although they were not exceptional. In 1927 and 1928, courts in Warsaw, Kalisz and Piotrków suspended less than 20% of all prison sentences (Skupiński, 1993, p. 65). The situation was similar in the former German part: in 1928, 19% of prison sentences issued within the jurisdiction of the appellate court in Poznań were suspended (Skupiński, 1993, p. 70). The greatest willingness to use suspended sentences seems to have been in the former Austrian part of the territory, where in 1927 58.6% of all prison sentences issued within the jurisdiction of the appellate court in Lwów (*Lviv*) were suspended, while in 1928 this proportion was 40 % (Skupiński, 1993, p. 69).

A unified suspended sentence model applicable across the entire territory of pre-Second World War Poland was introduced in 1932 with the new penal code. The inclusion of suspension provisions within the new code was quite natural, given that the main creator of the new code, Juliusz Makarewicz, and other prominent penal lawyers of the time were strongly influenced by the sociological school of penal law. The model established in the 1932 code was in general retained by the two consecutive codes and thus remained in force until Poland's most recent penal reform in 2015.

The provisions in the 1932 code on sentence suspension, or "conditional suspension of the execution of penalty" (*warunkowe zawieszenie wykonania kary*), were quite concise (Art. 61–64). Prison sentences whose duration did not exceed 2 years could be suspended. The operational period for such a suspended sentence was to last no less than 2 years and no more than 5 years. The substantive condition for suspension was a positive criminological prognosis: the offender's personal characteristics, the circumstances of the offence and the offender's conduct since committing the offence had to indicate that he/she would not commit a new offence despite not having to serve a penalty for the original offence. The option of suspending a prison sentence was not applicable to cases involving recidivists as defined under Art. 60. A convicted offender could be placed under probationary supervision by a person or institution of trust for a period equal to the operational period and could also be obliged to repair the damage resulting from his/her offence. A suspended sentence was revoked, i.e. an "order to carry [the sentence] out" (*zarządzenie wykonania kary*) was to be issued if the convicted person committed a new offence similar to the original offence or resulting from a similar type of motivation. If he/she committed any other offence, evaded supervision or otherwise misbehaved during the operational period, revocation was optional. These provisions remained in force until 1969.

Figure 6.1 and Figure 6.2 present the available statistical data regarding sentencing practices in 1933–1937 and 1956–1969. Initially, the proportion of suspended prison sentences was rather high and fairly stable (36%–40%), while the use of imprisonment increased and the use of fines decreased. Prior to 1937, suspended prison sentences played an important role but were not the most significant instrument of penal policy. After 1937, the use of both fines and non-suspended prison sentences dropped sharply, while the proportion of suspended prison sentences rose to more than half of all sanctions imposed. It was at this point that suspended prison sentences became the most frequently used type of penal sanction. The reasons for this radical change are unclear and, because there is no data from the subsequent years, we do not know whether this tendency continued in 1938 and 1939.

Criticisms of the growing role of suspended prison sentences began to appear in the literature already at that time (Skupiński, 1993, pp. 84–86). Indeed, the arguments raised at that time bore strong similarities to those that appeared after 1990. The most frequent criticism was that, in most cases, a suspended sentence meant practical impunity for the offender: apart from participating in the proceedings, and perhaps having to cover the costs of them, the offender suffered no other consequences and no hard treatment of any sort. At that time, provisions on supervision were seemingly not used at all. There was no probation system or probation officers, and the task was evidently not entrusted to other persons. There were also no other means of controlling offenders on suspension, which meant that suspended sentences were rarely revoked except when the offender was convicted again. Another general criticism was that it was quite common for an offender to receive several consecutive suspended sentences, which was considered to be profoundly wrong.

Between 1956 and 1969, when the 1932 penal code was still in force, a "balance" appears to have been reached between the use of custodial sanctions and suspended sentences. The proportion of custodial sentences oscillated around 35% in this period, with a slight decreasing tendency. The proportion of suspended prison sentences remained at around 40%, with a slight increasing tendency. The use of fines increased slowly, oscillating between 20% and 25%.

Under the 1969 penal code, provisions regarding suspended prison sentences (Art. 73–77) were more restrictive. The character of the offence determined the possibility of suspending the sentence: it was possible in cases of sentences of up to 2 years of imprisonment for intentional offences, and of sentences of up to 3 years of imprisonment for negligent offences. The operational period remained unchanged, at between 2 and 5 years regardless of the type of offence. The main substantive condition remained a positive criminological prognosis, based on the appraisal of the offender's personal conditions and previous way of life supporting and assumption that he/she would not reoffend. However, a positive criminological prognosis alone was no longer a sufficient condition for suspension. Additionally, it was necessary to establish that "reasons related to the social impact of the penalty" do not speak against its suspension. In other words, a prison sentence could not be suspended if general preventive considerations required this. This was certainly a more restrictive approach than under the 1932 code, and – at least theoretically – should have resulted in less frequent use of suspended sentences. Like the 1932 code, its 1969 counterpart ruled out suspension in cases involving recidivists (Art. 60).

Suspended prison sentences could be accompanied by various other measures, although this was always optional. These possibilities were broader after 1969 than under the 1932 code. First, it was always possible for a suspended prison sentence to be accompanied by a fine, even if the offence did not otherwise carry a fine. Second, it was possible to require the offender to repair damage caused, to apologise to the victim, to carry out their legal duty to support another person, to perform specified work or make a specific contribution for the common good, to refrain from alcohol abuse or to undergo specific medical treatment, and to refrain from frequenting specific milieus or places. If an offence was committed against social property,[23] the sentenced person was obliged to repair the damage. Third, during the operational period, the court could (or was obliged to, in the case of adolescents) place the sentenced person under the supervision of a designated person, institution or social organisation.[24]

A suspended prison sentence was necessarily revoked if, during the operational period, the sentenced person committed an intentional offence similar to the previous one and was sentenced to deprivation of liberty (i.e. a prison sentence, whether suspended or not) for it. Suspension was also revoked if the offender did not comply with his/her obligation to repair damage to social property. Otherwise, the court could decide to revoke suspension in cases of what the code referred to as "flagrant violation of legal order", which could include commission of an offence of a kind different from the previous one, failure to pay a fine accompanying the suspended sentence, or failure to comply with other obligations imposed by the court.

The new provisions of the 1969 code entered into force on 1st January 1970. They had no dramatic impact on the use of suspended prison sentences in practice. In general, numbers of convictions were lower in 1970–1989 than they had been previously; this was mainly due to the fact that under a new contraventions code that entered into force in 1971, certain types of petty offences were reclassified as contraventions (e.g. theft or damage to property under a certain value). The structure of sanctions did not change substantially. Non-suspended prison sentences amounted on average to 30% of all sanctions imposed, while suspended sentences made up about 35%. Both non-suspended and suspended prison sentences were thus used somewhat less frequently than before 1970, but the relation between them remained similar, with suspended prison sentences being used somewhat more frequently than custodial prison sentences. The somewhat diminished role of both these types of sanctions under the 1969 code likely resulted from the introduction of a new sanction, restriction of liberty, which was intended to be equivalent to community service and was primarily brought in to substitute short-term imprisonment, which had been heavily criticised during the 1960s. With respect to this intention, the new penalty was rather a moderate success. Its introduction had paradoxical consequences, as in practice it was frequently used in place of fines, and did not often substitute for imprisonment. However, it did also have some impact on the role of suspended prison sentences.

Regulations regarding suspended prison sentences under the 1932, 1969 and 1997 codes resulted in some controversy, in particular centred on the suspended prison sentence as a penal sanction. None of the codes listed suspended sentences as a separate type of penalty. Instead, suspension was considered a special *mode* of implementing a prison sentence. In other words, nominally it was still a prison sentence, even if conditionally suspended. Critics of this position emphasised the fact that when suspended, the custodial sanction is not implemented, which makes a huge difference: a suspended sentence must at least *de facto*, if not *de iure*, constitute a separate non-custodial type of penal sanction. This argument was supported by the observation that suspended prison sentences were playing a growing role in sentencing policy. They were no longer an exception to the norm of custodial sanctions, but had become an independent and frequently used alternative sanction. Therefore, to treat suspended sentences as a form of custodial sanction would be not only inaccurate, but also inappropriate.

These theoretical discussions had practical implications. For instance, revoking a suspended sentence was mandatory if a new, similar offence committed during the operational period resulted in a deprivation of liberty or prison sentence. Did this mean only a non-suspended prison sentence, or also a suspended one? If, as the law defined at the time, a suspended prison sentence was a form of prison sentence, then the suspension of the first sentence would need to be revoked when a new suspended prison sentence was imposed. Many considered this rather absurd: the second sentence could remain suspended, but the first would need to be served out in custody. Therefore, it was argued that revocation of a suspension should only be mandatory in the case of a new conviction to a non-suspended prison sentence (Skupiński, 1993, p. 311). Yet several Supreme Court rulings, under both the 1969 and 1997 codes, contradicted this (Stefański, 2010, pp. 22–23). The controversy culminated in a decision made by the Constitutional Court in 2013 that partially invalidated the provisions mandating revocation of suspension in response to a conviction to another suspended prison sentence.[25] As mentioned earlier, the 2015 reform changed the wording of these provisions, terminating the practical controversies, but the underlying theoretical debate remains unsettled.

Conclusion

In Poland, as in many other countries of Central and Eastern Europe, the history of suspended prison sentences is little more than 100 years long. Sentence suspension was introduced in 1917 for limited use in cases involving petty offences committed by young offenders. This corresponded closely to the Franco-Belgian model. Since then, Poland has moved well beyond the limited Franco-Belgian concept and vastly expanded its use of suspended sentences. During the 1920s, provisions introduced on the territories of the former Austrian and German partitions enabled broader use of suspended prison sentences, and this tendency continued under the 1932 penal code, which gave sentencing judges broad discretionary powers and emphasised the need to individualise sanctions. Unfortunately, the grounding continued to be in the original Franco-Belgian model, and no effort was made to supplement the use of suspended sentences with additional supervision and assistance measures modelled on the Anglo-American concept of probation. Under communist rule after the Second World War, suspended prison sentences remained an important sentencing tool, but did not dominate sentencing policy. This continued to be the case under the new code of 1969, despite some attempts to limit the use of suspension. The rehabilitative rhetoric dominant in theoretical penological discourse at this time had, perhaps surprisingly, no noticeable impact on reshaping suspended sentences to make them a properly probationary measure.

After 1989, and especially under the 1997 penal code, there was a boom in the use of suspended sentences and they began to dominate sentencing practice, becoming *the* alternative to imprisonment. Although contemporary penal policy is clearly in great need of alternatives to custodial sanctions, the suspended sentence is not necessarily the best one (Krajewski, 2007). Its advantage, over fines and restriction of liberty, is that it is quite easy to administer.

In practical terms, suspended prison sentences imposed without a more comprehensive criminological prognosis, and without a real probationary character involving elements of social work, have proven extremely ineffective. A huge proportion of suspended prison sentences imposed in Poland were later revoked, and the offenders ended up behind bars. This was a crucial factor behind the country's extremely high imprisonment rate. Further reform in 2015 was partly successful in limiting the use of suspended prison sentences and encouraging the use of other alternatives to imprisonment, but it failed to substantially reduce the imprisonment rate, as the use of short-term custodial sentences increased. Therefore, the dilemma of the suspended sentence in Poland remains to a large extent unsettled. It will probably remain so unless a shift can be achieved towards a model combining suspension with meaningful probation involving effective use of social welfare approaches to assist, rather than merely restrict and supervise, convicted offenders.

Notes

1 Extensive amendments to the penal code were adopted by the Law and Justice government in December 2022 and entered into force on 1 October 2023. These revolutionise many of the penal code's provisions with the intention of increasing the punitiveness of penal law substantially, including many provisions related to sentencing principles. Many of these modifications constitute a dramatic throwback in the development of Polish penal law and a return to regulations of the kind that were previously in force under the communist regime. The impact of those changes on the sentencing practice so far is not clear, and the new government in power since December 2023 intends anyway to renege on those "reforms". However, regulations regarding suspended sentences and other probationary measures remained largely untouched by that amendment. New regulations will be mentioned here only when necessary.

2 Before the mentioned reform of October 2023, the upper limit for the limitation of liberty was 12 months.

3 Before October 2023, the upper limit of imprisonment sentences was 15 years. There was additionally a separate type of fixed imprisonment term of 25 years (and life imprisonment).

4 Equivalent to German *Vergehen* or French *délits.*

5 Equivalent to German *Verbrechen* or French *crimes.* These also correspond roughly to felonies in the USA.

6 During the years 1998–2015, it was also possible to suspend fines or restrictions of liberty; these options were very seldom used in practice.

7 The closest equivalent in Anglo-American jurisdictions is probably conditional discharge.

8 This was the regulation in force before October 2023, and therefore applicable during the period subject to analysis in this essay. Reform of 2023 deleted rehabilitative purposes of sentencing and substituted formulation on positive general prevention with the new one suggesting plain deterrence as the purpose of sentencing.

9 Adolescents are offenders aged between 17 and 21 years. Offenders under 17 years of age are treated as juveniles. Juveniles are generally not held criminally responsible but are subject to a special type of juvenile responsibility involving measures based almost exclusively on the principle of child welfare. In exceptional circumstances, juveniles between 15 and 17 may be considered criminally responsible, but in practice, this is rarely the case (Stańdo-Kawecka 2006).

10 Apart from some changes in the definitions of particular offences, the only substantive change in the provisions of the general part of the penal code regarded removing the provisions that had mandated draconian aggravations of penalties for recidivists. The drafting of the new penal code started very soon after the regime change and to aid its quick adoption, a decision was made not to engage in any piecemeal changes of the old one. Poland was the first of the former Warsaw Pact countries to adopt a new penal code.

11 Figures 6.1 and 6.2 depict data for the years 1933–1937 and 1956–2020 (omitting 1998). Data for the year 1938 were never published due to the outbreak of the Second World War. Similarly, no data are available for the periods of Soviet (1939–1941) and German (1939–1945) occupation. Between 1945 and 1955, no statistical data on crime or criminal justice were published. Data for the year 1998 are omitted: the new penal code entered into force on 1st September of that year, which makes any presentation of the data on sentencing outcomes under two different legal regimes quite complicated. Figure 6.3, for the sake of clarity, provides data only for selected years since 1990.

12 Under Polish law, contraventions (*wykroczenia*), are not considered to be offences (*przestępstwa*), but a separate category of prohibited acts.

13 In 2000, before this change came into force, there were 228,815 convictions altogether. In 2001, this number increased to 315,013, of which 86,271, or 27.4%, were convictions for DUI. This means that the entire increase in the total number of convictions in 2001 can be accounted for by convictions for DUI. In 2003, convictions for DUI constituted 31.2% of all convictions (129,910 out of 415,933). Without convictions for DUI, the total number of convictions after 2000 would likely have increased anyway, but not so substantially. In subsequent years, the number of convictions for DUI dropped, but in 2018 these still made up 16.1% of all convictions. A substantial decrease in the total number of convictions after 2004 was the result of various factors, including a general drop in the rate of registered offences and demographic change.

14 It is important to note that for many years now, restriction of liberty has involved real community service in the form of unpaid, supervised work for community purposes. A popular earlier version of this sanction that was based on wage deductions now applies only to a tiny minority of such sentences. For instance, in 2018, there were 78,172 convictions to restriction of liberty, out of which only 851 involved monthly wage deductions, i.e. 1.1%. In 2001, these amounted to 1.6%, and in 2010 to 0.9% of all sentences for restriction of liberty.

15 The 2015 reform introduced the possibility of "mixed sentences", involving a short prison sentence (up to 3 or in some cases 6 months) and a subsequent period of restriction of liberty. However, as the data in Figure 6.1 show, the proportion of convictions making use of these sentences remains tiny. Additionally, it may be mentioned that since 2009 imprisonment sentences – at the moment not exceeding 18 months – may be implemented in the system of electronic monitoring (Stańdo-Kawecka & Grzywa-Holten, 2015). In recent years on average, between 6,000 and 7,000 sentences were implemented in this system, something separate from suspended sentences.

16 The requirement under the 1969 code that considerations related to the social impact of penalty (i.e. related to general prevention) should not speak against suspension was dropped.

17 Under the 1997 code they included: keeping the court or probation officer informed about the progress of the operational period; apologising to the victim; providing support to another person; obtaining employment, attending vocational training or education; refraining from abusing alcohol or drugs; undergoing medical treatment; attending rehabilitative or educational courses; refraining from frequenting specific milieus or places; refraining from contacting the victim or other persons; leaving residential premises shared with the victim; undertaking any other appropriate conduct that may prevent future criminal behaviour.

18 Probation officers were introduced during the 1970s, but until 1997, their role was not formally acknowledged in regulations regarding suspended prison sentences. Under the new code, the probation system was professionalised.

19 The notion of a similar offence is defined in Art. 115, § 3 as follows: similar offences are those which belong to the same type. Offences involving violence or threats of violence and offences committed with the intent of gaining material advantage are deemed similar offences.

20 Data show that in some cases offenders were sentenced to more than 20 consecutive suspended prison sentences (Mycka & Kozłowski, 2017, p. 26).

21 For adolescent offenders and in cases of domestic violence, this remains – as before – 2 to 5 years.

22 In the years 2005–2015, the average incarceration rate in Poland amounted to 214 per 100,000 inhabitants. Although in the years 2016 – 2022 it dropped to 190, it remained still probably much above the expected results of the 2015 reform.
23 The differentiation between social (or state) property and individual property was typical in "socialist law". Social property – state or cooperatively owned – was granted much more intensive protections than individual or private property.
24 The respective provision contained no reference to probation service or officer, because at that time probation officers were practically non-existent in Poland (with the exception of the juvenile justice system).
25 Judgement of 17 July 2013, SK 9/10.

References

Busch, R. (1936). *Kritische Bemerkungen zum polnischen Strafgesetzbuch.* Zeitschrift für die gesamte Strafrechtswissenschaft, *55*, 621–640.

Drápal, J. (2018). Day fines: A European comparison and Czech malpractice. *European Journal of Criminology, 15*(4), 461–480.

Drápal, J. (2023). Punitive by negligence? The myths and reality of penal nationalism in the Czech Republic. *European Journal of Criminology, 20*(4), 1549–1567.

Faulkner, N. (2012). *The criminal code: Kodeks karny.* Warszawa.

Frankowski, S., & Wąsek, A. (1993). Evolution of the Polish criminal justice system after World War Two – An overview. *European Journal of Crime, Criminal Law and Criminal Justice, 1*(2), 143–166.

Frankowski, S., & Wąsek, A. (1995). Polish criminal law and procedure. In S. Frankowski & P. B. Stephan (Eds.), *Legal reform in post-communist Europe: The view from within.* Dordrecht–Boston–London: Martinus Nijhoff.

Glaser, S. (1933). Das neue polnische Strafgesetzbuch und die deutsche Strafrechtsreform. *Zeitschrift für Ostrecht, 7*, 348–358.

Kennedy, W. S., & Sadowski, T. (1973). *The penal code of the Polish People's Republic* (with introduction by W. S. Kennedy). F.B. Rothman.

Krajewski, K. (2004). Crime and criminal justice in Poland. *European Journal of Criminology, 1*(3), 377–407.

Krajewski, K. (2007). Too many suspended sentences? Polish or Central and Eastern European Problem? *Socjologija. Mintis ir veiksmas, 20*(2), 108–120.

Krajewski, K. (2016). Sentencing in Poland: Failed attempts to reduce punitiveness. In M. Tonry (Ed.), *Sentencing policies and practices in Western countries: Comparative and cross-national perspectives, Crime and justice: A review of research, 45*, 175–219). University of Chicago Press.

Krajewski, K. (2022). Przemiany polityki karnej po nowelizacji Kodeksu karnego z 2015 r. In M. Grzyb & K. Krajewski (Eds.), *Polityka kryminalna: między teorią a praktyką. Księga jubileuszowa prof. Janiny Błachut.* Kraków.

Makarewicz, J. (1933). Das Strafgesetzbuch für die Republik Polen. *Zeitschrift für Ostrecht, 7*, 316–331.

Mycka, K., & Kozłowski, T. (2017). Zarys aktualnych tendencji w polskiej polityce karnej w oparciu o dane statystyczne. *Probacja, 9*(2), 5–32.

Skupiński, J. (1993). *Warunkowe skazanie w prawie polskim na tle porównawczym*, Oficyna Naukowa.

Skupiński, J. (2009). Warunkowe zawieszenie wykonania kary pozbawienia wolności. In A. Błachnio-Parzych, J. Jakubowska-Hara, J. Kosonoga, H. Kuczyńska, B. Kunicka-Michalska, C. Nowak, & J. Skupiński (Eds.), *Alternatywy pozbawienia wolności w polskiej polityce karnej*. Wydawnictwo Naukowe Scholar.

Stańdo-Kawecka, B. (2006). Continuity in the welfare approach: Juvenile justice in Poland. In J. Junger-Tas & S. H. Decker (Eds.), *International handbook of juvenile justice*. Springer.

Stando-Kawecka, B., & Grzywa-Holten, J. (2015). Offender electronic monitoring in Poland: Expectations and results. *Neue Kriminalpolitik, 27*(2), 158–170.

Stępniak, P. A. (2005). Formy probacji a praca socjalna ze skazanymi. *Przegląd Więziennictwa Polskiego, 47–48,* 5–14.

Stefański, R. (2010). Obligatoryjne zarządzenie wykonania kary zawieszonej warunkowo. *Probacja, 1*(2), 5–27.

van Kalmthout, A. M., Roberts, J., & Vinding, S. (Eds.). (2003). *Probation and probation services in the EU accession countries*. Wolf Legal Publishers.

Weigend, E. (1998). Das neue polnische Strafgesetzbuch von 1997. *Zeitschrift für die gesamte Strafrechtswissenschaft, 110*(1), 114–142.

Wzorek, D. (2024). Polityka karna w Polsce w latach 2008 – 2020. Ucieczka od racjonalności? *Państwo i Prawo*, *79*(4), 53–80.

7 Suspended prison sentences in Romania

Gabriel Oancea

Introduction

After the historic revolution in 1989, Romania embarked on a tumultuous journey of transformation. The overthrow and execution of Nicolae Ceaușescu marked the end of decades of communist rule and set the stage for a new era. In the 1990s, Romania embraced the challenges of transitioning to democracy and a market-oriented economy. This was a time of political awakening and economic restructuring. The country faced hardships and uncertainties, but also witnessed the emergence of civil society and the birth of a new political landscape. In 2004, Romania achieved a significant milestone when it joined NATO, solidifying its security ties with Western nations. Three years later, another pivotal moment came when Romania became a member of the European Union. However, the road to progress was not without obstacles. Romania struggled with corruption, political instability, and economic disparities. The fight against corruption intensified since the middle of the last decade, leading to the conviction of high-ranking politicians and officials.

For Romania, as for many other Central European countries, 1989 marked the end of the period of political totalitarianism that had lasted since the end of the Second World War, and the beginning of a period of democratic transition, which involved three stages: liberalisation and the collapse of the authoritarian system, democratisation and social modernisation, and consolidation of democracy (Welsh, 1994).

The penal reforms that took place after 1990 must be understood in the context of this transformation. Their aim was to create a legal system that guaranteed the respect of the new social values, such as human rights and dignity, freedom of speech, cultural freedom, and individual autonomy. In line with this aim, the reforms altered the sanctions system, placing a new emphasis on the avoidance of incarceration and the social reintegration of offenders.

To begin with, a series of modifications was made to the Criminal Code of 1968. However, it was clear that these amendments were insufficient to address the complexity of the desired reforms. A new criminal code was therefore adopted in 2009 (Law No. 286/2009), which entered into force on 1st February 2014. The development of this new criminal code had been a priority and several

DOI: 10.4324/9781003568667-10

draft versions had been formulated in the intervening years since 1989 but these had struggled to garner political consensus. The implementation of the new criminal code was repeatedly postponed between 2009 and 2014 due to various factors, including the need to provide training for legal professionals, the absence of infrastructure compliant with the code of criminal procedure's requirements (e.g. hearing rooms equipped with recording equipment), and objections voiced in the public sphere by various non-governmental organisations.

The introduction of suspended sentences with supervision is a representative example of the developments mentioned above. It was first introduced in 1992 as a solution to the problem of prison overcrowding. With the creation of the probation system, the use of suspension with supervision increased and led to a reduction in the prison population. As we will show in this chapter, the legal provisions that regulate suspension have been modified over time, with the aim of circumscribing more precisely the applicability of suspension with supervision and of providing an adequate framework to facilitate offenders' social reintegration.

Sentencing overview

The current sentencing framework consists of the provisions of the Criminal Code and additional laws on the execution of sentences.[1] Section III of the Code distinguishes between principal, accessory, and supplementary sanctions. According to Article 53, the principal penalties are life imprisonment, imprisonment, and penal fine.

Life imprisonment, governed by Article 56 of the Criminal Code, is the most severe penalty; it is custodial and lasts for the rest of the offender's life. This penalty was first introduced by Decree-Law No. 6/1990 on replacing the death penalty. Parole may be granted to offenders serving life imprisonment after they have effectively served 20 years of imprisonment.

The penalty of imprisonment consists of deprivation of liberty for a fixed term of between 15 days and 30 years. These limits are fixed and cannot be exceeded by the judge when individualising the sentence. Offenders serving prison sentences can be released on parole upon the simultaneous fulfilment of several criteria: the execution of the legally mandated portion of the sentence, full payment of all compensation specified in the sentencing judgment unless proven impossible, and the court's confidence in the individual's rehabilitation and ability to successfully reintegrate into society.

Under certain conditions, set out below, the execution of a prison sentence of up to 3 years may be suspended.

Compared to the previous penal code, the current regulations offer more extensive opportunities for imposing fines, with a larger number of offences for which fines can be applied as the only penalty or as an alternative to imprisonment. The amount of the fine is determined by a day-fine system. The fine is imposed in the form of a number of day-fines, and the amount of one day-fine is determined by the court within certain limits laid down by law. The amount of the total fine is determined by multiplying the amount corresponding to one day-fine by the number of day-fines imposed in the sentence.

Romanian criminal law distinguishes between supplementary and accessory penalties. Supplementary penalties are criminal law sanctions, whether restrictive or disqualifying, regarding particular rights or military degradation. They are applied in addition to the main penalty (prison sentence or penal fine) and are intended to supplement the punishment imposed by the main penalty. Their enforcement begins after the prison sentence (if applicable) has been served.

Accessory penalties are also imposed in addition to the main custodial penalty (imprisonment or life imprisonment) and consist of restrictions to certain rights during the execution of the custodial sentence (e.g. the right to hold an office involving the exercise of state authority; the right to vote; parental rights, etc.), because these rights are considered incompatible with imprisonment.

The courts impose individualised sentences by taking into account factors such as the degree of social danger of the offence, the offender's personality and any mitigating or aggravating circumstances as provided in the Criminal Code. The provisions of the Criminal Code detail how these factors should influence the length of prison sentences.

The institution of appeal ensures the uniform application of criminal law. The Code of Criminal Procedure does not place any limitation on the types of issues that may be the subject of such an appeal. The only requirement is regarding different interpretations of the same legal issue by the courts. Appeals in the interest of the law have dealt in the past with questions relating to: the calculation of the operational period; the interpretation of provisions relating to mitigating and aggravating circumstances; the application of legal provisions related to the commission of several offences; the application of a more favourable criminal law, among other issues.

The Code of Criminal Procedure provides a mechanism for avoiding prosecution (*diversion*), which waives prosecution when there is no public interest in pursuing it.[2] This waiver may be applied in cases involving offences for which the Criminal Code provides a fine or imprisonment of up to 7 years, on condition that the prosecutor considers there to be no public interest in prosecuting the offence. Public interest is assessed according to several criteria laid down in the Code of Criminal Procedure, such as: the substance of the offence and the specific circumstances under which it was committed, the aim pursued through the crime, the consequences that arose, or might have arisen as a result of the offence, and so on. In addition, the prosecutor may impose one or more of the following obligations on the person in relation to whom the decision not to prosecute has been taken: to rectify the consequences of the criminal act or repair the damage caused, or to agree a means of reparation with the injured person;

to publicly apologise to the injured party; to perform unpaid community service for a period of between 60 and 120 hours or to attend a counselling programme.

The court may order a discharge of penalty as a diversion procedure for offences of reduced gravity. This decision considers the nature and extent of the offence's consequences, the motive and purpose pursued, and the offender's person and conduct before the offence. If the court deems that a penalty would be inappropriate due to its consequences on the offender's person, it may order a discharge of penalty.[3]

Principles governing suspended prison sentences at present.

The Criminal Code exclusively regulates the suspension of the execution of a prison sentence with probationary supervision, which is not a penal sanction *per se,* but rather a measure of judicial individualisation in relation to the sentenced offender. If the conditions for suspension are met, the judge may decide to suspend the execution of the imposed prison sentence for an operational period, during which the offender is subject to supervision measures and must comply with one or more obligations imposed by the court (Udroiu, 2014).

This institution is regulated by Articles 91–98 of the Criminal Code. When suspending the execution of a prison sentence with probatory supervision, the court requires the sentenced offender to comply with the following supervision measures:[4]

(a) to report to the Probation Service on the dates set by the probation officer;
(b) to receive visits from the probation officer appointed to supervise them;
(c) to notify the Probation Service of any change of domicile and of any travel for a period longer than 5 days, as well as of their return date;
(d) to notify the Probation Service of any change of job;
(e) to provide information and documentation enabling the Probation Service to check their livelihood.

As mentioned in the academic literature (Udroiu, 2014), these supervision measures are mandatory and cumulative. This means that if the court decides to individualise the prison sentence by applying suspension with probationary supervision, it must require the convicted offender to comply with all these supervision measures.

In addition, the court must also require the sentenced offender to comply with one or more of the following obligations:[5]

(a) to attend a course of educational or vocational training;
(b) to attend one or more social reintegration programmes run by the Probation Service or organised in cooperation with institutions in the community;

(c) to undergo medical supervision, treatment or care;
(d) not to leave Romania's territory without the court's consent.

The purpose of the supervision measures is to enable stricter control over various aspects of the offender's daily life (his/her place of residence, professional activities, sources of income) and to regulate the interaction between the offender, the Probation Service, and the allocated probation officer.

The purpose of the obligations is to facilitate the social reintegration of the sentenced offender, addressing criminogenic needs relating to, for example, education, vocational training, health problems or addictions that facilitated the criminal behaviour. The obligation not to leave the territory of Romania without the court's consent is intended to limit the convicted person's freedom of movement beyond the limitations that can be brought about through standard probationary supervision measures. This obligation can also contribute to the offender's social reintegration when, for example, their involvement in criminal activities is transnational.

All sentenced offenders are additionally obliged to perform community service for a period of between 60 and 120 days, unless prevented from doing so due to ill health, as well as to pay, in full and by the end of the operational period, all compensation laid down in the court's judgment.

Suspension with probatory supervision may be applied to prison sentences of up to 4 years. The operational period is between 2 and 4 years but cannot be shorter than the duration of the prison sentence imposed.

Suspended prison sentences are imposed in two steps (Udroiu, 2014), although these take place at the same time. In the first step, the court determines the length of the prison sentence to be imposed. In the second step, the judge decides that the prison sentence should not be served in prison, applies suspension and sets the length of the operational period.[6] The court is obliged to provide reasons both for the conviction and for its decision to suspend the execution of the prison sentence.[7] The defendant is informed at the pronouncement of their sentence that he/she will not serve the sentence in prison.

The Criminal Code adopted in 1968 excluded the possibility of suspension in cases of bodily harm, rape, torture or other crimes committed with intent for which the law prescribes a prison sentence of more than 12 years. In the current criminal law, no such limitations exists. In theory, suspended prison sentences with probationary supervision can be imposed for any offence, provided the prison sentence imposed does not exceed 4 years.

A prison sentence can further only be suspended if the offender has not previously been sentenced to more than one year of imprisonment, unless the offence for which he/she was convicted is no longer criminalised, an amnesty has taken place, the conviction was for an offence committed through negligence, or the conviction has been expunged.

There are three additional situations in which a sentence cannot be suspended: (1) when the main penalty imposed is a fine; (2) when the prison sentence was initially deferred (see below), and the deferral was subsequently revoked; and (3) when the offender has evaded prosecution or trial or attempted to prevent the identification of other participants in the crime. In other words, if the defendant failed to appear when summoned during the investigation or trial or if attempted to influence a witness or tamper with evidence, the suspension of execution under the supervision of a prison sentence cannot be applied to their sentence. The reason for this limitation is that the convicted person has either already been granted clemency or has shown an attitude that indicates that he/she does not regret committing the offence or does not take responsibility for it.

When judges consider whether or not to suspend a sentence, they must take into account several factors relevant to the offender's personality, such as their conduct before committing the offence, any efforts made to eliminate or mitigate the consequences of the offence, and their potential for correction. Judges also assess the degree of social danger of the offence by evaluating elements such as the manner in which it was committed, the damage it caused, or the resonance that the offence had in public opinion. Before applying suspension, the judge must be convinced on the basis of this deliberative process that the offender possesses the means to successfully reintegrate into society without serving a prison sentence.

In practice, judges evaluate various aspects of the offender's personality through means such as psychological assessments, testimonies from witnesses, or the examination of documents provided by the offender. Both the prosecuting authorities and the judge may also ask the probation service to draw up an assessment report on the defendant. While such reports are optional for adults, they are mandatory whenever cases involving juvenile defendants are sent to trial. The advantage of these reports is the objectivity of the information they provide, given the probation officer's obligation to obtain information from other sources, including by carrying out interviews with other people and consulting documents, in addition to the information provided by the defendant themselves (Oancea, 2010, 2012; Schiaucu, 2010). The Probation Service's reports provide evaluations of defendants' risks of reoffending and their potential for future criminal activity, using specialised risk assessment instruments.

There are no legal provisions that limit the judge's discretion when deciding whether or not to suspend the execution of a prison sentence. However, the existing literature (Băncilă, 2020) and training sessions for magistrates have consistently emphasised the benefits of non-custodial sanctions and thus, implicitly, suspended prison sentences with probationary supervision, both for the sentenced offender and for the community. These benefits include avoiding prison overcrowding, enabling the convicted individual to continue their educational or professional activities, and significantly reducing the budgetary impact of the sentence.

Community service is imposed on all persons whose prison sentence is suspended with probationary supervision, except those exempt for medical reasons. Before imposing the sentence, the judge must first obtain the defendant's consent and agreement to work. In the decision on sentence suspension (which is taken at the same time as the decision on guilt and on the sentence), the court determines two institutions where the work may be carried out. The probation officer will decide on one of these two institutions after consulting the sentenced person. One day of community service entails two hours of work, so the 60–120 days of community service provided in the Criminal Code corresponds to 120–240 hours.

The legislation relating to probation defines the supervision process as comprising all activities and interventions carried out directly by the service or under its coordination that are designed to support the supervised offender's social rehabilitation, repairing the damage caused to the community by the committed crime and increasing the community's safety.

In probation practice, social reintegration is a complex process directly influenced by the assessed risk of reoffending and the factors that facilitated the emergence of conflict with criminal law (e.g. substance abuse, peer pressure, insufficient problem-solving skills, etc.). If the risk of recidivism is assessed to be high, the intervention required to address the underlying issues that contributed to the criminal behaviour will be intensive. To achieve the objective, probation officers aim to enhance supervised individuals' motivation for change and involve them in accredited individual or group rehabilitation programmes, which may be administered by the Probation Service itself or by community partners. Collaboration with community agencies is also essential in areas such as education, vocational training, medical treatment, detoxification programmes, and shelter provision. These services can be initiated by the offenders themselves or by their probation officer, who can also request the imposition of additional obligations by the court. If new reasons arise during the operational period that justify modifying the obligations or conditions of the suspended sentence, the court may order these changes.

The aim is to provide the convicted person with a better chance of reform. The court may also order the removal (cancellation) of some of the obligations it had previously imposed if they are no longer necessary. The probation officer or the responsible judge may request modifications or terminations of the obligations. This can also be done at the request of the probationers.

These options for modifying or terminating the obligations of a suspended sentence likely reflect the legislator's intent to create a regulatory framework geared to meeting the offender's criminogenic needs and, in turn, to reducing the risk of recidivism. For example, suppose that during the operational period, the probation officer discovers that the supervised person is experiencing problems related to drug use. In that case, the officer may ask the court to impose an obligation requiring the supervised person to undergo a course of treatment or medical care. Only the obligations under Art. 93 para. 1 (a–e) can be modified or removed.

There are three situations in which the judge must revoke the suspension of a prison sentence with probationary supervision, which are: (1) if the supervised person breaches the measures and/or obligations of the suspension in bad faith (e.g. settles in another locality without first notifying the probation service, fails to perform community service, refuses to report to a required detox programme, etc.); (2) if the offender fails to pay the required compensation in full by the end of the operational period, and has not proven that he/she lacks the necessary financial means to do so;[8] (3) if during the operational period of the suspended sentence, the offender is found to have committed a new offence.[9] The suspension of the original sentence will always be revoked following the intentional commission of an offence during the operational period; if the new offence was committed through negligence, the court must decide whether or not to revoke the suspension of the original sentence.

Most offenders whose sentences are suspended successfully complete the operational period without having the suspension revoked. In accordance with the provisions of the law on criminal records, suspended sentences with probationary supervision are mentioned in criminal records. The convicted person is automatically (*de jure*) expunged and the data relating to their conviction deleted from the criminal record three years after the end of the operational period, provided that he/she has not committed any further offence by that time.

The 2021 annual report of the National Probation Directorate, which oversees both suspended prison sentences with supervision and deferred sentences, reveals that 89.4 % of offenders placed under supervision successfully completed the operational period. The rate of revocation due to non-compliance with measures and obligations was 0.7%, while the rate of revocation due to non-payment of compensation was 0.1%, and the revocation rate due to the commission of an offence during the term of supervision was 1.7%. The low rate of recidivism is due to these data including offenders serving deferred sentences, usually for committing traffic offences (drunk driving, driving without a licence etc.), who are also under the supervision of the Probation Service and who are usually assessed as being at low risk of reoffending.

Additionally, in 1.5% of cases, supervision was terminated as a result of the death of the supervised person. In 6.4% of cases, the non-custodial sanction was revoked and the prison sentence enforced due to the existence of concurrent offences. In the Romanian legal context, concurrent offences refer to a person committing multiple criminal offences in the same act or during a series of acts in a closely related context. These offences are usually prosecuted together, and the person's criminal liability will be considered for all the offences involved, often leading to cumulative sentences. However, sometimes these offences may be part of different criminal cases, and the probation service will need to notify this situation in order to be applied a single penalty.

The reports drawn up by the Probation Service for judges include information about the distribution of cases across assessed risk levels. Risk is evaluated in probation practice using an officer software application, and the results are then compared with the probation officers' subjective opinions, based on their professional experience. The informed opinion may in some cases prevail over the evaluation achieved through the software application.

There is no difference in the evaluations provided for offenders whose sentences are suspended and those whose sentences are deferred. A low risk of reoffending was assessed in 44.8% of cases, a low-to-medium risk was assessed in 29.5% of cases, and a high risk was assessed in 2.4% of cases.

How and why the system developed

Until 1918, parts of Romania were under the dominion of the Austro-Hungarian Empire (Transylvania province) and the Russian Empire (Bessarabia province). In Hungary (under whose jurisdiction the province of Transylvania fell), a law known as the Penal Novela was adopted in 1908, which regulated the institution of the suspended prison sentence, among other things. After the 1918 unification, this legislation remained in force in Transylvania until 1st January 1937, when the Criminal Code known as the Carol II Code came into force.

Between 1918 and 1937, regulations related to suspended prison sentences were introduced in the Labour Disputes Act of 1920 (Art. 43) and the Trade Unions Act of 1921 (Art. 59). These two laws covered both labour law issues and criminal law provisions. For example, the Labour Disputes Act provided that, for certain offences, judges could decide to suspend the execution of the sentence for one year from the date of the final judgment of conviction. This provision could benefit first-time offenders. Similar provisions can be found in laws regulating professional unions (Gladchi & Bucur, 2011; Tipa, 2007).

The Carol II Criminal Code, which came into force on 1st January 1937, regulated the institution of suspended prison sentences in line with the Franco-Belgian model (Lejeune Law and Berger Law). These legal provisions remained almost unchanged until the Criminal Code was repealed in 1968.

According to the 1937 regulations, a sentence could be suspended if the case fulfilled certain conditions related to the offence and the offender's character and past behaviour. Prison sentences not exceeding 2 years could be suspended, and the operational period of their suspension would consist of the length of the prison sentence plus a fixed period of three years. The offender should not have been previously convicted of a custodial sentence (even if it was expunged). In addition, suspension was applied if it was expected to have a positive impact on the offender's future conduct.

The judge was obliged to provide a clear explanation for the decision to suspend the execution of the prison sentence and to inform the convicted individual about the potential consequences of failing to comply with the terms of the suspension (Gladchi & Bucur, 2011; Toader & Safta, 2018). There were also several provisions on when suspension could not be applied (for example, in the case of a plurality of offences when the prison sentence exceeds one year).

Any disqualifications or prohibitions arising from the conviction were also suspended, while security measures, civil obligations, and court costs were not affected. The court could also oblige the convicted person to compensate for damages caused by the offence, make restitutions and pay court fees before the expiry of the operational period.

If the sentenced person committed a new offence during the operational period, the suspension would be revoked and the offender would be ordered to serve the previously suspended prison sentence. However, if the offence was committed with negligence or was punishable only by a fine, the judge could order suspension once again, and could suspend the execution of the new punishment.

After 1945, Romania came under the influence of the Soviet Union, whose communist values were soon reflected in the criminal justice system and used to eliminate opponents of the new regime (Bădescu & Done, 2019; Cracănă, 2013). The Criminal Code that came into force in 1937 continued to apply, with some changes specific to the new context, and no substantial changes were made to the institution of the suspended prison sentence.

In 1968, a new criminal code was adopted to reflect the changes that had taken place in Romanian society since 1945. The institution of the suspended prison sentence was regulated much as it had been under the previous criminal code (Articles 81–86). Like the 1937 Code, the 1968 Code required the courts to justify all decisions to suspend sentences. The courts could order the suspension of a sentence if the punishment imposed was a maximum of 2 years of imprisonment or a fine and the court was satisfied that the purpose of the sentence could be achieved without the need for executing that punishment. The offender in question must not have previously been sentenced to imprisonment. Because of the increased protection of public property provided by criminal law under the totalitarian regime, it was stipulated that for offences against public property, only sentences not exceeding one year of imprisonment could be suspended. Furthermore, the execution of the sentence could only be suspended if the damage caused by the offence was fully repaired before the judgment was rendered.

The operational period of suspension differed based on whether the suspended sentence entailed imprisonment or a fine. For prison sentences, the operational period consisted of the duration of the prison term plus two years. For fines, the period was fixed at two years.

Punishment was defined as a measure of coercion and a means of re-educating the convicted person. Its purpose was to prevent further offences, while also aiming to foster a proper attitude toward work, respect for the rule of law, and adherence to the norms of social coexistence.

Suspension of the execution of a sentence did not automatically place the sentenced person under any additional measures and obligations, except for the requirement not to commit any further offences during the probation period and the requirement to pay civil liabilities. The expungement of the convicted person occurred *de jure* at the end of the probation period. Suspension was revoked if the offender committed a new offence during the probation period, although such revocation was at the judge's discretion if the new offence was committed through negligence. Failure to pay civil liabilities by the end of the operational period could lead to the revocation of the suspension (and hence to the execution of the sentence) unless the offender was able to prove that he/she could not pay them.

Like many other Eastern European countries, Romania's prison system was also a tool for political repression during the totalitarian years (Bichescu et al., 2005; Szalontai, 2002). Since it was a militarised system, the public had little information about the realities behind prison walls, and the state did not communicate openly about the problems the system faced, which – as it later became clear – included overcrowding, substandard detention conditions, compulsory inmate labour, and a lack of emphasis on rehabilitation. The pre-1990 literature mentions the increased rehabilitative potential of suspended sentences but fails to point out that they could help to decongest the prison system.

The prison system's problems worsened after 1977 as a result of several socialist ideological decisions made by Nicolae Ceaușescu, who believed that there were too many prisons in Romania. Without a detailed analysis, he established that there should be no more than 15,000 inmates in the penal system per year. This decision was reflected in Decree no. 225/1977, and it had a significant impact on the Romanian penal system, leading to a series of major changes and mass releases. As a direct consequence of this decision, 27 prisons were closed. Although some of them were subsequently reopened before 1989, the capacity remained insufficient and the resulting overcrowding problem was solved through periodic collective amnesties or pardons presented as part of the ruling party's humanist penal policy (Oancea, 2012; Oancea & Micle, 2020; Stefan, 2006).

After **the overthrow of the totalitarian regime in December** 1989, the new socio-economic reality meant that systematically amnesties and pardons for substantial numbers of convicted individuals were no longer a suitable strategy for addressing prison overcrowding. Additional prisons were built or reopened to solve the overcrowding problem, and the legal framework was reformed to give judges more options for individualising sentences. Pressure on the prison system post-1989 was substantial not least because there was a substantial increase in crime in this period (Kurkó-Fabian, 2005) .

Under these circumstances, the first significant reform of the Criminal Code took place in 1992, with the adoption of Law No. 104/1992. The new legal provisions allowed for more extensive application of suspended sentences and the introduction of suspended prison sentences with probationary supervision, in order to reduce pressure on the prisons. This reform was partly driven by Romania's accession to the Council of Europe and, consequently, its signature of the European Convention on Human Rights.

With the 1992 Code came an increase in the maximum length of prison sentence that could be suspended, from 2 to 3 years. The previous provisions establishing differentiated protection of public and private property under criminal law were removed. Suspended prison sentences with probationary supervision could be imposed for prison sentences of up to 4 years, provided that the offender had not previously been sentenced to more than one year of imprisonment (or that their previous conviction had been expunged). Suspension remained conditional in all cases on the court's conviction that the mere imposition of the sentence would be effective in preventing any future criminal activity, eliminating the necessity for carrying out the actual execution of the sentence.

The length of the operational period was determined as the length of the prison sentence plus an additional period of between 2 and 5 years, as determined by the judge. During the operational period, the sentenced person was obliged to comply with four supervision measures: to report to the supervising judge or other court-appointed bodies on fixed dates, to give prior notice of any changes in domicile, residence or place of abode and any trips longer than eight days, to communicate and justify changes in their place of work, and to provide information to demonstrate their means of subsistence.

In addition, the court could impose one or more of the following obligations: to carry out an activity or to follow a course of educational or vocational training; not to change their place of domicile or residence or to remain within a given territorial area, except under the conditions fixed by the court; not to frequent certain places; not to come into contact with certain persons; not to drive a vehicle or specific vehicles; to undergo medical tests, treatment or care, in particular for substance abuse.

Before the introduction of the Probation Service, the responsibility for ensuring compliance with these measures and obligations rested with the judges who were assigned to oversee sentence execution. At the end of the operational period, the offender was expunged *de jure*. If the offender failed to comply with the court-ordered supervision measures or obligations, the court could revoke the suspension and order the full execution of the sentence, or alternatively extend the operational period by up to 3 years. The regulation of the revocation and annulment of suspension with probationary supervision was identical to that of suspension without supervision.

Law no. 104/1992 established the obligation for all offenders whose sentences were suspended to repair all damages by the date of the court's decision pronouncement. Subsequently, the Constitutional Court ruled that these provisions were unconstitutional.[10] The court argued that tying the suspension of a prison sentence to the resolution of an issue outside the realm of criminal law led to unequal treatment among citizens. A defendant's access to non-custodial sanctions could not be denied based on non-criminal-justice grounds, such as repairing damages.

Some changes to the suspension of prison sentences were introduced in 1996. Suspension was no longer allowed for certain categories of intentional crimes that carried prison sentences of more than 12 years, nor for specifically enumerated offences such as grievous bodily harm, rape, and torture.

The Romanian Probation Service was created in response to the institution of suspended prison sentences with probationary supervision. Between 1994 and 2000, a series of experimental probation centres were set up in several localities, based on cooperation between courts, public prosecutors' offices and prisons, to pilot probation activities, with the aim of relieving the prison system, which was facing severe overcrowding. One of the main activities carried out by these centres was the supervision of how offenders serving suspended prison sentences with probationary supervision complied with the measures and obligations imposed by the courts.

The Criminal Code lacked explicit provisions regarding the supplementary institutions responsible for overseeing the fulfilment of measures and obligations set by judges. Hence, the requirement for offenders to report to experimental probation centres did not contradict the reference to "other institutions" mentioned in the law. Later on, once the Probation Service was fully established, this provision was modified to specify that sentenced individuals must report to the Probation Service.

Until the new Criminal Code came into force in 2014, supervision of compliance with the measures and obligations relating to suspension could be carried out either by the supervising judge or by the Probation Service, as decided by the court. During the period 2001–2014, the number of offenders subject to probationary supervision grew steadily, mainly due to judges' increasing confidence in the efficiency of the probation system (Oancea, 2012; Szabo, 2009).

The 2014 code made explicit two further provisions that had been used in practice during the previous years, namely the involvement of offenders in rehabilitation programmes and in community service during the operational period of their sentence suspension: sentenced offenders may be required to carry out an activity or to follow a course of educational or vocational training.[11]

In 1996–2000 the application of suspension with supervision was rather exceptional, but the development of the Probation Service was to change this. Between 2000 and 2014 the number of suspended prison sentences under supervision, managed by the probation services, increased steadily.

Following the implementation of the new Criminal Code, the Probation Service became overburdened, because the rising number of probationers outpaced the increase in probation officers. The National Probation Directorate's 2015 annual report revealed a 177% increase in the number of supervised individuals between 2011 and 2014, while the number of probation officers had only grown by 33% (from 271 to 360). From 2014 until 2015, the number of individuals under supervision increased by a further 58%, while the number of probation officers decreased by 3% (from 360 to 352). The substantial increase in the number of individuals subject to probationary supervision can be attributed to several factors. First, the new penal provisions provided for suspended prison sentences with probationary supervision as the only possible method of individualising the execution of prison sentences: suspension without supervision was no longer possible. Additionally, the new provisions introduced sentence deferment, which also entailed supervision by the Probation Service to oversee offenders' adherence to the measures and obligations imposed by the courts.

Probation staffing became a priority for the Ministry of Justice and, as a result, by the end of 2022 there were 683 probation officers. Furthermore, to enhance the quality of case management, the Ministry envisions that probation officers will become specialised officers through the establishment of dedicated offices within the Probation Service focused on assessment, supervision, and community work.

The new criminal law regulations introduced new types of obligation, such as community service, rehabilitation programmes, and the ability to individualise court-imposed obligations, without prior training to familiarise probation officers with these new practices. This placed additional demands on probation officers' time spent monitoring compliance with measures and obligations, reducing their capacity to provide assistance and counselling. The frequency of home visits decreased, and rehabilitation programmes were sometimes outsourced to community partners.

The establishment of the Probation Service led to an increase in the amount of multidisciplinary research focusing on the institution of suspended prison sentence with probationary supervision. In recent years, studies have been carried out on supervised offenders' motivation for behavioural change (Micle et al., 2012); the individualisation of sentences by judges (Oancea, 2010); unpaid community work (Szabo, 2009); and other relevant topics.

As can be seen from Table 7.1, in the years before 2014, judges consistently preferred the application of simple suspension rather than suspension with probationary supervision. We have not identified any systematic studies that explain why this was, but observations from the related literature (Oancea, 2012) lead us to believe that it was driven by the initial regulation of supervision, whereby a judge was allocated to oversee the sentenced offender's compliance with the court-imposed measures and obligations during the operational period. Although the criminal code mentioned the possibility of other institutions handling such oversight, this only really became applicable once the Probation Service had been established. Until then, applying suspension with supervision would have added to judges' workloads, which was already steadily increasing.

Moreover, the Criminal Code's provisions regarding suspended sentences with supervision lacked detailed legislation as to how compliance with the

Table 7.1 Dynamics of the application of criminal law sanctions 2000–2013

Year	*2000*	*2001*	*2002*	*2003*	*2004*	*2005*	*2006*	*2007*	*2008*	*2009*	*2010*	*2011*	*2012*	*2013*
Suspended prison sentence	15,430	25,285	26,821	26,012	25,822	24,860	22,644	20,977	18,391	17,962	21,098	25,014	25,584	24,592
Suspended prison sentence with probationary supervision	445	1,267	1,298	1,601	1,538	1,658	1,278	1,336	1,257	1,389	2,164	3,068	4,243	4,127
Prison	34,448	30,694	29,639	28,354	23,618	20,798	17,044	13,608	10,883	9,759	12,992	13,435	13,905	12,891
Criminal fine	18,235	18,729	16,850	13,817	12,003	11,514	9,564	5,162	2,621	2,075	2,356	2,678	2,423	2,609

Source: National Statistical Institute (statistical yearbooks of Romania).

measures and obligations was to be effectively monitored. Most of the time, this involved a formal process whereby sentenced individuals had to present themselves at the court's headquarters and sign declarations regarding their compliance. Legislation on effective supervision came into effect only eight years later, with the establishment of the Probation Service. Consequently, it was only after the introduction of the Probation Service that judges began to make more extensive use of suspended sentences with supervision.

The Criminal Code that entered into force on 1st February 2014 introduced fundamental changes to the penal system. In the explanatory memorandum, the legislator stresses that the effectiveness of criminal law enforcement is not correlated with the severity of sanctions, and that increasing punitiveness does not increase deterrence from committing further offences. The predictability of the penalty and its appropriateness to the specific characteristics of the offender are much more important. In line with this perspective, the new Criminal Code retained only the option of suspending the execution of a prison sentence with probationary supervision, and no longer provided for suspension without supervision.

The statement of reasons accompanying the new criminal regulations does not explain the decision to eliminate suspension without supervision, nor is the rationale behind the legislator's decision to do this addressed in any literature, as far as we have found. It is likely that the legislator viewed the new provisions enabling the deferment of a sentence as an alternative to the simple suspension of a sentence.

Deferment of a sentence, which was newly introduced in the 2014 Code, consists in the court imposing a sentence and concurrently deferring its execution for an operational period (Udroiu, 2014). The legislator introduced this possibility out of a desire to offer the courts more opportunities to impose non-custodial sanctions. A fine or prison sentence of up to 2 years can be deferred, provided that the offender has not previously been sentenced to more than one year of imprisonment, and conditional upon the offender agreeing to perform community service. Prior to deferring a sentence, the court must consider that it is not necessary to execute the imposed punishment, but that it is necessary to place the offender under supervision.

There are several similarities between deferring the enforcement of a sentence and suspending its execution with supervision. In both cases, the offender is required, during the operational period, to comply with the supervision measures provided for in the criminal code (reporting to the probation service, receiving visits from the probation officer, notifying of changes in their residence or workplace, and providing information and documents to justify their means of livelihood). In the case of deferment, no additional obligations to these measures or community service are required, although the court may decide to impose them, whereas for suspension at least one obligation must be imposed. In both cases, the Probation Service supervises the offender's compliance with the measures and obligations laid down by the court. The operational period for deferment is fixed at 2 years, after which the conviction is expunged. The possibility of revocation upon failure to comply with the measures and obligations laid down by the court, re-offending, or failure to pay damages in full, applies similarly to both deferment and suspension.

One of the important differences between a suspended prison sentence with probationary supervision and deferment of sentence is the sentence imposed in case of re-offending. If suspension is revoked, the originally suspended prison sentence is served in full in addition to the new sentence imposed for the new offence. If deferment of a sentence is revoked, the court imposes just one (combined) sentence for the original offence and the new offence. A deferred sentence may thus result in a more lenient sentence upon reoffence, compared with a suspended prison sentence.

Table 7.2 illustrates the changes in imposition of different sentence types following the implementation of the new Criminal Code. Although this code no longer includes suspended prison sentences (without supervision), the statistical reports issued after 2014 still use this category. Consequently, deferred sentences are classified as conditional suspension in the statistics, even though these two concepts are not equivalent. The table shows that suspended prison sentences were largely replaced by deferred sentences. Five years after the Criminal Code entered into force, there is a continuing decreasing trend in the number of prison sentences, and a clear preference for non-custodial sanctions.

Conclusions

Normative aspects of the institution of suspended prison sentences have been present in Romania since the early 20th century. The first comprehensive regulation of this institution was established in 1937.

Significant changes occurred after 1989, when socio-economic transformations necessitated a new approach to criminal sanctions, with a new emphasis on the rehabilitative aspect of punishment and on non-custodial sanctions that were partly motivated by problems with overcrowded and underfunded prisons.

Suspended prison sentences with probationary supervision were newly introduced in 1992, but there was a lack of organisational infrastructure for the effective supervision of probationers' compliance with court-imposed measures and obligations. Consequently, suspended prison sentences without supervision continued to be widely applied. The Probation Service was then established, which initially shared responsibility for supervision alongside the enforcing judges before later assuming full responsibility for probationary supervision. Over time, activities like community service and rehabilitation programmes were piloted and implemented within the probation system.

A new criminal code was enacted in 2014, bringing several changes to the suspension of prison sentences. Suspended prison sentences without supervision

Table 7.2 Dynamics of the application of criminal law sanctions 2014–2021.

	2014	*2015*	*2016*	*2017*	*2018*	*2019*	*2020*	*2021*
Deferred or suspended sentences (total)	22557	22565	12995	15007	13301	14083	14059	15779
Of which: Suspended prison sentences with probationary supervision	2764	3711	6030	6480	6166	6415	5579	6900
Prison sentences	10010	11268	9413	8988	7588	7718	7208	7308
Fines	2370	2467	3369	4129	4321	4763	4024	4696

Source: National Statistical Institute (statistical yearbooks of Romania).

were abolished, while suspended prison sentences with probationary supervision were retained. Additionally, a new institution called deferred sentencing was introduced. Although it was not explicitly stated, the intent was for this new institution to replace suspended prison sentences. There are substantial similarities between the institutions of suspended sentences and deferred sentencing in the Romanian context (both involve compliance with specified measures and obligations during a defined period), although the two institutions are not identical. Importantly, a deferred sentence is not generally considered a conviction, whereas a suspended sentence is treated as one.

The regulatory framework providing for suspension with supervision demonstrates the legislator's intention to enhance the prospects of rehabilitation for supervised individuals and to facilitate the recovery of damages by injured parties.

Notes

1 In particular Law no. 253/2013 on the enforcement of sentences, educational measures and other non-custodial measures ordered by judicial bodies during criminal proceedings and Law no. 254/2013 on the enforcement of sentences and custodial measures ordered by judicial bodies during criminal proceedings.
2 See Article 314, paragraph 1, lit. b and Article 318. Criminal Procedure Code.
3 See Article 80 para. 1 Criminal Procedure Code.
4 Officer Article 93 align. 1 lit. a–e of the Criminal Code.
5 Article 93(2). 2 (a-d) of the Criminal Code.
6 Article 92 align. 1 of the Criminal Code.
7 Article 94 align. 4 of the Criminal Code.
8 Article 94 para. 2 of the Criminal Code.
9 Article 96 para. 4 of the Criminal Code.
10 Decision no. 463/1997.
11 Article 86 para. 3 (a) of the Criminal Code.

References

Bădescu, V.–S., & Done, D. L. (2019). Unele considerații privind dreptul penal românesc în perioada regimului comunist. Tranziția postcomunistă şi reconstrucţia justiției române. Poziţii actuale privind identitatea naţională şi procesul integrării europene. PARTEA I. *Revista „Acta Universitatis George Bacovia. Juridica, 8*(1), 5–73.

Băncilă, A.–D. (2020). Măsurile de probaţiune. Prezentare generală. *Revista Română de drept penal al afacerilor* (1), 91–117.

Bichescu, D., Schauer, M., Saleptsi, E., Neculau, A., Elbert, T., & Neuner, F. (2005). Long–term consequences of traumatic experiences: An assessment of former political detainees in Romania. *Clinical Practice and Epidemiology in Mental Health, 1*(1), 1–11.

Cracănă, I. (2013). Justiţia populară în România O radiografie instituţională, 1948–1960. *Arhivele Totalitarismului, 21.*

Gladchi, G., & Bucur, C. (2011). Evoluţia istorică a instituţiei condamnării cu suspendarea conditionată a executării pedepsei ca instituţie a dreptului penal al României şi al RM. *Revista Naţională de Drept, 126*(3), 43–51.

Kurkó–Fabian, A. (2005). Dinamica şi tendinţele delincvenţei generale şi juvenile din România după 1989. *Studia Universitatis Babes–Bolyai–Sociologia, 50*(2), 173–192.

Micle, M. I., Oancea, G., & Saucan, D. Ş. (2012). Tipuri de motivaţii în reabilitarea condamnaţilor aflaţi în evidenţa serviciilor de probaţiune. *Social Work Review/Revista de Asistenta Sociala, 11*(3).

Oancea, G. (2010). Spre o evaluare a perceptiei judecatorilor cu privire la activitatea serviciilor de probatiune (Towards an assesment of judges's perception on probation services activities). *Revista de Asistenta Sociala* (3), 109.

Oancea, G. (2012). Probaţiunea în România: Evaluări normative şi sociologice [Probation in Romania: Normative and sociological evaluation]. *Bucureşti: CH Beck.*

Oancea, G., & Micle, M. I. (2020). The emergence of community control sanctions in the Romanian sanctioning system: Wdrożenie kar probacyjnych do systemu kar w Rumunii. *Archiwum Kryminologii* (XLII/1), 207–224.

Schiaucu, V. (2010). Influenţa referatului de evaluare în individualizarea pedepsei. *Revista "Dreptul"* (12), 159–171.

Stefan, B. (2006). Istoria si reforma inchisorilor romanesti (History and Romanian prison reform). *Revista Română de Sociologie, anul, XVII*(5–6), 485–512.

Szabo, A. (2009). *Perspective ale dezvoltării instituţiei probaţiunii în România.* Editura Universităţii din Bucureşti.

Szalontai, B. (2002). The dynamic of repression: The global impact of the Stalinist model, 1944–1953. *Russian History, 29*(2–4), 415–442.

Tipa, I. (2007). Viziune retrospectivă asupra instituţiei liberării de pedeapsa penală. *Studia Universitatis Moldaviae (Seria Ştiinţe Sociale)* (6), 205–210.

Toader, T., & Safta, M. (2018). The Great Union, premise for the unification of the criminal law. *Rev. Stiinte Juridice, 158.*

Udroiu, M. (2014). *Drept penal: partea generală: noul Cod penal.* CH Beck.

Welsh, H. A. (1994). Political transition processes in Central and Eastern Europe. *Comparative Politics, 26*(4), 379–394.

Part IIb

Suspended sentences in the former USSR

8 Countries of the former USSR

Gennady Esakov

Criminal Law in the Russian Empire pre-1917

To understand the history of the USSR's criminal law, we must first consider the pre-1917 context. The history of Russian criminal legislation can be traced back to the eleventh century, when the first compilation of laws known as "Russian Law" (*Русская правда*) appeared. Further, similar compilations of laws followed during the next few centuries. However, criminal law as a specific branch of the legal system and its doctrine appeared only at the beginning of the nineteenth century when "original scientific research on positive criminal law" began to emerge (Фельдштейн, 2003, p. 235).

Russian criminal law continued to develop during the nineteenth century; this was reflected in the Code of Laws of 1832 (volume XV of which was the Criminal Code of Russia), the Code on Criminal and Corrective Punishments of 1845 (*Уложение о наказаниях уголовных и исправительных*) and the Criminal Code of 1903 (*Уголовное уложение*, also known in Poland and the Baltic States as *Tagantsev's Code*[1]).[2] The last of these was one of the best European codifications of criminal legislation at the time and its provisions (especially the general provisions on fault, complicity, and inchoate offences) are still reflected in Russian criminal legislation today. This significant progress in criminal law doctrine also gave rise to a voluminous literature on criminal law towards the end of the nineteenth century.

Initially, Russian criminal law theory was noticeably influenced by German doctrine. The textbook *Lehrbuch des gemeinen in Deutschland gültigen peinlichen Rechts* by Paul Johann Anselm von Feuerbach (1775–1833) was translated and published in Russia in three editions (1810, 1811, and 1827) and served as the leading doctrinal source on criminal law until the mid-1860s. Up until 1917, links between German and Russian criminal law scholars were strong, and even today the Russian criminal law system is closer to the German system than it is to other European criminal law systems. Later, original Russian works on criminal law were published, in particular Ivan Foinitskii's *Course of criminal law: Crimes against person and property* (*Курс уголовного права. Посягательства личные и имущественные*) and *Course of criminal procedure*, Nikolai Sergeevskii's *Criminal law: The General part* (*Уголовное право.*

DOI: 10.4324/9781003568667-12

Общая часть) and Nikolai Tagantsev's *Russian criminal law: The General part* (*Русское уголовное право. Общая часть*).

Suspension of prison sentences[3] was seriously addressed for the first time in the 1890s (see also Тимашев, 1914, pp. 199–234; Люблинский, 1924, pp. 39–46): in 1890, an academic committee on penitentiary formed by the Saint Petersburg Law Society discussed the idea and recommended its implementation into legislation. The first monograph focused on suspended prison sentences was published a few years later by Piontkovskii (Пионтковский, 1894); in it, he strongly recommended that suspended prison sentences should be included in Russian legislation. Nevertheless, it was not until 1907 that the first draft law was presented to the Russian parliament as part of Stolypin's large-scale social reforms. This was passed by the lower chamber, the State Duma, in 1909, but was rejected in the upper chamber, the State Council, in 1910 and never enacted thereafter.

Both the defeat of the draft bill in the upper chamber of parliament and the 1903 Criminal Code's silence on the topic of suspended prison sentences may to some extent be attributable to Professor Tagantsev, who was both a member of the State Council and a leading drafter for the 1903 Code. Tagantsev was opposed to the concept of suspended prison sentences for two main reasons. First, on the theoretical level, he viewed suspended sentences as contrary to the idea of just retribution, which he saw as the main foundation of punishment. Tagantsev considered that just retribution can only be achieved through confinement. Second, he identified many practical difficulties in applying such a sanction. For example, he mentioned that suspended prison sentences could raise suspicion about corruption in the courts, since the general reasons the court would formulate for implementing suspended prison sentences could lead to a belief that this was a sanction for the rich. Further, he stated that it would be difficult to designate the list of crimes for which a suspended prison sentence might be an appropriate response and that it would be difficult to implement post-conviction supervision in practice (Таганцев, 1902, pp. 1392–1404; Государственный совет, columns 2146–2157: his speech in the State Council dated 7 April 1910). His personal views, coupled with the novelty of the institution and a lack of reliable experience in using the sanction in European countries, led to the drafters of the 1903 Code opposing the discussed concept.

The draft law of 1909 proposed enabling suspension for offenders sentenced to a fine, arrest,[4] or imprisonment of no more than 1 year and 4 months' duration (for the text of the law, see Столыпин, 2011, pp. 227–229). It provided, in general terms, for such a sentence to be suspended if it was feasible to do so based on the personal characteristics of the convicted person and of the crime committed (neither of which were specified in detail). There was a long list of exceptions; for example, suspended sentences would not be allowed for recidivists, nor for those guilty of horse theft (due to the particular importance of horses for agriculture). The proposed operational period for suspended sentences was 3 years for a fine or arrest and 5 years for a prison sentence. Any new crime committed during the operational period would be viewed as a breach of the suspended sentence.

The Early Soviet Period (1917–1958)

The Bolshevik *coup d'etat* of 1917 had an ambivalent impact on criminal legislation. On the one hand, the legislation was "Sovietised" in line with the dominant Communist ideology. It was framed in the style of the Communist rhetoric, which was biased against the "bourgeois" class of the population. Analogy – under which criminal liability could be established even in the absence of a specific prohibiting statute – was enacted as the key instrument of criminal law, and this remained in force until 1958. Between the 1920s and 1950s, Russian criminal legislation was used as a tool for large-scale repression and it embodied provisions that strongly protected the Communist ideology, state property and interests.

On the other hand, the criminal law doctrine framed within the Soviet phraseology continued to develop. While particular aspects inseparably connected with the Communist rule, such as negative attitudes towards international criminal law, the use of analogy in criminal law, and punishment for anti-Soviet beliefs and ideas, lasted only as long as the Communist regime, doctrinal works written during the Soviet period by scholars like Vladimir Kudriavtsev (1923–2007), Andrei Piontkovskii (1898–1973) and Aron Trainin (1883–1957) are still used in contemporary scholarly research and continue to form the basis of criminal law doctrine in Russia today. As Starosolsky points out, "[t]he real ambition of the Soviet law makers […] was to create a criminal law that would be revolutionary in its substance. They succeeded in many respects and experimented throughout nearly twenty years. But […] in the minds of the Soviet jurists an evolution had taken place back towards the old pre-revolutionary principles" (Starosolsky, 1950, p. 360). In the 1990s, it was easy enough for criminal law theorists to cast away the Soviet phraseology and make a smooth transition into a common legal language with continental European lawyers on guilt, punishment, and other key concepts of criminal law.

A special law enacted on 22 November (5 December[5]) 1917 (known as the Decree on Courts No. 1) allowed the use of former criminal legislation (that is, the Russian Empire's criminal legislation) insofar as it was not abolished by the new regime or not in itself against "revolutionary conscience or revolutionary legal ideology". In 1918, the Statute on People's Court (*Положение о народном суде*) completely prohibited the use of old "tsarist" legislation.

The first sporadic cases of sentence suspension by the new Bolshevik courts appeared immediately after the *coup d'etat* (see also Люблинский, 1924, pp. 47–52). *De iure,* this option for sentencing was introduced by the legislation known as the Decree on Courts No. 2, enacted on 15 February 1918. However, the relevant provision was quite unclear: suspended sentences were mentioned amongst the rights of the "people's assessors" (*народные заседатели*), who were lay judges accompanying the professional judge. Article 29 of the Decree provided that "people's assessors decide not only on the fact of a crime but also on the measure of punishment provided that they, following their belief, have the right to reduce the punishment prescribed by the law up to conditional or full discharge of the defendant from any punishment".

In early Soviet times, criminal legislation on the territory of the former Russian Empire developed along two main lines. The first affected countries that were under Soviet influence at the beginning of their (formal) independence: Ukraine and Belarus. The second affected Finland, Poland, Bessarabia (today's Moldova), and the Baltic states.

Russia, Ukraine, and Belarus

The first "Sovietised" Russian Criminal Code was enacted in 1922; this was declared valid for Belarus and also served as a textual basis for the Ukrainian Criminal Code (Гродзинский, 1927, p. 583). It provided for suspended sentences to be pronounced against defendants who (i) had committed a crime for the first time, (ii) as a result of bad living conditions, and (iii) who were not so dangerous as to require isolation (Art. 36).[6] The operational period for a suspended sentence was set at between 3 and 10 years (Art. 37). The only reason for revoking a suspended prison sentence was if the offender committed the same or a similar crime[7] during the operational period. On the one hand, it was possible to apply Art. 36 to sentences for any crime, irrespective of its gravity and the type or extent of the sentence imposed. On the other hand, Art. 36 expressly prohibited the use of suspended sentences for offenders whose case called for the "deprivation of rights", i.e. the deprivation of political, civil and certain other rights as a supplementary punishment, as provided under Art. 40 of the Code (Art. 42). While such "deprivation of rights" was an option applicable in any criminal case before the court, the court was obliged, at the very least, to discuss the suitability of imposing such deprivation in any case of conviction to imprisonment lasting more than 1 year. If the court also sentenced the offender to "deprivation of rights", their primary sentence could not be suspended.

On 29 December 1922, Russia, Ukraine, Belarus, and the united Caucasian Republic signed the treaty that established the USSR, and in 1926–1927 revised criminal legislation was enacted in all the Soviet republics. However, the newly enacted criminal legislation was not significantly different from that encoded within the 1922 criminal codes. Article 53 of the Russian Criminal Code of 1926 reduced the requirements for suspended sentences from the three conditions provided in the previous legislation to just one – that the offender was not sufficiently dangerous as to require isolation.[8] This change was motivated by a desire to simplify sentencing procedures. The operational period for suspended sentences was set at between 1 and 10 years. The only reason provided for revoking a suspended sentence was that the offender committed a new crime of the same or greater gravity than the first. Again, suspension of a prison sentence was not allowed when any term of imprisonment was accompanied by "deprivation of rights". With the exception of these cases, it was possible to suspend any sentence.

Once again, the Russian Criminal Code of 1926 served as the basis for the Ukrainian Criminal Code of 1927 and the Belarusian Criminal Code of 1928. For example, Article 56 of the 1928 Belarusian Criminal Code was similar in wording to Article 53 of the 1926 Russian Criminal Code: the only difference was in the operational period for suspended sentences, which was set to 1–3 years for prison sentences not exceeding 1 year, and 3–10 years in all other cases.

The practice of the first Soviet courts regarding the suspension of sentences was confused, both in terms of the numbers of suspensions imposed and in terms of the reasons for imposing them (see also Люблинский, 1924, pp. 52–63). For example, in 1920–1922 as many as 44% of all prison sentences were suspended; in 1922–1923 this percentage dropped to around 30%.[9]

Finland, Poland, Bessarabia, and the Baltic states

Finland, Poland, Bessarabia and the Baltic states began (or continued) to develop their own criminal legislation, which was not substantially influenced by the Soviet regime. Finland and Poland preserved their independence, and their criminal legislation will not be discussed in detail here. Bessarabia joined the USSR in 1940, largely becoming the Moldavian Soviet Socialist Republic (later to be Moldova). From 1940, the Ukrainian Criminal Code of 1927 applied in the Moldavian Soviet Socialist Republic.

After gaining their independence from Soviet Russia, the Baltic states reverted to earlier versions of the Russian criminal code. Latvia and Lithuania used *Tagantsev's Code* of 1903; in Latvia, this was superseded by a new code in 1933, while in Lithuania the 1903 code remained in force until 1940. Until 1935, Estonia used the Russian criminal code of 1845. It is interesting to note that a suspended sentence regime was introduced into Estonian law in 1920. In 1940 the Soviet regime took control of the Baltic states and all three new "Soviet Socialist Republics" were forced to abide by the Russian Criminal Code of 1926.

The Late Soviet Period (1958–1991)

The development of Soviet legislation in the late Soviet period, i.e. after the Second World War, was characterised by new codifications in all major branches of law that remained in force until the collapse of the USSR. With regard to criminal legislation, the late Soviet period started in 1958, when the new Basic Principles of Criminal Legislation of the USSR and the Union Republics (hereinafter "the Basic Principles") were enacted.

The constitutional framework of the USSR provided that the Union may enact specific legislative acts known as the Basic Principles (see also Berman, 1947, pp. 807–808; Osakwe, 1976, pp. 443–444). These acts were binding for the Union's Republics and constituted the basis for the respective Republic's codes. In criminal law, the Basic Principles covered only the general part of the criminal legislation and were copied verbatim into the general part of the Republic's criminal codes. The first Basic Principles in criminal law were enacted in 1924.

Between 1936 and 1957, the USSR Constitution of 1936 provided that the unified Criminal Code of the USSR should be enacted. There were some legislative drafts of this Code, but this idea was eventually abandoned, and the 1957 constitutional amendment returned to the concept of mixed jurisdiction of the Union and the Republics over the criminal law sphere.

Although the Basic Principles did not provide liability for specific crimes, the Union was able to legislate in this sphere. Firstly, liability for some crimes (for example, pertaining to military service) was provided only by the Union's legislation. Secondly, the Union's government sometimes increased liability for particular crimes or provided liability for new ones, and such laws were directly applicable in all Republics even before their reception into the respective Republic's criminal codes.

The new Basic Principles in 1958 closed, at least nominally, the era of analogy in criminal legislation, punishment without fault or even deed, family members' criminal responsibility for their relatives' behaviour and all other deviations of the revolutionary and Stalinist periods (see also Grzybowski, 1960).[10]

Following the enactment of these new Basic Principles, all Soviet republics revised their criminal legislation (see also Feldbrugge, 1963, pp. 252–256). The general part of that legislation, which included provisions on suspended sentences, was worded in language similar to that of the new Basic Principles.

The Russian Criminal Code of 1960 provided in Art. 44 that:

"[I]f, when assigning punishment in the form of imprisonment or corrective labour, the court, having taken into account the circumstances of the case and the character of the convicted person, is convinced that it is not desirable for the convicted person to serve the sentence assigned, it may take a ruling as to the conditional non-application to the convicted person of the punishment in question, mandatorily setting forth in the sentence the reasons for the conditional conviction. In this case the court rules that the sentence shall not be executed, provided that during the probationary period fixed by the court the convicted person does not commit a new crime of a similar nature, or a more serious crime".

This provision was taken verbatim from Art. 38 of the Basic Principles. The operational period for suspended sentences was fixed by the court at between 1 and 5 years (a maximum of 3 years in the Ukrainian and Moldovan Republics).

De iure any term of imprisonment could be suspended. However, there was a widespread understanding, both in theory and in practice, that sentences involving more than 5 years of imprisonment should not be suspended (Курс, 1970, p. 241).

Additionally, Art. 44 of the 1960 code (following Art. 38 of the Basic Principles) introduced suspended prison sentences with probationary supervision for the first time:

"[t]aking into account the circumstances of the case, the character of the convicted person, and petitions filed by social organisations or by the collective of workers, employees, or kolkhoz farmers at the place of employment of the convicted person, the court may make such organisations or such a collective responsible for the reeducation and reformation of the convicted person. If the court decides upon conditional conviction in the absence of the above-mentioned petitions, it may impose upon a particular collective of workers, or a person, with their permission, the responsibility for surveillance of the conditionally convicted person, and for doing educational work with him".

Two major reforms to suspended sentences took place in 1969 and 1982. In accordance with the usual practice in Soviet times, these legislative changes were first made in the Basic Principles and subsequently incorporated into the criminal legislation of all the Union's republics. In 1969, the legislation began to consider "any intentional crime" to breach suspension conditions, and no longer only crimes "of a similar nature, or a more serious crime". In 1982, "any negligent crime" was also included in the list of reasons for revoking a suspended prison sentence (hence reoffending in any way became a reason for revocation), as was systematic public disorder punishable as an administrative offence[11] and evasion of "reeducation and reformation" or of work for the supervising organisation or collective.

The criminal legislation enacted in the late 1950s and early 1960s remained in force until the collapse of the Soviet Union. Thereafter, the common legal history of the former Union's republics came to an end. Some of them adopted new legislation, while others have continued to apply heavily Russian-influenced legislation.

Notes

1 Tagantsev's Code was named after its main author, Professor Nikolai Tagantsev (1843–1923), who was the leading professor of criminal law during the late Empire and the presiding judge in the Criminal Cassation Department of the Governing Senate, the highest criminal court of Russia, between 1896 and 1905.

2 In terms of the legal system, Finland was a separate region in this period. The Finnish criminal code was enacted in 1889 and came into force in 1894.

3 In Russia, suspended sentences are referred to as "conditional conviction". However, for consistency, we here refer to them as "suspended sentences" throughout.

4 Arrest referred to short-term imprisonment (up to 6 months); this was viewed as a non-degrading punishment for petty offences. The conditions under which arrest was served were more lenient than those applicable to ordinary imprisonment (for example, arrest lasting up to 7 days could be served at home, and persons serving arrest sentences were not dressed in prison uniform).

5 In Russian tradition, all events in Russian history before 31 January (13 February) 1918 have two dates, following the Julian and Gregorian calendars.

6 Note that Art. 32 of the Criminal Code mentioned suspended sentences amongst types of punishment. This was the only case of such a classification; none of the criminal codes enacted thereafter refer to suspended sentences as punishment.

7 The concept of "the same or similar crime" refers to committing a new crime that is either identical or close in its nature to the crime previously committed. For example, intentional homicide is only "the same" crime as another intentional homicide, whereas theft is "similar" to fraud, violent theft and some crimes against property. The court decides *ad hoc* whether the new crime is similar to the previously committed crime or not. Usually, crimes covered within a single chapter of the Special part of the Criminal Code would be treated as "similar" to one another.

8 Suspended sentences were also accepted in cases of sentencing to compulsory labour (known as corrective labour since 1960). Corrective labour is served at the convicted person's usual workplace, part of the salary from which is paid to the state authorities.

9 In the satiric novella *Heart of a Dog* (Собачье сердце), written in 1925, the prominent Russian author Mikhail Bulgakov refers to the widespread practice of suspending prison sentences as ridiculous. For instance, he gives the following brief description of the life of one of the main characters, Klim Chugunkin: "Name: Klim Grigorievich Chugunkin. Age: 25. Marital status: Unmarried. Not a Party member, but sympathetic to the Party. Three times charged with theft and acquitted – on the first occasion for lack of evidence, in the second case saved by his social origin, the third time put on probation with a conditional sentence of 15 years hard labour. Profession: plays the balalaika in bars".

10 Of course, there were differences between the law "on paper" and the law "in action". At the practical level, in the day-to-day business of the Soviet era criminal courts, procedures often left much to be desired as regards standards of legality. However, given that this chapter is primarily historical and introductory in character, I believe it is sufficient to engage with the law "on paper".

11 The Russian approach to the classification of "public wrongs" differs from that in many other European jurisdictions because there are two separate penal branches of law in Russia: criminal law and law of administrative violations. In brief, criminal law encompasses the offences that are classified as *crime* or *délit* in France, *Verbrechen* in Germany. All other minor offences (known as *contravention* in France, *Vergehen* in Germany) are administrative violations in Russia. These types of offences are generally subject to milder punishments (a maximum imprisonment of one month for administrative violations in contrast with a minimum of two months' imprisonment for crimes) and a simplified procedure, where the punishment is decided in most cases by the administrative body (police, executive bodies, etc.) with the possibility of appealing to the court.

References

Гродзинский, М. (1927). Новый уголовный кодекс УССР. *Вестник советской юстиции, 17*, 583–588.

Курс советского уголовного права. (1970). том III. Москва.
Люблинский, П. И. (1924). Условное осуждение в иностранном и советском праве. Москва.
Пионтковский, А. А. (1894). Об условном осуждении, или системе испытания. Уголовно-политическое исследование. Одесса.
Столыпин, П. А. (2011). Программа реформ. Документы и материалы, том 1. Москва.
Таганцев, Н. С. (1902). Русское уголовное право. Часть Общая, том 2. Санкт-Петербург.
Тимашев, Н. С. (1914). Условное осуждение. Санкт-Петербург.
Фельдштейн, Г. С. (2003). Главные течения в истории науки уголовного права в России. Москва.
Berman, H. J. (1947). Principles of Soviet criminal law. *Yale Law Journal*, *56*, 803–836.
Feldbrugge, F. J. (1963). Soviet criminal law – The last six years. *Journal of Criminal Law, Criminology, and Police Science*, *54*, 249–266.
Grzybowski, K. (1960). Soviet criminal law reform of 1958. *Indiana Law Journal*, *35*, 125–142.
Osakwe, C. (1976). Contemporary Soviet criminal law: An analysis of the general principles and major institutions of post-1958 Soviet criminal law. *Georgia Journal of International and Comparative Law*, *6*, 437–492.
Starosolsky, G. V. (1950). Basic principles of Soviet criminal law. *North Carolina Law Review*, *28*, 359–374.

9 Suspended sentences in Estonia

Jaan Ginter

History of Estonia

Estonia has been dominated by many different foreign powers throughout history, from Danes and the Teutonic Order in the late 12th century through the Livonian Order and the Baltic German aristocracy to Danish, Swedish, and finally Tsarist Russian rule (Demuth, 2003, p. 32; Piirimäe, 1997, p. 50; Meissner, 1992, p. 329).

This history of domination by outside forces was finally brought to an end when the country gained independent statehood in 1918, secured with the Treaty of Tartu in 1920, after which Estonia stood firmly on its own feet (Demuth, 2003, p. 32). However, this period of independence did not last long: the signing of the Molotov-Ribbentrop Pact on 23 August 1939 signalled the prelude to the annexation of the Baltic states by the Soviet Union (Rauch, 1995, pp. 189–234). After the Second World War, the Estonian territory was re-occupied by the USSR (Demuth, 2003, p. 75) and Estonia eventually regained its independence only in in 1991 (Titma, 1997, p. 8).

In the field of criminal law, the main historic influences have come from Russia. German influences were also significant in the field of civil law, but did not have a major impact on criminal law until the Penal Code of 2002[1]. Although there are close connections between legal scholars in Estonia, Finland, and Sweden, neither Swedish nor Finnish criminal law has substantially influenced Estonian criminal law. The Penal Code of 2002 was primarily influenced by German and French criminal law (Sootak, 1998, pp. 23–27).

Sentencing in Estonia

According to Supreme Court practice, the starting point for sentencing must be the average sanction rate specified in the special part of the Penal Code. For instance, if the minimum sanction is three years' imprisonment and the maximum is seven years' imprisonment, then the starting point would be five years' imprisonment[2]. The punishment is individualised on the basis of the offender's guilt (Penal Code, § 56, first sentence). The Supreme Court has interpreted this provision and asserted that the magnitude of the guilt must be assessed primarily

DOI: 10.4324/9781003568667-13

in terms of the circumstances in which the offence was committed, which include the character of the act, its consequences and the offender's motive and purpose.[3] When imposing a punishment, the court or body conducting out-of-court proceedings[4] takes into consideration any mitigating and aggravating circumstances and the possibility of preventing the offender from committing further offences in the future (individual prevention), as well as the protection of public order (general prevention) (Penal Code, § 56, second sentence). There are no other specific sentencing guidelines, reference punishments or normal punishments in Estonian criminal law. Currently, there are only two types of principal punishment provided for in the Penal Code, which are fines (Penal Code, § 44; the Penal Code uses the term "pecuniary punishment" to distinguish this penalty for a crime from the penalty for misdemeanours known as a "fine") and imprisonment (Penal Code, § 45).

If a court imposes a prison sentence of up to two years, it may decide to substitute the imprisonment with community service[5] (Penal Code, § 69). Prison sentences of up to one year may be substituted by electronic surveillance (Penal Code, § 69). For sex offenders and drug addicts, prison sentences of up to two years may be substituted by treatment (Penal Code, § 69). Prison sentences of up to five years can be suspended for an operational period of up to five years (Penal Code, §§ 73–74). In all these cases, the court must first decide whether the characteristics of the offence and the offender warrant a prison sentence, i.e. that the aims of the punishment cannot be achieved by a less onerous punishment (Penal Code, § 56). Only after it has reached that conclusion may the court decide whether substitution or suspension of the imprisonment is warranted.

In Estonia, under the 2002 Penal Code, a suspended prison sentence has never been seen as a distinct type of punishment: it has always been considered an alternative means of enforcing a prison sentence. In practice, the court must first conclude that the appropriate punishment for the offence committed is imprisonment and must impose a prison sentence of a specific duration. Suspension of a prison sentence[6] "is not an independent type of punishment and it can be applied only after the basic punishment has been sentenced".[7] The Estonian Penal Code initially contained 431 offences, which were punishable by:

(1) pecuniary punishment or imprisonment (252 offences, 56%);
(2) imprisonment only (150 offences, 36%);
(3) pecuniary punishment only (29 offences, 8%).[8]

In other words, the majority of offences can be punished by imprisonment and initially only 8% of the specified offences could not be punished by imprisonment.

For decades, the most prevalent punishment has been a suspended prison sentence, followed by imprisonment, while pecuniary punishment (i.e. fine) is the least frequent punishment. The rate of suspended prison sentences has been increasing and the rate of fine imposition has been decreasing (see Figure 9.1).

The significant increase in the use of suspended prison sentences, and the decrease in pecuniary punishment began already in 2000, following the establishment of the Estonian Probation Service in 1998. The 2002 Penal Code introduced a new system of pecuniary punishment (a day-fine system), but there was no indication that this would be burdensome for the judges to apply, nor any discussion of such difficulties. In 2002, all income tax return data was already available to the courts in digital form (online) and court clerks were capable of finding the data necessary for calculating the day-fines.

There has been some criticism of the extensive use of suspended sentences in the Estonian media (See e.g. Rätsep, 2016; Meelak, 2002), but there has not been any such criticism in the scholarly discussion and if we look at recent changes in the legislation, these have made the use of suspended sentences more available rather than less so. Initially, the 2002 Penal Code required that if an offender serving a suspended prison sentence commits an intentional offence during the operational period, then the suspension must be revoked and the sentences for the two offences aggregated and enforced. Since 1 January 2007, it has been possible to substitute that aggregated prison sentence with community service. Moreover, since 1 January 2015 it has been possible to suspend the resulting aggregated prison sentence provided that the offender is placed under behavioural supervision and electronic monitoring.

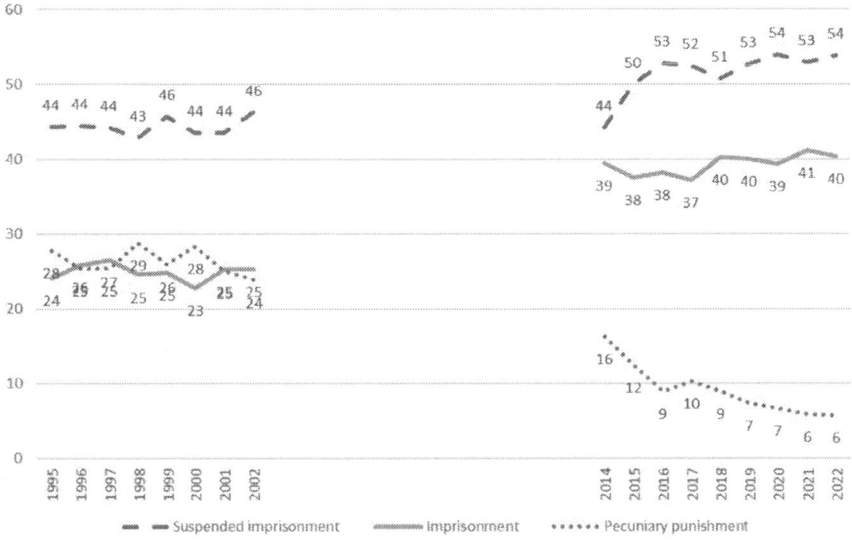

Figure 9.1 Punishments imposed in %.

Source: Data from Statistics Estonia and the Ministry of Justice.

Note: The data for 1995–2002 describe the situation as it was under the Criminal Code that was then in force. The data for 2014–2022 describe the situation under the Penal Code, which entered into force on 1 September 2002. There is no reliable data available for the years 2003–2013.

The rate of supervised suspended sentences as a percentage of all suspended sentences declined from 61% in 2010 to 37% in 2022 (see Figure 9.2).

This decline was supported by the substantial increase in the use of suspended prison sentences since the establishment of the probation service in 1998, which led to many offenders who did not need such an intensive measure being placed on supervised suspended prison sentence.[9] On the other hand, this may also have led to probation officers being overwhelmed by the huge number of persons serving supervised suspended prison sentences and unable to pay them sufficient attention. The conditions stipulated in the Penal Code initially and in early court practice had favoured the use of supervised suspended prison sentences rather than unsupervised suspended prison sentence (Salla, 2014, p. 598). Hence, it is possible that supervised suspended imprisonment was initially overused and that the observed decrease reflects a wider shift away from extensive supervision. There is only very limited public data available on the effectiveness of suspended sentences. One 2013 study revealed that 25% of suspended prison sentences resulted in re-offence. The study indicated that re-offending is more frequent among younger offenders aged below 30 years (32%) than among offenders over the age of 30 (15%) (Lobjak, 2013, p. 30).

Current legislation on suspended prison sentence

On 6 June 2001 the Estonian parliament (*Riigikogu*) adopted the new Estonian Penal Code, which entered into force on 1 September 2002. The most recent

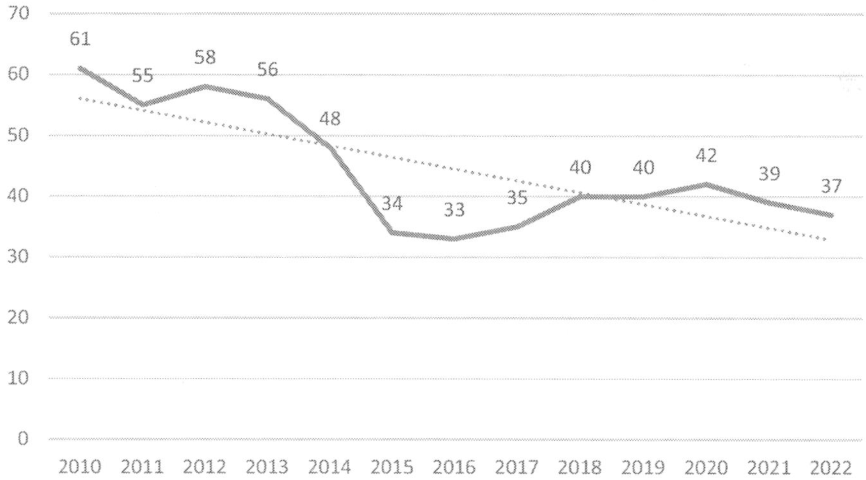

Figure 9.2 Supervised suspended sentences as a percentage of all suspended sentences.

Source: Data from Statistics Estonia and the Ministry of Justice.

amendments to the Penal Code regarding suspended prison sentences entered into force on 1 November 2017. The 2002 Penal Code provides for the following modes of suspended sentences:

Suspended prison sentence (Penal Code, § 73)

If a court, taking into consideration:

- the circumstances relating to the commission of a criminal offence;
- the personality of the offender.

finds that it **is not necessary for the offender to serve** the specified term of imprisonment or pay the specified amount of pecuniary punishment, the court may order the suspension of the sentence in full or in part. Suspension of the sentence **may be ordered in full**, unless otherwise provided for in the Special Part of this Code.

If a sentence is suspended in full, the imposed punishment is not enforced at all unless the offender commits a new intentional criminal offence within the operational period determined by the court (unless otherwise directly provided for in Penal Code).

As we have seen, § 73 of the Penal Code also permits the part-suspension of some prison sentences, resulting in a phenomenon known as shock imprisonment. If a court decides that part of the prison sentence or pecuniary punishment imposed is not to be executed, it must determine which part of the sanction is to be served or paid immediately and which part is conditionally suspended.

The Penal Code does not specify what period of time the offender should be required, in such cases, to spend in prison. Initially, some courts decided to impose non-suspended prison sentence in such cases that exceeded 6 months (e.g. 12 months in the Tartu County Court judgment of 18 September 2018 in Case No 1-18-7437[10]). Later analysis concluded that this was too long and suggested that the Penal Code should be amended to specify that the non-suspended prison sentence in such cases should not exceed 2 months (Ahven et al., 2013, p. 21). However, that proposal was not accepted. The later amendments to the Penal Code introduced a limit of 30 days for the non-suspended part of the sentence, but only for offenders below eighteen years of age.[11]

Shock imprisonment is applied in situations in which the characteristics of the offence and the offender make it impossible to suspend the sentence in full, but where the court considers it unnecessary for the sentence to be fully served in prison. Judges impose shock imprisonment, usually for a period of 1 to 4 months, if they consider it important for the offender to suffer some hardship.

Use of shock imprisonment was quite frequent in 2019, but has since declined considerably (see Figure 9.3).

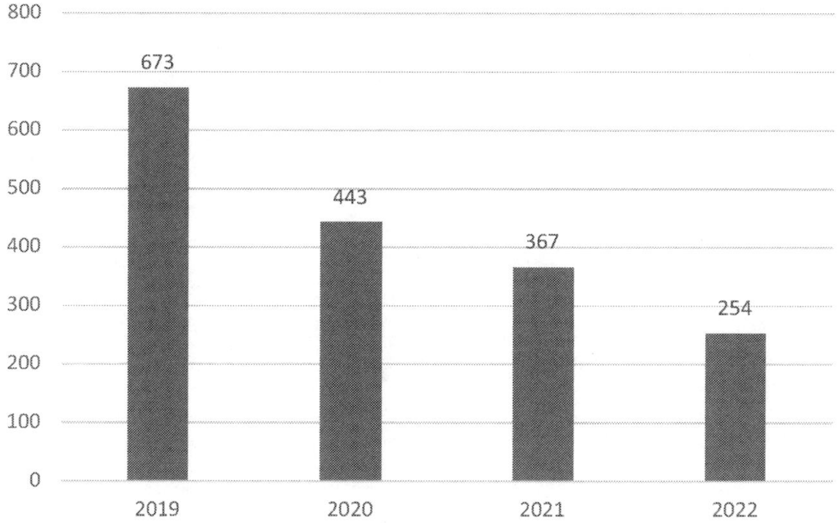

Figure 9.3 Use of shock imprisonment (number of cases of part-suspension of a prison sentence).

Source: Data from the Ministry of Justice.

The Special Part of the Penal Code lists several offences and circumstances under which the sentence imposed cannot be suspended in full. This list mostly consists of repeat sex offences, but its logic is not entirely clear. For example, it includes causing serious damage to the health of a person or causing the death of a person through negligence by an intentional violation of traffic regulations while intoxicated (Penal Code, § 422) but does not include the same if not in an intoxicated state, even if the offender has caused the deaths of two or more people.

Suspension, whether for part or all of a sentence, is ordered for an **operational period of between one and five years**. The Penal Code does not limit the length of custodial sentences that may be suspended, but the Supreme Court has ruled that the operational period must be longer than the sentence that is suspended. Consequently, offenders who have been sentenced to imprisonment for a period exceeding five years cannot have their sentences suspended.[12] Although the Supreme Court has long maintained this position, the lower courts frequently neglect to comply with it.[13] This restriction applies to all modes of suspended prison sentence (unsupervised and supervised ones).

If an offender commits a new criminal offence during the operational period and is sentenced to imprisonment for the new offence, an aggregate punishment is imposed, meaning that the previously suspended sentence is added to the sentence for the new offence. If life imprisonment is one of the punishments imposed, life imprisonment is imposed as the aggregate punishment. If the new criminal offence was committed through negligence, the court may suspend the aggregate punishment. If the new criminal offence was committed intentionally, the court may suspend the aggregate punishment as long as it also places the offender under electronic surveillance. If the new prison sentence is not suspended, the court may still substitute it with community service.[14]

If an offender commits a new criminal offence during the operational period and is sentenced to a pecuniary punishment for the new offence, the court may decide not to enforce the original (previously suspended) sanction and order separate enforcement of the pecuniary punishment imposed for the new offence. Supplementary punishments of various types are also executed independently.

Suspended prison sentence with behavioural supervision (Penal Code, § 74)

This option differs from unsupervised suspended prison sentence in that it imposes supervision of the offender's behaviour. If this type of suspension is ordered, the imposed punishment is not enforced as long as the offender does not commit a new criminal offence within the operational period determined by the court **and complies with all supervisory requirements and obligations imposed on him or her during the operational period,** unless otherwise directly provided for in Penal Code.

The **operational period** for this type of suspension is **between six months and five years**. If, during the operational period, the offender fails to comply with the supervisory requirements or perform other obligations imposed on him/her or commits a misdemeanour similar to the original criminal offence for which they were sentenced, the probation officer or court may decide to do one of the following:

- issue a written caution;
- impose additional obligations;
- extend the operational period by one year;
- enforce the punishment.

The Supreme Court has decided that courts must use discretion and that while they may apply some of these possible consequences when a violation is detected, they are also permitted not to apply any of these measures described in the law.[15] If an offender commits a new criminal offence during the operational period and is sentenced to imprisonment, the same consequences apply as in the case of suspension under §73 (see above).

Behavioural supervision entails a number of mandatory measures that "constitute a formal framework for behavioural control, the main purpose of which is to ensure that the convict who is at liberty is available to the state and can be monitored".[16] These mandatory measures require offenders:

(1) to reside in a permanent place of residence determined by the court;
(2) to report at intervals determined by the probation supervisor to the probation supervision department. The Supreme Court has interpreted this requirement as meaning that the offender must appear in person at the probation department, at the time specified by the probation officer, where his/her arrival is recorded. The offender is not obliged, as part of this requirement, to participate in any additional individualised activities, e.g. discussions with the probation officer;[17]
(3) to enable the probation officer to supervise him/her at his/her place of residence, and provide the probation officer with information relating to the performance of the offender's obligations and his/her means of subsistence;
(4) to obtain permission from the probation officer before leaving his/her place of residence for longer than fifteen days;
(5) to obtain permission from the probation officer before changing his/her place of residence, study or employment;
(6) to obtain permission from a probation officer before leaving the territory of Estonia.

Taking into consideration the circumstances of the criminal offence committed and the characteristics of the offender, the court may decide, in addition to the above-listed mandatory requirements, to impose any or all of the following obligations on the offender during the operational period of behavioural supervision:

(1) to remedy the damage caused by the criminal offence within a deadline determined by the court. The damage must be repaid in full (not in part) and the deadline cannot exceed the length of the operational period;[18]
(2) not to consume alcohol. The Supreme Court has ruled that the courts may oblige offenders subject to this requirement to present the results of blood tests to the probation officer at regular intervals and to bear the cost of such tests;[19]
(3) not to possess or use narcotic drugs or psychotropic substances;
(4) not to possess, carry or use weapons;
(5) to seek employment or acquire general education or vocational training within a deadline determined by the court;
(6) to undergo prescribed treatment to which the offender has previously consented;
(7) to pay maintenance (alimony);
(8) not to frequent specific places as determined by the court or communicate with specific persons as determined by the court;

(9) to participate in social programmes;
(10) to submit to electronic surveillance to which the offender has previously consented;
(11) to submit to surveillance relative to the prohibition of alcohol consumption by means of an electronic device, if the offender has previously consented to such surveillance;
(12) other obligations with the purpose of improving the offender's conduct, to which the offender has agreed.

The introduction of the last of these optional obligations is a welcome indication of support for restorative justice, and in private communications prosecutors have indicated that this option is becoming more and more popular.

The courts may, during the operational period, taking into consideration the circumstances of the criminal offence and the characteristics of the offender, decide to **mitigate or annul** obligations that were imposed on an offender for the period of behavioural supervision, **or impose additional obligations** on the offender.

Compliance with supervisory obligations is not required from offenders who are serving the custodial part of a partially suspended prison sentence. If an offender has complied with the supervisory requirements determined for him/her on the basis of subsections 1–4 of this section for at least six months of the operational period and has fulfilled the obligations imposed on him or her, the court may release the offender from further compliance with the supervisory requirements and obligations imposed on him/her for the operational period. The offender is nevertheless still required to refrain from committing new criminal offences within the operational period.

Electronic surveillance (Penal Code, § 75[1])

Electronic surveillance is a measure sometimes used in combination with suspended prison sentences and supervised suspended prison sentences, or release on parole. Electronic surveillance is an obligation imposed on an offender for a period of time determined by the court, requiring the offender to comply with the use of electronic devices:

- to monitor their compliance with restrictions on freedom of movement; or
- to monitor their consumption of narcotic drugs, psychotropic substances or alcohol.

The type of device used for electronic surveillance (this may be either a device attached to the offender's leg that communicates with a home security device or a GPS active tracking device that allows determining the location of a person serving a suspended prison sentence in real time) is chosen by the probation officer. Prior to initiating the use of electronic surveillance, the court orders a medical examination of the offender as necessary in order to verify whether the offender's state of health permits his/her electronic surveillance. The court may order electronic surveillance for a period of between one and twelve months. That period begins on the date on which the electronic surveillance device is attached to the offender's body. The court may extend or shorten the period of electronic surveillance imposed on an offender, but the total period of electronic surveillance must still be in the range of 1–12 months. If an offender withdraws his/her consent for electronic surveillance prior to the end of the allotted period, the court may order the enforcement of the part of the punishment that was not served.

The work of the probation service

Since the new probation system was established in 1998, the proportion of suspended prison sentences has increased in judicial practice year by year, reaching half of all sentences (47.6%) by 2003. In 2004, more than twice as many suspended prison sentences (supervised and unsupervised; 3175 sentences in total) were imposed as non-suspended prison sentences (1630). At the same time, the average length of non-suspended prison sentences imposed by the courts has also become shorter (Brügel, 2006, p. 81). During the last ten years, the use of suspended sentences has increased due to a decrease in the use of pecuniary punishments (see Figure 9.1) that has resulted from these being very difficult to enforce due to offenders lacking official income and property.[20]

The probation system is regulated by the Probation Supervision Act, which was adopted on 17 December 1997 and entered into force on 1 May 1998. To begin with, probation departments were established at county and city courts. Ten years later, a new law established a probation service within the prison system (Ministry of Justice, 2013). The number of probation officers has increased over the years; by the end of 2005, there were 195 probation officers in Estonia and a total of 8099 persons serving suspended prison sentences under their supervision (Ministry of Justice, 2006, p. 11). Since 2005, the number of persons serving suspended prison sentences has declined in correlation with the reduction in the crime rate (see Figure 9.4). The number of probation officers has not declined (Ministry of Justice, 2020).

Figure 9.4 depicts the fact that suspended prison sentences are used significantly more than imprisonment (non-suspended prison sentences). The imprisonment rate has declined constantly over the period shown. Since the crime rate has also been declining, the number of persons serving suspended prison sentences has also been declining since the probation service became fully operational in 2009.

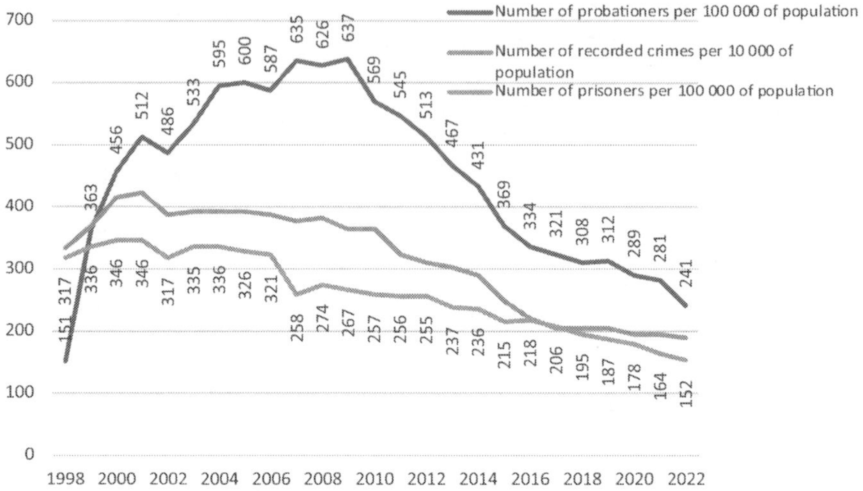

Figure 9.4 Comparison of suspended prison sentences, recorded crimes, and imprisonment rates from 1998 to 2022.

Source: Data from Statistics Estonia and the Ministry of Justice.

Situations in which suspended prison sentence is not available

There are several circumstances in which the Supreme Court has decided that supervised suspended prison sentences should not be applied. These include:

(1) If the offender has committed a serious crime against another person, i.e.:
- intentional homicide;[21]
- extremely serious bodily harm resulting in death;[22]
- aggravated rape or sexual gratification in an unnatural manner;[23]
- repeated humiliation of the dignity of fellow human beings through violent actions.[24]

(2) If the offender has committed a traffic offence under aggravating circumstances, for example:
- caused a traffic accident while under the influence of alcohol, as a result of which the victim died;[25]
- caused a serious traffic accident, then left the scene and went into hiding, but later tried to hide the traces of the crime to avoid responsibility for the death of two persons and mislead the investigation;[26]
- caused the deaths of two people while driving a car at 90 km/h (40 km/h above the speed limit) in a crowded place in the city centre;[27]

- drove a motor vehicle under the influence of alcohol three times; the last crime was committed during the operational period;[28]
- was punished 13 times for driving a motor vehicle while intoxicated, but these administrative punishments have not persuaded him to behave law-abidingly.[29]

(3) If the offender has committed a dangerous crime, for example:
- has used an official weapon issued to him by the state to criminally attack others; [30]
- has acquired narcotic substances for the purpose of distribution; [31]
- has committed a large number of crimes (e.g. nine second-degree crimes within two weeks).[32]

The history of suspended prison sentences in Estonia

Before gaining its independence in 1918, Estonia was under Russian rule. The Baltic provinces (Estland, Livland, and Courland) had their own law, based on the privileges confirmed in the Acts of Capitulation of 1710 and the Peace Treaty of Uusikaupunki in 1721, and later confirmations of these privileges by the Russian rulers. On 15 August 1845, Tsar Nicholas I decreed that Russia's first systematised set of criminal law norms would enter into force on 1 May 1846 in the whole of the Russian Empire, including the Baltic provinces (Kivistik, 2012, pp. 169–170).

After Estonia gained its independence in 1918, the Penal Code of the Russian Czar of 1845 (Уложение о наказаниях уголовных и исправительных) remained in force. The first legislative initiative in the field of criminal law during the first period of Estonian statehood (i.e. before the Second World War) was the adoption of suspended sentencing law by the Riigikogu on 2 July 1920, entering into force on 16 August 1920 (Seadus tingimisi süüdimõistmise kohta, 2.juuli 1920.a.-Riigi Teataja 1920, 119/120, 247). This legislation introduced suspended prison sentences for offences usually punishable with prison sentences of up to 18 months, for which the offender had been sentenced to up to 6 months' imprisonment. The sentence could not be suspended if the offender "had been earlier punished by a stricter punishment than a short-term arrest or suspended prison sentence". The sentence could be suspended for up to 3 years. If during this period the offender was punished for an offence by up to three months' arrest, the suspension could be revoked and if punished by more severe punishment than three months' arrest the revocation was mandatory.

The 1920 Act did not include any provisions regarding supervised suspended prison sentence.

In essence, this legislation meant that the Estonian courts could begin to suspend prison sentences for certain offenders, as a result of which those offenders would not need to serve their sentences in custody. Initially, the courts and police oversaw offenders serving suspended sentences; later, prisoner care societies were formed which were tasked with taking care of offenders after their release from prison, supervising persons placed under supervision by the court, and taking care of incarcerated prisoners' moral development and cultural needs. Hence, although the 1920 Act did not create a probation authority nor any detailed rules for supervision during the operational period, the resulting system was a combination of the French and US models of suspended prison sentence.

The new legislation was designed to help criminals not to be a danger or a loss to society, but to learn to act according to common norms and rules. Thus, in early 20th century Estonia, the principles were similar to the modern suspended prison sentence: on the one hand, supervision and control, and on the other hand, promoting adaptation into society and personality development (Laane, 2013, p. 2). After Estonia was occupied by Russia in 1944, the 1926 Criminal Code of the Russian Federation was enforced. According to Articles 53 and 54 of that code, a prison sentence could be suspended if the court was satisfied that the offender's degree of dangerousness did not require the execution of the prison sentence. If an offender whose prison sentence had been suspended committed a new crime during the operational period, the court might partially or fully add the original suspended sentence to the new sentence for the new crime.

The Criminal Code of the Estonian Soviet Socialist Republic entered into force on 1 April 1961. In this code, suspended prison sentences were provided for in § 47. The measure was referred to not as suspension but as "conditional conviction", which the court could apply in the event of a positive special prognosis, i.e. if the court found that it was not appropriate for the offender to serve the imposed sentence. The idea was that the offender's behaviour could be corrected and the offender re-educated through the "active participation of the Soviet public". The operational period was set for between one and five years. In the event that the offender committed a new intentional act during the operational period, which was punishable by imprisonment, the court would sentence him/her to an aggregated punishment. Conditional conviction (suspension) was considered justified if there were one or more mitigating circumstances, but special attention had to be paid to the characteristics of the offender, in particular whether they were a person "whom the release from punishment stimulates to a blameless life" (ENSV KrK, § 47). Assessment took into account the offender's behaviour after committing the crime (confession of guilt, reparation of damage) as well as whether the crime could be considered incidental in the context of the offender's life. Conditional conviction (suspension) was usually applied for crimes of low social danger (Rebane, 1980, § 47, comments 3–4).

Shortly after Estonia regained its independence in 1991, an amended Criminal Code was introduced in 1992 to reflect the changes in society. The measure described in § 47 was now "conditional non-application of deprivation of liberty", but in essence, the instrument remained the same. The 1992 Criminal Code provided that if the court, taking into account the circumstances and characteristics of the offender, found that serving the prison sentence was not expedient, that sentence could be suspended. In this case, the court would determine that the sentence need not be executed, provided that the offender did not commit a new intentional crime punished by a prison sentence during the operational period set by the court, and provided that the offender fulfilled all obligations imposed on him/her. The operational period was set for between one and three years. When applying this measure, the court could oblige the offender to repay damages by a certain deadline, to start work or study, to inform the police authority of any change of residence, work or study, to appear periodically for registration at the police authority and/or to undergo a course of treatment for alcoholism, drug addiction, abuse of toxic substances or venereal disease.

If the offender did not fulfil the obligations imposed on him/her by the court, or violated public order or work discipline during the operational period, for which administrative or disciplinary sanctions were applied, the court could, at the request of the police authority, revoke the suspension and order the offender to serve the sentence originally imposed. If the offender committed a new intentional crime during the operational period, for which he/she was sentenced to imprisonment, the court would impose an aggregate punishment (Penal Code 1992, § 47). Suspended prison sentences are thus currently a longstanding and stable part of the Estonian system of criminal punishment. More than half of all criminal trials result in suspended prison sentences and there is no major opposition to their broad usage.

Notes

1 Penal Code, Official Gazette RT I 2001, 61, 364 as amended by RT I, 06.07.2023, 6, https://www.riigiteataja.ee/akt/106072023040?leiaKehtiv, English translation available: https://www.riigiteataja.ee/en/eli/ee/502012024009/consolide/current.

Penal Code, 1992, Official Gazette RT 1992, 20, 288, https://www.riigiteataja.ee/akt/22221.

2 RKKKo 1-19-4150, p. 26, https://rikos.rik.ee/?asjaNr=1-19-4150/132. RKKKo is an abbreviation that stands for "Judgment of the Supreme Court's Criminal Chamber".

3 RKKKo 3-1-1-18-11, p. 26, https://www.riigikohus.ee/et/lahendid?asjaNr=3-1-1-18-11.

4 In Estonia, misdemeanor cases may be decided by a court, or the Police and Border-Guard Board, or another administrative body. The latter are referred to in legal acts as "a body conducting out of court proceedings".

5 Community service and electronic monitoring are not principal punishments. These measures can be applied only if the court has first imposed a prison sentence and subsequently decides that under the circumstances of the case imprisonment is not necessary and may be substituted for community service or electronic surveillance. These measures are referred to as "substitute punishments".

6 "Conditional release from punishment" is the term used by the Estonian legislator.

7 RKKKo 3-1-1-66-10, p. 11.4, https://rikos.rik.ee/LahendiOtsingEriVaade?asjaNr=3-1-1-66-10.

8 Penal Code (01.09.2002), https://www.riigiteataja.ee/akt/106082022027.

9 Estonian Penal Code differentiates between unsupervised suspended prison sentence and supervised suspended prison sentence that imposes supervisory requirements on the offender and allows requiring the person to perform certain obligations.
10 Tartu County Court judgment of 18 September 2018 in Case No 1-18-7437, https://www.riigiteataja.ee/kohtulahendid/fail.html?id=234114515.
11 The same conditions apply to the non-suspended part in the case of a supervised suspended prison sentence.
12 RKKKo 3-1-1-96-11, 7.4, https://www.riigikohus.ee/et/lahendid?asjaNr=3-1-1-96-11.
13 RKKKo 1-19-7945, p. 31, https://www.riigiteataja.ee/kohtulahendid/fail.html?id=293282227.
14 The length of community service is calculated based on the rule that one day of imprisonment corresponds to one hour of community service.
15 RKKKo 5-20-11/9, p. 17, https://rikos.rik.ee/?asjaNr=5-20-11/9.
16 RKKKo 1-21-5058/25, p. 10, https://rikos.rik.ee/?asjaNr=1-21-5058/25).
17 RKKKo 1-21-5058/25, p. 8, https://rikos.rik.ee/?asjaNr=1-21-5058/25.
18 RKKKo 3-1-1-126-03, p. 8, https://rikos.rik.ee/?asjaNr=3-1-1-126-03.
19 RKKKo 5-20-11/9, p. 21, https://rikos.rik.ee/?asjaNr=5-20-11/9.
20 There is no data suggesting that the percentage of offenders who are unable to pay fines has increased. Just the perception of difficulties in enforcement has indicated that fines are not a suitable punishment for many offenders.
21 RKKKo III-1/1-5/95, https://www.riigikohus.ee/et/lahendid?asjaNr=III-1/1-5/95. The statutory minimum sentence for intentional homicide is 6 years' imprisonment. But Penal Code § 61 allows the court to take special circumstances into consideration and to impose a less onerous punishment than the minimum term provided by law. Suspended prison sentences have sometimes been imposed for aiding in homicide.
22 RKKKo III-1/1-31/95, https://www.riigikohus.ee/et/lahendid?asjaNr=III-1/1-31/95.
23 RKKKo 3-1-1-100-96, https://www.riigikohus.ee/et/lahendid?asjaNr=3-1-1-100-96. Before 23 December 2013, anal and oral intercourse against the victim's will were qualified separately. Since 23 December 2013, these have been classified as rape.
24 RKKKo 3-1-1-11-02, https://www.riigikohus.ee/et/lahendid?asjaNr=3-1-1-11-02.
25 RKKKo 3-1-1-90-97, https://www.riigikohus.ee/et/lahendid?asjaNr=3-1-1-90-97.
26 RKKKo 3-1-1-13-99, https://www.riigikohus.ee/et/lahendid?asjaNr=3-1-1-13-99.
27 RKKKo 3-1-1-82-00, p. 7.3, https://www.riigikohus.ee/et/lahendid?asjaNr=3-1-1-82-00.
28 RKKKo 3-1-1-77-01, p. 8.1, https://www.riigikohus.ee/et/lahendid?asjaNr=3-1-1-77-01.
29 (RKKKo 3-1-1-26-03, p. 5, https://www.riigikohus.ee/et/lahendid?asjaNr=3-1-1-26-03.
30 RKKKo 3-1-1-47-98, https://www.riigikohus.ee/et/lahendid?asjaNr=3-1-1-47-98.
31 RKKKo 3-1-1-111-01, p. 5.1, https://www.riigikohus.ee/et/lahendid?asjaNr=3-1-1-111-01.
32 RKKKo 3-1-1-129-97, https://www.riigikohus.ee/et/lahendid?asjaNr=3-1-1-129-97.

References

Ahven, A., Kruusement, A., & Salla, J. (2013). Tingimisi vabastamise ja käitumiskontrolli kohaldamise analüüs. *Kriminaalpoliitika analüüs* Nr *3/2013* Tallinn.
Brügel, V. (2006). *Alternatives to imprisonment* (in Estonian). Tallinn.

Criminal Code (Kriminaalkoodeks). Official Gazette ÜVT 1961, No. 1(54). https://www.digar.ee/viewer/et/nlib-digar:271718/246293/page/5

Demuth, A. (2003). *Politics, migration and minorities in independent and Soviet Estonia, 1918–1998* [Dissertation, Universität Osnabrück].

Kivistik, (2012). Kohtuniku ees seisab kaks jumalat, kaks õigust ja kibe tarvidus ühte kui teist ehk mõlemaid korraga teenida. *Juridica, 2012*(3).

Laane, E. (2013). Kriminaalhooldus – võimalus vabaduseks. *Vangla Ekspress, 2013*(6).

Lobjak, O. (2013). *Kriminaalhooldusaluste retsidiivsus ja retsidiivsuse riskitegurid, Rapla maakonna näitel*. Tallinn.

Meelak, I. (2002, March 12). Pros and cons: Are the courts too lenient? *Eesti Päevaleht*.

Meissner, B. (1992). Baltic states. In R. Bernhardt (Ed.), *Encyclopedia of public international law* (Vol. 1). Elsevier.

Ministry of Justice. (2006). *Estonian prison system and probation supervision yearbook, 2006*. https://www.vangla.ee/sites/www.vangla.ee/files/elfinder/dokumendid/aastaraamat_2006_kodulehele.pdf (in Estonian)

Ministry of Justice. (2013). *15 years have passed since the re-establishment of Estonian probation*. https://www.just.ee/et/uudised/moodus-15-aastat-eesti-kriminaalhoolduse-taasasutamisest (in Estonian)

Ministry of Justice. (2020). *Prison service 2020 review*. https://www.vangla.ee/et/uudised-ja-arvud/vanglateenistuse-2020-aasta-ulevaade (in Estonian).

Piirimäe, H. (1997). Historical heritage: The Relations between Estonia and her Nordic neighbors. In M. Lauristin & P. Vihalemm (Eds.), *Return to the Western World: Cultural and political perspectives on the Estonian post-communist transition*. Tartu University Press.

Rätsep, L. (2016, October 18). Are the sentences too soft? *Saarte Hääl*. (in Estonian).

Rauch, G. (1995). *The Baltic states: The years of independence. Estonia, Latvia, Lithuania 1917–1940*. St. Martin's Press.

Rebane, I. (1980). *Eesti NSV kriminaalkoodeks: Kommenteeritud väljaanne*. Eesti Raamat.

Salla, J. (2014). Karistuse asendamist ja karistusest vabastamist puudutavad muudatused. *Juridica, 2014*(8).

Sootak, J. (1998). Kuriteomõiste ja õigusriiklik kriminaalõigus. Kolme-elemendilisest kuriteomõistest karistusseadustiku üldosa eelnõus. *Juridica, 1998*(1), 23–27.

Titma, M. (1997). Estonia on the eve of independence. *International Journal of Sociology, 26*(1), 7–19.

Penal Code (Karistusseadustik) (01.09.2002). Official Gazette RT I 2001, 61, 364. https://www.riigiteataja.ee/akt/184411

Penal Code (Karistusseadustik), as amended by RT I, 06.07.2023, 6. Official Gazette RT I 2001, 61, 364. https://www.riigiteataja.ee/akt/184411?leiaKehtiv; English translation available: https://www.riigiteataja.ee/en/eli/ee/530092022005/consolide/current

Probation Supervision Act (Kriminaalhooldusseadus), as amended by RT I, 06.08.2022, 5. Official Gazette RT I 1998, 4, 62. https://www.riigiteataja.ee/akt/106082022024?leiaKehtiv; English translation available: https://www.riigiteataja.ee/en/eli/ee/525082022004/consolide/current

10 Suspended prison sentences in Russia

Gennady Esakov and Ekaterina Khodzhaeva

Introduction

Like any other punishment, the regime in which suspended prison sentences are imposed depends substantially on the social and legal background in each jurisdiction. It is influenced by the jurisdiction's general penal policy and crime level, and also by informal penal policy, which includes the conflicting interests of prosecutors, courts, and defendants. This regime should thus be analysed not as a single penal option among many, constituting a small part of the criminal legislation, but rather as a part of the complex machinery of criminal justice.

This chapter explains how the suspended prison sentence regime (or conditional conviction[1], as it is known in Russian criminal law) works in Russian criminal law today. Unlike some other legal systems, Russia has only one such regime, which combines the suspension of the prison sentence with supervision. It is regulated by the current Russian Criminal Code (hereafter "the RCC"), which was enacted on 13 June 1996 and came into force on 1 January 1997.

In this chapter, we describe the legal groundwork for this punishment policy, shaped by the legislation and Russian Supreme Court decisions. We also use a corpus of official statistics provided by the Judicial Department of the Supreme Court (JDSC) for the general public[2] and on request[3] together with some data from the Penal Service[4] to show the main dynamic trends in this punishment policy. We focus primarily on the period 2002–2020. The chapter begins with a short overview of the main outcomes of criminal trials. We then consider trends in the use of punishment options during the last two decades, in particular suspended sentencing, and finally, we look at the role this punishment plays in the current Russian criminal system, given that system's pro-conviction bias.

Sentencing overview

Russian criminal justice is usually described in the literature as very repressive and with a strong pro-conviction bias. Focusing on criminal justice outcomes and in particular the low level of acquittals (only 0.2% of publicly prosecuted defendants are acquitted) in the criminal statistics, academic scholars refer to an *accusatorial bias of the Russian criminal courts* as a result of the pretrial

DOI: 10.4324/9781003568667-14

screening of all cases (Solomon, 2015, 2018) and the mutual cooperation of all state agencies (including the courts) to achieve better key performance indicators (KPI) during the pretrial and trial stages of criminal cases (Paneyakh, 2014; Paneyakh et al., 2018). The current KPI rules count acquittals and other total rehabilitation outcomes as indicators of very bad quality work on the part of all state agencies involved in the criminal case (prosecutors, investigators, detectives, and others), forcing them to appeal against any acquittal. This practice effectively makes the judiciary the final module in a massive criminal case conveyor. As a result, judges are very loyal to the decisions made by investigators and prosecutors during the pretrial stages of the investigation.

The pro-conviction bias is a result of extralegal factors and the everyday routine inside the Russian court system (which also includes police and other investigatory bodies; McCarthy, 2015; Moiseeva, 2014; Pomorski, 2001). In these conditions, the formal opportunities for the defence party to obtain an acquittal or other equivalent dismissal of the case[5] are very limited (Moiseeva, 2016; Khodzhaeva & Rabovski, 2016). As a result, the type and duration of punishment are the key focus of plea bargaining in Russia.[6] Suspended sentences, together with other kinds of sanctions without real imprisonment, may in many cases be considered quasi-acquittals.

However, it is important to note that the pro-conviction bias does not mean that practically all outcomes are convictions. Only three-quarters of defendants are convicted in criminal courts in the strict sense, i.e. declared guilty and sentenced to punishment. This rate has remained quite stable during the last two decades despite reductions in the total flow of criminal offenders passing through the criminal justice system, from more than 1.2 million per year in the mid-2000s to less than 800,000 per year in the 2020s. The majority of defendants who are not convicted are *released from criminal liability due to the dismissal of the criminal case.* This means that the defendant is released unconditionally (despite pleading guilty during the investigation or trial phase[7]) without a full trial, sentencing or punishment. As a rule, this release is applicable only to petty crimes and is conditional upon active repentance or reconciliation with the victim (Arts 75, 76 of the RCC), compensation for inflicted damages in specifically listed crimes, mainly economic crimes (Art. 76^1 of the RCC), or the payment of a "judicial fine" (Art. 76^2 of the RCC).[8] These releases from criminal responsibility (commonly known as non-rehabilitative grounds for release) are the second most common outcome: 20–24% of defendants; the majority (18–13%) of such dismissals were issued upon reconciliation of the parties.

A defendant accused of a non-severe crime has two options, the first of which is to get their case dismissed on non-rehabilitative grounds. This is a much more lenient option than the second, i.e. a conviction, because the offender does not get a full entry on his/her criminal record but only a note indicating that s/he was under criminal trial. In 2021, only 76.6% of all defendants in criminal trials were convicted and sentenced; all the other defendants (not taking into account acquittals, the rate of which is less than 0.5%) were released from criminal liability on non-rehabilitative grounds.

The suspended prison sentence regime may be applied only when the defendant has been convicted and sentenced.

After a conviction decision, there are currently 12 types of sanctions (Art. 43 of the RCC)[9] that may be imposed. The most commonly used types are as follows:

- fine; this is a very popular sanction for non-severe crimes and is imposed nowadays for every eighth convicted offender. In 2021, fines were used as the main sanction for 12% of convicted offenders (68,232 offenders) and as an additional punishment for 1.5% (8,588 offenders);
- compulsory work; this has been permitted since 2005 and nowadays every sixth convicted offender (i.e. 16–17%) receives this kind of punishment;
- corrective labour[10] is also a popular punishment (8–10% per year). In the majority of cases, this is effectively a fine: if the convicted person has a permanent job, he or she must pay between 5% and 25% of the salary for a period of between two months and two years;
- imprisonment for a fixed term (at least 2 months and at most 20 years for a single crime or 35 years for multiple crimes); this is a dominant type of punishment. In 2021, about 56% of all convicted offenders were sentenced to fixed-term imprisonment. Of them, 158,923 offenders were handed non-suspended prison sentences (incarceration) and 158,768 persons received suspended prison sentences.

These punishments may be applied either: (i) only as a principal sanction (compulsory work; corrective labour; restriction of military service; compulsory labour; arrest, imprisonment in a disciplinary military unit; imprisonment for a fixed term; life imprisonment); (ii) only as a secondary sanction, i.e. in addition to another sanction (deprivation of a special or military rank or honorary title, class rank, or government award); or (iii) as either a principal or secondary sanction depending on the crime committed (fine; deprivation of the right to hold specific offices or to engage in specific activities; restriction of liberty). Some punishments have restrictions on their enforcement based on the personal characteristics of the defendant (for example, life imprisonment cannot be applied to any offender who is less than 18 or more than 65 years of age).

Judicial discretion in sentencing is considerable. As a basic rule, the court has wide discretion in choosing the type of punishment,[11] or at least in determining the exact length or amount of that punishment.[12] The judge should determine this on the basis of his/her appraisal of the deed and of the offender's personal characteristics. There are two long lists of mitigating and aggravating circumstances (Arts 61, 63 of the RCC) but they (with limited exceptions) do not have any quantitative effect on sentencing.

In cases of multiple crimes, the court may use either an all-inclusive approach to determine the final punishment – the most severe punishment becomes the final one – or a summative approach, in which the final punishment does not exceed one-and-a-half times the most severe punishment, or 25 (in specified cases 30) years of imprisonment.

To summarise the main numbers related to convictions, sentencing, and acquittals, in 2021 565,523 persons were convicted and sentenced (of these, 317,691 persons were sentenced to imprisonment); 162,521 persons were released from criminal liability in court proceedings; and 2,315 persons were acquitted.

Principles governing suspended prison sentences at present

In terms of criminal legislation, the suspended prison sentence regime is a type of *release from punishment*, a category of outcome that includes not only the widely applied suspended (prison[13]) sentence (Art. 73 of the RCC), but also conditional early release from punishment (Art. 79 of the RCC); release from punishment due to illness (Art. 81 of the RCC); and deferral of punishment for pregnant women, women with dependent children aged below 14 years of age or men who are single parents to children below 14 years of age (Art. 82 of the RCC). Release from punishment may only be imposed by the court after the full trial and sentencing procedures.

Given that suspended prison sentences are a type of release from punishment, they are applied as a twofold construct. Firstly, the legal prerequisites for a release must be established and secondly, the court determines the factual basis for such a release.

(i) The legal prerequisite of suspended sentences. Article 73(1) of the RCC provides that a suspended prison sentence[14] shall be imposed only on convicted persons who are sentenced to imprisonment for a term of up to eight years. It does not matter what punishment is prescribed for the crime in question – the suspension of the prison sentence depends on the punishment actually imposed in the given case.

The eight-year limit is a legislative accident caused by one abnormal case and introduced in 2003. Before 2003, conditional conviction was theoretically applicable to *any* term of imprisonment. However, there was a widespread tradition, both in practice and in theory, that suspension should not be applied to any sentence of more than five years of imprisonment[15]. This limit was in line with the maximum term for the operational period of a suspended sentence: it would be strange to suspend a sentence that was longer than the operational period of its suspension. However, in 2001, the former Minister of Justice, Valentin Kovalev, was sentenced for bribery and larceny to nine years of imprisonment with a five-year operational period. This verdict was controversial within the legal community, and thereafter, the eight-year limit was proposed without any detailed discussion about why precisely such a limit should be adopted.

In 2012, a number of crimes were introduced for which a suspended prison sentence could not be imposed; the list of such crimes has since been enlarged and now includes (a) sexual crimes against minors under fourteen years old;[16] (b) specifically designated crimes of a terrorist nature; (c) severe or especially severe crimes[17] committed during the operational period of a suspended prison sentence or during the operational period of conditional early release from punishment, if the person was earlier sentenced for an intentional crime; (d) any crime committed under circumstances of dangerous or especially dangerous recidivism.[18]

(ii) The criminal legislation provides that there is a single factual basis on which a suspended sentence may be imposed, which is the court's conclusion that it is possible to rehabilitate the convicted person without him/her actually serving the punishment. In reaching this conclusion, the court must take into account "the nature and degree of the social danger of the crime committed, of the personality of the guilty person, and of mitigating and aggravating circumstances" (Art. 73(2) of the RCC). This provision is not further elaborated by either criminal legislation or jurisprudence. The factual basis for suspended sentences is thus often viewed as an intuitive decision by the judge.

To impose a suspended prison sentence, the judge must first find the person guilty of the crime(s) they were charged with and second sentence him/her to one of the punishments applicable to those crimes (as mentioned above). If the person is found guilty of several crimes, the cumulative sentence may be suspended if it does not exceed eight years of imprisonment. In terms of criminal procedure, the decision to suspend is taken at the same stage as the decision on guilt, i.e. during the deliberations and delivery of the final verdict on the case. There is no option to suspend only part of a sentence.

When imposing a suspended prison sentence, the court determines an operational period for that suspended sentence (in Russian, this is known as the *испытательный срок*). Article 73(3) of the RCC provides that during the operational period "the person [whose sentence is suspended] should prove their rehabilitation by his behaviour".

Suspension is only possible for principal punishments. If the offender is also sentenced to secondary punishments, these punishments cannot be suspended, but must be executed. For example, if a convicted person is sentenced to both imprisonment and a fine, then the prison sentence may be suspended, but the fine must be paid.

For prison sentences of up to one year, and for more lenient punishments (corrective labour, restriction in military service, or service in a disciplinary military unit), the operational period must be no less than six months and no more than three years. For prison sentences of more than one year, the operational period must be no less than six months and no more than five years.

A court may impose specific obligations on a person whose sentence has been suspended, such as not to change his/her permanent place of residence, work or study without notifying the specialised state body that supervises the behaviour of convicted offenders, not to visit certain localities, to undergo a course of treatment for alcoholism, drug addiction, toxicology or venereal disease, to work (to find employment) or to continue studying at a general education establishment. A court may also impose other duties on a convicted person, which will assist in his/her reformation. During the operational period, the court may revoke such duties in full or in part, or supplement them, if recommended to do so by the body exercising control over the behaviour of the convicted person.

The probation period is calculated from the day on which the sentence is delivered. This legal nuance does not mean that the sentence becomes valid immediately; it may be appealed and if upheld at the appeal, will become valid only after the appeal. However, if the probation period were to be calculated from the day of appeal, the period between the trial and the appeal would constitute procedural limbo: the convicted person would not be subject to the limitations of the operational period in the time before the appeal and supposing they were to commit a new crime at that time, it could not be viewed as committed during the operational period of their suspended prison sentence. Hence a rule was introduced in 2010 that enables a suspended sentence to be revoked if the offender reoffends after the imposition of the suspended prison sentence by the first-level court, but prior to the appellate court's decision.

Supervision of the behaviour of convicted offenders is exercised by a specialised state body which is part of the Russian penitentiary service (the Federal Penitentiary Service of Russia, which is itself under the supervision of the Ministry of Justice), and is known at the local level as the "criminal executive inspection". Such supervision is mandatory and consists mainly in observation of the convicted person's fulfilment of his/her specific duties and in addressing any violations of the conditions of their operational period. Supervision of the behaviour of convicted persons who are carrying out military service is exercised by their military commanders.

Behaviour can have both positive and negative results during the operational period. Good behaviour may lead to the early termination of the suspended prison sentence. If the convicted person proves that they have changed their ways and has repaid all damages inflicted by the crime either in full or at least in part before the end of the operational period, the court may order the early termination of the operational period (Art. 74(1) of the RCC). In this case, the convicted person is fully discharged. The suspended prison sentence may be revoked once no less than half of the fixed operational period has passed. The operational period cannot be terminated before expiration of the term of the secondary punishment (in such a case, the operational period and the term of the secondary punishment are calculated concurrently, and the last one shall expire before the early termination of the operational period). This practice is rarely used by the courts. In 2021, there were only 16,449 such motions, three-quarters of which were granted (whereas 240,485 persons were under supervision related to suspended sentences). The small number of such motions is explained by the fact that they may only be initiated by the supervising body and not by the convicted offender.

Negative behaviour during the operational period, meanwhile, may lead to the mandatory or optional revocation of the suspended prison sentence, or to the extension of the operational period.

(i) The only grounds for the mandatory revocation of a suspended prison sentence are the commission of an intentional severe or especially severe crime[19] during the operational period. In this case, the court shall revoke the suspended prison sentence. The punishment determined at sentence imposition is taken as non-executed in full, irrespective of the period of time that has passed between the imposition of the suspended sentence and the revocation of the suspension.
(ii) The operational period may be extended if the convicted person has evaded the duties placed on him by the court or failed to repay the damages inflicted by the crime, or has breached public order, for which he/she has been found civilly responsible. The court may extend the operational period for up to one year, even if such extension leads to the operational period exceeding the statutory maximum in total.
(iii) A suspended prison sentence may be optionally revoked if: (a) the convicted person continues to evade restitution of damages inflicted by the crime even after the operational period has been extended; or (b) the convicted person systematically[20] breaks the public peace during the operational period and has been found responsible[21] for that behaviour, or if he/she systematically[22] fails to discharge the duties placed on him/her by court, or if he/she has evaded supervision measures for more than 30 days; or (c) if the convicted person commits a negligent crime or an intentional crime of low or average severity during the operational period.

The official statistics show that the numbers of early terminations of suspended prison sentences have recently decreased. In 2008–2011, every tenth supervised convict serving a suspended sentence was granted an early termination, while in 2020–2021, this rate was approximately 5%.[23] At the same time, the judiciary more frequently supports applications from the penitentiary service to prolong the operational period: in 2008–2009, one in every five or six offenders under supervision had their probation extended; today (2020–2021), this happens to almost one in three.[24]

If the convicted offender successfully completes the operational period and fulfils the conditions set for it, he/she is not obliged to serve the sentence that was suspended. Nor is that conviction recorded on his/her criminal record; hence he/she will not be treated as a repeated offender[25] if committing a new intentional crime in future.

How and why has the system developed?

The suspended prison sentence regime is a legacy of the Soviet era. Legal scholarship has not questioned its validity or necessity as a legal concept. Rather, it is so elaborate that practically all legislative changes to this regime during the 1990s–2020s should be viewed as minor non-essential corrections. The single important innovation in the 2010s was the introduction of a set of crimes that could not be sanctioned with a suspended prison sentence. This was not the result of any negative attitudes towards suspended prison sentences (which, as a rule, were not imposed for these crimes even prior to the change) but merely a reflection of general criminal policy on severe crimes.

Firmly rooted in Russian criminal law, the suspended prison sentence is designed *de jure* as a non-repressive penal measure. As explained above, a suspended prison sentence can be imposed only if the court concludes that it is possible to rehabilitate the convicted person without that person serving a punishment.

The courts generally grant suspension in appropriate situations, it would seem: the rate of re-offence during the operational period of a suspension is quite low. During the last few decades, this rate has halved, from 9% to 4.5%.[26] This effect was even larger among juvenile offenders: in the early 2000s, 13% of convicted juveniles committed a new crime during the operational period; nowadays (2020–2021) this is only true for 4% of such persons. However, these low figures may also be partly explained by the inner motivation of the courts. In the knowledge that recidivism during a suspended sentence usually resulted in the revocation of suspension and hence in imprisonment, judges may have avoided granting suspended prison sentences to people at risk of reoffending. Remember that to impose a suspended prison sentence, the court must be satisfied that the convicted person can be rehabilitated without actually serving a punishment. Those at greater risk of criminal behaviour in future do not obviously meet this criterion.

On a practical level, suspended prison sentences have long been used *de facto* as a tool for keeping the prison population under control. This may be explained via criminal statistics.

Unfortunately, the criminal statistics of 1985–2003 do not contain detailed data on all outcomes of criminal cases. We have collected available data from various reports on the percentages of different sentences imposed (Figure 10.1). Non-suspended prison sentences remained the most popular outcome until the

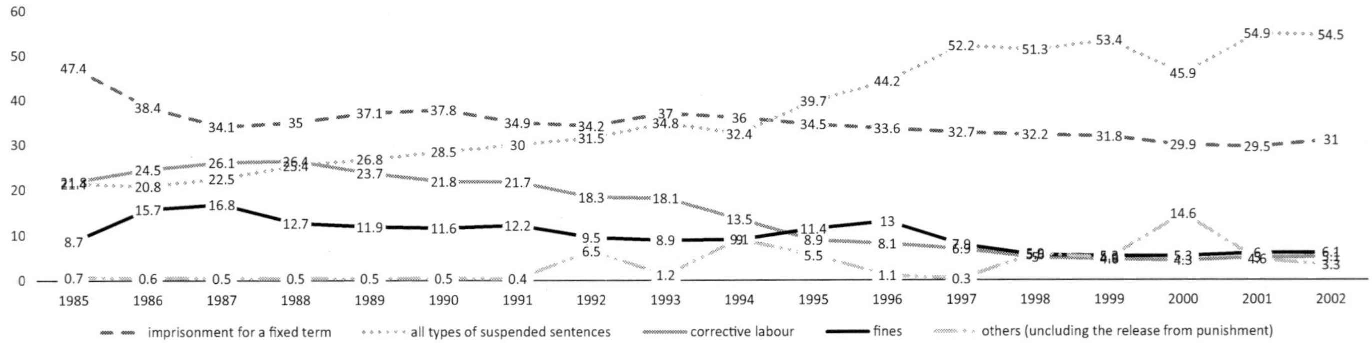

Figure 10.1 The dynamics of sentencing outcomes for convicted defendants in late Soviet and early post-Soviet Russia (1985–2003).

Source: The national economy of the RSFSR in 1989, p. 263; Crime and offences, 1991, pp. 128–129; and Russian statistical yearbook, 2002, p. 275. All data collated and recalculated by Ekaterina Khodzhaeva.

beginning of the 1990s, when suspended sentences became almost as common as imprisonment. After 1995, the use of suspended prison sentences increased rapidly, soon being awarded in more than half of all convictions, before dropping slightly following the Second World War amnesty in 2000 (that year, some offenders were pardoned under the amnesty rather than being handed suspended sentences).

As a result, during the early 2000s, more than half of all convicted offenders were handed suspended prison sentences.

In 2021, the picture is quite different: suspended sentences are used as much as non-suspended prison sentences.

Meanwhile, the share of custodial prison sentences has remained very stable: between 1987 and 2021, one in every three convicted defendants has been sent to prison.

The decreasing use of suspended prison sentences may be explained by the rise of new types of non-custodial punishment. In 2005, compulsory work was introduced and its use has grown from 3–5% in the mid-2000s to 16% in 2021. Similarly, corrective labour has been imposed more frequently, especially during the mid-2010s, and the use of fines has also increased.

It is important to note that there are no significant gender, age, and social disparities in suspended prison sentencing *de jure* in Russia.[27] As mentioned above, not all types of sanctions may be applied to women, elderly men, or minors. Both custodial sanctions (imprisonment) and some non-custodial punishments are restricted. As the criminal statistics reveal, female offenders, especially older women, are *de facto* sentenced to imprisonment less frequently than men. Men of retirement age are also less frequently imprisoned. These reductions are not, however, reflected in a significantly higher rate of suspended prison sentencing for these groups of offenders; rather, the judiciary prefers to turn to alternative non-custodial sanctions for women and older men. This is particularly true for women of retirement age, who are sentenced to fines more frequently than other categories of offenders. This approach is likely driven by humane and social reasons: the judiciary prefers to impose fines, which may sometimes be paid in instalments, over suspended prison sentences with the socially restrictive conditions they entail. The rate of suspended prison sentencing is only higher for female offenders who are pregnant or have very young children, perhaps because punishments involving work are less suitable for this group of offenders and hence judges must realistically choose between just two non-custodial sanctions: suspended prison sentences or fines. Given that these offenders face the financial burdens of childcare, judges logically prefer to impose suspended prison sentences in such cases; the conditions these entail, such as not changing one's permanent place of residence or not visiting certain localities, are not perceived as problematic for this group of offenders.

To summarise our main empirical findings, the suspended prison sentence regime has three main penal functions in Russia today. Firstly, it enables the

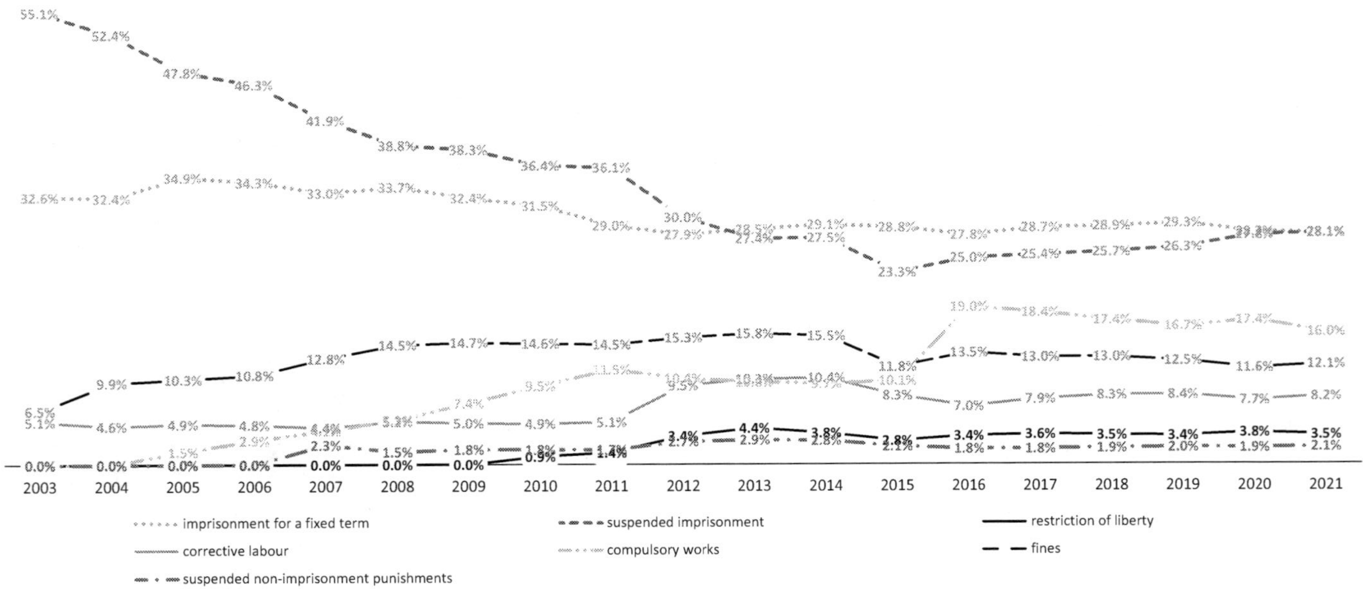

Figure 10.2 The dynamics of sentencing outcomes for convicted offenders (2003–2021). (In 2015, there was a large amnesty to mark the anniversary of Russia's victory in the Great Patriotic War and the Second World War. That year again, some offenders were pardoned under the amnesty rather than being handed suspended sentences. This reduced the share of suspended prison sentences imposed in 2015 to 23% of convicted offenders.)

prison population to be kept at what is considered a reasonable level. Secondly, it serves as non-custodial punishments when other non-custodial sanctions are not available. Thirdly, they are used as a mitigation instrument to reduce the over-penalisation of certain crimes.

The use of suspended sentences to maintain the prison population at a reasonable level may be illustrated using the example of drug crimes. During the last decade, the number of reported drug crimes rose. Meanwhile, the prison sentencing ranges for those crimes also increased, and as a result, convicted drug criminals soon made up approximately one-third of the prison population.[28] The Russian judiciary used two strategies to keep the prison population at what it considered an acceptable level for these crimes. For those who were convicted of more severe drug crimes (illegal behaviour with drugs on a large scale and without intent to sell which is subject to imprisonment for between 3 and 10 years: 22,158 convicted offenders in 2021), judges widely used suspended prison sentences: the rate of this outcome rose from 52% in 2009 to 64% in 2021 (Figure 10.3). For less severe crimes (illegal behaviour with drugs not on a large scale and without intent to sell, which is punishable by a fine, certain types of work, or imprisonment for up to 3 years; 34,409 convicted offenders in 2021), the judiciary did not choose to award suspended prison sentences so frequently, but made greater use of other non-custodial outcomes (especially fines) (Figure 10.4).

Suspended prison sentences are also widely used by the courts in cases where non-custodial sentences are not available. As a result, when additional non-custodial options are enabled, the rate of suspended prison sentencing decreases.

For example, in 2010 the sanction known as restriction of liberty was introduced. As a result, the rate of suspended prison sentences imposed in cases involving illegal behaviour with weapons and ammunition (Art. 222(1) of the RCC) decreased from 73% in 2009 to 45% in 2021 (Figure 10.5). 40% of offenders convicted of these offences are now sentenced to the non-custodial punishment known as restriction of liberty (Figure 10.6).

On the other hand, for a similar crime introduced into the criminal legislation in 2014, Art 222[1] of the RCC states that illegal behaviour with explosives or explosive devices has no other type of punishment prescribed except imprisonment. As a result, the rate of suspended sentences awarded for this crime is high.

Lastly, courts sometimes use suspended prison sentences to mitigate for mistakenly over-penalised crimes.

For example, since 2018 the number of offenders convicted under Art. 158(3) of the RCC (aggravated theft) has increased. This crime was introduced to the criminal code following an increase in the number of "card thefts" (i.e. improper use of stolen credit cards, etc.), and is punishable with a fine, compulsory work, or imprisonment of up to 6 years. However, its introduction led to an obvious disparity in sentencing: cash theft of up to 2500 roubles is not a crime at all (it is an administrative offence and only considered a crime in special circumstances) but under the new law, theft with a card was a serious crime irrespective of the

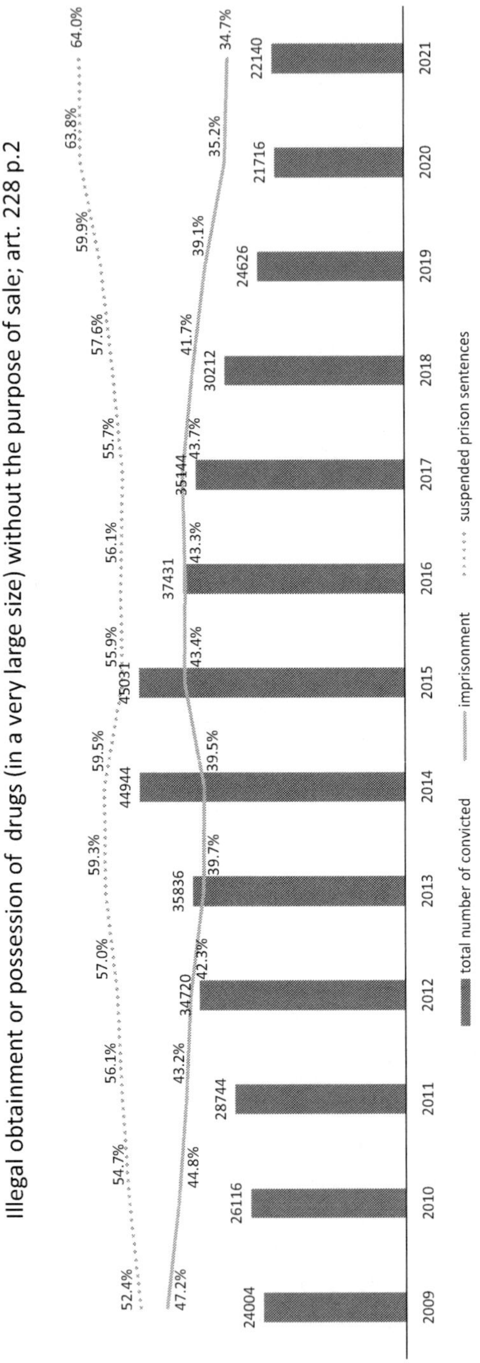

Figure 10.3 Illegal obtainment or possession of drugs (on a large scale) without the purpose of sale; art. 228(2).

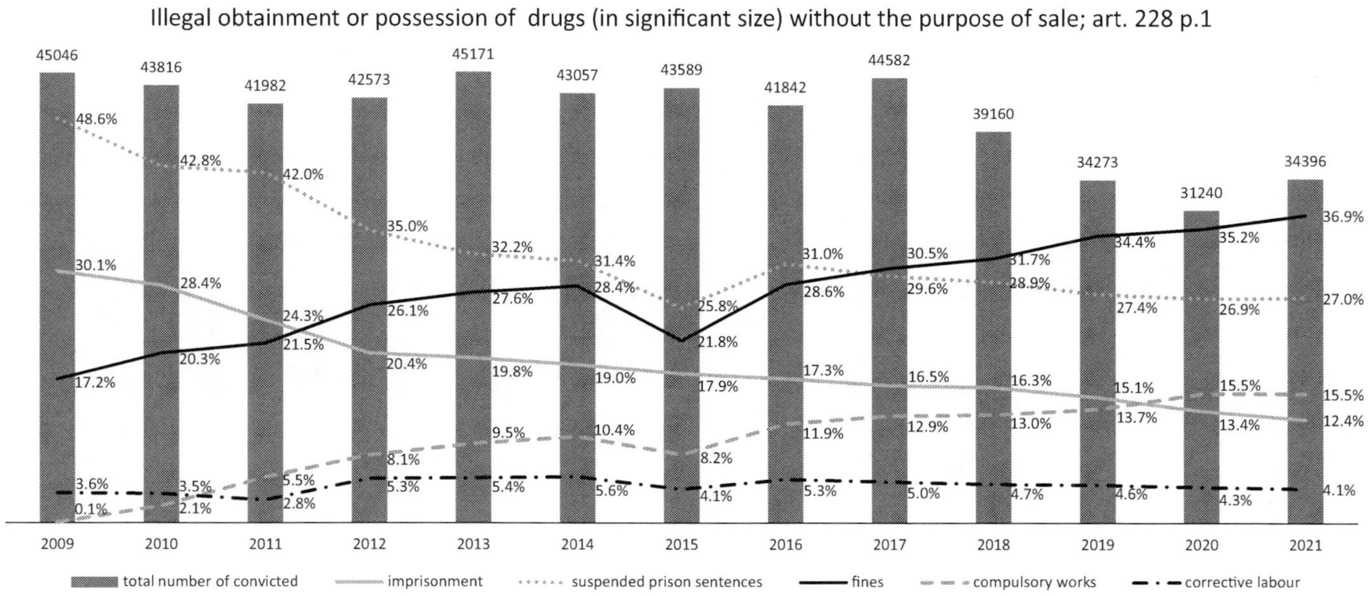

Figure 10.4 Illegal obtainment or possession of drugs (in significant size) without the purpose of sale; art. 228(1).

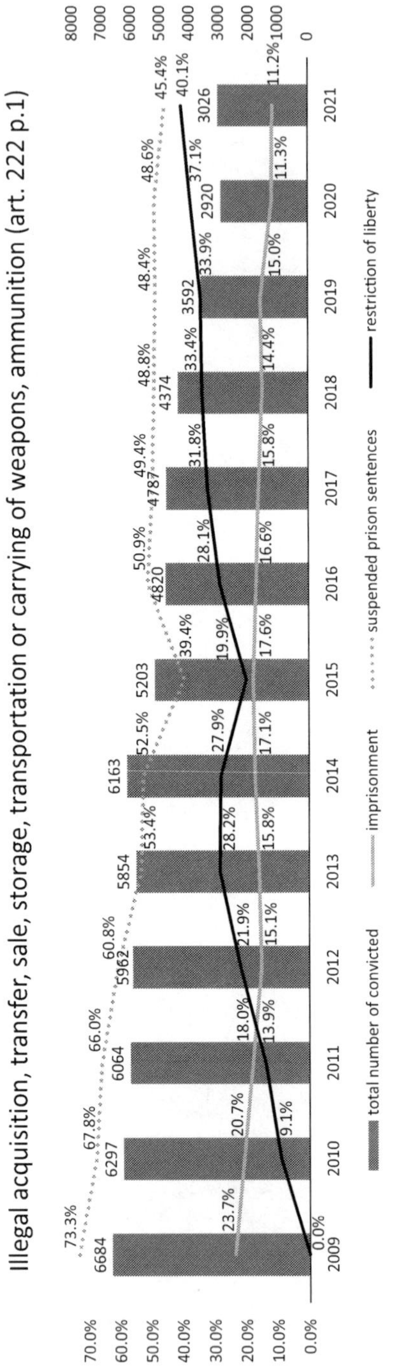

Figure 10.5 Illegal acquisition, transfer, sale, storage, transportation or carrying of weapons and ammunition (art. 222(1)).

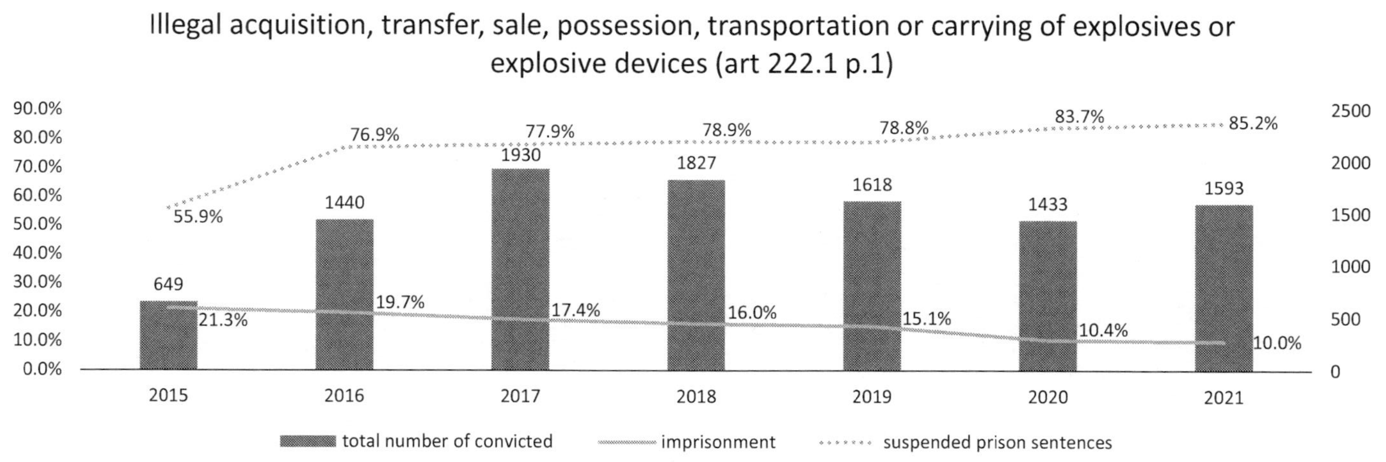

Figure 10.6 Illegal acquisition, transfer, sale, storage, transportation or carrying of explosives or explosive devices (art. 222[1](1)).

sum stolen. Moreover, there was no option to be released from liability after repaying the damages.

The courts were understandably dissatisfied with the resulting over-penalisation in cases of petty card thefts and tend to use suspended prison sentences to reduce the impact of that over-penalisation, along with awarding an increasing number of fines for this crime. For example, in 2017 there were 33,457 offenders convicted of this crime, of whom 48.4% were sentenced to imprisonment while 46.5% were handed suspended prison sentences. In 2021, there were 50,624 convicted offenders, 32.1% of whom were sentenced to imprisonment while 50.7% were handed suspended prison sentences.

A similar situation arose in relation to the crime of large-scale payout fraud as specified in Art. 159^2(3) of the RCC, which is punishable by imprisonment of up to six years. Offenders in these cases are typically women (64–66% convicted persons in 2015–2021) who have illegally obtained a child benefit on falsified grounds.[29]

The courts are unable to sentence such offenders to fines (because they will clearly be unable to pay them) or to compulsory work (this sanction is expressly forbidden in the criminal legislation if the offender has a child less than 3 years old). The only available option, as a result, is a prison sentence of up to 6 years. This meant that, in 2021, 84.6% of offenders convicted of this crime were handed suspended prison sentences.

Conclusion

Suspended prison sentences serve a variety of purposes in Russia's criminal justice system today. Historically, these were the only real alternative to custodial sanctions. Nowadays, while still considered a means of rehabilitating offenders without punishment, suspended sentences serve multiple functions, which correct certain situations perceived by the courts as otherwise unfair. These include situations relating to the defendant's personal circumstances, the nature of particular crimes, and the courts' perception of the punishments prescribed for the given offences in the criminal code.

There is no discussion currently in the legal sphere about suspended prison sentences. They are seen as an effective legal instrument in sentencing and punishment that has remained a stable part of the penal system for years, and there are no significant legislative proposals to change that. Society, too, is content with the status quo – most citizens view suspended prison sentences as just trial outcomes. For these reasons, there is no prospect of the suspended prison sentence regime being either abolished or substantially amended in Russian criminal law in the near future.

Notes

1 Literally translated from Russian "*условное осуждение*" [uslovnoye osuzhdeniye]
2 http://www.cdep.ru/index.php?id=79
3 Upon official request, the aggregated data of the JDSC that is not publicly accessible is made available. This data is aggregated at the court level and some of the data is aggregated at the regional level.
4 https://fsin.gov.ru/statistics/
5 The criminal case may be closed in court without an official acquittal based on so-called "rehabilitating grounds" for the defendant due to the non-involvement of the suspect in the criminal incident as an offender; absence of an event or corpus delicti.
6 Plea bargaining in Russia is an interesting combination of formal and informal practices. On the one hand, it is legally permissible to plead guilty and to speed up the criminal procedure (to conduct the trial without hearing evidence) in cases of crimes that carry a sentence of no more than 5 years of imprisonment. In such a case, the maximum punishment shall not exceed 2/3 of the statutory maximum provided for this crime. On the other hand, in cases of all other severe crimes (carrying sentences of more than 5 years of imprisonment), a guilty plea does not speed up the criminal procedure but *de facto* enables it to be conducted in a simplified manner (that is, without any real contest between prosecution and defence, with nominal study of the evidence, etc.) and the resulting punishment is more lenient.
7 Investigators have the right to dismiss criminal cases during the pretrial stage, but they do this very rarely due to the KPI, which forces them to send their cases to court. In 2021, investigators dismissed 62,000 cases on non-rehabilitative grounds during the pretrial stage.
8 The "judicial fine" was introduced as an option in 2017 and became very popular: the rate of its use has grown from 2% of defendants in 2017 to 7.9% in 2020. In 2021, this type of dismissal was used for 5% of defendants.
9 These punishments are as follows: fine; deprivation of the right to hold specific offices or to engage in specific activities; deprivation of a special or military rank, or honorary title, or class rank, or government award; compulsory work; corrective labour; restriction of military service; restriction of liberty; compulsory labour; arrest, imprisonment in a disciplinary military unit; imprisonment for a fixed term; and life imprisonment. The death penalty, although still included in this list, was finally abolished in 2009 by the Constitutional Court of the Russian Federation.
10 The difference between three types of work (labour) known to Russian penal policy is as follows: compulsory work is done on behalf of the local community; non-payable, corrective labour is served at the convicted offender's usual workplace with payment of part of his salary in favour of the state authorities. Compulsory labour is served instead of imprisonment for crimes of low or average severity at specially designated workplaces.
11 For example, theft (Art. 158(1) of the RCC) may be sanctioned with a fine of up to 80,000 roubles (min. 5,000 roubles), or amounting to the convicted offender's wage/salary or any other income for a period of up to 6 months (min. 2 weeks), or by compulsory work for a period of up to 360 hours (min. 60 hours), or by corrective labour for a period of up to 1 year (min. 2 months), or by restriction in liberty for a period of up to two years (min. 2 months), or by compulsory labour for a period of up to two years (min. 2 months), or by arrest for a period of up to 4 months (min. 1 month), or by imprisonment for a period of up to 2 years (min. 2 months).
12 For example, murder (Art. 105(1) of the RCC) is punished with imprisonment for a period of between six and 15 years. Aggravated murder (Art. 105(2) of the RCC)

is punished with imprisonment for a period of between eight and 20 years or by life imprisonment. Causing serious bodily injury (Art. 111(1) of the RCC) is punishable with imprisonment for between 2 months and 8 years.

13 Some other types of punishment can also be suspended, not only prison sentences. However, in practice, this happens rather rarely (only 11,704 cases in 2021).

14 The suspended sentence regime also includes suspension of corrective labour, restriction in military service (this type of punishment is de facto corrective labour for military personnel), and service in a disciplinary military unit (applied to military personnel instead of imprisonment for up to two years). However, as stated above, the courts rarely suspend these types of sanctions. The legal mechanism of all suspended sentences is the same.

15 See Курс, 1970, с. 241.

16 These crimes are specifically designated in the explanatory note to Art. 73 of the RCC (примечание in Russian being viewed as an integral part of the legislative text) and include sexual crimes against minors and crimes related to prostitution and pornography if they are committed against minors.

17 According to Art. 15 of the RCC, all crimes are divided into four categories: crimes of low severity, crimes of average severity, severe crimes, and especially severe crimes. The classification is based on fault requirements and prescribed punishments and is used mainly for imposing sanctions and for release from sanctions. Severe crimes are intentional crimes punishable by between 5 and 10 years of imprisonment and negligent crimes punishable by more than 10 years of imprisonment; especially severe crimes include only intentional crimes for which the prescribed punishment is more than 10 years of imprisonment.

18 In general, recidivism means committing a new intentional crime after conviction for a previously committed intentional crime (Art. 18 of the RCC). Depending on the number of previous convictions and the nature of the old and new crimes, there are three classes of recidivism: simple, dangerous and especially dangerous.

19 As provided by Art. 15 of the RCC, a severe crime is any intentional crime punishable by imprisonment for more than 5 years (or negligent crime punishable by more than 10 years of imprisonment). An especially severe crime is an intentional crime punishable by more than 10 years of imprisonment.

20 "Systematically" (Art. 190(5) of the Criminal Enforcement Code of the Russian Federation of 1997) means that the convicted person was punished twice during one year for an administrative offence and commits that new offence again.

21 See endnote on administrative offences in Russia in chapter 8.

22 "Systematically" (Art. 190(5) of the Criminal Enforcement Code of the Russian Federation of 1997) means that the convicted person fails to discharge the duties placed on him/her by court at least three times during one year or fails to discharge the duties placed on him/her by court for more than 30 days.

23 The proportion is calculated from two sources: official court statistics on the number of positive decisions by the judiciary on the early termination motions (Art. 74(1) of the RCC) and statistics from the Federal Penitentiary Service on the total number of offenders serving suspended sentences.

24 The proportion is calculated from two sources: official court statistics on the number of positive decisions by the judiciary on penitentiary service officers' motions to prolong the operational period of suspended sentences (Art. 74(2) of the RCC) and the statistics of the Federal Penitentiary Service on the total number of offenders serving suspended sentences.

25 See above, n 24.

26 Official court statistics provided by the Judicial Department at the Supreme Court of the Russian Federation.

27 Hereinafter, the analysis of the data from the Supreme Court's Judicial Department was conducted by Ekaterina Khodzhaeva.

28 There are two main drug crimes in the Russian Criminal Code, namely Art. 228 (illegal behaviour with drugs without intent to sell) and Art. 228^1 (illegal behaviour with drugs with intent to sell, including drug dealing). Here we explain the function of keeping the prison population to reasonable numbers with regard to the first of these (56,654 convicted offenders in 2021).

29 Every mother is eligible to receive a state benefit after the birth of their child. However, the money they receive must be used for designated purposes, which are education, medical care, buying a home for the child, etc. Obtaining this benefit for any other purpose constitutes fraud.

References

Chetverikova, I. V. (2014). Роль семьи, профессиональной карьеры и пола подсудимых при вынесении приговоров российскими судьями [The role of the family, professional career and sex of the defendants in sentencing by Russian judges]. *Journal of Sociology and Social Anthropology (Журнал социологии и социальной антропологии)*, *17*(4), 101–123. (in Russian)

Khodzhaeva, E., & Rabovski, J. (2016). Strategies and tactics of criminal defenders in the context of "accusatorial bias". *Russian Politics and Law*, *54*(2–3), 191–226.

Kurmangaliyeva, M. (2018). Missing rich offenders: Traffic accidents and the impartiality of justice. *Review of Law & Economics*, *14*(1).

McCarthy, L. A. (2015). *Trafficking justice: How Russian police enforce new laws, from crime to courtroom* (pp. 84–114). Cornell University Press.

Moiseeva, E. (2016). Plea bargaining in Russia: The role of defense attorneys and the problem of asymmetry. *International Journal of Comparative and Applied Criminal Justice*, *41*(3), 163–184.

Moiseeva, E. N. (2014). Рабочие группы в судах Санкт-Петербурга [Courtroom working groups in St Petersburg]. *Journal of Sociology and Social Anthropology (Журнал социологии и социальной антропологии)*, *17*(4), 86–100. (in Russian)

Paneyakh, E. (2014). Faking performance together: Systems of performance evaluation in Russian enforcement agencies and production of bias and privilege. *Post-Soviet Affairs*, *30*(2–3), 115–136.

Paneyakh, E., Titaev, K., & Shklyaruk, M. (2018). *Траектория уголовного дела: институциональный анализ*. European University at St. Petersburg.

Pomorski, S. (2001). Justice in Siberia: A case study of a lower criminal court in the city of Krasnoyarsk. *Communist and Post-Communist Studies*, *34*(4), 447–478.

Pozdnyakov, M. L. (2015). *Система оснований отмены и изменения судебных актов в российском уголовном процессе* [System of grounds for overturning and amending the judicial decisions in Russian criminal process]. Moscow. (in Russian)

Solomon, P. (2015). Understanding Russia's low rate of acquittal: Pretrial screening and the problem of accusatorial bias. *Review of Central and East European Law*, *40*(1), 1–30.

Solomon, P. (2018). Accusatorial bias in Russian criminal justice. In M. Kurkchiyan & A. Kubal (Eds.), *Sociology of justice in Russia* (pp. 170–204). Cambridge University Press.

Volkov, V. V. (2016). Legal and extralegal origins of sentencing disparities: Evidence from Russia's criminal courts. *Journal of Empirical Legal Studies*, *13*(4), 637–665.

Курс советского уголовного права, том 3 [The treastise on Soviet criminal law, volume iii] (1970). Moscow. (in Russian)

Part IIc

Suspended sentences in countries of the former Yugoslavia

11 General tendencies of criminal law and penal policy in Yugoslavia (1945–1990s)

Milena Tripković

Introduction

From 1945 until the 1990s, today's countries of Bosnia and Herzegovina, Croatia, Kosovo (a state with partial international recognition), Montenegro, North Macedonia, Serbia, and Slovenia were all constituent entities of the Socialist Federal Republic of Yugoslavia (hereinafter Yugoslavia). In this introductory section, I seek to explain the principles of criminal law and penal policy that were dominant in Yugoslavia in this period, in order to account for two things. First, the chapter traces the legal and political trajectory in Yugoslavia during this period in order to help us understand the starting point from which the subsequently independent states of former Yugoslavia further developed after 1991, and hence to understand the relative similarity of both substantive and procedural criminal law in those countries today. Second, this shared background can explain why, at the time of Yugoslavia's dissolution, the newly independent countries mostly possessed the institutional and legal capacity necessary for swiftly enacting the kind of democratic and human rights-based transformation of criminal law that would subsequently take place also in other formerly Communist countries in Europe. Overall, I aim to show in this introduction that in the early 1990s, despite its socialist background, former Yugoslavia exhibited progressive tendencies in respect to criminal law and penal policy, especially in comparison to the Warsaw Pact countries. This resulted in a relatively painless transformation of criminal law post break-up, which is further detailed in the two separate chapters on Serbia and Slovenia.

I outline developments in criminal law in Yugoslavia by focusing on three distinct (though interrelated) domains – historical, constitutional, and academic – in which key developments and characteristics of the Yugoslav system took place. I begin by outlining the historical development of criminal law after 1945, in particular the tensions between the "Soviet" model of criminal law (formally abolished in 1951 but with longer-lasting ideological tendencies) and the more progressive, rights-based tendencies which grew stronger as Yugoslavia moved towards its dissolution. I then go on to explain the constitutional transformation of Yugoslavia that began in 1974 and was geared towards giving its constituent republics and provinces greater autonomy, broadening their institutional and

DOI: 10.4324/9781003568667-16

legal competences, which paved the way for a relatively swift transformation of criminal law after the dissolution of Yugoslavia. Finally, I explain trends in the academic study of criminal law and criminology in Yugoslavia at this time which – albeit undertaken within the state system – demonstrated a high level of resilience, independence and maturity that proved essential in the post-independence, state-building period in which criminal law no longer needed to serve ideological purposes.

General characteristics of Yugoslav criminal law and penal policy

The first common state of Southern Slavs – as Yugoslavia was commonly described – was formed in 1918, in the aftermath of the First World War. Known as the Kingdom of Serbs, Croats, and Slovenes until 1930 and thereafter as Yugoslavia, this country brought together what had hitherto been a legally disintegrated territory, in which criminal laws based on various foreign criminal codes applied. The Serbian criminal code (adopted in 1860) was modelled on the 1851 Prussian criminal code (Živanović, 1935), while the 1878 Hungarian penal code (the *Csemegi* code) applied in Vojvodina, the northern province of today's Serbia. The remaining territories of today's Croatia, Bosnia and Herzegovina, and Slovenia all applied criminal legislation based on the 1852 Austrian criminal code (Mirković, 2017).

Post-unification, this existing legislation was retained until 1929, when the first Criminal Code of Yugoslavia was adopted; this was modelled on the German criminal code (1872) and founded on the classical school of criminal law (Stojanović, 2005, p. 56). After the end of the Second World War, Yugoslavia aligned politically with the USSR, which led to substantive changes in its social, economic, political, and legal system. Those changes were reflected in its newly adopted and comprehensively transformed criminal code of 1947, which replaced the previous "German" model of criminal law with a markedly "Soviet" one. The general tone of the 1947 Criminal Code promoted a specifically Soviet understanding of the nature and place of crime in a communist society, and was "notoriously punitive" (Krajewski, 2004). To reflect the particularity of the Soviet society, criminal law referred to sociological categories, such as the "social dangerousness" of an act (the Soviet equivalent of "crime") and "social defence" (the Soviet word for "punishment"), while the "supremacy of law [was replaced] by revolutionary legal conscience" (Berman, 1947, p. 805).[1] Criminal law, like many other social instruments, sought to invoke a distinct vision of unity between Soviet citizens and the Soviet state, which had no place for or tolerance of crime: the hope was that crimes, as remnants of the bourgeois society, would eventually "wither away" (Osakwe, 1976, p. 437; the notion of "withering away" was originally developed by Friedrich Engels). The system was, however, based on abstract categories that defied common legal approaches, and was therefore unstable and insufficiently respectful of individual rights – these were postulated as second-order considerations, while the principal concern was the protection of the communist system.

This distinct understanding of crime and punishment developed through various principles and ideas. For example, crimes were defined as "socially dangerous" acts, i.e. not as acts that impact on citizens' individual rights and interests but instead acts "directed against the Soviet system or infringing the legal order established by the workers and peasants in the period of transition to communism" (article 6 of the Russian Federation Criminal Code of 1926, cited in Berman, 1947, p. 811). Additionally, the law permitted extensive use of analogy, which allowed for the discretionary expansion of grounds for prosecution beyond those stipulated in the law.[2] In that regard, analogy was not "just another institution of criminal law" but rather symbolised "the basic attitudes toward the function and role of the state in relation to the individual" (Fletcher, 2007, p. 129). Finally, punishment could be imposed by non-judicial organs: most commonly by administrative and "security" agencies.

In 1948, just a year after adopting its new criminal code, Yugoslavia distanced itself politically from the USSR and its hard-line communism was substituted with a more relaxed self-managing socialism, in which "the economy was planned only to a certain degree, enterprises enjoyed comparative independence from state authorities, creating a more liberated atmosphere, greater autonomy and more incentives to produce and sell more" (Šelih, 2012, p. 5). This led to a further transformation of the legal system.[3] The subsequent 1951 Criminal Code readopted the "German" model (in fact, it closely followed the Swiss criminal code), which meant that many ideological norms were abolished (Srzentić et al., 1998; Stojanović, 2005). The new rules followed the tripartite system of criminal law (Fletcher, 2007), under which, for an act to constitute a crime, it has to be: (a) prescribed as a crime, (b) unlawful, and (c) perpetrated by a guilty offender. The most important effect of this new system was that it prohibited the use of analogy: even though the definition of crime still retained the material element of "social dangerousness", this merely served as a justification for the criminalisation of a particular act, but gave no authority to state organs when deciding whether to prosecute.

To qualify the post-Soviet period as entirely progressive would, however, be somewhat misleading. Specific categories of offenders – such as, for instance, those perceived as Stalinists and Soviet sympathisers – were subjected to harsh punishment. Albeit outwardly concerned with "unity and brotherhood", the political system frequently exploited criminal law to eliminate opposition: for example, at least 13,000 people were interred of which about subsequently 300 died in a secret prison at *Goli Otok* (Barren Island) off the Croatian shore in the period between 1949 and 1956 (Previšić, 2019). Most of these people were, in effect, political prisoners against whom the criminal law and criminal norms "protecting" the socialist system were used. Therefore, even though most of the ideological and regressive criminal law tendencies were abolished after the

Yugoslavia-USSR rift, it would take decades for the country's criminal law to fully eradicate its ideological inclinations.

Increasing autonomy in the Yugoslav republics after 1977

The new constitutional framework set up by the last Constitution of Yugoslavia (1974) increased the autonomy of the six constitutive Republics and two autonomous provinces (Kosovo and Vojvodina, integral parts of the Republic of Serbia), including in criminal matters. Nevertheless, the Federation still retained jurisdiction for regulating the basic principles of criminal law and criminal sanctions (the "general part" of criminal law) along with particular groups of crimes that were considered of specific interest for the federation (such as crimes against the social and constitutional order, international crimes, crimes against the reputation of the country and its organs, crimes against the armed forces, and so on).[4] A new Yugoslav criminal code was adopted in 1976, which did not differ substantially from the previous one adopted in 1951 (and modified a number of times since), though it was more liberal in many respects. The six republics and two autonomous provinces also each adopted their own criminal code in 1976, which contained provisions for the "special part" (criminal offences other than those provided for by the federal criminal code). All nine codes entered into force on 1st July 1977.

Even though the new system of criminal legislation was based on "unity of conceptual-political foundations of the society" (Franko, 1977, p. 7), it nevertheless increased the sovereignty of Yugoslavia's various federal units and paved the way towards a more independent, context-specific criminal legislation (Đorđević, 1977, p. 16). In reality, the separate federal republics' and autonomous provinces' criminal codes were very similar, but the wide scope of their autonomy when it came to criminal legislation allowed them to accommodate penal policy and sentencing practices to their particular needs. While the federal code required them all to subscribe to the same types of criminal sanctions (these were: (a) punishments – imprisonment and fine; (b) suspended prison sentence and judicial admonition; (c) security measures), each constituent republic or autonomous province could tailor penal and sentencing policies to their circumstances. Therefore, for instance, while the federal criminal code stipulated that suspension could only be applied to prison sentences of up to two years, the republics and autonomous provinces could significantly influence the number of suspended sentences imposed by prescribing the sentence ranges for the crimes within their legislative authority. In addition, judges – who were more independent than ever before under the new constitutional arrangements – could further mould their sentencing practices in the ambient that was conducive to promoting the social, cultural, political and economic specificities of their particular federal unit (Aćimović, 1969). The overall effect of the new constitutional framework was a growing sense of independence, both in general and specifically in the domain of penal law and policy, which put the constituent units of Yugoslavia (most of which would soon become independent states) in a good position from which to further democratise, liberalise, and humanise their penal systems.

Development of criminal law and criminology as an academic field

In former Yugoslavia, academic study in the fields of criminal law and criminology was inseparable at first; criminology began to gain more traction as a separate area of study in the mid-twentieth century. In 1954, the first Yugoslav Institute of criminology was founded in Ljubljana (Slovenia), and this was followed during the 1960s by another three similar research centres in Belgrade (Serbia), Sarajevo (Bosnia and Herzegovina) and Zagreb (Croatia) (Aćimović, 1969; Šelih, 1972). The researchers affiliated with these institutions, who usually also held teaching roles at higher education institutions, studied crime in relation to both its concrete phenomenology in the Yugoslav context and its legal frameworks and responses (Institute of Criminology, 2022). Researchers from the various Yugoslav republics and autonomous provinces collaborated closely within the framework of the Yugoslav Society for criminal law and criminology (*Jugoslovensko udruženje za krivično pravo i kriminologiju*), which, from 1963 onwards, regularly published the Yugoslav Review for Criminology and Criminal Law (*Jugoslovenska revija za kriminologiju i krivično pravo*). In addition to the federal association, most of the republics – good examples are Croatia and Slovenia (see Shelley, 1979; Getoš-Kalač & Karlović, 2014) – also had their own criminal law and criminology associations and journals (such as the Slovenian *Revija za kriminalistiko i kriminologijo*), which was conducive to the decentralisation of criminological research. This was immensely important given the specificity of Yugoslav criminology, which had to account for criminal phenomena in a country that was nationally, religiously, economically, and socially diverse, and was also characterised by geo-political specificities, enhanced urbanisation, migration, and industrialisation (Aćimović, 1969).

The criminology research conducted in former Yugoslavia was closely linked to the country's existing criminal law and policy, but profited immensely from engagement with foreign colleagues (especially those in German- and French-speaking jurisdictions). In that regard, the role and impact of academic criminal lawyers and criminologists was significant, and their engagement with the problems of crime (apart from political crimes) was largely unobstructed by the state. As a result, Yugoslav criminology research achieved high quality, diversity and analytical sophistication and therefore gained "international recognition" (Shelley, 1979). In comparison to Soviet criminology, for example, Yugoslav criminology was not only better organised, but enjoyed more academic freedom and was less ideologically driven, therefore providing room for criticism, reflection and "unrestricted intellectual development" (Shelley, 1979, p. 143). Yugoslav lawyers and criminologists were thus better equipped to deal with the necessary transformation of criminal law that would occur with the transition to democracy.

Conclusion

The dissolution of Yugoslavia began in the early 1990s. Owing to a set of complex circumstances (see Glenny, 1992) related to previous unresolved conflicts, ethno-nationalist hostilities, and the general downturn of the Yugoslav economy, a bloody civil war engulfed large parts of its territory and lasted for a decade. One by one, the former federal republics became independent states: Slovenia, Croatia, and North Macedonia in 1991, Bosnia and Herzegovina in 1995, Montenegro in 2006 and Kosovo (which unilaterally declared itself independent from Serbia) in 2008.

After gaining independence, each of these states soon renounced the old political system and introduced various democratic changes, not least in the field of criminal law and policy. As we have seen, their ability and propensity to transform these systems was positively impacted by their history of progressive change, which had begun back in 1929 and was especially pronounced from the late 1960s onwards. The new countries did not suddenly "break away" from Communism and build their new penal systems from scratch: they had already been treading a solid path toward a non-ideological outlook on criminal law for decades. The multiple changes that the former Yugoslav republics introduced after their independence largely centred around human rights, and a more dignified, parsimonious approach to punishment. These changes, including the abolition of the death penalty, stronger procedural guarantees, improvement of prison conditions and prisoner rights, and so on, were introduced in both substantive and procedural law, and were substantially prompted by the conditions for joining the Council of Europe.

That said, it would not be accurate to suggest that the penal transformations in the countries of former Yugoslavia have been entirely progressive; some worrying tendencies have also been observed. For example, penal governance has been marked by authoritarian tendencies in Serbia (Tripković, 2016), and punitiveness and sensationalism in Slovenia (Meško & Jere, 2012). These tendencies seem to be present in the wider Central and Eastern European context (Kossowska et al., 2012): for instance, Hungarian penal policy has been premised on "zero tolerance" (Levay, 2012), Poland follows a "law and order" model (Krajewski, 2004), Estonia is described as "populist" (Saar, 2004), Lithuania as "punitive" (Dobryninas & Sakalauskas, 2011), while Czechia seems to be punitive "by negligence" (Drápal, 2021). Recent penal transformations across the region therefore seem to be multifaceted and not always unidirectional – and we must keep that in mind when considering the use of any penal instrument, including suspended prison sentences.

Notes

1 Fletcher (2007) explains that this understanding required the adoption of the *quadripartite* system of crime, a model that differs from both the *tripartite system* used in most of Continental Europe and the *bipartite system* used in common law countries (see below for an explanation of the difference between these systems). The *quadripartite system* distinguishes between (a) the subject, (b) the subjective aspect of liability, (c) the object, and (d) the objective aspect of liability. While the subject and subjective aspect of liability are not particularly important for our current discussion, the object of the offence "brings to bear a distinctively Communist way of thinking about criminal offences as directed in all cases to some harm" (Fletcher, 2007, p. 48). The object, therefore, is the threatened harm, but for the offence to be "prosecutable" it also had to be "socially dangerous", a notion that was undefined and discretionary.

2 Article 16 of the Russian Federation's criminal code of 1926 stipulated: "If a socially dangerous act is not directly provided for by the present code, the foundations and limits of liability for it shall be determined according to those articles of the code which provide for those crimes most similar to it in kind" (quoted in Berman, 1947).

3 Soviet criminal law also underwent substantive and progressive changes, beginning in 1958 with the adoption of the Fundamental Principles of Criminal Legislation of the USSR and the Union Republics, as well as numerous other acts which re-conceptualised the criminal law system (see Gsovski, 1960; Grzybowsky, 1960; Osakwe, 1976). These changes constituted "the most radical turning point in this field since the inception of the Soviet regime" (Gsovski, 1960, p. 315). They led to a reduction in the number of incriminations and created a less strict system of criminal sanctions; the ideas of "social dangerousness" and "social defence" were transformed, analogy was abolished and the retroactive application of law was scrapped, and criminal punishment could be imposed only by the court.

4 See article 280, paragraph 12 of the Constitution of the Socialist Federal Republic of Yugoslavia.

References

Aćimović, M. (1969). Proučavanje kriminoloških problema Jugoslavije. *Zbornik radova pravno-ekonomskog fakulteta, 8*, 229–242.

Berman, H. (1947). Principles of Soviet criminal law. *Yale Law Journal, 56*, 803–836.

Dobryninas, A., & Sakalauskas, G. (2011). Country survey: Criminology, crime and criminal justice in Lithuania. *European Journal of Criminology*, *8*(5), 421–434.

Đorđević, M. (1977). Osnovne karakteristike novog krivičnog zakona SFRJ sa stanovišta primene u praksi. *Jugoslovenska revija za kriminologiju i krivično parvo, 2*, 15–34.

Drápal, J. (2021). Punitive by negligence? The myths and reality of penal nationalism in the Czech Republic. *European Journal of Criminology*, *20*(4), 1549–1567.

Fletcher, G. (2007). *The grammar of criminal law: American, comparative, and international*. Oxford University Press.

Franko, I. (1977). Pristupna izlaganja – pozdravni govori. *Jugoslovenska revija za kriminologiju i krivično parvo, 2*, 5–8.

Getoš-Kalač, A. M., & Karlović, R. (2014). Kriminologija i pogibeljni kriminal u Hrvatskoj i u globalnom kontekstu – stanje jučer, danas i sutra. *Zbornik Pravnog fakulteta u Zagrebu, 64*(5–6), 1121–1145.

Glenny, M. (1992). *The fall of Yugoslavia*. Penguin.

Grzybowski, K. (1960). Soviet criminal law reform of 1958. *Indiana Law Journal*, *35*(2), 125–142.

Gsovski, V. (1960). Reform of criminal law in the Soviet Union. *Social Problems, 7*(4), 315–328.

Institute of Criminology. (2022). *History of the institute*. Retrieved July 19, 2022, from https://www.inst-krim.si/en/history-of-the-institute-instituta/

Kossowska, A., Buczkowski, K., Klaus, W., et al. (2012). Politicians, media, and society's perception of crime. In A. Šelih & A. Završnik (Eds.), *Crime and transition in Central and Eastern Europe*. Springer.

Krajewski, K. (2004). Crime and criminal justice in Poland. *European Journal of Criminology, 1*(3), 377–407.

Levay, M. (2012). Penal policy, crime and political change. In A. Šelih & A. Završnik (Eds.), *Crime and transition in Central and Eastern Europe*. Springer.

Meško, G., & Jere, M. (2012). Crime, criminal justice and criminology in Slovenia. *European Journal of Criminology*, *9*(3), 323–334.

Mirković, Z. (2017). *Srpska pravna istorija.* Univerzitet u Beogradu.

Osakwe, C. (1976). Contemporary Soviet criminal law: An analysis of the general principles and major institutions of post-1958 Soviet criminal law. *Georgia Journal of International and Comparative Law*, *6*, 437–492.

Previšić, M. (2019). *Povijest Golog Otoka.* Fraktura.

Saar, J. (2004). Crime, crime control and criminology in post-communist Estonia. *European Journal of Criminology, 1*(4), 505–531.

Šelih, A. (2012). Crime and crime control in transition countries. In A. Šelih & A. Završnik (Eds.), *Crime and transition in Central and Eastern Europe*. Springer.

Selik, A. (1972). Criminological researches in Yugoslavia. *Journal of Offender Therapy and Comparative Criminology, 16*(2), 148–150.

Shelley, L. (1979). Soviet and Yugoslavian criminology. *International Journal of Comparative and Applied Criminal Justice, 3*(2), 143–156.

Srzentić, N., Stajič, A., & Lazarević, L. J. (1998). *Krivično pravo Jugoslavije - opsti deo.* Savremena administracija.

Stojanović, Z. (2005). *Krivicno pravo - opšti deo.* Justinijan.

Tripković, M. (2016). Beyond punitiveness? Governance of crime and authoritarian heritage in Serbia. *Punishment and Society*, *18*(3), 369–386.

Živanović, T. (1935). *Osnovi Krivičnog prava Kraljevine Jugoslavije: Opšti deo.* Gundulić.

12 Suspended prison sentences in Serbia

Milena Tripković

Introduction

Suspending an imposed prison sentence is a common way of administering justice to a select group of criminal offenders in Serbia. This has been the case for nearly a century since the sanction was first introduced in 1929, and this practice has proven broadly resistant to both the legal changes and the substantial transformation of social, political, and economic conditions that the country (formerly part of Yugoslavia) has since experienced. As the introductory chapter on the former Yugoslav region points out, the development of criminal legislation there was consistent and gradual and – with the exception of the period 1948–1951 when the Soviet model of criminal law prevailed – premised on a penal model that was mostly devoid of ideological tendencies.

Furthermore, suspending imposed prison sentences is a practice consistent with other "mild" sentencing practices that have been dominant in Serbia for decades. Identifying a discrepancy between policymakers' intentions and the sentencing decisions made by judges – a discrepancy made possible by imprecise sentencing rules and broad judicial discretion – Stojanović argues that "penal policy" as created by judges (i.e. the sum of decisions made in individual cases) is "in conflict" with noticeably stricter legal provisions (Stojanović, 2012). In the case of imprisonment, for instance, judges rarely impose prison sentences in the upper half tier of the sentencing range and almost never use the top third of the range, although this might presumably be justified in some cases (Stojanović, 2012). Suspending imprisonment is another tool in that penal policy, and its nature and purpose should be interpreted with that in mind.

In this chapter, I begin by providing a summary of key issues that pertain to sentencing in Serbia, with the aim of specifying how suspended prison sentences (henceforth: SPS) fit into the Serbian system of criminal sanctions. I then conduct a more thorough analysis of the legal rules that apply to SPS, focusing particularly on their key features, the conditions for their imposition, and the possible consequences of their breach. In the final part of the chapter, I explain the historical trajectory of SPS' development and the dominant understanding of their nature and purpose, and I present empirical data on their use. I argue that SPS, as used in Serbia (and arguably other countries of former Yugoslavia), are

DOI: 10.4324/9781003568667-17

distinct from other criminal sanctions due to their inclusive, communicative, trust-building nature, and that for that reason they fulfil an important function in the penal system, catering for some important but commonly ignored penal aims.

Sentencing overview

According to the current Criminal Code,[1] the purpose of sentencing is the "suppression of acts which harm or endanger values protected through criminal legislation" (article 4.2). This may be pursued by imposing four types of sanctions: (1) punishments, (2) warning measures, (3) security measures and (4) educational measures (for juvenile offenders).

1) The five punishments stipulated in the Criminal Code are:

- **Life imprisonment** – for a small number of the most serious crimes (such as murder and other crimes resulting in death) and perpetrators aged above 21 years (article 44a);
- **Imprisonment** – the statutory range is between 30 days and 20 years (note that a period of imprisonment greater than 20 years and less than life imprisonment cannot be imposed); imprisonment of a duration no more than 1 year can – under specific conditions – be carried out within the offender's home (*house arrest,* article 45);
- **Fine** – judges can either use an established system of daily amounts or impose the fine in an absolute amount (articles 48–51);
- **Work in the public interest** – i.e. community service, which may serve as a substitute sanction in place of a fine or up to 3 years' imprisonment (article 52);
- **Suspension of driving licence** – for perpetrators who used a vehicle when preparing or perpetrating a crime (article 53).

Sentencing rules are stipulated in the Criminal Code to assist judges when deciding on the appropriate punishment in a given case. These rules are sufficiently specific to significantly reduce judicial discretion while at the same time leaving substantial scope for choice. The rules relate to aggravating and mitigating factors, such as the level of guilt, the motive, the level of harm caused, the circumstances of the crime, the perpetrator's earlier life, their behaviour after the crime – especially towards the victim – and so on (article 54.1). There are also particular rules on reoffending, which is generally considered an aggravating factor (articles 55, 55a). In certain circumstances, punishment can also be reduced below the statutory minimum or a milder form of punishment can be imposed (articles 56–57): in some very specific cases, no punishment may be imposed even if the offender is found guilty (articles 58–59).

When an offender is sentenced to imprisonment, he/she is (save for some serious crimes such as aggravated murder or qualified cases of rape) eligible for conditional discharge after serving two-thirds of the sanction. The decision on conditional discharge is premised on their behaviour in prison and their propensity to reoffend (article 46).

2) The two warning measures stipulated in the Criminal Code are:

- Suspended prison sentence;
- Judicial admonition (see Section 4).

3) The 11 security measures stipulated in the Criminal Code, whose purpose is to remove criminogenic circumstances or conditions and, by so doing, influence offenders to refrain from future offending (article 79) are:

- Psychiatric treatment in a closed mental health institution;
- Psychiatric treatment as an outpatient;
- Drug addiction treatment;
- Alcohol addiction treatment;
- Prohibition from performing specific occupations, functions, or duties;
- Driving prohibitions;[2]
- Appropriation of objects;
- Deportation (for foreign offenders only);
- Publication of the verdict;
- Prohibition from approaching and communicating with the victim;
- Prohibition from attending particular sports events.

The special part of the Criminal Code outlines specific crimes, which it systematises according to their "protected object" (for example, "crimes against life and limb", "crimes against rights and liberty", "crimes against sexual freedom", "crimes against intellectual property"). For each specific criminal offence, the Criminal Code determines: (a) the type or types of sanctions that may be imposed, and (b) the specific range (minimum to maximum) within which the duration or amount of the sanction may be determined. For example, the crime of murder (basic form) is punishable by imprisonment within the range of 5–15 years (article 113); in the case of aggravated murder, the punishment must be a prison sentence lasting at least 10 years, or life imprisonment (article 114); manslaughter is to be punished with imprisonment lasting between 6 months and 5 years (article 118).

Courts and judges are independent when deciding in particular criminal matters. Jurisdiction in criminal matters is split between Basic and Higher courts: Basic courts decide on crimes for which the possible punishment is a fine or imprisonment of up to 10 years in duration, while the Higher courts decide on more serious crimes or in cases involving circumstances that require special knowledge or care, such as juvenile offences (*Zakon o uređenju sudova,* articles 22–24). Appeals against decisions made by Basic courts are resolved by the Higher court, while appeals against decisions made by Higher courts are dealt with by the Appellate court. Other than this, there is no formal hierarchy between the courts – each decides within its own authority.

In recent times (and to some extent in the more distant past, as I explain in the section pertaining to the development of the system), suspended prison sentences have been by far the most frequently imposed criminal sanction in Serbia. Figure 12.1 demonstrates the recent stability in the imposition of suspended prison sentences and the two next most frequent criminal sanctions (fines and imprisonment). Suspended prison sentences make up more than half of all criminal sanctions imposed in Serbia, and are thus very clearly preferred above other criminal sanctions, despite the rather limited legislative scope for their imposition, which is the focus of the next section.

Principles governing suspended prison sentences at present

As I explained above, four types of criminal sanction are currently used in Serbia: (1) punishments, (2) warning measures, (3) security measures and (4) educational measures (article 4.1). A suspended prison sentence, which is called *uslovna osuda* ("conditional sentence") in Serbian, is categorised as a "warning measure", along with a measure called "judicial admonition" – *sudsko upozorenje,* which I discuss briefly in part 4. These "warning measures" are cautionary sanctions or forms of admonition (Stojanović, 2003, p. 331) designed to be used with the *specific* purpose – as defined by the Criminal Code – to "abstain from imposing punishment on a perpetrator of a non-serious criminal offence

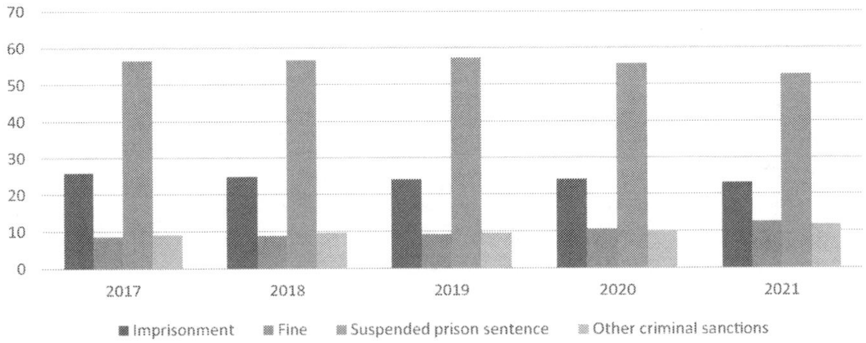

Figure 12.1 Imposed criminal sentences in Serbia, 2017–2021.

when it can be expected that the warning accompanied by a threat of punishment … will be sufficient to influence the perpetrator to refrain from reoffending" (article 64.2).

SPS are therefore not only distinct from other punishments, but are explicitly defined as a means of *avoiding punishment* if particular circumstances of the case and/or perpetrator justify it. In Serbia, unlike some other post-communist countries, SPS thus do not constitute punishment or a particular modality of imposing punishment, even though they are closely related to imprisonment (Miladinović, 1980, p. 386). For that reason, the essence of the suspended prison sentence as a sanction lies not in its *determination*, but rather in its *suspension* (Dragojlović, 2017). Contrasting the general purpose of *criminal sanctions* with the special purpose of *warning measures*, allows us to observe an apparent paradox: it seems that the "suppression of [criminal] acts" can be achieved by not imposing any criminal sanction and therefore abstaining from pursuing any penal aims (such as incapacitation, retribution, prevention, and so on). The mere *threat* of a future sanction is considered sufficient as a means of pursuing the penal aims of special prevention, as it is premised on social-ethical and educational-pedagogical grounds (Dragojlović, 2017). But even under this interpretation, special prevention is pursued by avoiding the imposition of any harmful consequences, which explicitly distinguishes this criminal sanction ("warning measure") from punishments.

Key features. Article 65.1 of the Criminal Code specifies two key elements of suspended prison sentences – their *modality of imposition* and their *operational period.* When imposing a suspended prison sentence, the court "[1] decides on punishment and at the same time determines that it will not be executed [2] if the convicted, during the time determined by the court, which cannot be shorter than 1 year nor longer than 5 years (operational period), does not perpetrate a new criminal offence" (article 65.1). The provision is somewhat contradictory because it implies that the court *first* decides on punishment but *at the same time* determines that it will not be executed. This provision effectively conveys that the court first needs to decide on a punishment of exact duration (not only that *some* punishment will be imposed) and then suspend its immediate execution. The provision also suggests that the decisions about punishment and about suspending its immediate execution are together the result of a single reflective process taking place within a single court session.

Various *security measures* (see above) can be imposed alongside SPS, but their execution cannot be suspended (article 65.3).

Conditions for imposition. The only sanction that can be suspended is a *prison* sentence (not a fine, although that was possible prior to 2005) **of less than 2 years' duration** (article 66.1). There are two further limitations. First, a prison sentence cannot be suspended when the sentencing range maximum for the sentenced offence is 8 years or more (article 66.2); this excludes crimes that can assume a very serious form. Second, prison sentences cannot be suspended for repeat offenders, unless 5 years have passed since the offender's previous prison sentence or suspended prison sentence for an intentional crime became final (article 66.3).

The decision to suspend a prison sentence of less than two years is left to the court's discretion, and it is difficult to state with any level of certainty whether the legislator intended suspension to be an exception or not. When making that decision, the court should take into account "the perpetrator's character, his earlier life, his behaviour subsequent to the perpetrated criminal offence, his level of guilt and other circumstances under which the offence was perpetrated" (article 66.1). There are apparently no particular forms of crimes which are automatically removed from consideration for suspension. Circumstances pertaining to the *offender* appear to be equally (if not more) relevant to this decision than those pertaining to the *offence*: it is the former that inform the court's expectation about the convicted person's likelihood (or otherwise) to reoffend if not punished. While the main condition for suspension is the short duration of the prison sentence, the court's decision is also based on evidence of non-criminogenic context and circumstances, i.e. proof that the perpetrated crime is unlikely to be repeated. In other words, SPS is tailored to offenders who do not need punishment in order to change *who they are* but who must nevertheless be sanctioned on account of *what they have done*. This latter can be adequately achieved by threatening punishment, without its immediate implementation.

As stipulated, the operational period for SPS is between 1 and 5 years. There are no further provisions to instruct the court in deciding its exact duration in each case, so judges have sufficient leeway to accommodate the period to the circumstances of the case. In theory, the presumption is that the operational period should correspond to the length of the sentence that is being suspended (Dragojlović, 2017).

Breach. There are two main situations in which the court will revoke a suspended prison sentence. One relates to events that occur *after* the sentence is imposed, and the other to events that happened *before* the sentence was imposed but of which the court was not aware at the time of sentencing.

A suspended sentence is breached if the convicted person perpetrates a new criminal offence or fails to fulfil other obligations during the operational period. The sentence imposed for the new crime determines whether or not the suspended prison sentence is revoked.

If the offender is sentenced to two years of imprisonment or more for new crime(s) (meaning that the new sentence is equally as serious as, or more serious than the sentence for the previous crime), the suspended prison sentence is *automatically* revoked and the judge may not decide otherwise (article 67.1).

If the offender's sentence for new crime(s) is a prison sentence of less than two years or a fine (meaning that the new sentence is less serious than the sentence for the previous crime), the court *must decide* whether to revoke the suspended prison sentence or not (article 67.2). When deciding, the court must take into account all circumstances that relate to the offender and offence, especially the similarity between the new and old crime(s), the significance of the crime and the offender's motives (article 67.2). However, if the combined sentence for the old and new crime(s) amounts to more than two years of imprisonment, the court *must* revoke the suspended prison sentence (article 67.2).

A particular case of breach exists when the initial suspended prison sentence was accompanied by one or more additional obligations for the offender. Such obligations may include, for instance, the return of criminal proceeds or payment of damages to the victim. When suspending the prison sentence, the court imposes deadlines for fulfilling these obligations within the general operational period (article 65.2). A breach is considered to have occurred if the obligations are not fulfilled by the stated deadline, even if the convicted person has not reoffended (article 69). In this case, the court may decide to prolong the deadline for fulfilling the obligation(s) in question, relieve the offender from completing them (if it is impossible for him/her to fulfil), substitute them with other obligation(s) in accordance with the law, or revoke the suspended prison sentence (article 69).

Deadlines for recalling suspended prison sentences. SPS can only be revoked for new crime(s) perpetrated during the operational period (which lasts between 1 and 5 years, as determined by the court) and can be recalled up to one year after the operational period has passed (article 70.1). The same applies if one or more of the obligation(s) attached to the suspended sentence are not fulfilled – the absolute deadline for the court to revoke suspension of the prison sentence is one year after the operational period has passed (article 70.2).

A suspended prison sentence with probationary supervision (*uslovna osuda sa zaštitnim nadzorom,* i.e. "conditional sentence with protective supervision") is a particular form of suspended prison sentence in which one or more "measures" are attached to a prison sentence that has been suspended in the regular way. The purpose of these measures is to provide "help, care, supervision and protection" (article 71.2), and they can be imposed when it is expected that they will contribute to the purpose of the suspended prison sentence being achieved "more fully" (article 72.1.). Article 71 stipulates that the measures imposed (see below) can last for a period shorter than or equal to the operational period: the court can, furthermore, decide to terminate any measure if it decides that its purpose has already been fulfilled, or to substitute certain imposed measures with others (article 71.3; 75.3). This particular type of suspended prison sentence is premised on the acceptance of some elements of the Anglo-Saxon model, in that it requires activity on the part of the state in order to achieve the purpose of the suspended prison sentence (Lazarević, 1967; Stojanović, 2003). Even though the intention was for this sanction to be used in only a small number of borderline cases (Stojanović, 2012), it undermines the nature of suspended prison sentences to some extent, given that, as defined in Serbian law, SPS are premised on the state's passivity. For this reason, a suspended sentence with probationary supervision is often thought of as an intermediate or alternative sanction (Tešović, 2020), rather than a genuine "warning measure".

When deciding whether to impose measures in addition to a suspended prison sentence, the court looks at the offender's personality, previous life, conduct after the criminal offence was committed, and – in particular – the circumstances of the crime and the offender's conduct towards the victim(s) (article 72). The court may impose one or more measures, such as (article 73): maintaining contact with the probation officer and providing information upon request; engaging in education or work; fulfilling family obligations; undergoing (medical) treatment and therapy; and ameliorating the effects of the committed crime.

When deciding which measure(s) to impose and for how long, the court is required to take into account the offender's age, health conditions, inclinations and habits, motives for perpetrating the crime, behaviour after the crime, earlier life, personal, and family circumstances, conditions for complying with the measures, and other circumstances (article 74). Should the offender fail to abide by the imposed measures, the court has four options: (1) issue a warning, (2) substitute the imposed measure(s) with others, (3) prolong the duration of the measure(s), or (4) revoke suspension of the prison sentence (article 76).

Suspended prison sentences are entered into offenders' criminal record but are automatically erased (without any action on the convicted person's part) if the person does not reoffend within one year after the end of the operational period (article 98). If the criminal record is erased, the person in question is considered as never having been convicted (article 97).

How and why did the system develop?

The general purpose and aims of suspended prison sentences in Serbia (1929–2022)

Suspended prison sentences have been in use in Serbia for nearly a century. They have demonstrated remarkable stability throughout this period in terms of the dominant understanding of their purpose and place within the system of criminal sanctions. While the general conditions for their imposition have changed over time (albeit hardly dramatically, see section 4.2) and their practical use must be understood in the context of similarly conceived intermediate sanctions that have appeared in more recent times (see section 4.3.), SPS have always been the preferred penal reaction to less serious offences, and in particular cases in which offenders are considered not to have been profoundly "criminally infected" (Dragojlović, 2017, p. 505) or committed to a "life of crime". This "diagnosis" is premised on the court's assessment of the offender's personal qualities, life, and other relevant circumstances, which provide evidence that the offender is, in fact, an "accidental delinquent" (Lazarević, 1967, p. 26).

The legal rules pertaining to SPS applied across the territory of former Yugoslavia between their introduction and the dissolution of the country in the 1990s. The possibility of suspending imprisonment was first introduced in 1929, with the adoption of the 1929 Criminal Code of the Kingdom of Serbs, Croats, and Slovenes (the country changed its name to "Yugoslavia" in 1930) – the first unified criminal code to apply equally across the whole of Yugoslavia, a country formed in 1918 after the end of the First World War. This was a hitherto legally disintegrated territory: prior to unification, the various regions within it had subscribed to different legal regimes and instruments, which had been heavily influenced by Austrian penal legislation (Mirković, 2017). The 1929 Code was a modern, progressive, and comprehensive legal instrument based on the principles of legality and equality, and was substantially influenced by the 1871 German Penal Code (Mirković, 2017). The introduction of SPS was considered a progressive solution in place of short prison sentences, which would help to keep the number of prisoners under control (Stojanović, 2003).

Suspended prison sentences appeared again in the 1947 Yugoslav Criminal Code (*Krivični zakonik,* Official Gazette of the Federal People's Republic of Yugoslavia, 106/47). Although this code was soon substituted by the 1951 Yugoslav Criminal Code,[3] which broke away from the Soviet model of criminal law that had applied from 1947, the 1951 provisions largely returned to the legal solutions provided in the 1929 Criminal Code; hence, suspended prison sentences remained.

The 1951 Code was substituted by the 1976 Criminal Code, which entered into force in 1977;[4] again, suspended prison sentences were retained. In line with the new constitutional framework drawn up in the 1974 Constitution of Yugoslavia, the authority to enact criminal legislation was split between the Yugoslav federation and its six federative republics. The federation retained jurisdiction for the general part of the criminal code and some groups of crimes with relevance for the whole country (such as crimes against the constitutional order and security, and military crimes).

In 2005, after the dissolution of Yugoslavia and shortly before the dissolution of the State Union of Serbia and Montenegro, Serbia adopted a new Criminal Code, which retained suspended prison sentences in their previous form, but further expanded the system of alternatives to imprisonment. This Code has been amended a number of times since 2005 and remains in force today.

Academic commentators have argued that there are substantive and important differences between the *models* of suspended prison sentences as stipulated in the various laws since 1929. The alleged extent of these differences has led some commentators to propose that the "nature" of suspended prison sentences has profoundly changed over time (Stojanović, 1977), such that we can distinguish three separate models:

(1) Under the 1929 Code (the provisions of which were largely replicated in the 1951 Code), suspended prison sentences are not stipulated as a criminal sanction (examples of which include the death penalty, imprisonment, limitation of civic rights, or fines). The 1951 Code (article 48) explicitly states that *once the penalty of imprisonment* of up to two years or a fine has been imposed, the court may decide to suspend the execution of the sentence. Rather than constituting a separate criminal sanction, suspension of a prison sentence is thus merely *a modality* of its imposition and is dependent on a previously made decision on imprisonment.
(2) Under the 1976 Criminal Code, the decision to impose imprisonment and suspend it came *at the same time* (article 52). This means that the decision that suspension is warranted might actually be made *before* the exact length of imprisonment is set, which allows the judge to tweak the latter to enable its suspension. In this way, sentence suspension seems to come into its own as a sanction; this has been seen as increasing its "independence" from imprisonment (Stojanović, 1977).
(3) In 2005, the new Serbian code provided the first explicit definition of the nature of the suspended prison sentence as a "warning measure" (*mera upozorenja*) alongside judicial admonition. This postulates these measures as criminal sanctions with a lower level of intrusion. Unlike punishment whose purpose is stipulated to be incapacitation, special and general prevention, expression of public censure, strengthening of moral and law-abiding and achievement of fairness and proportionality (article 42), the "warning measures" explicitly seek to avoid punishment if a positive prediction can be made that the offender will not re-engage in crime. Thus, the suspended prison sentence was here for the first time explicitly formulated as a non-punishment, further divorcing it from imprisonment.

While there are established differences in nuance between these three models, the idea that they are fully separate seems somewhat exaggerated. Historically, there is consistency in how suspended sentences have operated, and the understanding of suspended prison sentences as *non-punishment* has been dominant since they were first introduced, even though this was not explicitly specified in the criminal code until 1976 (for an alternative interpretation of the nature of SPS arising from ambiguous legal norms, see Miladinović, 1980). While it is directly dependent on punishment – because it suspends imprisonment of a certain duration (not just punishment *in abstracto* as is the case under the Anglo-Saxon model), the nature and aims of suspended prison sentences are profoundly distinct from those of punishment (Stojanović, 1977). Since its introduction, the suspended prison sentence has been understood as a *sui generis* sanction that promotes self-government, self-control and personal responsibility. The operational period (in Serbian: *rok proveravanja,* which translates into "period of checking") is commonly described as *kušnja,* which means "temptation" or "trial" (Dragojlović, 2017), conveying the idea that offenders must apply their own efforts and devices to resist re-offending, rather than relying on the state to prevent them from doing so by imprisoning them. The operational period exists so that offenders can show that (by not re-offending) they deserve to be forgiven (Babić & Marković, 2008). It is these characteristics of SPS, as they are used in Serbia – *trust* placed in the offender, *confidence* that they will not reoffend, and the resulting *liberty* for the offender (Lazarević, 1967) – that separate it very clearly both from imprisonment and from the Anglo-Saxon model of probation based on supervision and control.

Conditions for the imposition of suspended prison sentences

Since 1929, when SPS were first introduced, very few changes pertaining to the conditions for their imposition have occurred. Additionally, the place, purpose, and understanding of the legal nature of this sanction have for the most part remained the same. The offender's personality, character traits, and social context have remained central to the use of this sanction. Here, I offer a brief overview of how the sanction has evolved; for a more detailed analysis (see Bejatović, 1986).

According to the first (1929) criminal code, suspension could pertain to imposed fines, imprisonment under strict conditions of less than 6 months or (regular) imprisonment of less than 1 year. Under the 1951 Code, which abolished the previous differentiation between different forms of imprisonment, fines or imprisonment of less than 2 years' duration could be suspended. This policy was retained in the 1976 code. The legal provisions governing the operational period have not changed since 1929: it must not be shorter than 1 year or longer than 5 years. Similarly, the additional obligations that can be imposed alongside the suspension of the sentence (such as paying damages to the victim) have also remained the same. Finally, a distinction has always been made between mandatory and optional revocation of suspension, acknowledging the range of circumstances that might influence revocation.

The most notable change to suspended prison sentences in Serbia occurred with the adoption of the 2005 Criminal Code, which limited suspension to cases of *imprisonment only;* it excluded the possibility of suspending a fine, which had always been controversial (see Dragojlović, 2017). Additionally, the law now makes clearer reference to the seriousness of crime as judged by the *potential* sentence and not just the *imposed* sentence: while suspension can only be applied to prison sentences lasting up to 2 years, it cannot be applied when the sentencing range maximum for the relevant crime is 8 or more years. The relevance of previous conviction(s) in decisions about whether to suspend prison sentences has also changed, although these (especially recent convictions) had always had an impact.

These changes must, however, be interpreted within the wider context of the gradual expansion in alternatives to imprisonment that occurred in parallel with them. The gradual toughening of suspension conditions was accompanied by the introduction of new alternatives to imprisonment from 1976 onwards: judicial admonition, work in the public interest, driving licence suspension, and house arrest.

Trends in the use of suspended prison sentences

Similar consistency can be observed in the prevalence of suspended prison sentences, at least since 1973, the earliest year for which statistical data are available.

Figure 12.2 demonstrates a continual reliance on SPS over time, both in absolute numbers and as a proportion of the overall number of imposed criminal sentences.[5] Nevertheless, while the most recent data (2021) demonstrate that suspended prison sentences are the most used criminal sanction in Serbia (making up **52.7% of all sanctions for adult offenders**), this has not always been the case. A substantive rise in the use of this sanction occurred in the early 1990s, and there is an evident correlation between this increase and the simultaneous significant drop in the use of fines. For example, in 1989 fines constituted about 48% of all criminal sanctions imposed; by 2021 this had dropped to only 12%. This decreasing use of fines was caused by judicial reluctance to impose financial sanctions in circumstances of hyper-inflation, when the currency was losing its value very quickly (in January 1994, for instance, the daily rate of inflation in Serbia was 113%, see BBC, 2021). High rates of unemployment, economic instability, and civil war further impinged negatively on the propensity to impose fines. Suspension of imposed fines (which was possible until 2005)

Figure 12.2 Criminal sentences imposed in Serbia (1973–2021).

became a necessary solution when enforcement was impossible. The prevalence of fines further decreased more recently, in particular since 2006–2007, after Serbia adopted a system of day fines that requires judges to obtain a significant amount of information about the offender's life and socio-economic situation, which significantly complicates the process and is sometimes impossible. Particular criminal procedure rules also provide incentives to use SPS. This is notably the case following the offender's admission of guilt, when the judge is not required to provide reasons for the judgement, which they must otherwise do (article 429, Code on Criminal Procedure). This relieves the judge of the burdensome and demanding process of articulating why a particular sanction was chosen over other(s) and significantly simplifies sentencing.

Overall, SPS are easy and comfortable to use: they require little judicial effort and do not involve other agencies or state organs. The primary motivation for using suspended prison sentences is that they achieve maximum results with minimum engagement by the state; they are not premised on a particularly humanistic penal philosophy (Stojanović, 2006), although the humane treatment of the offender is a welcome bonus. The suspended prison sentence can also be seen as an efficient sanction: while official data are not available, research conducted at the beginning of this century indicates that SPS are recalled in only about 6–7% of cases (Stojanović, 2003, p. 334).

That the inference about the utility of SPS is correct can be corroborated by examining the use of other alternatives to imprisonment. Since the adoption of the 2005 Criminal Code, the range of non-custodial sanctions, i.e. alternatives to imprisonment, has expanded substantially to include *work in the public interest* (to substitute a fine or imprisonment of up to three years, available since 2005) and *house arrest* (to substitute imprisonment of less than one year, available since 2009) in addition to *judicial admonition* (in place since 1976, intended for perpetrators of crimes for which the threatened sanction is a fine or imprisonment of up to one or, in special cases, three years) and suspended prison sentences.

Figure 12.3 shows that while these additional alternative sanctions are used, their use is negligible in comparison to suspended prison sentences. The most used among them is house arrest, which, like SPS, requires less monitoring and control by the state than imprisonment. Work in the public interest has been imposed only rarely and with caution since its introduction, due to a lack of capacity among the agencies in charge of enforcing it (Škulić, 2007). Judges have expressed a reluctance to impose this sanction due to a lack of collaboration with other state organs, uncertainty about legal rules, and fear of negative reactions from the supposedly punitive public (Tešović, 2020). While significant improvements have been made to the conditions for its imposition in the last decade (Garić & Stepanović, 2018), more effort and resources are needed for judges to become comfortable and accustomed to using it. Should this happen, it would be reasonable to suggest that the number of SPS will eventually drop.

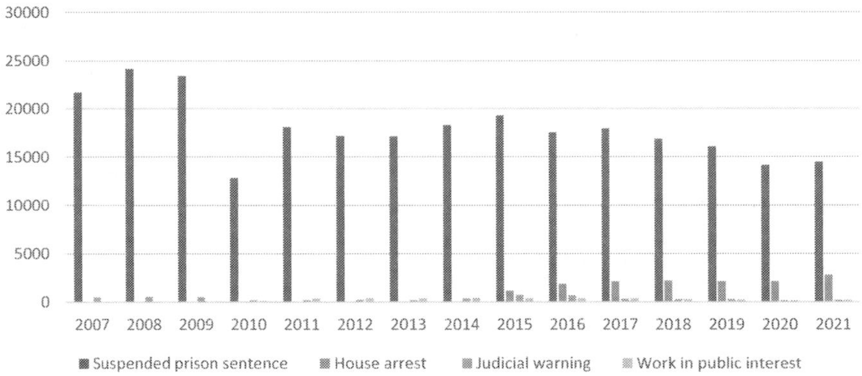

Figure 12.3 Suspended prison sentences and other alternatives to imprisonment in Serbia (2007–2021).

A more profound and comprehensive understanding of the use of SPS in Serbia is, unfortunately, lacking both because statistics are only available for the period since 1973 and because the available statistics lack nuance. For example, the available data indicate only the total number of prison sentences suspended each year. They do not record, for example, the length of the prison sentences that were suspended, whether additional obligations were added to those suspended prison sentences, what percentage of the suspended sentences were revoked, or other important details. What we do know comes from small-scale academic research; for instance, Stevanović and Vujičić (2018) show that SPS with probationary supervision is rarely used because the necessary provisions for its enforcement have not been made, and Dragojlović (2017) finds that there is scepticism towards it because it imports elements of probation that are foreign to the Serbian system.

Despite the patchy data, it is possible to draw some conclusions about the use of SPS. Although suspended sentences can only be imposed for relatively minor crimes (in place of prison sentences of up to two years), these represent a significant proportion of all crime, which may explain why SPS are used in such a high number of cases. Furthermore, comparing the use of suspended prison sentences with comparable prison sentences (up to two years) that are not suspended – see Figure 12.4 – reveals that eligible prison sentences are suspended roughly 2–3 times more than not: suspension is, therefore, a regular occurrence. Further comparison is impossible without data on the exact length of the suspended sentences.

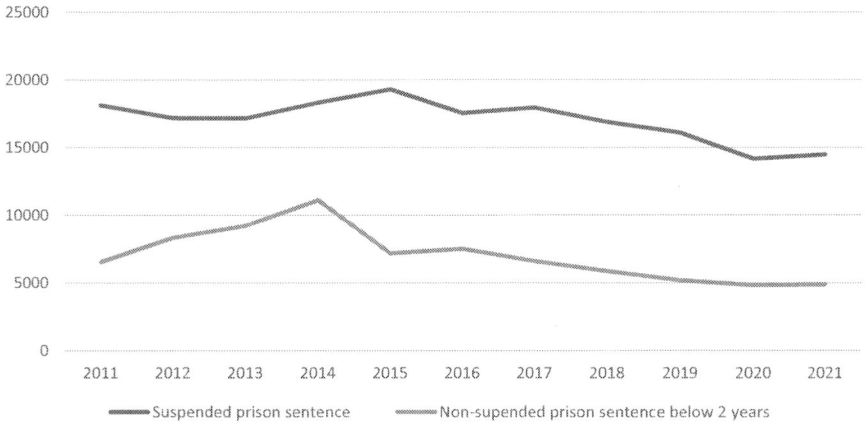

Figure 12.4 Use of suspended and non-suspended prison sentences (up to two years) in Serbia, 2011–2021.

Looking at what particular crimes are sanctioned using suspended prison sentences provides insight into how judges perceive the purpose of suspension (Figure 12.5).

First, we can see that SPS is frequently used for illegal possession of drugs, which is a behaviour that has been repeatedly criminalised and decriminalised in Serbia, for failure to pay alimony, a matter that is usually regulated through civil law but enjoys additional criminal law protection, and for endangering public traffic, a graver form of acts that are normally misdemeanours. All three of these crimes are relatively more serious forms of behaviours that are not considered criminal and as such, these may be considered to be "not proper" crimes, for which a criminal sanction must be imposed but punishment seems inappropriate: SPS thus becomes the preferred choice. Second, suspension pertains on the contrary to imprisonment for milder forms of crimes that are normally considered serious. Examples of this are the theft of objects of little value, which is still prosecuted even though in 2005 a legal provision was adopted which allows the prosecutors and courts to hold further proceedings: this provision is rarely used (Stojanović, 2012), and the crime of family violence which – apart from physical violence – can include psychological violence or coercive control;[6] in such cases, judges have considered that sentence suspension is appropriate except in situations of prolonged violence or alcohol abuse (Nikolić-Ristanović, 2013).

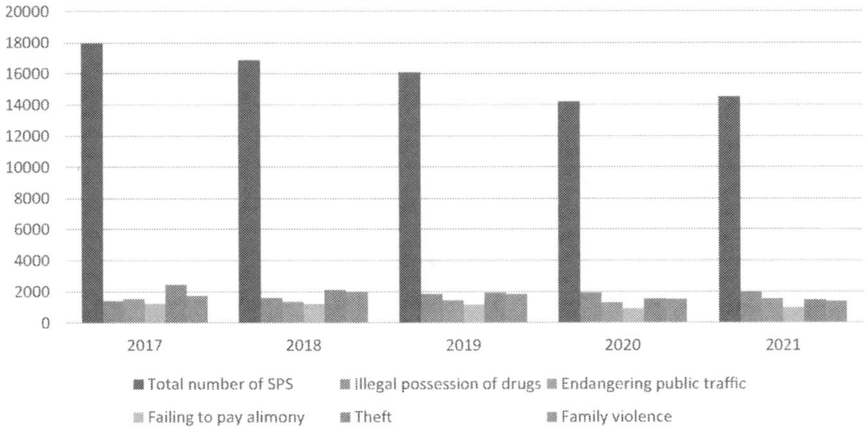

Figure 12.5 Most frequent crimes for which SPS were imposed in Serbia, 2017–2021.

Conclusion

The current Serbian system of suspended prison sentences has developed along a largely stable and continuous legal trajectory since the sanction first appeared in the 1929 Yugoslav Criminal Code. The dominant understanding and philosophy behind the sanction, its nature as a non-punishment, and the conditions for its imposition have remained largely unaffected by more general changes to the criminal law. In contrast to other former Communist countries, the system of suspended prison sentences in Serbia has never been thoroughly "reimagined" (Drápal, this volume), even when the fundamental premises of criminal law and criminal justice were modified, particularly with a view to satisfying the conditions for joining the Council of Europe (Tripković, 2016).

As the statistical data demonstrate, suspended prison sentences have been widely used by judges in Serbia for at least half a century, with a prominent increase over time. This was not only premised on the desire to achieve cost-effectiveness – the notion that maximum results can be achieved with minimum effort – but also on the idea that, by avoiding imprisonment, further "criminal infection" of those who are not "proper" criminals can be avoided. However, this notion of "criminal infection" as a basis for judicial decisions can be criticised from at least two perspectives. First, it is dubious whether such a distinction between "proper" and "accidental" offenders can ever reasonably be made: it is not based on any thorough understanding of criminological factors but relies heavily on the judge's own propensity to predict future criminal behaviour, which is impossible. Second, it is highly questionable whether judges should be allowed to make decisions that ultimately undermine the principle of equality, based on their own (ungrounded) impression of what a "real" criminal looks like.

A better way to conceive of the purpose of this sanction – albeit one that again relies on making *some* distinctions between criminal offenders with regard to their unknown future behaviour – is to understand SPS as suitable for offenders who can be trusted not to reoffend. The idea of "trusting" offenders links to broader penal tendencies rejecting the retributive purpose of punishment and instead viewing punishment as a form of inclusion and communication, grounded in the idea of criminal offenders' perpetual citizenship as members of the political community (Duff, 2001).

It is in this regard that SPS may be described as the "least worst sanction" (Drápal, this volume): in imposing this sanction, unlike many others in Serbian criminal law, the state expresses confidence that the offender can refrain from reoffending and abstains from imposing the harsh consequences of punishment. This is also what makes SPS a unique sanction in Serbian law: even though other intermediate sanctions also seek to avoid imprisonment, suspension of a prison sentence shows a more robust level of confidence that no intervention is needed to "fix" the offender.

On the other hand, when we understand this sanction in this positive light, with its promotion of self-governance and personal responsibility, it might then place too heavy a burden on the offender. While not intrusive in the sense of limiting the offender's liberty, the consequent "responsibilisation" of the offender, who becomes an instrument and tool in achieving their own change (Garland, 2002), is intrusive in a psychological sense.

By now, the Serbian public is accustomed to the concept of SPS. Public opinion was initially wary and suspicious of suspended prison sentences when they appeared in 1929, considering them unjustified from the standpoint of criminal repression and taking them as a signal that the state was "easy" on criminal offenders (Mirković, 2017). Yet over time, the Serbian system's reliance on three principal sanctions: suspended prison sentences for less serious crimes, imprisonment for more serious crimes and fines in specific (and rare) cases, has become widely accepted (Tešović, 2020). A small survey conducted among younger inhabitants in four Serbian cities in 2016 found that more than half of respondents think that SPS can achieve the same purpose as punishment and about two-thirds of respondents support the existence of SPS (Dragojlović, 2017). Suspending a prison sentence is now a traditional, normalised, and widely accepted way of administering justice to a select group of offenders in Serbia, and as such, will probably remain just as relevant in the years to come.

Notes

1 *Krivični zakonik,* Službeni glasnik Republike Srbije, 85/2005; 88/2005; 107/2005; 72/2009; 111/2009; 121/2012; 104/2013; 108/2014; 94/2016; 35/2019.
2 Although they have similar effects, this security measure is different from the criminal sanction "Suspension of a driving licence" that was mentioned above. In the former case, the aim of the sanction is to prevent the offender from driving when using a vehicle is a modus operandi for committing crimes (for instance, armed robbery). In the latter case, the driving prohibition is premised on the fact that the offender's driving is dangerous (because they have, for instance, caused a traffic incident before).
3 *Krivični zakonik,* Official Gazette of the Federal People's Republic of Yugoslavia, 13/51.
4 *Krivični zakon,* Official Gazette of the Socialist Federal Republic of Yugoslavia, 44/76.
5 The "drop" in all numbers in 2010 is due to reform of the judiciary (including reelection of the judges) which prevented courts from working for a few months at the beginning of the year. See: Stojanović, 2012.
6 This crime was first introduced in 2002.

References

Babić, M., & Marković, I. (2008). *Krivično pravo – opšti dio.* Pravni fakultet.

BBC. (2021). *Raspad Jugoslavije, inflacija i dinar.* Retrieved October 5, 2022, from https://www.bbc.com/serbian/lat/srbija-58629879

Bejatović, S. (1986). *Uslovna osuda.* Poslovna politika.

Dragojlović, J. (2017). Uslovna osuda i novčana kazna. *Kultura polisa, 32*, 497–507.

Drápal, J. (this volume). Key features of suspended prison sentences and some associated problems. In J. Drápal, K. Krajewski, & M. Tripković (Eds.), *Suspended prison sentences: Elusive punishment in Central and Eastern Europe.*

Duff, R. A. A. (2001). *Punishment, communication, and community.* Oxford University Press.

Garić, D., & Stepanović, A. (2018). Alternativne krivične sankcije (stanje u Srbiji i mere unapređenja praktične primene). In S. Bejatović & I. Jovanović (Eds.), *Alternativne krivične sankcije (regionalna krivična zakonodavstva, iskustva u primeni i mere unapređenja.* OEBS.

Garland, D. (2002). *The culture of control.* Oxford: Oxford University Press.

Miladinović, V. (1980). Pravna priroda uslovne osude. *Zbornik radova Pravnog fakulteta u Nišu, 20*, 381–394.

Mirković, Z. (2017). *Srpska pravna istorija.* Univerzitet u Beogradu, Pravni fakultet.

Nikolić-Ristanović, V. (2013). *Praćenje primene zakonskih rešenja o nasilju u porodici u Srbiji: Nalazi pilot istraživanja.* UN Women. https://www.vds.rs/File/PracenjePrimeneZakResONasiljuUPorodiciUSrbiji.pdf

Plesničar, M., Tripković, M., & Lazarević, D. (1967). Uslovna osuda i kratkotrajna kazna zatvora. Jugoslovenska revija za kriminologiju i krivično pravo, 17.

Stevanović, I., & Vujičić, N. (2018). Rad u javnom interesu i uslovna osuda sa zaštitnim nadzorom u Republici Srbiji i povrat (analiza uspešnosti primene iz ugla istraživača). *Crimen, 3*, 267–284.

Stojanović, Z. (1977). Odnos uslovne osude i kazne u Krivičnom Zakonu SFRJ i pitanje samostalnosti uslovne osude. *Zbornik Radova Pravnog Fakulteta u Novom Sadu, 11*, 265–272.
Stojanović, Z. (2003). *Krivično pravo, opšti deo* (8. izd.). Univerzitet u Beogradu, Pravni fakultet.
Stojanović, Z. (2006). *Komentar krivičnog zakonika.* Službeni glasnik.
Stojanović, Z. (2012). Kaznena politika u Srbiji: Sukob zakonodavca i sudske prakse. In Đ. Ignjatović (Ed.), *Stanje kriminaliteta u Srbiji i pravna sredstva reagovanja, I deo.* Univerzitet u Beogradu, Pravni fakultet.
Škulić, M. (2007). Alternative sanctions, some other measures and probations in the criminal law system of Republic of Serbia. In Đ. Ignjatović (Ed.), *Stanje kriminaliteta u Srbiji i pravna sredstva reagovanja, I deo.* Univerzitet u Beogradu, Pravni fakultet.
Tešović, O. (2020). *Priručnik za primenu alternativnih sankcija.* Forum sudija Srbije.
Tripković, M. (2016). Beyond punitiveness? Governance of crime and authoritarian heritage in Serbia. *Punishment and Society, 18*(3), 369–386.

13 Slovenia

Suspended sentences as a pillar of penal moderation[1]

Mojca M. Plesničar and Aleksej Jankovič

Introduction

In terms of sentencing, Slovenia is an outlier when we compare it to the surrounding region, and the same is true in the broader European context. This small country in Central Europe, with some two million inhabitants, has remained steadily moderate in how it punishes its offenders for the better part of the last century, ever since criminology first emerged as an academic endeavour in Slovenia. Both from a conceptual, ideological point of view and on a practical level (with the exception of politically motivated trials in the communist period), there have been no significant excesses (Flander et al., 2023). Indeed, Slovenia's sentencing was exceptional within the former federation of Yugoslavia post-Second World War and remains a considerable exception in today's European context, where it is commonly compared with Scandinavian systems (Dünkel, 2013; Hacin et al., 2022; Flander & Meško, 2016; Plesničar & Drobnjak, 2019).

Slovenia's sentencing system is traditionally continental, both in terms of its normative framework – with wide statutory sentencing ranges – and in terms of the practical problems encountered due to disparity issues. Its sentencing outcomes are less continental, however: the proportion of prison sentences is relatively stable at around 20% of all sentences, and the vast majority of these sentences are shorter than two years. This means that Slovenia is significantly less punitive than other countries in Central and Eastern Europe, as will be apparent later in the chapter. This leniency is not solely due to the extensive use of suspended sentences, which consistently make up more than 60% of all sentencing decisions, sometimes even 70%.[2] However, combined with the fact that suspended sentences rarely, if ever, lead to actual prison sentences, it is apparent that these play a substantial role in perpetuating the "Slovenian exception". In the Slovenian context, suspended sentences are known as "conditional sentences" and are independent sanctions, set apart from prison sentences, although they serve purposes similar to suspended prison sentences in other European countries.

In this chapter, we begin by giving an overview of sentencing in Slovenia. We then expand on how suspended sentences are conceptualised, understood

DOI: 10.4324/9781003568667-18

and used in practice, with particular emphasis on their independent status within the catalogue of sanctions. Finally, we look at how the system was developed and the factors that led to the dominance of suspended sentences in modern times.

Sentencing overview

The Slovenian penal landscape is permeated by the principle of individualisation. Individualising the sentence is an ideal to be followed at all three stages of penal intervention: when defining abstract sentences for abstract crimes (differentiating between offences and offence types when defining the sentencing ranges and providing broad sentencing ranges that allow for later individualisation), when sentencing specific offenders for specific crimes (considering guilt, harm, and an unrestricted number of mitigating and aggravating circumstances), and when imposing such individualised sentences (allowing for individual treatment plans, diverse prison regimes, prison restrictions, and rewards) (Plesničar, 2013b).

The sentencing stage of the process is regulated by the Criminal Code (CC) and additionally moulded by judicial practice. The CC establishes the basic principles of sentencing, defining the aims, sentencing options and limitations in general terms. Moreover, it defines all criminal offences and variants of each offence (aggravated and mitigated forms), and sets forth a sentencing framework for each offence type. However, the provisions in the CC are abstract and general in nature, and its sentencing framework leaves substantial discretion to judges in making individual decisions in specific cases.

Aims of punishment

Punishment aims were only written into the CC in 2016, having previously been omitted since the country gained its independence (see Plesničar, 2013b). These aims are multiple. Art. 45.a stipulates that through choosing the proper punishment, *"the State protects the fundamental values and principles of the rule of law, creates awareness among the offender and others of the inadmissibility of the commission of criminal offences, and, above all, while respecting the human dignity and personality of the offender, enables the offender to be integrated with dignity into the common social environment by means of an appropriate sanction".*[3] Note – in comparison to other countries – the lack of emphasis on retribution and the ample emphasis on social rehabilitation, reinforced through the use of the words *"above all"* (see also Carroll et al., 2015; Shames, 2011; Oswald et al., 2002). In any case, the permissible rationales are numerous and largely non-hierarchical, leaving ample room for individual judges' preferences (Hogarth, 1971).

Discretion and sentencing options

The discretion left to judges in individual cases is very broad. This is most evident in two aspects. First, there is a multitude of sentencing options available to judges, depending on the specific features of the case. Generally, sanctions for adult offenders are grouped into (1) sentences; (2) admonitory sanctions; and (3) safety measures (see Table 13.1). The last group applies to specific situations (e.g. confiscation of objects or restraining orders), specific crimes (e.g. bans from practising particular professions) or specific offenders (e.g. compulsory psychiatric treatment). Among sentences, imprisonment is the most important one, and the one that is used in the CC to determine the ordinal and cardinal proportionality of the offences (Ashworth, 2015).

Offences, for which the CC defines individual sentencing ranges, are further divided into different modalities: regular, mitigated, and aggravated forms. However, the sentencing ranges prescribed by the CC for each offence type are still very wide (for example, non-aggravated rape can be sentenced with a prison sentence of between one and ten years). Furthermore, these ranges may be further mitigated below the sentencing minimum (Art. 50), remitted (Art. 52), combined, or executed as an alternative sanction (Art 87): most typically, a sentence of up to two years of imprisonment may be served in the form of community service upon the request of the offender and at the judge's discretion.

Admonitory sanctions encompass simple judicial admonition and two types of suspended sentence. Contrary to other solutions across Europe and in line with the Yugoslav tradition (see Tripković, this volume), suspended sentences are systemically separate from prison sentences and constitute an independent measure. They may be used when the court would otherwise impose a fine or a

Table 13.1 Criminal sanctions in Slovenia

Sentences (direct translation: punishments)	Imprisonment Fine Driving ban for motor vehicles Deportation of an alien
Admonitory sanctions	Suspended sentence Suspended sentence with custodial supervision Judicial admonition
Safety measures	Compulsory psychiatric treatment and confinement in a health institution Compulsory psychiatric treatment at liberty Ban from practising a profession Restraining order and prohibition of communication with the victim Revocation of driving licence Confiscation of objects

prison sentence not exceeding two years in length, and only for offences with a statutory minimum term of imprisonment lower than three years.

The CC offers little general guidance on sentencing. It emphasises the hard limits set by the statutory ranges in the CC and gives most relevance to the principle of proportionality: the sentence must respect the gravity of the offence as well as the offender's culpability (Art. 49). Moreover, it leaves plenty of room for judges to interpret the specifics of the case, emphasising the court's obligation to take into account *"all the [mitigating and aggravating] circumstances, and in particular the degree of the offender's culpability, the motives for committing the offence, the degree of threat or violation of the protected legal value, the circumstances in which the offence was committed, the offender's previous life, their personal and financial situation, their behaviour after the offence [...] and the expected effect of the sentence on the offender's future life in the social environment"* (Art. 49/II). In so doing, the CC effectively grants judges great autonomy (as well as responsibility) in imposing just, fair, and individualised sanctions upon particular offenders.

In addition, the Slovenian penal system enables sentences to be further individualised throughout their enforcement via back-door sentencing (Padfield, 2014), i.e. the option of parole (in Slovenian: conditional release). Decisions on parole are not, however, made by judges but by an administrative committee governed by the Ministry of Justice. In theory, two conditions must be met for a prisoner to be conditionally released: one formal condition, i.e. that the offender has served more than half of their sentence in prison, in practice usually more than three-quarters; and one material condition, i.e. that the committee reasonably expects that the offender will not reoffend while at liberty – this is known as a "positive prognosis" (Ambrož & Šugman, 2011; Plesničar, 2012; Arnež & Plesničar, 2025).

Individualisation vs disparity

That emphasis on the individualisation of punishment is further reinforced by case law. There are not many Supreme Court or higher court decisions that specifically address sentencing, even though these courts have the power to enforce judicial self-regulation with regard to sentencing (Drapal & Plesničar, 2023; Plesničar, 2013a). The ones that have been passed in recent years largely addressed the aims of punishment (Plesničar, 2013b) prior to the amendment of the CC in 2016, while one rather prominent high court judgement re-emphasised the importance of the principle of individualisation over consistency by stating that *"the factual circumstances of a particular crime, as a unique life event, cannot be identical to the circumstances of other specific cases, and therefore, when deciding on the choice and imposition of a criminal sanction, [...] the Court's consideration of circumstances of allegedly comparable offences [...] is irrelevant"* (Decision III Kp 23259/2017, 10.10.2018, point 14).

Considering this apparent lack of stringent formal sentencing requirements and general guidance, and adding recent research on the effects of bias and stereotyping on sentencing (Hafner et al., 2020), it is not surprising that recent studies have shown a variety in sentencing outcomes that could be categorised as disparity (Plesničar et al., 2023). These studies have only recently spurred discussions within the academic community, relevant stakeholders and government authorities about the ways to address the situation; no formal steps have yet been taken.

Principles governing suspended prison sentences at present

As we have seen, suspended sentences occupy a particular place in the Slovenian context, both in theory and in practice – due to their frequent use. Whereas in many other systems, suspended sentences function as modified prison sentences or a post-sentencing afterthought, suspended sentences in Slovenia are a type of admonitory sanction. This is very much in line with the Yugoslav tradition and similar to several other ex-Yugoslav systems (cf. Tripković, this volume). It has been criticised for being duplicitous, in the sense that suspended sentences may eventually transition into custodial sentences and the distinction is thus less clear than it should be. Moreover, the tradition is not upheld everywhere. For example, one of the newer Croatian amendments to the Criminal Code changed the Croatian system in such a manner that suspended sentences are no longer independent (Verdel Kokol, 2021).

Admonitory nature of suspended sentences

Admonitory sanctions are a separate type of sanction, classified in a special chapter of the Slovenian CC. The systemic placement implies a desire to avoid using sentences, and especially the prison sentence, where this would be justified. Admonitory sanctions are intended to be imposed when the nature and gravity of the offence, the circumstances of the offence and the personality of the offender make a custodial sentence unnecessary. In other words, they are to be used when the purpose of punishment (which, in short, is to prevent the offender from reoffending) can be achieved by merely warning the offender that such a sentence will be imposed if they breach the conditions imposed (in the case of a suspended sentence) or by an act of reprimand (in the case of a judicial admonition)[4]. The qualitative difference between admonitory sanctions and prison sentences is that the former do not impinge on the offender's rights and personal integrity to the same extent as a sentence involving a restriction of his or her liberty (Verdel Kokol, 2021).

A key feature distinguishing admonitory sanctions from sentences is that they do not involve any actual restriction of the offender's liberty (Verdel Kokol, 2021).[5] Suspended sentences are exhausted in the warning: either accompanied by a fixed penalty of imprisonment or a fine, which is not actually imposed (suspended sentences) or in the warning itself (judicial admonition). Bačić (1998) explains that admonitory sanctions may even be categorised as "parapenal" sanctions, since they lack the repressive element of traditional sanctions. In other words, they offer a lot of "bark", but lack the "bite" we traditionally associate with penal sanctions. Using the Damocles' sword metaphor, the "bite" consists in the threat that hangs over the offender's head.

However, this lack of bite is purposeful and driven by a realisation that, in many cases, custodial sentences are neither necessary nor the most appropriate way of achieving penal aims (Plesnicar & Tripković, 2024). Admonitory sanctions replace custodial sentences when the latter are not absolutely necessary (imprisonment is viewed as an *ultima ratio* measure; see Bavcon et al., 2013). In particular, they are used in place of short-term prison sentences. This may be justifiable when dealing with cases of lesser importance (for minor, less dangerous offences (i.e. petty crime) and less dangerous offenders (e.g. first-time offenders who committed the crime for transient (non-chronic) reasons). In these cases, the imposition of a custodial sentence would likely have more harmful than beneficial effects; hence the legislature allows for the admonitory approach instead (Verdel Kokol, 2021).

In theory, it is reasonable to impose an admonitory sanction if a comprehensive assessment of both the circumstances of the offence and the personality of the offender concludes that a cautionary sanction will be sufficient to achieve the aims of punishment – in the Slovenian system mainly a special and general preventive effect (aimed at the offender and the general public respectively). This means that before such an admonitory sanction can be imposed, there must first be a complex assessment of its justifiability and appropriateness (Verdel Kokol, 2021).

Judicial admonition is the most lenient sanction available to Slovenian courts and was used very sparingly, albeit consistently, in about 2% of all cases. Its use has slowly declined over recent decades, and it has not been used at all since 2015. This development can hardly be the result of changes in the types and qualities of crime considering recent trends in crime (Urbas, 2020). It seems more likely that the change came as a result of courts assessing these sanctions as inappropriate, which might be attributed to the slow slide towards harsher penalties (Plesničar & Drobnjak, 2019).

On the other hand, as Figure 13.1 below shows, suspended sentences entail a large proportion of all passed sentences. This may be a consequence of the types of crimes prevalent in Slovenia, the vast majority of which are theft-related crimes and minor drug offences. However, it seems that this is the default sentencing policy among Slovenian courts, except for the most serious crimes, even though there is no formal requirement for this to be so.

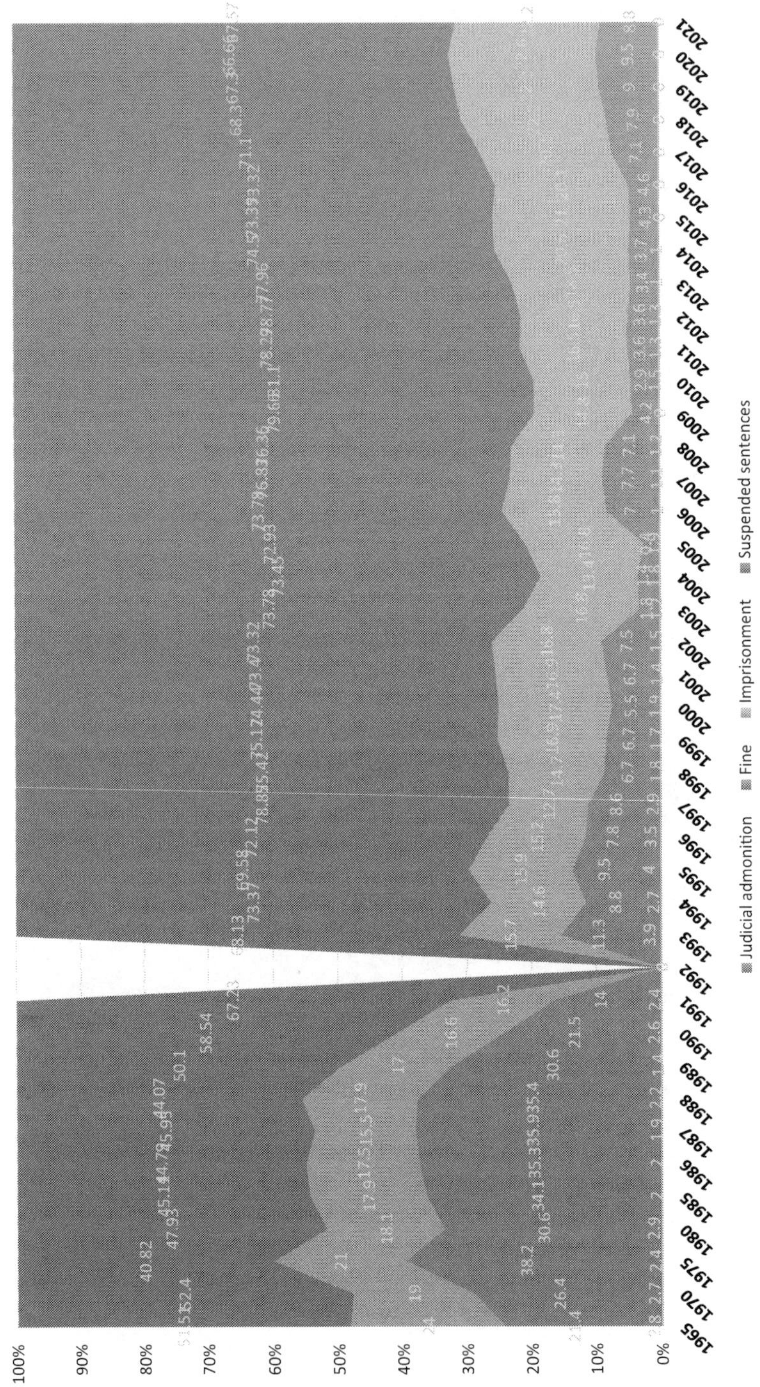

Figure 13.1 Distribution of sanctions in Slovenia, 1965–2022.

Note: There is no data available for 1992.

Formal and material criteria

According to Slovenian law, the possibility of suspending a sentence is dependent on two conditions or criteria: the formal and the material. The first refers to the criterion of the stipulated imprisonment sentence, and the second to the reasonable expectation that the convicted person will not reoffend while at liberty – the so-called "positive prognosis". The CC stipulates that a sentence will only remain suspended if, within the operational period determined by the court, the convicted person does not commit another criminal offence (Art. 57/II).

The CC formulates the formal criterion in two ways, considering both the abstract sentence prescribed for the offence and the specific sentence passed in the given case. The former is set in negative terms: the court may not impose a suspended sentence if the prescribed minimum sentence for the given offence is three years or more (Art. 58/III). The latter is set in positive terms: the court may impose a suspended sentence instead of a (non-suspended) sentence (Art. 57/I) when the latter would be imprisonment of up to two years or a fine (Art. 58/I). In theory, suspension is thus available for both prison sentences and fines, but in practice, suspension of fines is very rarely used; fines overall amount to less than 10% of all sentences imposed.

The material criterion refers to the court's conclusion that the offender's "personality, previous life, behaviour after committing the criminal offence, degree of guilt, and other circumstances in which the act was committed" provide reasonable grounds to expect that the offender will not commit any further criminal offences (Art. 58/III).

The CC stipulates that the operational period must be at least one year and not more than five years (Art. 57/II). This period is determined in years (not months or days); when determining the duration of the operational period, the court considers the prognosis of the offender's future behaviour, determining what length of operational period is needed in order to prevent the offender from reoffending (Verdel Kokol, 2021). The length of the determined sentence and the length of the operational period are usually correlated – longer sentences typically carry longer operational periods when suspended (Verdel Kokol, 2021).

There are some exceptions to these requirements. Following the legislative introduction of confessions of guilt at pretrial hearings or in plea bargains with the state prosecutor, in 2012, Art. 58/V now stipulates that the court may suspend a prison sentence for which a minimum sentence of five years of imprisonment is prescribed if the offender pleads guilty during the pretrial hearing or in a plea bargaining agreement with the state prosecutor. In such cases, the court may impose a suspended sentence of up to five years' imprisonment with an operational period of up to ten years.

These options have been used in recent years and have caused some disruption in the system, which had not previously undergone significant change for decades. They have made it possible for suspended sentences to be used even more frequently and, despite some early reservations, these have indeed begun to be used even in cases where one might not have expected them, such as for sexual offences against children (Plesničar et al., 2023).

Conditions and accessory sentences

Slovenian legislation does not provide for the partial suspension of any sentence. However, the court may combine a suspended sentence with an accessory sentence, safety measures, additional special conditions, and probationary supervision.[6]

First, the court may decide to complement the imposition of a suspended sentence with one or more additional accessory sentences (e.g. a fine, driving ban, or deportation). Based on Art. 58/IV, the court may decide that one or all of these accessory sentences be enforced, even when the main sentence is suspended. The phrasing of this provision implies that the default is for the accessory sentences to be suspended, unless the court specifically decides that they are to be enforced (Verdel Kokol, 2021).

Second, any safety measure may be combined with a suspended sentence according to the CC (Art 69/I) and enforced regardless of whether the suspended sentence is later revoked (Art. 57/IV).

Furthermore, in addition to the general condition – that the offender refrain from committing any new criminal offence – the court may decide to condition the suspension of the sentence on three additional special conditions (Art. 57/III): the restitution of the proceeds of the crime within a specified time limit; the payment of compensation for damages caused by the crime; and performance of other obligations determined by criminal law provisions. While the meaning of the former two conditions is reasonably clear, the latter means, for example, that the court may decide to condition the suspension of a sentence upon e.g. the prohibition of pursuing a particular profession, and that the suspension may thus be revoked if the convicted person does not comply with that prohibition (Art. 71/III).

Finally, the suspension of a sentence may be combined with probationary supervision, which is seen as a modified form of suspended sentence (Verdel Kokol, 2021). The court combines a suspended sentence with probationary supervision when it determines that such supervision is necessary and appropriate, either for a specific period or for the duration of the operational period (Art. 63). In the Slovenian system, probationary supervision entails psychological and social support for the offender, with the aim of recognising problematic aspects of their behaviour and controlling their behaviour in line with social norms (Verdel Kokol, 2021), but also entails a certain level of monitoring and surveillance. The imposition of probationary supervision is not final or absolute: if the court later determines that probationary supervision is no longer required, it may order it to be discontinued even before the end of the previously specified probation period (Art. 64/II).

Like simple suspended sentences, suspended sentences with probationary supervision may be accompanied by one or more specific instructions to be followed by the convicted person,[7] individualised considering their age, their psychological characteristics, the motives for their act, their personal circumstances, their previous life history, the circumstances in which the act was committed, and their behaviour since committing the criminal offence. Probationary supervision is carried out by a probation officer appointed by the Probation Service (Art. 66 of the CC). Should the convicted person fail to comply with such conditions during the probation period, the court may either issue an admonishment, modify the conditions, extend the probationary supervision within the limits of the probation period, or revoke the suspension of the sentence (Art. 67).

However, the fact that the courts may use these variants of the suspended sentence does not mean they do so to any considerable extent in practice. Although there is no exact data on the types of suspension used, anecdotal information indicates that the vast majority of suspended sentences are simple suspensions. Data on suspended sentences with probationary supervision, only available for the last couple of years through the Probation Service, show that the number of these sentences has not exceeded 100 cases per year (Probation Service, 2021).

Breach

The Slovenian legal system does not explicitly define actions that constitute a breach of a suspended sentence. However, these may be extrapolated from the provisions governing the revocation of suspension. According to the CC, the court may revoke the suspension of a sentence due to: (1) newly committed crimes; (2) a previous criminal offence committed before the suspended sentence was imposed; and (3) non-compliance with imposed obligations – this can occur either when special conditions are not fulfilled, or when the offender fails to comply with instructions given within their probationary supervision.

There are two options for revoking a suspended sentence: obligatory and facultative revocation, and their use depends on the severity of the breach. In the first (more frequent) instance, revocation follows the convicted person committing, during the operational period, a new criminal offence for which the court decides to impose a sentence of two or more years of imprisonment (Art. 59/I). In such cases, the court has no option but to revoke the existing suspension.

In the second instance, facultative revocation, the court has broader discretion. This may follow the imposition of a new prison sentence of less than two years or of a fine, during the operational period. The decision as to whether to revoke the previously suspended sentence in such cases is left to the court, which should consider all the circumstances relating to the criminal offences committed and the perpetrator (Art. 59/II). If the court decides not to revoke the existing suspension, a new suspended sentence or punishment may be imposed for the new criminal offence. In such cases, the court issues an aggregate sentence for the previous and new offence and determines a new operational period (Art. 59/IV).

Facultative revocation is not frequent in Slovenian practice, and this is often a sore spot in public debates and feeds criticism of the system (Šugman Stubbs & Ambrož, 2012). There is no statistical data on how often it is used, but in our empirical research, we have encountered – not infrequently – case files in which offenders accumulated several suspended sentences that were never revoked.

Revocation for criminal offences that were committed before the imposition of the suspended sentence in question occurs if the court determines that there would not have been sufficient grounds for imposing a suspended sentence had the existence of the previous offence been known to the court at the time of sentencing (Art 60/I).

If additional obligations are imposed on the convicted person and they fail to comply with these within the time limit set out in the judgement, the court may either extend the time limit for compliance or revoke the suspended sentence (Art. 61). Through personal interaction, the probation service has been vocal about the courts' lack of action in this regard.

Expungement

The current regulation of the legal status of convicted persons after serving their sentences can be traced back to three key societal concerns: upholding human dignity, reintegrating the convicted individual into society, and, pragmatically, preventing the restriction of rights for a large number of citizens after they have completed their sentences (Polegek, 2021).

In the Slovenian legal system, expungement can take two forms: legal or judicial. Legal expungement, as defined in Article 82/I of CC, involves clearing the conviction from the criminal record, ending the application of legal consequences, and considering the convicted person as never having been convicted. For suspended sentences, this happens automatically one year after the end of the operational period (Art. 82/I, IV-2), provided that no new crime has been committed.

Judicial expungement, on the other hand, is at the court's discretion and must be requested by the convicted person (Art. 83). The court can decide to expunge the conviction and consider the person as never having been convicted if at least half of the prescribed period for legal expungement has passed since the conviction's expiration, and no further criminal offences have occurred. When deciding on expungement, the court considers the offender's behaviour since serving the sentence, the nature of the crime, and other relevant circumstances (Art 83.) Generally, courts only approve judicial expungement when specific, compelling reasons for doing so exist, such as benevolent actions towards the injured party or exceptional circumstances that significantly affect the convicted person's rights (Polegek, 2021).

Sentencing practice

As discussed above, Slovenia's sentencing is mild in practice compared to its neighbours and other European countries, and has been so consistently despite a slowly increasing trend in the use of imprisonment during recent decades (Meško et al., 2011; Plesničar & Drobnjak, 2019).

Data on sentences has only been officially recorded and made available in recent decades, and no one has yet attempted to access historical data from the early 20th century via substantial archive research.

The available data covers the period since the mid-20th century and clearly reveals that suspended sentences have consistently formed the backbone of the sentencing system in this period. In recent decades, as a proportion of all sanctions, these have not dropped below 67% in the observed period and rose at their highest to 81% of all sanctions.

Looking at the total number of convictions, we can observe that this slowly decreased from the 1960s to the early 1990s, reaching its lowest point in 1995 (when the criminal justice legislation was rebooted after Slovenia gained independence in 1991). It then rose slowly, peaking in 2013 and 2014 (after plea bargaining was introduced in mid-2012), and has been slowly descending since.

If we focus on prison sentences (in the Slovenian system, this means non-suspended imprisonment), we see that as a percentage of all sentenced cases, these decrease from a maximum of 24% in 1965, dropping gradually to around 15% in the early 2000s and then rising to the current 22%.

Moreover, it is apparent that since Slovenia became independent in the early nineties, the use of fines has significantly decreased, whereas there has been an increase in the use of suspended sentences.

The length of imposed prison sentences tends to be focused at the lower end of the prescribed ranges, with prison sentences of less than two years imposed in the vast majority of cases. Figure 13.2 shows that the longest prison sentences, above ten years, are imposed in only a handful of cases each year.

If we focus on suspended sentences (see Figure 13.3), we can observe not only that many such sentences are imposed, but also that they tend to be relatively short. The large majority fall into two length ranges: 2 to 3 months and 3 to 6 months. The smaller proportion of lengthier suspended sentences, especially those approaching 2 years, is somewhat understandable as those are the cases in which judges would generally consider the case approaching the custody threshold.

The presented data refers to all variants of suspended sentences – with and without supervision and other additional conditions. Until 2014, statistics were available for suspended sentences with supervision separately; there were

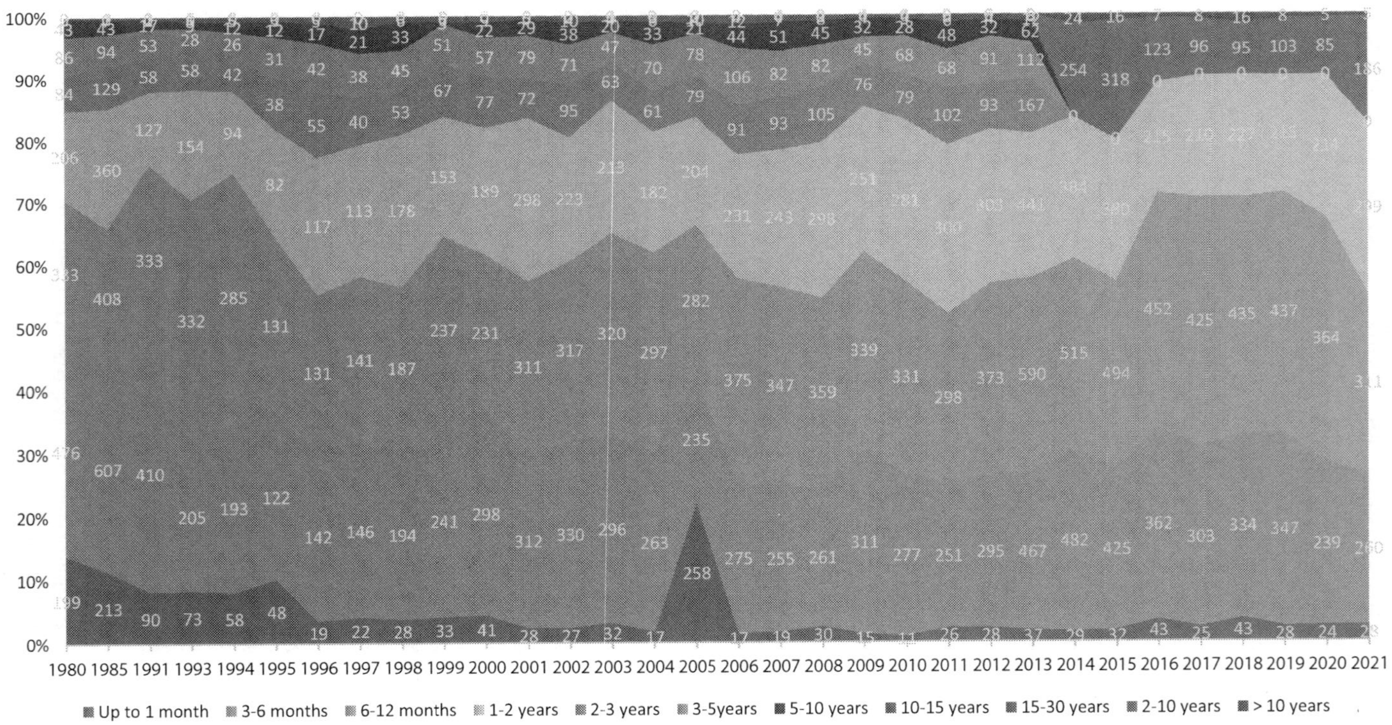

Figure 13.2 Length of prison sentences in Slovenia, 1980–2021.

Source: SURS

Note: In 2014 the statistical office (SURS) changed the categories in which it provides information on prison sentence length – the previous categories 2–3 years, 3–5 years, 5–10 years and 10-30 years have been merged into a single category of >10 years.

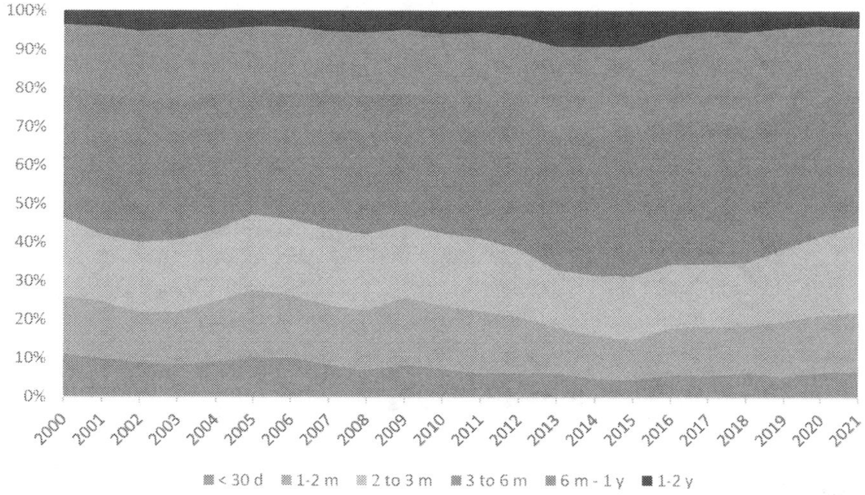

Figure 13.3 Length of suspended sentences in Slovenia, 2000–2021.

approximately 100 such sentences per year which, compared to the total number of around 6000 suspended sentences, means that their use was very infrequent. Anecdotal information suggests that other conditions are attached to suspended sentences more often than that, especially the obligation to repay damages to victims. However, there is no official data on the frequency of such conditions, as this information is not processed in the official statistics.

The same is also true when it comes to combinations of sanctions passed conjointly with the suspended sentence, such as bans on driving motor vehicles or restraining orders.

Moreover, there is no data available on how often reoffending occurs during the operational periods of suspended sentences nor on how many suspended sentences are revoked as a result.

How did the system develop?

In this section, we will explore how the current system of suspended sentences in Slovenia developed. We will consider which forces shaped the flow of events that resulted in this concept becoming part of the legal system; what major legislative and practice-related changes moulded suspended sentences into what they are today; and, finally, what the concept of suspended sentences tells us about Slovenia's legal and social system during that time.

Our exploration considers the ideas developed by the criminologists and criminal lawyers who have shaped sentencing in Slovenia for the past century, which reflect their interpretation of the evolution of society, sentencing and suspended sentences.

The background

At the turn of the 20th century, historical and economic transformations that took place in society prompted innovative approaches to addressing societal needs, which were gradually honed over time. Following the October Revolution in 1917, it became apparent that the previously dominant bourgeois conception of society and of the individual's role within it was no longer valid. An evolving social consciousness emerged that ultimately gave birth to the concept of psychological dynamics within individual personalities. This progression marked the point at which society assumed the responsibility for crafting strategies to meet its needs, while also placing upon individuals the duty to engage with and respect these evolving norms and practices (Vodopivec, 1966).

These changes prompted greater emphasis on social research and the expansion of the field of criminology, which combined social and legal aspects. These developments were significantly influenced by scholars adhering to the "socioantropological" or positivist theory of crime, notably Enrico Ferri (1856-1929). Unlike the classical and neoclassical schools, the positivists underscored the importance of the offender's personality. They argued that it was not the act itself, but rather the offender's criminal disposition and potential for future offences that posed a threat to society (Bavcon, 1958). According to Ferri, society approached crime prevention similarly to its approach to natural threats or wild animals by implementing protective measures. As such, Ferri proposed that society should combat crime in four ways: through preventive measures against "dangerous" individuals, measures to address the consequences of criminal acts, repressive measures with no fixed duration, and elimination measures targeting recidivists and incorrigible offenders (Ferri in: Bavcon, 1958).

Despite enduring controversy and criticism surrounding its deterministic philosophy (see Bavcon, 1966; Maklecov, 1948), the positivist school's enduring legacy lies in placing human beings and their individual personalities at the core of the philosophy of criminal law. This legacy firmly established the principle that sentences, whether punitive or corrective in nature, should be tailored to the specific circumstances of each individual offence and offender, emphasising the importance of individualisation.

In Yugoslavia, there were significant developments in criminological research during the early 20th century, which established that every criminal offence resulted from a complex interplay of individual, social, and physical factors. Consequently, the abstract notion of the *"homo delinquens"* was deemed to have no substantial basis (Bavcon, 1966).

As a response to this paradigm shift and the recognition that each offence was a product of an individual's actions within specific circumstances, the movement advocating for the individualisation of punishment began to gain momentum (Bavcon, 1966; see also Bavcon, 1958). Given the prevailing philosophical underpinnings of criminal law during this era, this concept of individualisation was primarily rooted in the abstract criterion of "sentencing fairness" (Bavcon, 1958) and was notably distant from the modern understanding of individualised sentencing as a means of rehabilitation. Nonetheless, this concept constituted a significant advancement and a pivotal starting point for further developments in criminal law and policy (Bavcon, 1958).

In the late 1930s, various movements with preventive or non-punitive agendas emerged that subsequently influenced post-Second World War criminal policy. One noteworthy movement in Slovenia during this period was the Social Defence movement, which advocated for the replacement of repression with a *"range of preventive, therapeutic, and only if necessary, repressive socio-economic, mental health, medical, educational, and similar measures"* (Bavcon, 1966, p. 21). Consequently, crime began to be viewed not merely as an abstract concept but as a tangible societal and individual phenomenon. Moreover, preventive doctrines and movements began to emphasise the need for a scientifically informed societal defence against crime (Bačić, 1978b).

The theoretical justifications for this shift in criminal policy varied, as one Yugoslav criminology textbook explains: *"some justify it on the basis of criminology in the narrow sense, others on the basis of social solidarity, the third on the basis of Christian compassion; we, however, refer the justification to socialist humanism"* (Bavcon, 1966, p. 21).

Criminal law

Suspended sentences have been used in Slovenia since the early 20th century. Slovenia's criminal law evolved alongside its neighbouring regions, beginning with the State of the Slovenes, Croats, and Serbs, and continuing through various subsequent iterations, culminating in the Socialist Federal Republic of Yugoslavia, reflecting the prevailing legal ideas of each era.[8]

The first unified Criminal Code was adopted in 1929, and with it came the option of using suspended sentences. Suspension worked in the traditional way – after a (short!) prison sentence was passed, there was the additional option of suspension, which was seen as an instrument for controlling the prison population (Stojanović, 2003).

Since then, suspended sentences have remained part of Slovenia's legal framework. The new criminal codes in 1947 and 1951 reflected significant ideological shifts but had no practical impact on suspended sentences, whose framework and modus operandi remained unchanged: a suspended sentence was an afterthought, decided after the main decision to impose a prison sentence.

The first significant shift came in 1977, when a new Criminal Code was passed, implementing reforms that gave new powers to the individual republics within Yugoslavia, which were now able to pass their own special parts of the Criminal Code, and thus also choose to (de)criminalise specific offences. The general part of the code – determining the conceptual framework and sanctions – remained uniform at the federal level. The new Slovenian criminal code embraced a more liberal approach, emphasising individual autonomy and reducing state repression (Bavcon, 1980). This shift involved depenalisation, moving away from traditional punitive notions of punishment, and promoting humanisation and new, less repressive values. It reshaped the concept of punishment, targeting not only past actions but also the person's future (Bačić, 1978b). The new legislation thus aimed *"to follow that idea of a self-governing social order which seeks to ensure that there is as much constructive economic, social, political, educational and similar action in society as possible, and as little coercion as possible"* (Bavcon, 1980, p. 5).

These humanistic shifts also affected suspended sentences. While in the 1951 Criminal Code, suspended sentences were mainly viewed as a modified form of punishment with a different mode of execution (Bačić, 1978a), the 1977 reform redefined them as more than just a method of execution. It now considered suspended sentences as an autonomous and independent type of sentence of a primarily admonitory nature (Bavcon, 1980; see also Radovanović, 1966).[9] In other words, the suspension of the sentence became less about retribution and more about replacing the punishment (Bačić, 1978b). According to the new legislation, the court's process involved two steps: first, imposing a suspended sentence, and then, substantively evaluating the penalty within the formal and substantive framework set by the legislator (Bavcon, 1980).[10]

What were the consequences of this conceptual shift? The reform had notable effects on suspended sentences at three levels (Bavcon, 1980). From a *theoretical perspective*, the reform greatly expanded the possibilities for a non-punitive and non-retributive societal response to less serious offences. The reformed suspended sentence represented a crucial tool in the criminal justice system aimed at individual prevention, socialisation, and resocialisation within the context of freedom. *Conceptually*, the distinction between imposing a suspended sentence and determining the penalty reflects the court's assessment of the offence's seriousness and the offender's level of criminal responsibility. It also serves as a warning to the offender that any future offences or failure to fulfil obligations outlined in the sentence may result in the imposition and enforcement of the suspended sentence. *Practically*, if a new offence occurs, the court considers both the previously imposed sentence and the sentence for the new offence, applying rules for multiple offences to determine a single sentence or reinstating the previously determined sentence if the suspended sentence is revoked due to non-compliance with its obligations. In practice, this difference was smaller and less obvious than it was in theory, as the courts, in reality, had already been in the habit of first deciding whether a sentence would be suspended or not and then determining its parameters; the only difference was that the new CC of the SFRJ required this (Bavcon, 1980).

The 1977 reform also brought in new variations of suspended sentences that blended the Anglo-Saxon "probation" model and the French-Belgian model (Bačić, 1978b). Yugoslavia's federal criminal code outlined a general framework for modified forms of suspended sentences in Article 58. It described probationary supervision as "assistance, care and supervision" while delegating more detailed regulation to individual republics (Bačić, 1978b). In response, the Slovenian legislators, recognising the growing post-Second World War trends towards humanisation and depenalisation in the criminal justice system, seized the opportunity and crafted not one but four variations of suspended sentences (which are still relevant today, as we saw above):

(1) Basic suspended sentences;
(2) Suspended sentences with special conditions/obligations;
(3) Suspended sentences with probationary supervision;
(4) Suspended sentences with probationary supervision and instructions (for further details, see Bavcon, 1980).

The criterion for selecting the appropriate type of suspended sentence was based on the sanction's expected success in rehabilitating the offender. The final decision on which of the four components of supervision should be implemented fell to the social worker, who, under the legislation, had the authority to enforce the sentence (Bavcon, 1980).

Unlike some other Yugoslav republics, such as Bosnia or Croatia, where the legislatures had established a rigid set of instructions as the sole substance of probationary supervision, Slovenian legislators adopted a more flexible and progressive approach. They structured the legislation in a way that allowed instructions to be just one of many options available to the court and the executive branch in their efforts to facilitate the offender's rehabilitation (Bavcon, 1980).

The rationale behind this approach was clear: rather than limiting the scope of probationary supervision to a predefined set of instructions, the legislation acknowledged the diversity of challenges offenders might face, including influences from harmful associates, medical conditions, homelessness, vagrancy, unemployment, personality disorders, frivolous behaviour, and wastefulness. It recognised the wisdom of consulting the social welfare service to determine the most promising path for success, whether through discreet guidance, assistance, supervision, or court-ordered instructions, depending on the specific circumstances (Bavcon, 1980).

The 1977 reform continued to apply in the independent Republic of Slovenia, whose first criminal law legislation in 1994 was to a large extent a copy of its Yugoslav predecessor. In the reformed criminal code of 2008, which is still applicable today, many of the provisions governing suspended sentences were unchanged. As explained above, suspended sentences remain separate from imprisonment sentences, falling under admonitory sanctions and retaining a specific, less punitive focus.

Prevalence of the suspended sentence

As the images towards the end of this chapter show, suspended sentences have gained a very significant, if not crucial, role in the landscape of Slovenian punishment. Over the years, the proportion of offences punished by suspended sentences has risen to about two-thirds of all cases. Combined with the prevalence of relatively short custodial sentences, this reveals a strikingly lenient approach to crime. Admittedly, crime in Slovenia is typically low-level, with the large majority of cases falling under (petty) theft and other non-violent crimes.

Unfortunately, precise data is not available for some of the years since suspended sentences were introduced, especially the earlier decades of the 20th century. However, the post-1977 period of statutory reform is of most interest, since this is when there was a substantial shift in the legislation and in practice as regards the use of suspended sentences. The system began to rely on suspended sentences more and more during the 1980s and in the post-independence years, with a peak around 2010 and a slight decrease after that.

Conclusion

When Slovenia's exceptionalism in punishment (Dünkel, 2013; Flander & Meško, 2016; Plesničar & Drobnjak, 2019) is discussed, suspended sentences are not always discussed in detail. This may be a significant oversight as it seems that the leniency of the system is heavily reliant on the use of suspended sentences.

The reforms of 1977, which were carried over into the contemporary penal system post-independence, created a suspended sentence that is regarded both in theory and in practice as a separate, independent sanction, and equally as important, if not more so, than imprisonment or fines. The tie between suspended sentences and custodial prison sentences, which is strongly implied or made explicit in most other systems, is relegated to a mere calculation of a "potential" period of imprisonment in Slovenia. Moreover, there is no data to show how prevalent breaches of suspension conditions are or how often suspended sentences are revoked, but we know that neither of these happen often (Šugman Stubbs & Ambrož, 2012). This occasionally causes public unease and professional annoyance with the "ineffectiveness" of suspended sentences; however, no serious investigation into how (in)effective the system actually is has been carried out.

The Slovenian legal and criminological strands of thought do not typically perceive the potential lack of "penal bite" in this system as problematic. Generally, retribution is only seen as one (rather small) part of the sentencing rationale, whereas much more emphasis is placed on rehabilitation. In other words, punishment is not meant to be painful but rather serves – in a Durkheimian vein – as means of reaffirming the compromised criminal norm (Dežman, 2021).

Suspended sentences, as used in the Slovenian context, place remarkable trust in the offender's capability to abstain from reoffending (Plesnicar & Tripković, 2024). On the one hand, this may be a result of a system born in a relatively small community where effective informal means of social control resulted in a lesser need for formal social control. However, the extensive use of suspended sentences even in cases where it may not be entirely appropriate (Plesničar et al., 2023), suggests that other dynamics may be at play as well. The status quo may very well be the result of inertia – to deviate from the norm would mean extra effort on the side of the decision-makers – which they may not be able or willing to give. For a long period of time, there were few alternatives to imprisonment other than suspended sentences. Despite significant changes in this regard during the past decades, especially due to community sentences evolving with the introduction of the probation service in 2017, the default decision has remained a suspended sentence, making the system lenient almost by inertia (the opposite has been observed in Czechia: see Drápal, 2023).

Notes

1 This chapter was prepared thanks to the project "Suspended Prison Sentences in Post-Communist Europe: The Unexplored Behemoth" (Grant no. 21-19485S), carried out at the Faculty of Law, Charles University and funded by the Grant Agency of Czechia and the research programme "Social Control, Criminal Justice System, Violence and the Prevention of Victimization in the Context of High-Technology Market Society" (P5-0221), carried out by the Institute of Criminology Ljubljana and funded by the Slovenian Research and Innovation Agency.
2 As the other chapters in this book demonstrate, similar proportions can be observed in other Central and Eastern European countries as well, including countries whose sentencing policies are substantially different – indicating that there are different factors at play.
3 All translations from Slovenian are the authors' own unless otherwise stated.
4 Judicial admonition lacks any kind of additional burden on the offender – the offender is simply found guilty and given a formal reprimand.
5 They do, however, carry all other consequences of a criminal conviction, such as a criminal record, ineligibility for certain positions, etc.
6 In Slovenian, this option is called "protective supervision".
7 For example, requirements to undergo treatment at a medical facility, or training in a specific professional field, as well as various sorts of restraining orders, etc. (Art. 65).
8 See chapter *General tendencies of criminal law and penal policy in Yugoslavia (1945-1990s)* (Tripković, this volume), and also see chapter *Suspended prison sentences in Serbia* (Tripković, this volume).
9 See chapter *Suspended prison sentences in Serbia* (Tripković, this volume), where such a shift in a later reform in Serbia is discussed. It seems that authors from different republics understood the changes differently.

10 This same process is still present at the conceptual level today with the idea of 1. qualitative individualisation (choosing the sanction), followed by 2. quantitative individualisation (choosing the appropriate "quantum") (Bavcon et al., 2013).

References

Ambrož, M., & Šugman Stubbs, K. (2011). Conditional release (parole) in Slovenia: Problems and possible solutions. *The Prison Journal*, *91*(4), 467–488. https://doi.org/10.1177/0032885511424394

Arnež, J., & Plesničar, M. M. (2025). Reconsidering Parole: The Interplay of Purpose, Expertise and Institutional Structure, In: H. Annison, N. Carr & T. Guiney (Eds.), *Parole futures: Rationalities, institutions and practices* (pp. 177–199). Hart.

Ashworth, A. (2015). *Sentencing and criminal justice* (5th ed.). Cambridge University Press.

Bačić, F. (1978a). Komentar krivičnog zakona socijalističke federativne republike Jugoslavije. In N. Srzentić (Ed.), *Komentar Krivičnog zakona Socijalističke Federativne Republike Jugoslavije* (pp. 236–257). Savremena administracija.

Bačić, F. (1978b). *Krivično pravo: opći dio*. Informator.

Bačić, F. (1998). *Kazneno pravo, opći dio* (5. prerađeno in prošireno izd.). Informator.

Bavcon, L. (1958). *Kriminalna politika in njene tendence v socialistični družbi: doktorska disertacija*. Cankarjeva založba.

Bavcon, L. (1966). Pregled razvitka kriminološke nauke. In K. Vodopivec (Ed.), *Kriminologija* (pp. 3–23). Narodne novine.

Bavcon, L. (1980). Pogojna obsodba in pogojna obsodba z varstvenim nadzorstvom v novi jugoslovanski zakonodaji. *Pravosodni Bilten*, *3/4*, 5–25. ISSN 1318-1459.

Bavcon, L., Šelih, A., Korošec, D., Ambrož, M., & Filipčič, K. (2013). *Kazensko pravo: Splošni del* (6. izdaja). Uradni list Republike Slovenije.

Carroll, J., Perkowitz, W., Lurigio, A., & Weaver, F. (2015). Sentencing goals, causal attributions, ideology, and personality. *Journal of Personality and Social Psychology*, *52*(1), 107–118 . https://doi.org/10.1037/0022-3514.52.1.107.

Dežman, Z. (2021). Sistem kazenskih sankcij (3. Člen). In *Kazenski zakonik (KZ-1) s komentarjem* (pp. 108–124). Lexpera, GV založba.

Drápal, J. (2023). Punitive by negligence? The myths and reality of penal nationalism in the Czech Republic. *European Journal of Criminology*, *20*(4), 1549–1567. https://doi.org/10.1177/14773708211063753

Drápal, J., & Plesničar, M. (2023). Sentencing elsewhere: Structuring sentencing discretion in post-communist Europe. *European Journal on Criminal Policy and Research*, *31*, 250–270. https://doi.org/10.1007/s10610-023-09568-4

Dünkel, F. (2013). Slovenian exceptionalism?—Die Entwicklung von Gefangenenraten im internationalen Vergleich. In *Essays in honour of Alenka Šelih. Criminal law, criminology, human rights* (pp. 61–93). Institute of Criminology Ljubljana.

Flander, B., & Meško, G. (2016). Penal and prison policy on the "Sunny side of the Alps": The swan song of Slovenian exceptionalism? *European Journal on Criminal Policy and Research*, 22, 565–591. https://doi.org/10.1007/s10610-015-9299-1

Flander, B., Meško, G., & Hacin, R. (2023). Punishment in Slovenia: Seventy years of penal policy development. *European Journal on Criminal Policy and Research*, *29*, 625–645. https://doi.org/10.1007/s10610-022-09524-8

Garland, D. (2001). *The culture of control: Crime and social order in contemporary society*. Oxford University Press.

Hacin, R., Meško, G., Aebi, M. F., & Flander, B. (2022). From apparent unity to diversity: Penal policies of (former) Yugoslav republics. *European Journal of Crime, Criminal Law and Criminal Justice*, *30*(3–4), 329–354. https://doi.org/10.1163/15718174-bja10038

Hafner, M., Plesničar, M. M., & Šugan Stubbs, K. (2020) *Searching for stereotypes and prejudice in sentencing: a study on professional judges*. Inštitut za kriminologijo pri Pravni fakulteti v Ljubljani

Hogarth, J. (1971). *Sentencing as a human process*. University of Toronto Press and Centre of Criminology, University of Toronto.

Horvatić, Ž. (1980) *Izbor kazne u jugoslavenskom krivičnom pravu i sudskoj praksi*. Informator.

Kury, H., Ferdinand, T. N., & Obergfell-Fuchs, J. (2008). Punitivity in Germany: Attitudes to punishment, sentencing, and prison rates. In H. Kury & T. N. Ferdinand (Eds.), *International perspectives on punitivity* (pp. 107–138). Universitätsverlag Dr. Brockmeyer.

Loader, I. (2006). Fall of the »platonic guardians«: Liberalism, criminology and political responses to crime in England and Wales. *British Journal of Criminology*, *46*(4), 561–586.

Loader, I. (2009). Ice cream and incarceration: On appetites for security and punishment. *Punishment Society*, *11*(2), 241–257.

Maklecov, A. (1948). *Naše novo kazensko pravo in njegove vodilne ideje*. Profesorski zbor Pravne fakultete.

Meško, G., Fields, C., & Smole, T. (2011). A concise overview of penology and penal practice in slovenia: The unchanged capacity, new standards, and prison overcrowding. *The Prison Journal*, *91*(4), 398–424.

Oswald, M., Hupfeld, J., Klug, S., & Gabriel, U. (2002). Lay-Perspectives on Criminal deviance, goals of punishment, and punitivity. *Social Justice Research*, *15*, 85–98. https://doi.org/10.1023/A:1019928721720.

Padfield, N. (2014). Front door and back-door sentencing. In G. Bruinsma & D. Weisburd (Eds.), *Encyclopedia of criminology and criminal justice* (pp. 1846–1855). Springer. https://doi.org/10.1007/978-1-4614-5690-2_492

Plesničar, M. M. (2012). Slovenska ureditev pogojnega odpusta v luči sodobnih razvojnih trendov. *Revija za kriminalistiko in kriminologijo*, *63*(2), 136–148.

Plesničar, M. M. (2013a). Odločanje o sankcijah v kontinentalnih pravnih ureditvah. In M. Ambrož, K. Filipčič, & A. Završnik (Eds.), *Zbornik za Alenko Šelih: Kazensko pravo, kriminologija, človekove pravice* (pp. 326–330). Inštitut za kriminologijo pri Pravni fakulteti v Ljubljani, Pravna fakulteta, Slovenska akademija znanosti in umetnosti.

Plesničar, M. M. (2013b). The individualisation of punishment: Sentencing in Slovenia. *European Journal of Criminology*, *10*(4), 462–478.

Plesničar, M. M., Babnik, A., Briški, L., Fišer, Z., Jankovič, A., & Pina-Sánchez, J. (2023). *Poenotenje odločanja o sankcijah v kazenskih postopkih*. Inštitut za kriminologijo pri Pravni fakulteti.

Plesničar, M. M., Briški, L., & Jankovič, A. (2023). *Kaznovalna politika pri spolni kriminaliteti*. Inštitut za kriminologijo pri Pravni fakulteti.

Plesničar, M. M., & Drobnjak, M. (2019). Kaznovanje in kaznovalna politika v Sloveniji: Konceptualni premiki in praktične posledice. *Revija za kriminalistiko in kriminologijo*, *70*(2), 10.

Plesnicar, M. M., & Tripković, M. (2024). Communicating confidence: Suspended sentences as communicative punishment. *Pravni Zapisi, 2024*(1), 239–271. https://doi.org/10.5937/pravzap0-50554

Polegek, B. (2021). Rehabilitacija, izbris obsodbe in pogoji za dajanje podatkov iz kazenske evidence. In M. Šepec (Ed.), *Kazenski zakonik s komentarjem* (pp. 1005–1018). GV Založba.

Probation Service. (2021). *Annual report 2020*. https://www.gov.si/assets/organi-v-sestavi/UPRO/Letna-porocila/UPRO-Letno_porocilo_2020.pdf

Radovanović, M. (1966). *Krivično pravo SFRJ: opšti deo*. Savremena administracija.

Shames, A. (2011). Sentencing within sentencing. *Federal Sentencing Reporter*, *24*, 1–3. https://doi.org/10.1525/FSR.2011.24.1.1

Stojanović, Z. (2003). *Krivično pravo, opšti deo (osmo izdanje)*. Univerzitet u Beogradu, Pravni fakultet.

Šugman Stubbs, K., & Ambrož, M. (2012). Recalling conditionally released prisoners in Slovenia. *European Journal of Probation*, *4*(1), 98–110.

Tripković, M. (this volume). General tendencies of criminal law and penal policy in Yugoslavia (1945-1990s). In J. Drápal, K. Krajewski, & M. Tripković (Eds.), *Suspended prison sentences: Elusive punishment in Central and Eastern Europe*.

Tripković, M. (this volume). Suspended prison sentences in Serbia. In J. Drápal, K. Krajewski, & M. Tripković (Eds.), *Suspended prison sentences: Elusive punishment in Central and Eastern Europe*.

Urbas, V. (2020). Kriminaliteta v Sloveniji v letu 2019. *Revija za kriminalistiko in kriminologijo*, *71*(3), 157–182.

Verdel Kokol, V. (2021). Uvodni komentar: Peto poglavje—Opozorilne sankcije. In M. Šepec (Ed.), *Kazenski zakonik (KZ-1) s komentarjem: Splošni del* (pp. 793–795). GV Založba.

Vodopivec, K. (1966). Pojam krivičnog djela i počinitelja kao individualnih pojava. In K. Vodopivec (Ed.), *Kriminologija* (pp. 39–69). Narodne novine.

PART III

14 Common and divergent pathways of suspended prison sentences in Central and Eastern Europe

Milena Tripković, Krzysztof Krajewski, and Jakub Drápal

Part 1: the historical trajectories of the suspended prison sentence in Central and Eastern Europe

Introduction

The development of penal norms pertaining to suspended prison sentences in the countries of Central and Eastern Europe can be divided into three periods. The first period, during which the concept of the suspended prison sentence initially emerged, consists primarily of the interwar period, 1918–1939, with the most important developments occurring during the 1920s. At that time, the examined countries were all newly independent states that had inherited their penal legislation from their former dominating powers. After gaining their independence, these new countries gradually began to introduce legal changes inspired by the laws of Western European countries, such as France and Italy. During this first period, suspended prison sentences were adopted in all the countries of the examined region and quickly became an established penal instrument that was founded on a newly developed understanding of the appropriate penal reaction to particular crimes. The sanction was predominantly modelled on the original Franco-Belgian solution and developed for the most part along a common pathway during this time. However, even during this first period, the first departures from that original model occurred, paving the way for subsequent divergence.

The second period began immediately after the end of the Second World War and lasted until the late 1980s, i.e. until the downfall of communism in the observed countries. This period encompasses Soviet rule in Russia and in the Baltic region, as well as the period of Soviet domination over the countries of the Warsaw Pact. While Yugoslavia remained formally independent from direct Soviet interference and orthodoxy, it was nevertheless a communist-governed country and thus exhibited many similarities to the rest of the region. In all these countries, Soviet penal ideology and legislative solutions had a strong impact during this second period. The suspended prison sentence remained present in the penal legislation across the region; moreover, its function as an alternative to custodial sanctions became more pronounced, which resulted in the abandonment of some of the original assumptions underlying the Franco-Belgian model. These developments were, however, adopted unevenly within the region, and

DOI: 10.4324/9781003568667-20

therefore the differences between the individual countries' understandings and uses of the sanction grew.

The third period began after the fall of the communist regimes during the "velvet revolutions" (1989–1990), which resulted in the collapse and disintegration of the Soviet Union and the Soviet Bloc, and was followed by the disintegration of Yugoslavia during the conflicts of the 1990s. Newly formed countries (the former Soviet and Yugoslav republics, Czechia, and Slovakia) began, along with the countries that had regained their independence (Bulgaria, Hungary, Poland, and Romania) to revise and amend their penal legislation and policies. Suspended prison sentences yet again survived this political and social transition, and it was at this time that they (in most cases) began their unhinged rise, becoming the most frequently used penal sanction and dominating the sentencing sphere.

Introduction of suspended penal sentences: the period between two world wars (1918–1939)

The development of suspended prison sentences began slightly later in Central and Eastern Europe than it did in the western part of the European continent. Prior to the First World War, most of the examined countries (with the exceptions of Bulgaria, Romania, Serbia, and to some extent Hungary) were not independent nations. Hence, their legislative developments, including penal legislation, were entirely dependent on related developments in the countries that dominated them: Austria, Germany and Russia. While discussions and proposals pertaining to the introduction of suspended prison sentences began in several of these countries before the outbreak of the First World War (most notably in Austria – then a part of the Habsburg Empire – and in Germany), the only country in which the sanction was introduced at this time was Hungary, which enjoyed substantive autonomy within the Habsburg Empire, including pertaining to autonomous penal legislation. Hungary, then, was the first country in the region to introduce the suspended prison sentence, which it did in 1908 through an amendment to the *Csemegi* Penal Code (1878). The sanction was next adopted by a region that is now part of Poland, which was dominated by Russia at the time, but fell under German occupation in 1914. In 1917, the German occupational authorities introduced amendments to the Russian Penal Code of 1905 (known as the *Tagancev* Code), which was in force at that time.[1] Czechoslovakia soon followed suit: in 1919, a special law was adopted introducing suspended prison sentences across the country, despite the fact that two different penal codes were in force at the time (the Austrian Code in Czechia, and the Hungarian *Csemegi* Code in Slovakia).

After that, suspended prison sentences spread quickly to other countries in the region. In Estonia, the sanction was adopted through amendments to the Russian penal code in 1920. That same year, the possibility of suspending a prison sentence was also introduced in Romania. Things were more complicated in what is now Poland: while the sanction had already been adopted (as mentioned) in the Russian part of Poland, the parts of the country governed earlier by Austria and Germany only embraced this new sanction in 1926 (former Austrian part) and 1927 (former German part). It was not until 1932, when a new penal code was adopted, that these regulations were substituted by uniform provisions for the entire Polish territory. One of the last countries to adopt the sanction in this region was the Kingdom of Serbs, Croats, and Slovenes (later known as Yugoslavia), which introduced it through the country's first penal code in 1929. By the late 1920s, all countries of the studied region had adopted the suspended prison sentence, a new and previously unknown type of penal sanction.

These first legal provisions were predominantly modelled on the Belgian (1888), and/or French (1891) models, both of which were premised on the idea of suspending (very) short prison sentences (such as a couple of months or up to six months in Belgium) for first-time offenders who were assessed as having a positive criminological prognosis – in other words, for whom the sentencing judge determined that there was sufficient reason to trust that the individual would not reoffend even in the absence of imprisonment. Alternative legal formulations in some countries were more demanding, requiring "good behaviour" as part of such a positive prognosis. The concept of the suspended prison sentence was also based on an underlying assumption of its exceptionality: while there were some differences and discussions regarding this aspect, it was generally assumed that the sanction would not be used routinely, but only for a narrowly defined group of offenders. The main idea guiding the introduction of suspended prison sentences was the perceived need for an "intermediary sanction" between a fine and imprisonment, which could serve as a substitute for short-term imprisonment (Radzinowicz, 1991, p. 13). Although the original conception emphasised the exceptionality of such a sanction, this was undermined by the existing reality: at the time, short-term prison sentences were used very frequently throughout Europe, so the pool of potential candidates for such a sanction was large.

Most of the differences between the initial suspended prison sentence provisions in different countries related to the length of prison sentences eligible for suspension. For instance, the Hungarian provisions allowed for the suspension of sentences of less than one month. In the part of Poland under Russian control, prison sentences of up to 6 months could be suspended, but only if the perpetrator was a young offender. Similar provisions were subsequently adopted for the other parts of Poland, though there suspension could also be applied to older offenders' sentences. Estonia adopted the same 6-month cut-off point. In Czechoslovakia, prison sentences of up to one year could be suspended.

Subsequently, the predominant trend across these countries was towards the expansion of the conditions for the imposition of suspended prison sentences, rendering them applicable to more offenders. For instance, the 1932 Polish penal code increased the sentence length cut-off point from 6 months to 2 years. The same upper limit was provided for in the new Romanian penal code of 1937. In the Yugoslav penal code (1929), sentences of up to 6 months or 1 year (depending on whether it was a case of "regular" or "strict" imprisonment) could be suspended. The Soviet legislation (penal codes of 1922 and 1926) did not stipulate any upper limit of imprisonment eligible for suspension. These provisions constituted a clear departure from the original Franco-Belgian model, mostly because they permitted the suspension of sentences imposed on offenders that could hardly be termed "petty", albeit many of the other initial provisions (such as positive criminological prognosis or a lack of prior convictions) were retained. As a consequence, the use of suspended sentences increased in many countries during the 1930s (one such example is Poland). Curiously, that increase in use applied not only to the countries that had made changes to the conditions for suspended prison sentences, but also to other countries (such as Czechoslovakia), where the provisions had remained unchanged.

Having departed from the original conception of exceptionality, it took little time for the countries in the region to fully embrace suspended prison sentences, using them frequently. The clearest example is probably Czechoslovakia where, one year after their first introduction, suspended prison sentences already accounted for more than 50% of all prison sentences. Similarly, in Poland – though the available data is fragmentary – these sentences soon amounted to between 20%–60% of all prison sentences (depending on the part of the country). In the second half of the 1930s, suspended sentences regularly made up about half of all sanctions imposed in Poland, making them the most frequent type of penal sanction. Far from being exceptional, suspended prison sentences quickly became one of the most important penal instruments. It is worth bearing this in mind as we move forward in time and uncover a similar phenomenon more recently. Finally, it should be noted that the initial period of development of this sanction was characterised by a high level of consistence and commonality throughout the region's perception of the nature and purpose of the sanction.

Expansion without genuine transformation: The communist period (1945–1989)

When communism took centre stage in the region during the second half of the 1940s, the suspended prison sentence was already a well-established penal sanction, possibly far better established than comparable sanctions in Western Europe. The importance of this sanction remained unchanged under communist rule; on the contrary, the use of suspended prison sentences further expanded, aided by the fact that the basic premises of the suspended prison sentence were consistent with the main principles of Soviet penology, which became influential throughout the region. Suspended prison sentences had been introduced in the Soviet Union itself during the 1920s, in a form that differed substantially from the original Franco-Belgian model as it permitted prison sentences of any length to be suspended.

To understand why suspended prison sentences held such appeal during the Soviet period, we may first recall that the original Franco-Belgian model had emerged from key ideas underpinning criminological positivism. The tendency to limit the use of short-term imprisonment by instead using suspended prison sentences was consistent with the positivist notion of the individualisation of punishment (Radzinowicz, 1991, p. 13; Wetzel, 2022, p. 61). Moreover, these sanctions were also consistent with the fundamental concept of criminological positivism that pertained to criminal policy, namely "social defence" (Cantor, 1936, pp. 36–37; Radzinowicz, 1991, pp. 32–47; Fijnaut, 2017, p. 305). While on the one hand "social defence" required an indeterminate sentencing system and indeterminate security measures towards dangerous offenders, on the other hand it also justified the use of suspended prison sentences, probation and suchlike measures for the least dangerous offenders. Suspended prison sentences offered a deviation from purely retributivist ideas and from the notions of proportionality that were fundamental to the classical school. They signalled a move towards the consequentialist approach, which was concerned with crime prevention and the individualisation of punishment, i.e. tailoring sanctions to offenders' particular needs.

Soviet criminology was strongly influenced by positivist ideas (Shelley, 1979), both in general and more specifically through the work of individuals such as Enrico Ferri, whose draft criminal code of 1921 had significant impact on Soviet penology despite never becoming law (Cantor, 1936, pp. 29–31). In spite of its origin, the suspended prison sentence was never considered a bourgeois or reactionary invention. It is, however, questionable quite how sincere the use of these positivist ideas was in practice. For example, we know that a distorted positivist conception of offenders' dangerousness served as a tool for indiscriminate political repression and inappropriately punitive penal policies (Radzinowicz, 1991, p. 91) and that the rehabilitation of offenders often deteriorated into a punitive approach to crime control, based on deterrence and incapacitation.

Even in this context, the suspended prison sentence found its place. This was not only due to legislative inertia in countries such as Poland or Romania, where the old, pre-war penal codes remained in force until the end of the 1960s, but also in other countries of the region where new, "progressive" penal legislation was adopted from the early 1950s onwards. As a matter of fact, the communist period seems to have provided optimal conditions for the further expansion of suspended prison sentences across Central and Eastern Europe. Despite the "rehabilitative" rhetoric in the Soviet Union and the Soviet Bloc, very little was actually done in this period to introduce proper rehabilitative programmes, either for imprisoned offenders, or for those handed suspended sentences. Probation services were either absent or poorly developed, and even in those countries whose legislation allowed for probationary supervision during the operational period, this was rarely used in practice. When it was used, it was not viewed as a way of supporting the offenders, but of controlling them. Therefore, despite the prevailing rehabilitative rhetoric, nothing approaching the western or Anglo-Saxon style of probation was introduced for suspended prison sentences in Central and Eastern Europe, nor even community corrections: suspended sentences remained simply a criminal sanction that had (perhaps paradoxically) been deprived of its penal bite, without any truly rehabilitative elements.

There is one more possible explanation for the expansion of suspended prison sentences in countries under communist rule. Communist penal law and criminal justice systems were – despite their official commitment to rehabilitation – notoriously punitive, which resulted in high incarceration rates, prison overcrowding and other associated problems. This tendency had to be countervailed one way or another, to avoid a serious crisis in the prison system. Various alternatives to imprisonment were hence considered and discussed in the region (community sentences, fines, probation, and so on), but most of these were not taken up to the extent seen in the West. In the countries of Central and Eastern Europe, various problems associated with such sanctions made their use impossible or impractical. For example, fines were considered ideologically suspect, not only because monetary sanctions seemed at odds with "working class paradises", but also due to (somewhat justified) concerns about their unequal effects that privileged more affluent offenders. As a result, their use remained modest. Sanctions similar to community service were introduced in some Central and Eastern European countries during the 1960s and 1970s, but these were also treated with suspicion by judges, in particular because they sometimes led to paradoxical outcomes. In Poland, for example, community service more frequently substituted a fine than a prison sentence. Given these countries' reluctance to make use of other alternatives, suspended sentences remained the most popular non-custodial sanction – they were easy to administer and helped to keep the prison population within manageable numbers (this situation persists today in some countries, such as Russia).

These developments in sanction use varied, of course, across the region. In particular, practices were slightly different in the Soviet Republics than elsewhere, since in the Soviet Republics no upper limit was set for the length of prison sentence that could be suspended. Meanwhile, Yugoslavia – which quickly distanced itself from hard-line communism after the Second World War – went on to have a milder and less ideologically coloured penal system. Hence, between 1945 and 1989, the countries of Central and Eastern Europe began to diverge more substantially in their approaches to suspended prison sentences, but at the same time they increasingly distinguished themselves from Western Europe, in what will eventually be described as the "penal divide" (Krajewski, 2014), between the West and the East. Nevertheless, suspended prison sentences remained a constant and popular penal instrument.

Suspended prison sentences after the fall of communism (1989 to today)

After the fall of communism, the suspended prison sentence continued to be one of the most frequently used sanctions in the Central and Eastern European countries; however, contrary to earlier complacency about this situation, the newly independent countries gradually began to turn a more critical eye to their frequent use and, after a few decades, eventually decided that this had turned into a problem that needed solving.

The unique role that suspended prison sentences have consistently played in the region's penal systems can be easily observed by comparing the statistical data for Western Europe with that for Central and Eastern Europe. Relevant data are provided here for two selected years (1999 and 2015).

The data presented in Figures 14.1 and 14.2 show that most Central and Eastern European countries included in the data made far more frequent use of

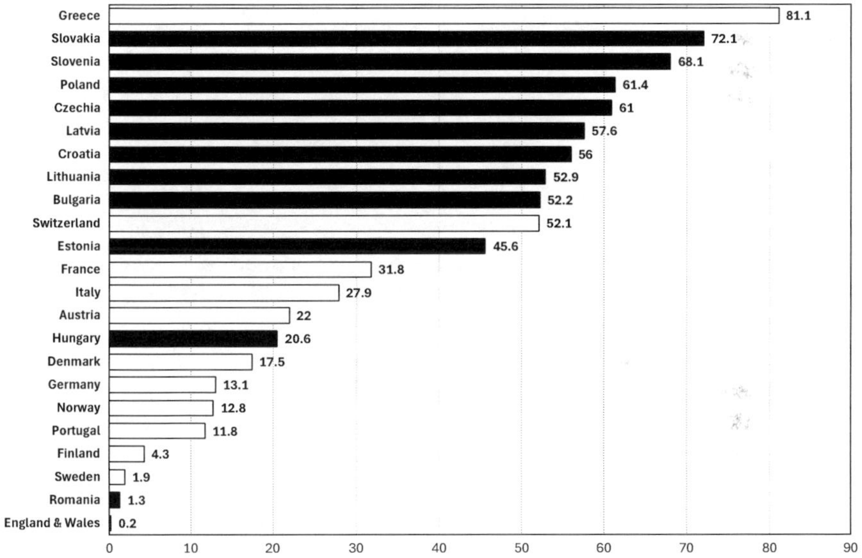

Figure 14.1 Proportion of suspended sentences in select European countries in the year 1999.

Source: European Sourcebook 2003, table 3.2.3.1, p.145.

Note: The data pertaining to Romania provided in the relevant chapter suggest that the proportion of suspended sentences in that country was much higher than suggested by the data relating to the year 1999 that can be found in the 2003 edition of the European Sourcebook of Crime and Criminal Justice Statistics; this would make their use in Romania similar to that in other countries of the region. Unfortunately, the 2021 edition of the European Sourcebook does not provide data on Romania for the year 2015. The authors of this chapter were not able to determine the source of this discrepancy, but we assume that the data provided in the chapter on Romania better reflect the use of suspended sentences in that country.

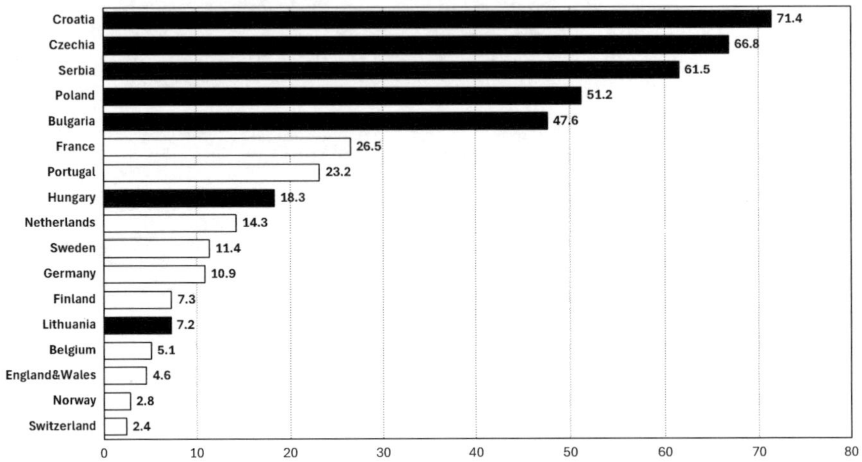

Figure 14.2 Proportion of suspended sentences in select European countries in the year 2015.

Source: European Sourcebook 2021, table 3.2.3.1, p. 217.

suspended prison sentences than Western European countries. Furthermore, no significant change can be observed in this respect between 1999 and 2015. In Bulgaria, Croatia, Czechia, Poland, and Serbia, suspended sentences were used more frequently than in Western countries. Among the Western European countries whose use of the sanction was relatively frequent, such as France, Portugal, and Italy, the proportion of such sentences was about half of the proportion of such sentences in the countries of Central and Eastern Europe in which its application was least frequent. When compared to the Central and Eastern European countries which used it the most, the proportion is about one-third. This further demonstrates that Western Europe and Central and Eastern Europe followed distinctively different pathways with regard to the use of suspended prison sentences.

The same data also enable us to observe distinct pathways within the region itself. Hungary is a clear outlier among the Central and Eastern European countries: its use of suspended prison sentences amounted (in both years) to only about 20% of all sanctions imposed, a much lower proportion than in other countries of the region, and even lower than in some Western European countries. Another curious case is Latvia: while in 1999 the country's use of suspended prison sentences was high, in accordance with the regional model, this country banned suspended prison sentences without probation supervision in 2024, replacing these with probationary supervision.[2] A similar effort in Poland also resulted in a significant decrease in the use of suspended prison sentences.

The year 2015 was thus the last year in which suspended prison sentences were used so frequently in Poland: a comprehensive reform of sentencing rules that occurred that year introduced substantial changes to the structure of sanctions imposed by courts. Increased use of community service and fines accompanied a slow reduction in the use of suspended prison sentences. Post 2022, suspended prison sentences dropped to below 20% of all sentences imposed, bringing the Polish situation closer to countries such as Hungary. A similar trend can be observed in Czechia where – as discussed in the relevant chapter – fines have to some extent substituted suspended prison sentences. Meanwhile, countries such as Serbia and Slovenia continue to use suspended prison sentences frequently and without much hesitation.

The increased use of suspended prison sentences in many countries of Central and Eastern Europe after the fall of communism led to a perception that they were out of control, primarily because at such high frequency it was clear that they had abandoned the original notion of exceptionality. The affected countries had gone through deep and agonising political, economic and social transformations, which had resulted in the growth of crime, and their criminal justice systems, themselves undergoing deep reforms, had begun to face serious difficulties. Suspended prison sentences offered an easy solution to certain problems, such as the enormous increase in the number of cases before the courts, growing prison populations, and prison overcrowding. Additionally, the changing social context in these countries and swift technical developments contributed to the frequency of suspended sentences: rising numbers of road traffic offences, for example, and of other similar negligent offences brought previously unknown types of offenders into the courts. The situation the region found itself in, with the need to respond rapidly to dramatically changing conditions, was vastly different to that of the Western European countries, which had been able to respond to these challenges and adapt their criminal justice systems to them over the course of several decades.

Under such circumstances, suspended prison sentences – in most cases devoid of any supervision or particularly demanding obligations – offered a simple solution to relieve the criminal justice system of various kinds of pressures. This, however, entailed abandoning the original model of the suspended sentence, and mass use of these sentences was considered a problem by legal theorists and practitioners, and increasingly also by the public, who perceived that a substantial majority of offenders were getting away with their crimes. In times of penal populism, such accusations have led to political abuse.

Part 2: main features of suspended prison sentences across the region

In Part 1, we presented the different phases in the development of suspended prison sentences in Central and Eastern Europe and outlined how and why, from a common starting point, this type of sentence went to have independent trajectories in different parts of the region. In this next section, we determine the main differences in the key features of suspended prison sentences today between the observed countries.

The penal philosophy and penal aims of suspended prison sentences

Suspended prison sentences are differently conceptualised in different countries. There are differences in the philosophical commitments that underlie the sanction, its place within the system of penal sanctions, and the penal goals it is seen as fulfilling. By gaining a better understanding of the nature and purpose of this sanction in different countries, we will be better able to understand how the sanction operates in practice (which we address in the last part of this chapter).

An overview of countries presented in this book reveals quite varied views on the nature of the suspended prison sentence. Our dominant impression is that many of these countries have often avoided or omitted to adopt a clear stance on this matter and have tended not to provide any comprehensive explanation of the nature or purpose of the sanction. In that sense, we can draw a clear distinction between two groups of countries: (1) those that explicitly define suspended prison sentences as *not punishment,* but another type of sanction, and (2) those that consider the sanction a *modality of imprisonment,* thus clearly recognising it as a form of punishment.

The only two countries that fall into the first group are Serbia and Slovenia. Both countries differentiate between three main types of criminal sanctions: those whose key purpose is a punitive response to the offending (punishment), those that are guided by security concerns (security measures), and those that merely warn the offender (warning measures). Suspended sentences fall within the last group of sanctions, warning measures, which are sanctions of an admonitory nature that are to be used in situations in which punishment is considered unnecessary or unjustified. This solution is somewhat counterintuitive given that the state avoids using its penal prerogatives, yet does so while still remaining within the framework of criminal law. In other words, the state expresses confidence in the offender's future propensity to desist from crime (by not imposing punishment), treating the perpetrated offence as some sort of lapse in judgement of an otherwise trustworthy offender. At the same time, however, the state still retains the safety net of criminal law through threatened punishment. The theoretical orientation of the approach in these two countries was not always entirely clear and coherent: historically, the sanction gradually gained independence from imprisonment, becoming a distinct, *sui generis* criminal sanction after the dissolution of Yugoslavia. This development was probably strongly influenced by general satisfaction with how the sanction operated in practice in these countries.

All other countries in Central and Eastern Europe belong (more or less obviously) to the second group. The criminal codes in these countries consider suspended prison sentences as prison sentences – they represent a form, or modality, of imprisonment. In Romania, for instance, suspended prison sentences are understood as "individualized" criminal sanctions. In Czechia and Poland, they formally represent prison sentences whose execution is postponed (until the operational period expires); this is expressed in the name of the sanction (Czech: *podmíněný trest odnětí svobody* = conditional penalty of deprivation of liberty; Polish *kara pozbawienia wolności z warunkowym zawieszeniem jej wykonania* = penalty of deprivation of liberty with conditional suspension of its implementation). The close ties between suspended prison sentences and custodial prison sentences in these countries align with the process for their imposition, whereby the judge first decides that a prison sentence is warranted in a given case and then decides whether or not to suspend its execution. This kind of process also takes place in countries that belong to the first group: the only difference is that, if the decision that imprisonment is not warranted, the judges will then decide that an entirely different sanction (and not just a modality) of imprisonment is appropriate. The outcomes for the perpetrator are similar in either case, but this difference of approach is indicative of a substantial difference in the way in which the state communicates with the offender, and in its promotion of personal responsibility and pro-social inclinations.

The implications of the distinction between these two groups of countries also play out in respect of penal goals. Serbia and Slovenia, on the one hand, clearly identify (in criminal law provisions and in academic writing) that suspended sanctions aim to achieve the general aims of punishment without resorting to punishment itself, in cases in which a warning with the threat of punishment can be expected to achieve the desired results. In other countries, in which suspended sentences represent a modality of imprisonment, the penal goals correspond to those of imprisonment. This is somewhat problematic: imprisonment clearly has punitive goals, whereas its suspension is motivated by a desire to avoid the use of punitive instruments to achieve the purposes of punishment. In some countries, such as Russia, attempts have been made to resolve this problem through a re-conceptualisation of the suspended sentence to be a "release from punishment", so that although it remains a modality of imprisonment, it is clearer that it pursues goals other than retribution, such as rehabilitation.

Ultimately, we do not wish to overstate these "legal qualification" distinctions. In all countries, without exception, suspended prison sentences are imposed when it is considered that such a sanction can achieve the purposes of punishment via the threat of imprisonment, whatever those purposes might be. Furthermore, the rules for the imposition of suspended prison sentences are quite similar in all countries, sometimes in spite of the formal legal frameworks; in Czechia, for instance, there is a lack of coherence between the legal provisions and the wider understanding of the nature of the sanction. While suspended prison sentences are formally a modality of imprisonment, both academics and the courts tend to think of them as a separate type of sanction.

The legal qualification is relevant, however, because it can help judges make decisions about appropriate sanctions. By defining suspended prison sentences as mere "warning" tools, Serbian and Slovenian policymakers clearly convey that criminal offenders are not a uniform group of individuals – and that some deserve to be trusted not to reoffend more than others. Having a separate category of sanctions for those who deserve to be trusted contributes greatly to the robustness, coherence and precision applied in criminal law. In that regard, these outwardly minor differences of classification have practical implications for the way in which decisions about the imposition (and possibly later, the revocation) of suspended sentences are made.

"Probationary" aspects of suspended sentences

As we noted above, one of the key features of suspended sentences in Central and Eastern Europe is their lack of genuinely "probationary" features: in other words, since their introduction about a century ago, these sanctions have been expected to operate largely autonomously, without any state organ to monitor, control and support the convicted person through the operational period.

This is true to a somewhat lesser extent today: we can observe a general trend towards increasing certain aspects of supervision. All the examined countries currently have provisions in force that allow them to impose suspended prison sentences with probationary supervision. In Romania and Russia that probationary element is obligatory, which means that only this form of suspended prison sentence exists. In all the other countries, suspension can be imposed with or without a probationary element. Practical matters of imposition, however, further complicate this distinction. Although all countries provide for suspension with probationary supervision, some countries are quite unaccustomed to this sanction and barely use it, preferring to impose suspension without any requirement to report to or engage with probation officers. Serbia and Slovenia are both examples of this practice – whether due to a dysfunctional probationary system or resistance on the part of the judges. Even in these countries, however, suspended prison sentences can be accompanied by a wide range of conditions, obligations, and measures that limit the "freedom" of the offender to go about their life unobstructed, albeit without amounting to full probation. Some countries use such measures rarely, and pay relatively little attention to offenders' needs and the risks they might pose, in some cases also because they are difficult to enforce.

The reasons for this can be linked to the nature and purpose of suspended prison sentences in different countries, which we discussed above. Slovenia and Serbia, which clearly designate suspended sentences as "warning measures" and not as a modality of imprisonment, might be naturally more reluctant to rely on probationary features since such "warnings" can only be imposed upon offenders who are trusted to abstain and desist from future crime on their own. Confidence in offenders' ability not to re-offend is arguably incompatible with the idea that they require supervision or even support. This may explain why, while both countries' legal provisions allow for suspended prison sentences with probationary supervision, this form is little used.

In countries that have more positive attitudes towards suspended prison sentences, trusting offenders to spend the operational period largely unsupervised seems to indicate a more forgiving and moderate stance towards crime and criminal behaviour in general. Bearing in mind the frequency with which suspended sentences are used in these countries, the implication is that these countries consider most offenders not to need any supervision or control, which is an extremely significant finding. Although leaving offenders to grapple with the challenges of life alone during the operational period of a suspended sentence might be perceived as a means of responsibilisation – making offenders responsible for their own destinies while absolving the state of its responsibility to impose proper penal treatment (Garland, 2001) – it can, too, be understood in a more positive light as contrary to infantilisation and as a way of demonstrating trust and confidence in offenders' abilities to change their ways.

Ultimately, the rules in all countries require judges, when deciding whether to suspend a prison sentence, to conduct an assessment leading to a "positive prognosis" that the offender will be able to abstain from crime until the operational period expires. This process is critically dependent on determining that the offender has the personal capacities necessary to do so. In other words, the court must positively establish that there is a discrepancy between the offender's personal characteristics and "usual" self (i.e. who the offender really is) on the one hand and the criminal "episode" that they engaged in (i.e. what the offender did in the given case) on the other. And although there is an interesting difference – which could be examined further – between countries that merely expect the offender "not to reoffend" and those in which the offender is expected to "behave well", it is obvious that the positive prognosis is key to suspending a prison sentence. This process is, however, reliant on the judge's ability to assess properly whether the offender is indeed the sort of person for whom a mere warning will be sufficient to terminate their criminal career. Whether judges are capable of making such an assessment, given the volume of work that they are expected to process, their lack of training in this domain, and their focus on the legal (and not psychological) features of the case, is a complex question. The situation in Poland, for example, where large numbers of suspended sentences have ultimately ended in revocation, might serve as a warning about judicial capacities to establish a positive prognosis.

The function of suspended sentences in the penal system

Finally, we turn our focus to how suspended prison sentences operate in practice and seek to understand some of the benefits and limitations that have arisen from their application in Central and Eastern European countries. In that sense, we aim to answer questions relating to the conditions and frequency of their use, their importance in achieving the stated penal goals, as well as the professional attitudes towards them. In doing so, we set the stage for considerations concerning the need for reform, which will be addressed in the final chapter of this book.

When they were first introduced, as we have discussed above, suspended prison sentences were intended as a substitute for short-term prison sentences in an attempt to avoid the more harmful effects of the latter, such as the perceived "criminal contagion" that could occur in prison conditions, and to reduce prisoner numbers. Nowadays, while many countries still maintain that suspended sentences should serve as an "exceptional" substitute for short prison sentences, some countries have expanded their use well beyond prison sentences that could be considered "short". Currently, the maximum length of prison sentence that can be suspended ranges from one to eight years: 1 year (Poland), 2 years (Hungary, Serbia and Slovenia), 3 years (Czechia), 4 years (Romania), 5 years (Estonia), 8 years (Russia). Furthermore, some of the countries that permit suspension more broadly, in terms of length of sentence, do nevertheless limit the use of suspended sentences in other ways, i.e. by specifying which crimes suspended sentences can be imposed for – such is the case with Russia, where several crimes are excluded from eligibility for suspended sentences. An additional caveat concerns the fact that it is quite difficult to compare countries based on the length of prison sentences that they are willing to suspend, because the sentencing ranges for imprisonment tend to be different.

Beyond these fundamental legislative discrepancies, the use of suspended prison sentences varies widely in different countries. For instance, some of the countries that allow only relatively short sentences (up to 3 years) to be suspended impose suspended sentences in large numbers of cases: in Czechia, Serbia and Slovenia, suspended prison sentences constitute more than half of all imposed criminal sanctions. However, this is not the case across the board: Poland, for example, limits the use of suspended sentences to sentences shorter than 1 year and imposes them in only about 20% of cases (the chapter on Poland also explains how the country recently achieved a significant reduction in the use of suspended sentences), while Estonia permits suspension of prison sentences up to 5 years and uses them in roughly half of all cases. A country's use of suspended sentences – as a proportion of all sentences, or in real numerical terms – does not serve as a direct proxy for that country's level of repressiveness or leniency: to make a judgement about a country's repressiveness, we would need to factor in the nature and seriousness of crime in that country. An interesting case in point is Slovenia, where most suspended sentences are very short, indicating that they respond to appropriately non-serious crimes, even though they are used very frequently (in some recent years, they were used in about 80% of cases).

In any case, suspended prison sentences play an important role in the penal systems of Central and Eastern Europe, largely thanks to their close links to imprisonment, and they have been considered effective instruments in rectifying key challenges in the penal system. For instance, there is evidence that suspended sentences are used strategically in Russia to reduce the level of imprisonment – their use is not only justified in individual cases, but is also motivated by broader penal concerns. In Poland, the use of suspended sentences had the unanticipated and unintended result of increasing the prison population (after many such sentences were revoked), which then required policy makers to introduce policies to reduce their use and provide conditions for a more frequent use of other alternatives to imprisonment.

Whether or not we can consider the suspended prison sentence to be a "successful" sanction largely depends, first, on the legal rules that specify the conditions under which suspension can be revoked. Most countries provide for obligatory revocation in the case of a repeat offence of particular seriousness, while in some cases such revocation is optional and a new offence will not necessarily lead to a revocation of the original suspension. In that way, optimal conditions for the "success" are created by legal rules, as judges are not obliged to take every infraction as the reason to revoke the sentence. There is substantial discrepancy between different countries in terms of the numbers of suspended sentences that are revoked. Relevant data are scarce and difficult to obtain, but those available suggest that some countries – such as Romania, Serbia and Russia – revoke suspension in only a small number of cases (some 5–10% of all suspensions), while in other countries, such as Estonia, about 25% of suspended sentences are eventually revoked.

Finally, the role and impact of a particular penal sanction can also be assessed by looking at criminal justice professionals' stance towards it. Here, once again, we observe a difference between two groups of countries. In Estonia, Hungary, Russia, Serbia, and Slovenia, suspended prison sentences have operated without any significant problems or disruptions. Professionals view this as a standard type of sanction and an appropriate response to particular levels of crime and particular types of offenders. It is therefore not contested, and there are no major proposals for change or reform, except in regard to the use of suspended prison sentences for sexual offences. In contrast, in Czechia and Poland, practitioners, academics and the public have expressed concerns about the suspended prison sentences being used in ways that were incoherent and unjustified, or which led to unanticipated outcomes, such as the rise of the prison population. This has given rise to critical debate and moves towards reform.

Conclusion

Suspended sentences have existed for a century in Central and Eastern Europe and – although different countries in the region have taken somewhat different pathways over time – these sanctions continue to play an important role in the penal system. They are favoured in some countries, taken as a matter of fact in some, and heavily contested in others. Various lasting conceptual and practical problems with suspended sentences deserve our attention and consideration of whether there might be a more optimal route to serving the purpose suspended sentences are intended to fulfil.

In order to construct a more normatively robust version of the suspended sentence, we must start by answering key questions that we have raised in this chapter (and throughout the book). These concern, *inter alia*: the nature of the sanction (is it a punishment?); its penal purpose and rationale (which penal goals it seeks to achieve); the place and purpose of probationary features and the incoherence between probationary features and the "positive prognosis"; the breadth of its potential use (which sentences should be eligible for suspension) and the notion of "exceptionality"; judges' ability to assess for a positive prognosis; the problem of sentence inflation (i.e. the imposition of longer suspended prison sentences instead of shorter non-suspended prison sentences); and the conditions and consequences of revocation. The final chapter of this book provides some possible answers to these questions, and develops an original, normatively sound proposal for the shape and substance of the suspended prison sentence, bearing in mind the differences in the contemporary appeal of this sanction in different countries of the region.

Notes

1 Interestingly enough, suspended prison sentences were not known in the German penal legislation at that time; this remained so until 1953.
2 https://bnn-news.com/suspended-prison-sentence-will-no-longer-be-applied-in-latvia-263249

References

Blachnio-Parzych, A., Jakubowska-Hara, J., Kosonoga, J., Kuczyńska, H., Kunicka-Michalska, B., Nowak, C., & Skupiński, J. (2009). *Alternatywy pozbawienia wolności w polskiej polityce karnej*. Wydawnictwo Naukowe Scholar.

Cantor, N. (1936). Measures of social defense. *Cornell Law Review, 22*(1), 17–38.

Donovan, J. M. (2022). The French judicial and political origins of Raymond Saleilles' individualization of punishment. In M. Pifferi (Ed.), *The limits of criminological positivism: The movement for criminal law reform in the West, 1870–1940*. Routledge.

European Sourcebook of Crime and Criminal Justice Statistics – 2003. (2003). Boom Juridische uitgevers.

European Sourcebook of Crime and Criminal Justice Statistics – 2021. (2021). Göttingen University Press.

Fijnaut, C. (2017). *Criminology and the criminal justice system: A historical and transatlantic introduction*. Intersentia.

Garland, D. (2001). *The culture of control: Crime and social order in contemporary society*. Oxford University Press.

Krajewski, K. (2014). Different penal climates in Europe. *Kriminologijos Studijos*, *1*, 86–111.

Radzinowicz, L. (1991). *The roots of International Association of Criminal Law and their significance: A tribute and a re-assessment on the century of the IKV*. Max-Planck-Institut für ausländisches und internationales Strafrecht.

Shelley, L. (1979). Soviet criminology after the revolution. *The Journal of Criminal Law & Criminology*, *70*(4), 391–396.

Wetzel, R. F. (2022). Penal reform in Imperial Germany: Conflict and compromise. In M. Pifferi (Ed.), *The limits of criminological positivism: The movement for criminal law reform in the West, 1870–1940*. Routledge.

15 Suspended (prison) sentences reimagined[1]

Jakub Drápal

Introduction

The original conception of the suspended prison sentence seems largely to have got lost. Suspended prison sentences are no longer imposed exceptionally; they are not considered *bona fide* prison sentences, they need not be particularly short, the decision to suspend is not clearly based on offence seriousness, and there is evidence of sentence inflation taking place frequently. While suspended prison sentences were already considered problematic in some respects when they were first conceived, they have become far more problematic today, because the prevailing paradigm has changed. The turn-of-the-century consequentialist paradigm is gone and the proportionality paradigm is now the key sentencing rationale. Suspended prison sentences, however, are not usually responsive to proportionality concerns. The result? We urgently need to re-imagine suspended prison sentences.

In this chapter I present a proposal for what re-imagined suspended (prison) sentences might look like. This proposal aims to retain the advantages of suspended sentences while reducing their shortcomings; in addition, the proposed solution is guided by a desire for coherency with proportionality requirements. There are at least three elements of the solution that respond directly to those requirements: (i) better consideration of offence seriousness when suspending a prison sentence, since sentencing cannot be proportional unless offence seriousness is among the factors considered at the moment of suspension, (ii) clear identification of the "penal bite" of the suspended sentence, enabling a better assessment of its proportionality, and (iii) consideration of the "penal bite" (intrusion into the offender's life) of any other measures imposed alongside the suspended (prison) sentence, both upon imposition and upon revocation, to ensure that the overall penal bite of the state's reaction to the offence committed is not disproportionate.

My proposal makes use of a concept devised in Sweden, namely the term "penal value" used to designate a quantified value describing the extent to which the offender's life is to be limited and corresponding to the seriousness of the offence committed (Holmgren, 2021; Jareborg, 1995). The simplest

DOI: 10.4324/9781003568667-21

representation of "penal value" is the length of prison sentence that would be imposed if a prison sentence were imposed as the only sanction (I refer to this as the "potential prison sentence"). Specifying penal value as the length of the potential prison sentence enables appropriate alternative sanctions to be identified by comparing their penal bite with the penal value.

My proposed re-imagined suspended sentence would operate within the following general framework. During the sentencing phase, the judge would impose the duration of the operational period of suspension and set the potential prison sentence. Typically, the judge would also impose (a) at least one additional punitive sanction/measure, such as a fine or community service,[2] and (b) rehabilitative and incapacitative sanctions and measures, such as various prohibitions or obligations, if the offender's needs and level of risk render these appropriate. Upon a breach of the suspension conditions, the judge would not be obliged to revoke the suspension of the sentence, but if suspension is revoked, the length of the prison sentence to be served would then be set by deducting the total "penal bite" of all punitive, rehabilitative and incapacitative sanctions and measures endured up until the moment of revocation from the "potential prison sentence" that was set at sentence imposition. A suspended sentence imposed according to this re-imagined framework would fulfil the requirements of proportionality, rehabilitation and incapacitation, while evading all the problems we have previously identified with regard to current systems of prison sentence suspension in Central and Eastern Europe.

This chapter is structured as follows. I first discuss why we need suspended prison sentences at all, by trying to identify the groups of offenders for whom such a sanction would be appropriate. After that, I outline the basic principles that should guide courts in deciding whether to impose a suspended sentence and how to decide on its execution. Lastly, I present in detail how these principles could be implemented within a specific penal system – that of Czechia – applying my proposed framework in context, with all due nuances, so as to provide inspiration for other countries, including but not limited to those discussed in this book. Of course, any country-specific solution would need to be prepared by experts with detailed knowledge of the jurisdiction in question; the presented detailed solution is not intended as a one-size-fits-all.

Before embarking on this discussion, it is important to note that the aim of this chapter is to propose a solution for systems that wish to retain a sanction that is broadly similar to the existing suspended prison sentence. I do not advocate here either for or against the partial or complete abandonment of suspended prison sentences (nor even their replacement by partially suspended prison sentences), albeit these routes might hold potential as alternatives to re-imagined suspended sentences. I do, however, believe that suspended prison sentences, re-imagined as I propose in this chapter, deserve to be considered in any continental legal system.

Intended position and recipients of suspended sentences

The purpose of any sanction is inevitably linked to the characteristics of the offenders to whom it is to be imposed. Those characteristics will also determine the sanction's place within the penal system. Together, a given system of sanctions should provide appropriate solutions for all offender characteristics. In this section, I discuss the characteristics of the offenders and offences for which a suspended prison sentence may be appropriate.

Punitive bite: filling the space between imprisonment and fine

A suspended sentence should be conceived as an intermediate sanction (Morris & Tonry, 1990): a type of punishment that imposes significant limitations on the offender, without resorting to his/her imprisonment. As such, a suspended sentence ought to be imposed in response to an offence more serious than those for which a fine is considered appropriate, but less serious than offences warranting a custodial prison sentence. The identification of these thresholds is most easily facilitated by using the concept of the penal value, or **potential prison sentence**: A fine could be thought to replace a potential prison sentence of e.g. up to 6 months, and a non-suspended prison sentence may be considered appropriate when the potential prison sentence is longer than e.g. 2 years.[3] Suspended sentences could operate between these two thresholds.

Most countries in Central and Eastern Europe do not currently have a very diverse system of intermediate sanctions. Community service is one possibility, but is limited to (charity) work, while electronic monitoring (home arrest) constitutes a very serious interference in offenders' lives (Durnescu, 2013). Devising a suspended sentence that would function appropriately as an intermediate sanction would benefit these systems. Such a sentence would, in contrast to the status quo, not constitute a prison sentence; as a result, certain difficulties seen under current frameworks, such as the need to cross the custody threshold, while not incarcerating the offender, would be resolved. For this reason, I prefer to refer to the re-imagined sentence as a "suspended sentence", rather than a "suspended prison sentence".[4]

Sanctions limiting offenders' rights or entitlements should be imposed as part of a suspended sentence to achieve an appropriate penal bite and clearly distinguish a suspended sentence from a fine. These sanctions would typically include fines and community service, which would form part of the suspended prison sentence rather than being imposed as standalone sanctions (their penal bite alone would be insufficient). The choice of such additional sanctions should be left to the court, whose responsibility it is to tailor the punishment to the offender and offence. The potential prison sentence remains the primary benchmark here: the longer the potential prison sentence, the more punitive sanctions and measures should be imposed. Thus, while the court would only be obliged to specify the length of the operational period, doing so without also imposing additional sanctions should be exceptional. For instance, if the offender committed a minor offence, a combination of a fine and a suspended sentence would be appropriate, while for a more serious offence, other sanctions such as community service and home arrest would be appropriate in addition to the suspended sentence.[5] Finally, for serious offences for which deprivation of liberty is considered necessary, a very short non-suspended prison sentence could be imposed alongside the suspended sentence.

An adjustable sentence: tailoring for different offences and different groups of offenders

In order for suspended sentences to fill that "intermediate" space between fines and imprisonment, they need to be adjustable at imposition so that they can be used appropriately for offences of varied seriousness. As in current systems, suspended sentences would thus be imposed for both minor and more serious offences. The necessary differentiation of the suspended sentence's penal bite would be achieved by imposing additional penalties, restrictions and obligations as part of a suspended sentence, ensuring the individualisation of the sentence. In its various forms, the penal bite of a suspended sentence would then be equal to the penal bite of a range of other possible sanctions, corresponding to a medium fine, house arrest, or a mid-long prison sentence. This would have the advantage of keeping the suspended sentence an appropriate sanction for a pool of offenders similar to those who are handed suspended sentences today. The ways in which the relevant decisions would be made, and penalties, restrictions, and obligations imposed as part of a suspended sentence, would change, but the range of offenders catered for could remain broadly similar.

The biggest differences would pertain to the farthest points on the seriousness spectrum. For low-level offences, fines should be imposed and suspended sentences should not normally be considered.[6] For the most serious offences, a prison sentence should be the rule. For rather serious offences, it would be conceivable to combine a suspended sentence with a short non-suspended prison sentence, and possibly other sanctions as well, so as to punish the offender in a way that is proportionate to the penal value of the offence, while at the same time avoiding long-term incarceration.

Another chance: responding appropriately to infrequent offenders

Given the high level of societal tolerance towards low-level breaches of social rules, offering infrequent offenders another chance by permitting them to continue to lead their day-to-day lives is generally acceptable. The same might also be warranted in the case of moderately serious offences, especially those committed by first-time offenders. At the same time, however, society should not resign from expressing the seriousness of the offence via the penal bite of the imposed sanction, even to infrequent and first-time offenders, especially in the case of moderately serious offences. That penal bite is necessary, even when the sanctions imposed refrain from restricting the offender's life to an extent that would prevent them from integrating into, or continuing to live within society.

If an offender handed the suggested suspended sentence fulfils their commitment to society – by behaving in accordance with the conditions of their suspended sentence – any part of the theoretical penal bite of their punishment that has not already been executed via various sanctions and measures will be forgiven at the end of the operational period. This is a consequence of limiting retributive purposes for the sake of achieving consequentialist aims through less restrictive punishment. If the offender does not re-offend, society is safer, and this result cancels out the need for a fully proportionate response to the original offence. If the offender re-offends, however, the response should result in a fully proportionate, yet not disproportionately harsh punishment. A suspended sentence would, under my proposal, typically entail punitive sanctions or measures alongside the suspension itself, ensuring the offender experiences some hard treatment, and not merely limiting censure to a pronouncement of the sentence, as is often the case with existing models of suspended prison sentences.

Protection of society: responding to offenders' risks and needs

Fines and community service sentences have a limited propensity to respond to offenders' risks and needs, as they do not motivate convicted offenders to complete treatment programmes or actively resist risk factors for re-offending. Once a fine is paid or the prescribed community service completed, offenders have little incentive to comply with any programmes or treatments. A suspended sentence provides a more suitable context within which to incentivise offenders, since it provides an ever-present threat of punishment.

Suspended sentences should thus be the preferred instrument in cases in which the court concludes that the offender's risks and needs must be addressed and that the offender has the capacity to respond to appropriate treatments and programmes. The court would also need to decide whether to opt for particular treatments and programmes or whether a comprehensive model of complex probationary supervision is appropriate. If used in this way, the suspended sentence would become a proper instrument of sentence individualisation capable of responding to the convicted person's particular risks and needs, fulfilling the individualisation requirement not only in terms of proportionality but also from the standpoint of consequentialist demands.

A restorative sanction: repairing harm and other restorative purposes

One of the objectives of criminal law is the restoration of social relations disturbed by criminal activity, including compensation for damages and reparation of harms (hereafter jointly referred to as "compensation of damages"). A suspended sentence provides ample opportunities to ensure that any damages are compensated. While offenders who are only sanctioned with a fine or community service might serve their sanctions and yet fail to compensate for the damages their offence caused, a suspended sentence ensures that even after payment of an accompanying fine or fulfilment of a community service sanction, the offender knows that their behaviour will be subject to the scrutiny of a judge at the end of the operational period, which increases their motivation to compensate the victim, even if this might be a purely "formal" restoration. Suspended sentences could thus be a useful sanction in situations in which the judge wishes to ensure that damages are compensated, and this aspect could reduce opposition to the use of suspended sentences (Roberts, 2004, pp. 168–169). Under certain conditions, suspended sentences could further be used to fulfil other restorative purposes. For instance, offenders might be motivated to complete restorative programmes, although in this particular case, since participation in such programmes is voluntary, the motivation ensuing from the suspended sentence would not be so substantial.

Offenders on the verge: suspended sentences for homeless offenders, offenders experiencing health problems and offenders with transient lifestyles

Suspended sentences could also be a back-up sanction for offenders upon whom other sanctions (such as fines, community service, or home arrest) cannot be imposed, when imprisonment (or home arrest) would be too severe. Fines can typically not be imposed on unemployed offenders, while community service cannot be imposed if the offender is unfit to work on a regular basis. In addition, home arrest cannot be used if the convicted person does not have a stable home address. In these cases, the imposition of punitive, rehabilitative, and/or incapacitative measures alongside the suspended sentence could be justified, but it would also be acceptable to use a suspended sentence alone if (i) no other sanctions can be imposed due to the offender's personal circumstances and (ii) the imposition of a prison sentence would be too punitive. The state should never over-punish; where no entirely suitable response is available, the state should under-punish. At the lowest end of the offence seriousness spectrum, a suspended sentence could be imposed instead of a fine for offenders without sufficient means.

Which offenders are good candidates for a remodelled suspended sentence, and which are not?

To summarise, my proposal is for a remodelled suspended sentence that would constitute a suitable sanction (albeit in different forms) for the following groups of offenders (alternatives are listed):

- Infrequent offenders who commit offences of moderate severity;
- Offenders who commit minor and moderate offences and present risks and needs that can be addressed without incarceration;
- Offenders who commit minor and moderate offences who cannot be sentenced to fines, community service, or house arrest for objective reasons;
- Offenders who commit minor and moderate offences and who have not voluntarily compensated the victim of the offence prior to sentencing may do so during the operational period.

Conversely, I believe that remodelled suspended sentences, based on my proposal, should not be imposed for the following groups of offenders:

- Offenders who commit low-level offences and do not have special risks or needs that require a particular response: in this case, a fine should be the preferred penalty;
- Perpetrators of very serious offences, for whom either imprisonment or house arrest is appropriate;
- In most cases, foreign offenders who are likely to be deported since a suspended sentence has broader purposes than a suspended prison sentence, which served only as a warning and a threat.

A suspended sentence, thus, could be imposed broadly. It would not be confined to a group of offenders with specific needs, but it also would not be considered appropriate for almost all offences, as is often the case with a suspended prison sentence. As a result, the use of suspended sentences could be lower than the current very extensive use in some Central and Eastern European countries, but this decrease does not have to be drastic.

The basic principles of a re-imagined suspended sentence

I now turn to an outline of the basic principles that should guide the imposition of a suspended sentence under my re-imagined model.

A proportionate penal bite

One of the main problems identified with current systems of suspended prison sentences is sentence inflation, i.e. the imposition of longer suspended prison sentences in place of shorter non-suspended sentences. There are two competing interests at the moment of front-door sentencing (when the sentence is first suspended): quantifying the seriousness of the offence, and translating that into hard treatment. Offence seriousness must be quantified in a consistent way so that this is both fair and transparent for the offender, the victim and society. If no quantification were made at this stage, and the length of the sentence to be served were to be determined only upon revocation of suspension ("back-door sentencing"), the offender, victim and society would be left uncertain as to the fair nature of the response and its specific impact on their lives; back-door sentencing would, in addition, be very impractical, since judges would end up having to assess the seriousness and other elements of offences committed a long time ago. To ensure legal certainty, the judge should determine the severity of the offence and the appropriate length of potential prison sentence to respond to it at the time of imposing the suspended sentence. Since that judge cannot fully predict at that time what will happen during the operational period, the sentence would remain a potential prison sentence until the operational period was complete, or until a breach of suspension conditions occurred. A second means of translating offence seriousness into hard treatment would be provided through the regular imposition of additional punitive sanctions and measures as part of a suspended sentence, which would increase the penal bite effective during the operational period and could thus offset sentence inflation by reducing the impression that there is no hard treatment except in case of a breach.

To take the penal bite of punitive, rehabilitative, and incapacitative measures during the operational period into account and ensure fair treatment, the length of the potential prison sentence should be set at front-door sentencing, as is the case in the current system, but not as definitively as it has traditionally been. The Swedish concept of penal value, expressed via a potential prison sentence, is useful here. Announcing the exact length of the potential prison sentence that could be imposed if the offender were imprisoned both communicates more effectively (to the offender and others) the seriousness of the offence and, upon an eventual revocation of suspension, provides the judge with a clearly defined penal value of the offence. In order for a suspended sentence to function properly – and to ensure legal certainty – this potential prison sentence should be stated in the guilty verdict. If the concept of the potential prison sentence were widely used in the system – not only for suspended sentences, but in all cases for comparison purposes – the potential for sentence inflation would further decrease, as the potential prison sentence would be determined independently of what sanction type was eventually imposed in the end. The detail of how such a broad application of the concept of the potential prison sentence would work both in theory and practice lies beyond the scope of this chapter, but I discuss its potential application in Central and Eastern Europe elsewhere (Drápal, 2025).

A simple (but not simplistic) suspended sentence

It should be relatively easy to impose a suspended sentence. In cases that do not seem to require any more detailed examination of the offender's risks and needs, a relatively simple sentence could be imposed, such as a suspended sentence combined with a fine or community service. At the same time, however, judges should not impose such a simple suspended sentence if the offender's risks and needs are significant. There should thus be a two-step consideration of offenders' risks and needs: first, a preliminary assessment indicating whether there is a need for a thorough examination of the offender's risks and needs, which should be carried out pretrial. Prosecutors might be directed to provide the judge with the basic assessment of the offender's risks and needs using information from pretrial proceedings (and possibly with reports prepared by probation/social services).[7] In the absence of such information and if the judge is furthermore unable to conduct their own assessment using information contained in the case file, the judge should him/herself conduct at least a basic investigation of the offender's risks and needs; this would effectively bar him/her from ruling via a simplified procedure (e.g. penal order).

If a preliminary assessment concludes that the offender may present significant risks and needs, judges should be directed to examine those risks and needs in detail before imposing appropriate sanctions and measures that respond to them. The detailed assessment of risks and needs should be carried out primarily through pre-sentence reports by the probation/social service and should not primarily be a task for the judges themselves, who have neither the skills nor the time to conduct such an evaluation. Suspended sentences could thus function properly only in systems capable of providing judges with the necessary assessments, either by default or upon request.

Penal bite: enabling consideration of sanctions and measures during the operational period

Punitive, rehabilitative and incapacitative sanctions and measures should be imposed alongside suspended sentences so that the latter carry punitive bite and as a means of responding to offenders' risks and needs. Subsequently, the impact such sanctions and measures have had on the offender's life should be considered if the suspended sentence is revoked, and should then be taken into account when determining the prison sentence the offender will have to serve. Taking these into account cannot be done at any other point in time than at the moment of revocation, because it is only then that a judge can determine the extent of hard treatment that the offender has experienced. Things such as participation in treatments, abiding by prohibitions and restrictions, payment of fines and completion of community work can only be quantified upon revocation. Hard treatment suffered during the operational period also includes the experience of having lived for a certain period of time under the "Damocles' sword" of a suspended sentence, due to the negative impact that such a sentence has on the offender's standard of living. This may be taken into account by, for instance, deducting one day from the prison sentence for every week during which the offender complied fully with the conditions of the operational period, to reward those who completed a longer period without breaching their sentence conditions.

Upon revocation, the overall impact of all sanctions and measures experienced up to the date of the breach would be deducted from the potential prison sentence announced at conviction, resulting in a revised prison sentence to be served. This would ensure that the overall penal bite of all sanctions never exceeded the penal value of the perpetrated offence. In order to make such decisions principled and straightforward, fixed ratios of equivalence should be established between units of sanctions and measures and days of potential prison sentence, either within the penal code, in explanatory documents accompanying the sentence reform, in jurisprudence or through other legal guidelines.[8] For example, two day-fine units or one day in residential treatment could be considered equivalent to one day of imprisonment.

Breach: a true and fair sanction

One aspect of the suspended prison sentence that would not change under my proposal, as compared with current models, is that each further offence committed during the operational period would have an additional impact on the offender's life. In other words, another offence committed would result in an additional punishment. Similarly, any breach of the conditions of a suspended sentence would warrant a response from the state. While a suspended sentence offers the offender another chance, this nevertheless implies an obligation on the state's part to respond if the offender fails to take advantage of that chance (Corda, 2025). That response, however, need not be the most punitive one available. Thus, it is possible to conceive of a response to a breach of suspension conditions that would not consist of a revocation of suspension or the imprisonment of the offender.

The judge might instead, for instance, impose an additional fine, a new requirement to carry out community service, make alterations to the offender's other obligations and restrictions and/or extend the operational period. Such alterations to the conditions of suspension and accompanying measures would not lead to a disproportionate penal bite should the suspended sentence ultimately be revoked, since their penal bite would be carefully quantified and deducted from the potential prison sentence upon such revocation. Judges should not only be presented with these options for responding to a breach of suspension conditions, but also given guidance on which responses are considered most appropriate in typified scenarios.

One judge decides upon revocation

If an offender commits a further offence during the operational period of a suspended sentence, it is necessary to decide which judge should decide on the appropriate response to the breach of the suspension conditions. In many countries, one judge decides on the sentence to be imposed for the new offence, while another judge decides on the revocation of the suspended sentence. I believe it is essential for these two decisions to be taken simultaneously by a single judge, to ensure a coherent and principled outcome. This would also likely make savings on judicial time, since the judge deciding on the new sentence would already have all the information necessary for making the decision on a response to the breach, including the length of the potential prison sentence in relation to the original (suspended) sanction, which sanctions and measures were imposed alongside suspension, and which of those have been served to date.

A possible argument against enabling one judge to decide on a breach of suspension conditions that were imposed by a second judge is that the new judge may have no previous interaction with the offender. While this criticism is warranted, all relevant information should be found in the case file and, should the "new" judge deem it necessary, he/she could procure additional information from the judge who imposed and oversaw the original suspended sentence. Furthermore, it is already the case in many systems that revocation of suspension is decided by a different judge than the one who imposed the suspended prison sentence. In some systems, special judges decide on the execution of sentences (in francophone countries *juge d'application des peines*) while in other systems, judges might leave courts for various reasons (quitting the bench or moving to a different court), resulting in different judges deciding on the revocation of previously imposed suspended prison sentences.

In the event of a breach, the offender does not end up in a hopeless situation

Sentence inflation is one of two reasons why offenders often end up serving disproportionately long prison sentences upon revocation. The second is the accumulation of prison sentences, which occurs when an offender serves multiple consecutive prison sentences, some of which are revoked suspended prison sentences (or other non-custodial sanctions), and others newly imposed non-suspended prison sentences. I have argued elsewhere that when sentencing an offender who is due to serve another sanction, the judge should take that previously imposed sanction into account when determining the new sentence; however, most European countries currently lack any provisions to allow for such consideration (Drápal, 2023b)[9].

How exactly the penal values of offences separated by sentence imposition should be combined is a complex issue for which I suggest possible solutions elsewhere (Drápal, 2023b). At this point, it suffices to say that re-offence during the operational period of an existing suspended sentence might lead a judge to incarcerate the offender for the new offence even when they might not otherwise have done so. Such a decision to incarcerate already represents a substantially harsher sanction for the offender. It could thus be acceptable to apply principles of concurrency to a substantive degree, given that an incarceration will always impact the offender much more than any sanction prior to it.

Broader issues of sentencing policy

Suspended sentences cannot exist in a vacuum, and even a very well-designed institution cannot properly function in an otherwise ill-conceived system. Currently, some sentencing systems in Central and Eastern Europe suffer from systemic problems that negatively impact the functioning of suspended sentences by undermining the achievement of principled sentencing. One example of such a problem is that of high sentencing range minimums. A high sentencing range minimum results in a high potential prison sentence, reducing the scope for deciding to impose a suspended sentence. This example illustrates the need for a more comprehensive reform, which cannot be limited to individual institutes within a sentencing system.

Difference from probation

A critical reader might wonder what difference there is between a suspended sentence and probation. The difference depends upon what is considered to be included within the term probation. Typically, probation entails supervision by a probation officer (Alexander et al., 2014), while a suspended sentence in and of itself does not, and nor do many of the other sanctions and measures that may be imposed alongside a suspended sentence – such as fines, prohibitions, and restitution. Probationary supervision is only one of a range of possible measures that may be imposed alongside a prison sentence. A further difference is that probation is often imposed without any prior decision about the length of prison sentence that would be served were probation not imposed (Frase, 2019).[10] Suspended sentence thus differs from probation in the emphasis put on proportionality, and it is to an extent still linked with the continental tradition of a court setting certain sanctions upon front-door sentencing and in only an occasional role played by probation officers. Suspended sentence is closer to probation than a suspended prison sentence was, yet it is still distinct.

The possible outline of suspended sentence in Czechia

In outlining my proposal for reformed suspended sentences, I cannot go into greater detail than a description of the general principles, since the specificities of the national legal systems in Europe differ sufficiently that the specific implementation in each would need to vary. So as to provide insight into how such a reformed solution might work in a particular legal system, and how it would address certain jurisdiction-specific issues that are difficult to capture if only broad principles are discussed, I here present my solution specifically for Czechia. This detailed presentation enables me to provide a clearer picture of how suspended sentences could be imposed in incremental steps. To facilitate comparison with existing systems, I adopt a similar structure as used in previous chapters for the national reports.

Czechia is one of the European countries that imposes suspended prison sentences most frequently, and its framework of suspended prison sentences is in many respects similar to the sanction's original design. Many common problems linked to the use of suspended prison sentences, such as sentence inflation, accumulation of prison sentences, and imposition of suspended prison sentences for rather serious offences, have been empirically identified in Czechia, which is otherwise a rather well-functioning, democratic rule-of-law country in which penal populism does not play a crucial role (Drápal, 2023a).

Positive and negative definitions (who should and should not be a good candidate for a suspended sentence): The Penal Code should not set any conditions in terms of which offences are eligible for a suspended sentence and which are not; this decision should be governed by the offence seriousness, which would be expressed primarily via the potential prison sentence.[11] Instead, the general condition for the imposition of a suspended sentence should be that (i) the behaviour is serious enough to render the imposition of a fine alone insufficient, (ii) the behaviour is not sufficiently serious to justify a non-suspended prison sentence (this could be expressed by a cut-off length of potential prison sentence, such as two years) and (iii) the offender has a positive prognosis, i.e. their probability of re-offending is low enough not to require the imposition of a non-suspended prison sentence or home arrest.

The decisive factor for imposition: All characteristics of the case should be taken into account, including the seriousness of the offence.

Exceptionality: A suspended sentence would not be considered exceptional and could be a commonly imposed sanction; there would not be any underlying reasoning why it should be exceptional. It would be a regular option in an arsenal of possible sanctions which could be appropriate for a broad set of offenders.

Procedure preceding sentencing: The risks and needs of the offender should always be examined in at least a very cursory way to determine whether a more detailed assessment (e.g. a pre-sentence report) is necessary. This should be carried out by prosecutors, who should then request a pre-sentence report from the probation service if needed. Judges should not decide by penal order unless a basic assessment has been carried out and has determined that a more detailed assessment is not required. Judges should also not decide by penal order if the offender has reoffended during the operational period of a suspended sentence.

Operational period: For all suspended sentences, the judge would be required to set the operational period. This could be any length within a slightly wider range than at present (1–5 years), such as from 6 months to 5 years. The minimum of 6 months would be sufficient for non-serious offences for which the judge imposed a punitive sanction that can be carried out easily and to allow sufficient, but not excessive, time during which the offender would need to compensate for damages caused. In such cases, an operational period of one year could be too long. The starting point for determining the length of the operational period would be between one-and-a-half times and double the potential prison sentence; the operational period should never be shorter than the potential prison sentence.

Potential prison sentence: The exact length of the potential prison sentence would be stipulated at sentencing in all cases, to ensure principled sentencing and limit the danger of sentence inflation. The length of the potential prison sentence would be included in the dispositive part of the verdict, so that an appeal could be filed also only against the length of a potential prison sentence in case of a suspended sentence.[12]

Additional sanctions and measures: As a rule, at least one additional punitive sanction or measure would be imposed with a suspended sentence, to ensure an element of hard treatment. If the offender's risks and needs warrant it, rehabilitative and incapacitative sanctions and measures should be imposed (these could be accompanied by probationary supervision if deemed necessary). Only in exceptional cases would it be possible to impose a suspended sentence alone, without any other sanctions or measures. Compensation for damages would not count as a punitive, rehabilitative or incapacitative sanction, meaning that it would not be sufficient to award a suspended sentence with a set operational period alongside a requirement for the offender to compensate for damages caused, but at least one additional measure would be required.

Conditions during the operational period: The offender would be required not to re-offend (possibly including administrative offences, especially those of a kind similar to the committed offence[13]) and to comply with all requirements set by courts and other agencies. They would not, however, be required to lead a "law-abiding life", as this term is unclear and does not provide sufficient certainty and guidance to the offender. Any failure to comply with the conditions of the sentence imposed – such as medical treatment, compensation for damages or requirements set by the probation service – would be considered a breach of the suspended sentence, prompting the judge to decide whether to revoke the suspension or take another action.

Changes to sanctions and measures during the operational period: During the operational period a judge could decide to lift or change the sanctions and measures imposed with the suspended sentence if he/she considers these no longer suitable due to changed circumstances. However, provided that the offender has not breached the conditions of the suspended sentence, the judge would not be permitted to impose new sanctions or measures, nor change the existing sanctions to the detriment of the offender. For example, if one of the imposed sanctions consisted in the electronic monitoring of movement, the judge could gradually narrow the restriction on movement, but she/he could broaden it only if the previously stipulated conditions had been violated. Additionally, it would be possible for the judge to alter the sanctions and measures while achieving an equivalent penal bite overall, typically with the offender's consent: for example, if an offender became unemployed and could not pay a previously imposed fine, this sanction could be converted into community service.

Possible responses to breaches of conditions: Judges would have a wide range of options when responding to breaches of sentence conditions, and careful guidance would be provided to them about which options to use in which situations. It would frequently not be necessary to revoke the suspension of a sentence, but the judicial reaction to a breach of sentence conditions should always carry an additional punitive bite. Appropriate reactions to breaches of conditions could be stipulated along the following lines:

- A first non-serious breach, such as a minor breach of electronic monitoring conditions or a failure to compensate the victim, should primarily result in a warning and in slight tightening of the existing sanctions and measures imposed on the offender, possibly accompanied by an extension of the operational period.
- A breach that is not serious enough to result in the revocation of suspension and ensues from the offender's lifestyle should result in additional rehabilitative and incapacitative sanctions and measures if newly arisen needs and risks are identified during the breach proceedings. If the breach indicates that the offender has limited respect for the rights of others and the rule of law, then a punitive sanction would be appropriate.
- A breach consisting of an offender displaying high disregard for the rights of others and the rule of law (especially by committing a more serious offence or multiple offences) should result in the revocation of the suspended sentence and thus in the offender serving a prison sentence (possibly in the form of house arrest with electronic monitoring).
- If the offender re-offends, the response should reflect both the seriousness of the offence committed and the elapsed time of the operational period. For example, a less serious offence committed halfway through the operational period or later should typically not lead to a revocation of suspension. Similarly, a non-serious offence committed very shortly after the imposition of a suspended sentence, given that the offender would not be imprisoned if he/she were sentenced for both the original offence and the new offence at the same time.
- Repeated breaches of conditions: the general rule would be that the offender should not be given an infinite number of chances. Similarly, the offender

should not be given multiple chances to compensate damages: in this case, the offender should first be warned, then a punitive sanction such as community service should be imposed in the case of the following infraction, and then the suspended sentence should finally be revoked (with incarceration or house arrest following revocation).

Procedure following a breach of conditions: The judge should respond to any breach of conditions swiftly, without waiting for the operational period to expire in order to consider the offender's behaviour in its totality. The procedural rules should be adapted to reflect this so that, for example, it would not be necessary to summon the offender by official letter, but it would be possible to invite him/her to appear by telephone (this would require an important change of procedural rules) since the response to a breach should be rapid (Roberts, 2004, p. 58). If an offender is unwilling to appear, this could be considered grounds for a stricter decision (albeit not necessarily a revocation).

Determination of the length of prison sentence upon revocation: If, as a result of a breach of the sentence conditions, a judge revokes the suspended sentence and incarcerates the offender, he/she would determine the length of the final prison sentence to be served using the potential prison sentence indicated during the original sentencing as the starting value. From that potential sentence, the judge would subtract the penal bite of all sanctions and measures served during the operational period. Served sanctions and measures would be evaluated and transformed into an equivalent length of prison sentence in line with set ratios, for instance: two day unit fines, two hours of community service or one day of house arrest should be considered equivalent to one day of imprisonment. Similar ratios should be applied to rehabilitative measures, for which the ratios should be established so as to encourage offenders to complete allocated programmes and treatments (not dropping out mid-way). For example, if the programmes were successfully completed, the time would be counted in full, but participation in incomplete portions of programmes would only be counted as half the time actually spent. Residential programmes (such as substance abuse rehabilitation) could be treated like house arrest (one day of a residential programme would count as one day of prison sentence) and other programmes could be considered in the same way as community service (two hours of a programme should result in one day deducted from the potential prison sentence). With regard to the operational period, every month of the operational period that passed without a breach (i.e. prior to the breach) could result in a reduction of the prison sentence by five days.

Sentence imposition in the case of re-offending: Upon re-offending, the judge deciding on the new offence would also decide on the suspended sentence. The new judge could request a report on the progress of the suspended sentence from the judge who imposed the suspended sentence. The new judge would decide on revocation (or the transformation of the suspended sentence) along with the imposition of the new sentence. The decision on the revocation should thus be made in the dispositive part of the judgement so that it could be appealed either together with the new sentence or independently from it.

Decision at the end of the operational period: At the end of the operational period, a judge should verify the execution of all sanctions, fulfilment of all measures, and compensation of damages, in order to establish whether the offender complied with the conditions. No "fiction of complying with conditions" would be possible – the judge would always decide[14]. The fact that a judge has certified compliance with the conditions would not, however, prevent that decision being reopened should it later be discovered that the offender committed a new offence during the operational period. However, there would be a time limit for this, after which the judge's decision on compliance with suspension conditions would be considered final and immutable. For example, the judge might have a one-year window within which he/she could begin an investigation and a five-year period thereafter within which to reach a final decision.

Terminology: So far, I have used the term suspended sentence, which I find useful as it clarifies the fact that this is indeed a sentence – and not simply a deferral of sentencing – while part of the penal bite is suspended. Such a sentence does not constitute probation; probationary supervision is merely one of the measures imposed alongside it. Whether a suspended sentence would be considered a form of punishment or a separate type of measure would depend on the traditions of labelling sanctions in each jurisdiction; in Czechia, it would constitute a separate type of sanction. Ultimately, how a suspended sentence is labelled is less significant than how it functions: this would very clearly not be a prison sentence. In this respect, I differ from e.g. Julian Roberts' idea of labelling a tough community sentence as "community custody" (Roberts, 2004, p. 161). Similarly, my proposal for remodelling the suspended sentence envisages it as a less onerous sanction than that proposed by Julian Roberts, who argues for house arrest to be a presumptive condition of all suspended sentences. That said, even house arrest is considered an alternative sanction in Czechia and not a type of prison sentence. In the Czech context, at the very least, it would be misleading to call a suspended sentence of the type I have outlined a prison sentence.

Conclusion

By the end of the 19th century, criminal lawyers were convinced that all guilty verdicts must be accompanied by clearly set sanctions. For this reason, suspended prison sentences were introduced in continental Europe, rather than probation. Over time, views on this have evolved, and it is now time to re-imagine the suspended prison sentence, retaining the good aspects (giving offenders another chance), removing the problematic aspects (such as its labelling as a prison sentence with all that entails) and enabling proper fulfilment of multiple sentencing rationales with an outcome that does not violate the principle of proportionality (i.e. with full consideration of risks and needs and allowing for the adjustment of the eventual custodial sentence based on the penal bite endured during the period of suspension).

The re-imagined suspended sentence, as outlined in this chapter, would resolve most of the challenges linked to suspended prison sentences that were described in the previous chapters of this book. Specifically:

- The penological paradox of having to cross a custodial threshold and yet not incarcerating the offender would disappear, since the re-imagined suspended sentence would not be considered a prison sentence.
- Offence seriousness could be considered when deciding on whether a suspended sentence should be imposed since the decision to suspend would no longer be a back-door sentencing decision.
- Suspended sentences would not be imposed for low-level offences, with fines being imposed for these instead.
- Suspended sentences would not be seen as let-offs, since they would always entail a punitive bite expressed via a fine, community service or another punitive sanction or measure.
- Contrary to the original conception of only offering offenders another chance to reform themselves, suspended sentences would respond to their risks and needs when appropriate.
- Sentence inflation would not take place since the concept of the potential prison sentence and its proportional calculation would be built into the criminal justice system and there would be clearly established rates of equivalence between different sanctions.
- The punitive bite of sanctions served and measures experienced during the operational period would not be ignored upon revocation: the eventual prison sentence to be served would be reduced from the originally set potential prison sentence accordingly.
- If the offender re-offended during the operational period, only one judge would decide both on the revocation of the original suspension and on the sentence for the newly committed offence.

By re-imagining the suspended prison sentence in this way, we would emphasise different paradigms than those that shaped its creation at the end of the 19th century. We no longer naively believe that suspension is a means of executing a prison sentence or that a 3-year suspended prison sentence and a 3-year non-suspended prison sentence are equally harsh. We no longer expect the primary purpose of a suspended sentence to be deterrence. Rather, we aim to respond to offenders' risks and needs and are better able to do so. We place ever more importance on proportionality, understanding that the penal bite needs to be assessed both at sentence imposition and at the moment when suspension is revoked. In short, we know we need a sanction that fulfils the proportionality requirement by impacting offenders' lives, providing an opportunity for the offender to continue to live in the community, and incentivising offenders to tackle their risks and needs. The re-imagined suspended sentence, as outlined above, could be such a sanction.

Notes

1 Some of the ideas developed in this chapter have been explored in publications in Czech on which this chapter is partly based (see: Drápal, 2024; Drápal & Kubů, 2023). I am grateful to Milena Tripković and Krzysztof Krajewski for their valuable comments and to Anna Barton for proofreading.
2 An example of a punitive measure which is not a sanction would be e.g. the withdrawal of the offender's driving licence for non-traffic offences in Czechia.
3 Defining this threshold is difficult and very country-specific (Roberts, 2004, pp. 163–164).
4 Finding the right name for this type of sanction is difficult. The term "suspended sentence" is less clear about what exactly is suspended (some countries, such as Poland, allow the suspension of e.g. fines or community service). This is less tricky, however, in most Slavic languages, where a "suspended (prison) sentence" is typically referred to as a "conditional sentence" or "conditional conviction". It would be a particular type of sentence in its own right, not a suspension of another type.
5 A suspended sentence could thus entail also a fine or community service. I do not find this problematic, since a suspended sentence would only be imposed in cases in which a fine or community service alone would not be considered a sufficient sanction.
6 A suspended sentence – as opposed to the current suspended prison sentence – would carry greater punitive bite than a fine, because it would entail the threat of future incarceration in addition to a fine, a community service requirement, or a similar punitive sanction.
7 The defendant could, of course, also submit his/her own statement about risks and needs.
8 For some sanctions – such as day fines or community service – judges should not have much discretion as these sanctions are very commensurable from the viewpoint of criminal law. With regard to other measures, such as various treatments, judges should have substantial discretion, as these measures might vary significantly in their content; nevertheless, judges should still be provided with certain guidance. Such clarification would not be a novel idea; the interchangeability of sanctions has long been discussed as a key requirement of proportionality (Lovegrove, 2001).
9 Whether some courts may allow for this even without specific legal provisions is unclear.
10 Similarly, a suspended sentence is not a deferred sentence or a diversion, but a fully fledged sentence that entails a punitive bite and, if needed, also rehabilitative and incapacitative sanctions and measures.
11 For additional reasons, such as unprincipledness and political interference, see Roberts (2004, p. 165).
12 If not included in the dispositive part of the judgement, the potential prison sentence would need to be included in the reasoning; this, however, would be problematic as very little reasoning (or none) is provided with many verdicts and it is not possible to appeal against the reasoning alone.
13 For example, DUI is dealt with under criminal law in Czechia only if the level of alcohol is above a certain threshold (approximately 1 per mille). Drunk driving with

a lower blood alcohol level is an administrative offence, but this should still be considered a breach of the requirement not to commit a new offence. Nevertheless, many other minor administrative offences, such as speeding slightly over the speed limit, should generally not be considered a breach of sentence conditions.

14 Currently, in Czechia, if the judge fails to decide within one year of the end of the operational period of a suspended prison sentence whether or not the offender has behaved appropriately during the operational period, the offender is automatically considered to have led a law-abiding life via what is known as a legal fiction.

References

Alexander, M., Lowenkamp, C. T., & Robinson, C. (2014). Probation and parole practices. In G. Bruinsma & D. Weisburd (Eds.), *Encyclopedia of criminology and criminal justice* (pp. 3973–3979). Springer New York. https://doi.org/10.1007/978-1-4614-5690-2_25

Corda, A. (2025). The legitimacy of criminal law and the performance crises of penality. *Criminal Law Forum*, *36*, 351–381. https://doi.org/10.1007/s10609-025-09509-2

Drápal, J. (2023a). Punitive by negligence? The myths and reality of penal nationalism in the Czech Republic. *European Journal of Criminology*, *20*(4), 1549–1567. https://doi.org/10.1177/14773708211063753

Drápal, J. (2023b). Sentencing multiple conviction offenders. *European Journal of Criminology*, *20*(1), 142–160. https://doi.org/10.1177/1477370821996903

Drápal, J. (2025). Towards proper sentence justification. In J. Drápal, *Justifying Punishment* (1st ed., pp. 95–114). Routledge. https://doi.org/10.4324/9781003470670-7

Drápal, J., & Kubů, O. (2023). Jak reformovat podmíněné odsouzení? Zavést skutečné podmíněné odsouzení namísto podmíněného trestu odnětí svobody. *Trestní Právo*, *3*, 50–65.

Drápal, J., Cioffi, V. A., Vanča, T., & Kubů, O. (2024). *Podmíněný trest odnětí svobody: Převládající, nepoposaný, nepřiměřený*. Wolters Kluwer.

Durnescu, I. (2013). Community sanctions. In S. Body-Gendrot, M. Hough, K. Kerezsi, R. Lévy, & S. Snacken (Eds.), *The Routledge handbook of European criminology* (pp. 409–421). Routledge. https://doi.org/10.4324/9780203083505.ch22

Frase, R. S. (2019). Suspended sentences and free-standing probation orders in U.S. guidelines systems: A survey and assessment. *Law and Contemporary Problems*, *82*(1), 51–79.

Holmgren, A. (2021). *Straffvärde: Som rättslig konstruktion* (Upplaga 1:1). Iustus Förlag.

Jareborg, N. (1995). The Swedish sentencing reform. In C. Clarkson & R. Morgan (Eds.), *The politics of sentencing reform* (pp. 95–123). Clarendon Press.

Lovegrove, A. (2001). Sanctions and severity: To the demise of Von Hirsch and Wasik's sanction hierarchy. *The Howard Journal of Criminal Justice*, *40*(2), 126–144. https://doi.org/10.1111/1468-2311.00196

Morris, N., & Tonry, M. (1990). *Between prison and probation: Intermediate punishments in a rational sentencing system*. Oxford University Press.

Roberts, J. V. (2004). *Virtual prison*. Cambridge University Press.

Index

Note: Page numbers in **bold** reference tables; page numbers in *italics* reference figures.